# Paul's Suffering and Weakness in 2 Corinthians

Reading From a Disability Perspective

Royal L. Pakhuongte

MONOGRAPHS

© 2022 Royal L. Pakhuongte

Published 2022 by Langham Monographs
*An imprint of Langham Publishing*
www.langhampublishing.org

Langham Publishing and its imprints are a ministry of Langham Partnership

Langham Partnership
PO Box 296, Carlisle, Cumbria, CA3 9WZ, UK
www.langham.org

ISBNs:
978-1-83973-591-2 Print
978-1-83973-647-6 ePub
978-1-83973-648-3 Mobi
978-1-83973-649-0 PDF

Royal L. Pakhuongte has asserted his right under the Copyright, Designs and Patents Act, 1988 to be identified as the Author of this work.

All rights reserved. No part of this publication may be reproduced, stored in a retrieval system or transmitted, in any form or by any means, electronic, mechanical, photocopying, recording or otherwise, without the prior written permission of the publisher or the Copyright Licensing Agency.

Requests to reuse content from Langham Publishing are processed through PLSclear. Please visit www.plsclear.com to complete your request.

Unless otherwise stated Scripture translations in this work are the author's own.

Scripture quotations marked (ESV) are from The Holy Bible, English Standard Version® (ESV®), copyright © 2001 by Crossway, a publishing ministry of Good News Publishers. Used by permission. All rights reserved.

Scripture quotations marked (NASB) are taken from the New American Standard Bible®, Copyright © 1960, 1962, 1963, 1968, 1971, 1972, 1973, 1975, 1977, 1995 by The Lockman Foundation. Used by permission.

Scripture quoted by permission. Quotations designated (NET) are from the NET Bible® copyright ©1996–2016 by Biblical Studies Press, L.L.C. http://netbible.com All rights reserved.

Scripture quotations marked (NIV) are taken from the Holy Bible, New International Version®, NIV®. Copyright © 1973, 1978, 1984, 2011 by Biblica, Inc.™ Used by permission of Zondervan.

Scripture quotations marked (NRSV) are from the New Revised Standard Version Bible, copyright © 1989 National Council of the Churches of Christ in the United States of America. Used by permission. All rights reserved.

Scripture quotations marked (RSV) are from Revised Standard Version of the Bible, copyright © 1946, 1952, and 1971 National Council of the Churches of Christ in the United States of America. Used by permission. All rights reserved.

**British Library Cataloguing-in-Publication Data**
A catalogue record for this book is available from the British Library

ISBN: 978-1-83973-591-2

Cover & Book Design: projectluz.com

Langham Partnership actively supports theological dialogue and an author's right to publish but does not necessarily endorse the views and opinions set forth here or in works referenced within this publication, nor can we guarantee technical and grammatical correctness. Langham Partnership does not accept any responsibility or liability to persons or property as a consequence of the reading, use or interpretation of its published content.

This book is dedicated to my grandmother,
*Dr. Lalrimawi Pudaite.*

# Contents

Acknowledgements ........................................................................................ xi

Abbreviations ............................................................................................. xiii

Chapter 1 ........................................................................................................ 1
*Introduction*
    1.1 Statement of the Problem ........................................................................ 1
    1.2 Elaboration of the Problem ..................................................................... 1
    1.3 Rationale ................................................................................................... 5
    1.4 Literature Survey ...................................................................................... 6
        1.4.1 Weakness and Suffering of Paul in 2 Corinthians
            from Different Perspectives ............................................................ 6
        1.4.2 Important Literature Applying Disability
            Perspectives to Pauline Texts ...................................................... 11
    1.5 Research Questions ................................................................................ 19
        1.5.1 The Primary Question .................................................................. 19
        1.5.2 Secondary Questions .................................................................... 19
    1.6 Scope and Limitations ........................................................................... 19
    1.7 Structure of the Thesis ........................................................................... 21

Chapter 2 ..................................................................................................... 23
*Disability Hermeneutic*
    2.1 Introduction ........................................................................................... 23
    2.2 The Term "Disability" ............................................................................ 24
        2.2.1 The Ambiguity of the Term "Disability" .................................... 24
        2.2.2 Justification for the Use of the Term "Disability" ..................... 26
        2.2.3 Multiple Approaches of Defining the Term "Disability" .... 27
        2.2.4 The Definition of the Term "Disability" for this Study ....... 30
    2.3 Trends of Disability Hermeneutics (DHs) in Current
        Biblical Studies ....................................................................................... 31
        2.3.1 DH Focusing on a Medical Diagnostic Perspective ............ 32
        2.3.2 DH Focusing on a Theological Perspective ......................... 33
        2.3.3 DH Focusing on a Socio-Cultural Perspective .................... 35
    2.4 Developing a Viable Method of DHs .................................................. 37
        2.4.1 Disability Hermeneutics: Rhetorical Criticism Explained ... 39
        2.4.2 The Sociological Approach of DHs Explained ..................... 54
    2.5 A DH Pressed into the Reading of 2 Corinthians ............................. 67
    2.6 Summarization ....................................................................................... 71

Chapter 3 ............................................................................................... 73
*Disability in the Greco-Roman, Jewish World*
   3.1 Introduction ..................................................................................73
   3.2 General Attitudes towards Disability among Greeks,
       Romans, and Jews ......................................................................74
       3.2.1 Disability and Ancient Greek Society and Culture ............75
       3.2.2 Disability and Ancient Roman Society and Culture ..........80
       3.2.3 Disability and Ancient Jewish Society and Culture ...........84
   3.3 Disability in Corinthian Society ....................................................88
       3.3.1 A Brief History of the City of Corinth .................................88
       3.3.2 Evidence of Disability in Corinth ........................................89
       3.3.3 The Attitude of Corinthian Society towards the PwD ........90
   3.4 Paul and Disability ........................................................................91
       3.4.1 Paul's Own Testimony ..........................................................92
       3.4.2 Evidence from the *Acts of Paul and Thecla (APT)* ..............99
       3.4.3 Establishing Paul as a PwD ................................................103
   3.5 Summarization ............................................................................105

Chapter 4 ............................................................................................. 107
*The Socio-Rhetorical Context of Paul's Second Letter
to the Corinthians*
   4.1 Introduction ................................................................................107
   4.2 Authorship and Date ..................................................................108
   4.3 Occasion and Purpose of Paul ...................................................111
   4.4 The Social Matrix of the Corinthian Congregation ..................115
   4.5 The Corinthians' Attitude towards Rhetoricians and
       Disability ...................................................................................119
   4.6 Literary Unity of 2 Corinthians Correspondence ......................121
       4.6.1 The Letter Is a Compilation ...............................................122
       4.6.2 The Letter Is Not a Compilation ........................................124
       4.6.3 The Integrity of 2 Corinthians from a Disability
           Perspective .........................................................................125
   4.7 Opponents of Paul in Corinth: Identities and Hypothesis ........126
       4.7.1 Judaizers ..............................................................................127
       4.7.2 Gnostics ...............................................................................129
       4.7.3 Θειος ἀνηρ (Divine Men) ...................................................130
       4.7.4 Pneumatics .........................................................................131
       4.7.5 Sophists ...............................................................................132
       4.7.6 The Opponents from a Disability Perspectives .................134
   4.8 Summarization ............................................................................135

Chapter 5 ..................................................................................... 137
*Excavating Insights for Disability Theology in 2 Corinthians:*
*An Exegetical Exploration of the Selected Passages*
   5.1 Introduction ............................................................................137
   5.2 Applying a DH to the Exegetical Analysis of
       2 Corinthians 1:3–11................................................................138
      5.2.1 Establishing the Rhetorical Unit: Paul's Self Defence
          of His Disability................................................................139
      5.2.2 The Rhetorical Problem: The Issue of Disability ...............141
      5.2.3 Paul's Statements in Defence of His Disability ..................147
   5.3 Applying a DH to the Exegetical Analysis of
       2 Corinthians 4:1–18................................................................159
      5.3.1 Rhetorical Unity of 2 Corinthians 4:1–18 ..........................161
      5.3.2 *Probatio*: Paul Defends His Apostolic Ministry................163
   5.4 Applying a DH to the Exegetical Analysis of
       2 Corinthians 6:3–13................................................................179
      5.4.1 Rhetorical Unit of 2 Corinthians 6:3–13 ............................181
      5.4.2 *Probatio*: Paul Defends Himself to the Corinthians..........183
   5.5 Applying a DH to the Exegetical Analysis of
       2 Corinthians 10–13.................................................................200
      5.5.1 Rhetorical Unit of 2 Corinthians 10–13 .............................201
      5.5.2 The Rhetorical Exigence: Corinthians' Negative
          Attitude to Paul's Disability.............................................203
      5.5.3 *Probatio*: Paul Defends Himself.........................................211
   5.6 Summarization........................................................................229

Chapter 6 ..................................................................................... 231
*A Critique of Paul's Sufferings and Weaknesses in 2 Corinthians*
*from a Disability Perspective*
   6.1 Introduction ............................................................................231
   6.2 The Socio-Anthropological Dimension of Paul's Suffering
       and Weakness...........................................................................232
   6.3 Paul's Disability Is at the Heart of His Suffering for His
       Ministry ...................................................................................235
      6.3.1 Paul's Disability as Crucial Components of His
          Ministry ...........................................................................236
      6.3.2 DHs on the Christological Dimensions of Paul's
          Suffering and Weakness...................................................239
   6.4 The Purpose and Functions of Paul's Suffering and
       Weakness in 2 Corinthians......................................................244

  6.4.1 Interpreting His Suffering and Weakness as a
    Symbol of His Strength ........................................................245
  6.4.2 Paul's Suffering and Weakness Was for the
    Corinthians' Salvation..........................................................249
 6.5 Summarization.................................................................................254

Chapter 7 ................................................................................................ 257
*Conclusion and Implications*
 7.1 General Conclusion .......................................................................257
 7.2 Implications....................................................................................263
  7.2.1 The Use of DHs within New Testament Studies...............263
  7.2.2 Implications for Pauline Studies.........................................264
  7.2.3 Contributing to Disability Studies in Christian
    Academia................................................................................264
  7.2.4 Implications to the Church and Her Members .................266

Appendix 1 ............................................................................................. 271
*Index of Some Rare Greek Words for Disability*

Bibliography.......................................................................................... 275

# Acknowledgements

Thank you, God, for your mercy and faithfulness each step of the way.

I am immensely grateful to you, my mentor, Dr. Roji Thomas George, for your excellent guidance both academically and pastorally. The final product of my thesis is due to your desires for perfection and meticulous scrutiny. I have learned so much from you. I am also very much grateful to the SAIACS New Testament department for giving me a chance to pursue my PhD degree. I am grateful particularly for the initial guidance of Dr. Idicheria Ninan and Dr. William J. Subash.

Thank you so much, the late Dr. Rochung Pudaite, Dr. Mawii Pudaite, Rev. John Pudaite, Rev. Rohminglien Pakhuongte, and Mr. Roland Z. Chonzik, for all your financial support throughout my studies.

Thank you very much Dr. Vanrammawi Pakhuongte, Ms. Mary Grace Pangamte (PhD-NT student), and Ms. Marina Laltlingzo Infimate (PhD Linguist) for proofreading my thesis.

Thank you to the SAIACS academic and administrative staff for working tirelessly behind the scenes. Thank you Dr. Havilah Dharamraj for the PhD writing sessions. To the principal, the faculty, and all the SAIACS library staff, thank you for all your dedication and hard work.

To my wife, Fidelia L. Pakhuongte, and daughter, Stephanie L. Pakhuongte, my heart overflows with gratitude for your patience with me in our struggles. I cannot ever imagine myself travelling this lonely road, let alone completing it, without your constant supports.

I am so grateful to God for my family, and to my mother, brothers, and sisters for your gifts, prayers, and support throughout my studies. I am also very much grateful to my in-laws for all their kindness and monetary support. My gratitude also goes to the leaders of Evangelical Free Church of India, as well as to all our well-wishers who have been generous to us during our stay here at SAIACS.

# Abbreviations

## General
| | |
|---|---|
| AD | Anno Domini |
| *APT* | *Acts of Paul and Thecla* |
| ATEM | Associate for Theological Education in Myanmar |
| BC | Before Christ |
| BCE | Before Common Era |
| BTESSC | Board of Theological Education of the Senate of Serampore College |
| CA | California |
| CE | Common Era |
| ch./chs. | chapter/chapters |
| cf. | confer, compare |
| CO | Colorado |
| Cic. | M. Tullius Cicero |
| DH/DHs | disability hermeneutic/disability hermeneutics |
| diss. | dissertation |
| ed./eds. | edited by |
| EDAN | The Ecumenical Disability Advocates Network |
| esp. | especially |
| et al. | *et alia* (and others) |
| FL | Florida |
| GA | Georgia |
| *Inst.* | *Institutio Oratoria* |
| *Inven.* | *De Inventione* |
| IVP | InterVarsity Press |

| | |
|---|---|
| Jr. | Junior |
| MA | Massachusetts |
| MN | Minnesota |
| LXX | Septuagint |
| n. | footnote |
| NY | New York |
| NCCI | National Council of Churches in India |
| no. | Number |
| NT | New Testament |
| P$^{46}$ | Papyrus 46 |
| PA | Pennsylvania |
| PDF | Portable Document Format |
| PhD | Doctor of Philosophy |
| Pla. | Plato |
| PTCA | The Program for Theology and Cultures in Asia |
| PwD/PwDs | person with disability/persons with disabilities |
| Quintilian, | Quint. |
| *Rep.* | *Republic* |
| rev. | revised |
| *Rhe. ad Her.* | *Rhetorica ad Herennium* |
| SBL | Society of Biblical Literature |
| S. C. M. | Student Christian Movement |
| Sec. | Seneca |
| SPCK | Society for the Promotion of Christian Knowledge |
| s.v. | *sub verbo* (under the words) |
| SATHRI | South Asia Theological Research Institute |
| SCEPTRE | Senate Centre for Extension and Pastoral Theological Research |
| St. | Saint |
| *TDNT* | *Theological Dictionary of New Testament* |
| TN | Tennessee |
| trans. | translated |
| v./vv. | verse/verses |
| vol. | volume |

| | |
|---|---|
| WCC | World Council of Churches |
| YTCS | The Yushan Theological College & Seminary |

## Modern Biblical Versions

| | |
|---|---|
| ESV | English Standard Version |
| KJV | King James Version |
| NASB | New American Standard Bible |
| NET | New English Translation |
| NIV | New International Version |
| NJB | The New Jerusalem Bible |
| NLT | New Living Translation |
| NRSV | New Revised Standard Version |
| RSV | Revised Standard Version |

## Biblical References

### Old Testament

| | |
|---|---|
| Gen | Genesis |
| Exod | Exodus |
| Lev | Leviticus |
| Num | Numbers |
| Deut | Deuteronomy |
| Josh | Joshua |
| Judg | Judge |
| 1 Sam | 1 Samuel |
| 2 Sam | 2 Samuel |
| 1 Chron | 1 Chronicles |
| Ps/Pss | Psalm/Psalms |
| Prov | Proverbs |
| Eccl | Ecclesiastes |
| Song | Song of Solomon |
| Isa | Isaiah |
| Ezek | Ezekiel |
| Dan | Daniel |

## New Testament

| | |
|---|---|
| Matt | Matthew |
| Rom | Romans |
| Gal | Galatians |
| 1 Cor | 1 Corinthians |
| 2 Cor | 2 Corinthians |
| Eph | Ephesians |
| Phil | Philippians |
| Col | Colossians |
| 1 Thess | 1 Thessalonians |
| 1 Tim | 1 Timothy |
| 2 Tim | 2 Timothy |
| Philem | Philemon |

## Intertestamental Period

| | |
|---|---|
| 1 Macc | 1 Maccabeus |
| 2 Macc | 2 Maccabeus |
| 4 Macc | 4 Maccabeus |
| Sir | Sirach |
| 1QM | War Scroll |
| 1QS | Community Rule or Manual of Discipline Qumran Scroll |
| 1QS$^a$ | Rule of the Congregation or Messianic Rule |
| 4Q | Qumran Cave 4 |
| 4QFlor. | Florilegium |
| 4QpNah. | The Nahum Peshar Qumran Scroll |
| CD. | Damascus Documents |
| M. Sanh. | Mishnah Sanhedrin |
| TGad. | Testament of Gad |
| TJud. | Testament of Judah |

CHAPTER 1

# Introduction

## 1.1 Statement of the Problem

Paul's Second Epistle to the Corinthians abounds with his narrations of weaknesses and sufferings. In recent years, several scholars have put forward their views to explain why Paul focuses so much on his weakness and suffering in 2 Corinthians, mainly from a theological and rhetorical point of view. This present study also attempts to understand why Paul was seemingly fixated on his weaknesses and sufferings in 2 Corinthians. However, unlike previous attempts of scholars, this present study seeks to analyse Paul's suffering and weakness in 2 Corinthians from a disability perspective. This is mainly because scholars have not dealt with the socio-cultural and historical dimension of Paul's weakness and suffering adequately, especially in relation to disability. Moreover, scholars do not seem to have seriously considered the possibility of Paul's disability as playing a crucial role in the understanding of his weakness and suffering in his arguments in 2 Corinthians. Therefore, this present study will critically analyse some selected texts from 2 Corinthians by employing a disability hermeneutic.

## 1.2 Elaboration of the Problem

There has been a great deal of scholarship on Paul's suffering (θλίψις) and weakness (ἀσθένεια) from a variety of perspectives. For instance, Bultmann has attempted to understand Paul's θλίψις and ἀσθένεια from a theological perspective in which Paul's struggle becomes validated as far as "Christ is revealed in his entire life."[1] On the other hand, Fitzgerald has examined it from a historical perspective in which he analysed Paul's θλίψις and ἀσθένεια in parallel to the "*peristaseis* catalogues" found in many ancient documents.[2] Recently, Lim has employed a narrative approach to identify Paul's suffering as intrinsically related to the story of Jesus.[3] Many other scholars have struggled to explain Paul's suffering and weakness in 2 Corinthians[4] with varying degrees of success.[5] Yet the problem seems far from being resolved. For instance, the marked tonal differences between Paul's emotional arguments in 2 Corinthians 1–9 and the sudden shift in the intensity of his defences and arguments in 2 Corinthians 10–13 is causing considerable difficulty among scholars. It is true that Paul's letter is, in the words of Barrett, "simply a letter in which he wears his heart on his sleeve and speaks without constraint, hiding neither his affection, nor his anger or agony."[6] This present study hopes that by employing a disability hermeneutic, one will get better insights into the rhetorical strategy of Paul.

All throughout the letter, one observes Paul using the Greek word θλίψις and ἀσθένεια multiple times, an implication of the importance of these words to Paul. For instance, one finds the Greek word θλίψις in 2 Corinthians 1:4–5, 1:8–9, 4:16, 4:10–11, and 4:17–18. On the other hand, the Greek word ἀσθένεια is present in 2 Corinthians 11:21, 30, 12:5, 9–10, and 13:3–4, 9. These two words have a wide range of meanings. While θλίψις can refer to pressure in a physical sense or, figuratively, to "harassment, affliction, or oppression,"[7] similarly, ἀσθένεια signifies "weakness or powerlessness of various kinds," be it "literally, of bodily ailment, weak, ill, sick, and of physical or intellectual inability, inadequate" or "figuratively, of what is less effective, weak, feeble, not strong."[8] From these definitions alone, it is not altogether a stretch to think

---

1. Bultmann, *Second Letter*, 16, 116; Thrall also believes that Paul's letters to the Corinthians are best understood in light of Paul's theological thinking (*Corinthians 1–7*).
2. Fitzgerald, *Cracks*, 1.
3. Lim, *Sufferings of Christ*, 150.
4. See Wan's, *Power in Weakness*; Becker, *Letter Hermeneutics*; Roetzel, *2 Corinthians*; Hafemann, *Suffering and Ministry*.
5. See section 1.4 of this chapter.
6. Barrett, *Commentary*, 32.
7. Schlier, "*thlibō* (to press, afflict)," in *TDNT* (abridged in one Volume), 334.
8. Zmijewski, "ἀσθένεια," 170.

that when Paul talked of his θλίψις and ἀσθένεια, he was actually referring to his own limitations both physically and mentally.

However, the problem is that the majority of scholars[9] have failed to focus on the significance of Paul's suffering and weakness from a viewpoint of physical and mental limitations and, most importantly, the social implications of those limitations. Instead, they are content in interpreting Paul's weakness and sufferings mostly from the theological perspective. Their explanations are not satisfactory because they fail to convey the true intentions of Paul when he was baring his heart and soul to the Corinthian congregation. One suspects that there are reasons beyond a theological explanation to Paul's argument, and it is the hope of this present study to unmask the deeper reason by analyzing his rhetoric of weakness and suffering from a disability point of view.

Current academic discourse understands disability not just as a biomedical condition but a socially constructed limitation upon the "disabled."[10] This means that "disability" is a condition in which one is *limited* not just because one is physically challenged but also because this *limitation* often comes from the humiliating treatment of a given society that imposes its prejudicial view on those whom it feels are different. As such, disability often entails social stigmatization. With this understanding, one may ask, will not an analysis of Paul's struggles in 2 Corinthians from a disability perspective make better sense? Case in point, in 2 Corinthians 4:8, Paul wrote of his "sufferings in all things" (ἐν παντὶ θλιβόμενοι); does this not imply the comprehensiveness of the reality of Paul's sufferings? If so, what occasioned him to say that he "suffers" on all sides? Further, in 2 Corinthians 10:10, Paul was criticized for the "weakness" (ἀσθένεια) of his bodily presence in relation to his contemptible (ἐξουθενημένος) manner of speaking (see also his illness in Asia; 2 Cor 1:8). Surely, this criticism levelled at Paul indicates some sort of disability compounded by some kind of cultural stigmatization.

According to Martin, in the ancient Greco-Roman world, it was customary to disregard public speakers who had weak physical structures and were weak in verbal communication, as these two features were closely interrelated.[11]

---

9. Please see footnotes @@1–4 as listing some of these "majority of scholars." Also, additional scholars' works will be analysed in the literature review (see sections 1.4.1 and 1.4.2).

10. The next chapter will deal with the proper definition of "disability" and the position of this present study. See Wasserman, "Philosophical Issues," 219–22.

11. Martin, *Corinthian Body*, 35.

Likewise, Parsons also admits, "It was commonplace to associate outer physical characteristics with inner moral qualities."[12] The ancient society, even close family included, did not spare their ridicule or stigmatization of those who exhibited physical symptoms of being different from what was considered normal. For instance, in the case of Emperor Claudius who had a speech impairment since birth,[13] his own mother, Antonia the Younger, called him "a monster of a man (*portentum hominis*), not finished by Mother Nature but only half-done (*tantum incohatum*)."[14] Seneca also made fun of Claudius's speech problem in his *Apocolocyntosis* by putting words into the deified Augustus who states, "In short, let him say three words in quick succession and I will be his slave."[15] Even an emperor did not escape the social prejudice when it came to disability.

Martin Albl has pointed out that, "Paul wrote in a bicultural context, and, in order to comprehend his thought, one must consider both the ancient Jewish and the ancient Hellenistic backgrounds."[16] It seems the social milieu in which Paul found himself was not kind to the disabled, and it will be best if one is to understand Paul's weakness and suffering through a conscientious exploration of his social and cultural context (i.e. his Jewish and Greco-Roman context) from a disability perspective.[17] Indeed, it will be to one's advantage if 2 Corinthians is analysed from a disability point of view. Therefore, this thesis will attempt to delve deeper by analyzing the selected texts of 2 Corinthians (1:3–11; 4:1–18; 6:3–13; 10–13) using a disability hermeneutic.

---

12. Parsons, "Character," 295.

13. Claudius, or Tiberius Claudius Caesar Augustus, was born in 10 BC and died in AD 54 (Wasson, "Claudius").

14. Laes, "Silent History?," 164–165.

15. Seneca, *Apocolocyntosis*, sec. 11. *Apocolocyntosis* is generally rendered as "The Pumpkinification of Claudius." It is a political satire on the Roman emperor Claudius, written around AD 55 by Seneca (see "Apocolocyntosis – Seneca the Younger – Ancient Rome – Classical Literature," *Classical Literature*, accessed January 24, 2017, http://www.ancient-literature.com/rome_seneca_apocolocyntosis.html). Seneca was born Lucius Annaeus Seneca, and his date of birth is not certain. Some say in 4 BC while others in 1 BC. However, his death date is certain (AD 65). He was born in Cordoba, Spain, and educated in rhetoric and philosophy in Rome (Vogt, "Seneca").

16. Albl, "Whenever I Am Weak," 145. (For a critical treatment on Albl's work, please see the literature review section in 1.4.2.)

17. See Albl, "Whenever I Am Weak," 145–146.

## 1.3 Rationale

The attempt to study biblical texts from a disability perspective is a recent activity among biblical scholars and theologians alike. Many scholars have started to take seriously the need to study biblical texts critically from a disability perspective in response to the accusation that biblical interpretation offers little to the disabled. For instance, Roji T. George has stated,

> The Church has been accused of contributing towards the socioreligious alienation and marginalization of the disabled people by her disability blind ableist theology. This has forced the biblical scholars to revisit the biblical texts with an aim to articulate a biblical response to the quest for dignity, honour, and accessibility of the nonconventional bodies within the Church.[18]

Surprisingly, in spite of the importance of Paul and his letters in developing the theological foundation for the church,[19] few attempts have been made to study his works from a disability perspective. In fact, the literature reviews done on this particular subject will reveal that very few substantive works have been carried out to study Paul's weakness and suffering from a disability perspective. This is surprising because one can hardly deny the central theme of Paul's θλίψις and ἀσθένεια in 2 Corinthians. If one fails to grasp the significance of Paul's weakness and suffering in 2 Corinthians, and the need to analyse it from a disability perspective, the present study contends that one cannot truly understand the nature of Paul's ministry and the reality of his struggle, as he ministers to the city of Corinth and the surrounding lands in and out of Asia Minor.

Since scholars have overlooked the more seemingly obvious and important aspect of his disability, arising from social constructs and not just physical limitations, this results in a rather skewed and shallow understanding of Paul's struggles and his relationship with the Corinthian Christians. Because they neglected the social dimension of Paul's struggle in 2 Corinthians, it becomes difficult to see the real Paul who was struggling to get the Corinthians to respect and love him as they did the other "super-apostles" (2 Cor 11:5). However, when Paul's θλίψις and ἀσθένεια are observed carefully through the

---

18. George, "(Dis)abled Jesus," 101; see also Eiesland, *Disabled God*, 74.
19. Paul's letters here refer to the canonically and traditionally accepted letters in the name of Paul the apostle.

lens of disability, this present study hopes to demonstrate that one will understand better the reason why Paul was in danger of losing the Corinthians' loyalty and respect.

The researcher is well aware of the social stigmatization accompanying any deviance from the physical structure that is considered normal within a society. Having struggled with the problem of weight since childhood, the researcher has (even without any medical issues) felt the jeers and humiliations from various sections of the society where being thin is considered the prime example of being human. Even the designs and settings of the infrastructure in a given society are geared towards a humiliating experience. As such, the researcher inhabits a unique position from which the texts of 2 Corinthians can be analysed and interpreted by employing a particular hermeneutical lens (i.e. the disability lens that critically examines the effect of societal attitudes in disabling a person who is already struggling with physical limitations).

Thus, from this interpretative location, a better grasp of Paul's struggle with the Corinthians can be achieved, which will then go a long way in contributing to the comprehensive understanding of Paul's thoughts and emotional arguments in 2 Corinthians. At the same time, one hopes to raise awareness for the church and its members to be better caretakers of those who are disabled and who are made more disabled by the attitudes of society.

## 1.4 Literature Survey

This present study will analyse selected scholarly literature under two headings. First, it will briefly deal with the important scholars who have done their work on Paul's θλίψις and ἀσθένεια from a different perspective than disability. Second, it will examine scholars who applied disability insights to their studies and particularly to the Pauline Letters.

### 1.4.1 Weakness and Suffering of Paul in 2 Corinthians from Different Perspectives

Among the more important works under this heading, it will be good to start with the work of Rudolf Bultmann, who in 1951 published a critical exegesis on 2 Corinthians.[20] His method in analyzing 2 Corinthians was mainly an

---

20. Bultmann, *Second Letter*, 9.

eclectic method that included methods like the philological, historical-critical, literary, and rhetorical (mostly his method of analyzing Paul's diatribe). One can claim that Bultmann was mostly interested in the theological outcome of Paul's suffering and weakness. For instance, he believed that 2 Corinthians should not be explained as a "biographical document or . . . a portrait of Paul's personality."[21] For Bultmann, the social and moral problems are not important.[22] However, the "sole concern is the question of the relation between the community and its apostle."[23] Therefore, for him, the guiding perspective was always to see it as an "apostolic writing."[24] Likewise, C. K. Barrett also felt that, even though this letter is intensely personal for Paul, one must not hand "the epistle over to psychological interpretation, for it would be equally true to say that he never wrote a more theological letter."[25] Barrett's analysis of 2 Corinthians started from a mindset that the Corinthian Christians, after the first visit by Paul, were starting to be corrupted and doctrinally twisted, and they could no longer differentiate between right and wrong.[26] Barrett believed that all of Paul's struggle, his weakness and affliction, can only make sense if viewed in the light of Christ crucified.[27]

Both of them believed that Paul's θλῖψις and ἀσθένεια only makes sense if one looks at his struggle from the christological point of view that the apostle was trying to make.[28] Bultmann stated, "The one who suffers is in fellowship with Christ and thus can understand his sufferings as those of Christ, can appropriate them in understanding by faith."[29] Bultmann's statement makes sense if one is to understand Paul's suffering purely from a theological point of view, but the overall tone, say of chapters 10–13, can hardly be justified from this theological perspective alone. Here one observes, aside from the theological tone, the primal nature of Paul screaming aloud for acceptance. It is true that theologically, a close and integral relationship exists between

---

21. Bultmann, 16.
22. Bultmann, 16.
23. Bultmann, 17.
24. Bultmann, 16.
25. Barrett, *Commentary*, 32.
26. Barrett, preface to *Commentary*, viii.
27. Barrett, 49.
28. See Barrett, 32.
29. Bultmann, *Second Letter*, 116.

the suffering of Jesus Christ and Paul. However, it seems that the way Paul connected their suffering had different dimensions apart from the theological overtone; it seems more likely that a big chunk of comparison had to do with the social dimension of his sufferings.

Frank J. Matera took an interesting approach in his commentary of 2 Corinthians when he tried to find a solution to the question of Paul's sufferings from an eschatological angle.[30] To the problem of affliction and suffering that marked Paul's ministry, Matera envisioned the Corinthians asking a question like, "if Paul is truly the minister of a new covenant that reveals the glory of God, where is the glory?"[31] To this, Matera argued that Paul showed the Corinthians the intimate relationship between his suffering and affliction and his new covenant ministry. Matera went a step further than what was argued by the likes of Bultmann, in that he would say that Paul's apostolic suffering on behalf of the Corinthians paradoxically revealed the eschatological power of Christ's resurrection life in his mortal body.[32] His drawbacks include the failure to draw out the many seemingly personal and social dimensions of Paul's θλίψις and ἀσθένεια. While he was right to point out the significance of eschatology in Paul's suffering and weakness, he ignored the possible reference to Paul's own condition. He therefore failed to grasp the full picture of Paul's struggle with the interpretation of Mosaic law in relation to the eschatological concern.

One of the first serious exegetical works done on 2 Corinthians was by Scott J. Hafemann.[33] In his exegetical analysis of 2 Corinthians 2:14–3:3, Hafemann argued that this passage talks about Paul defending his apostolic ministry that was characterized by suffering.[34] Granted, there were many hardships and much suffering involved along the way of spreading the gospel. However, can one firmly consider the notion that apostolic ministry carries with it suffering, and that this was somehow the source of Paul's weakness and suffering? In other words, did Paul mainly suffer because of his vocation? If Paul was suffering from an illness, as he made known in 2 Corinthians

---

30. Matera, *2 Corinthians*.
31. Matera, 105.
32. Matera, 105.
33. Hafemann, *Suffering and Ministry*.
34. Hafemann, 219–221.

1:8, was that because of his vocation, or was it a pre-existing condition that manifested while he was in Asia? Certainly, there are grounds for investigating the socio-cultural and historical context of Paul from a disability perceptive. Perhaps his illness as a disability was something that caused him suffering, not just physically but emotionally and mentally as well.

In 1991, Jerome Murphy-O' Connor published his exegetical work in which he saw the basis of Paul's letter to the Corinthians as their opposition to Paul's ministry.[35] It is interesting to see the difference in his work from others in that he believed there was a sort of alliance between the two opponents of Paul – Palestinian Judaizers and Hellenistic Jews. To the whole issue of Paul's sufferings, he seemed to derive his understanding from the insights he got from an analysis of the relationship between Paul and his opponents whom he identified as "the spirit-people."[36] Connor felt that Paul brought up his suffering in an attempt to justify his calling as God's chosen vessel. It is true that Paul defended his ministry by bringing up his suffering because it was an essential part of his ministry. However, the question of the origin of his suffering and the social dimensions of his suffering are still areas that can be further analysed.

Another significant work is that of Timothy B. Savage who posited that the opponents of Paul were the Corinthians themselves who made Paul suffer much.[37] It seemed to him that the enemies of Paul just took advantage of what the Corinthian congregation were guilty of in the first place.[38] Savage employed socio-historical description methods in his analysis of the text.[39] He looked at the Corinthians from a historical point of view and then tried to make sense of Paul's paradoxical statement that he made in 2 Corinthians 12:10b: "When I am weak, then I am strong."[40] Savage stated rather insightfully, "The Corinthians with the usual practice of their time wanted Paul to be like those leaders measuring up to their standards."[41] However, since Paul did not measure up to their standards, their accusation led him to suffer

---

35. Murphy-O'Connor, *Theology*.
36. Murphy-O'Connor, 44.
37. Savage, *Power Though Weakness*, 10.
38. Savage, 10.
39. Savage, 13.
40. Savage, 16.
41. Savage, 187.

even more. Savage did well to focus on the social dimension. If only he had employed a disability perceptive in his analyses, then his findings, and contribution to the understanding of Paul's weakness and suffering, would have been much more significant. One can say that he may have limited himself by his methodology or failed to extend his argument forward to its possible logical conclusion that the Corinthians could have despised Paul because of his limitations.

Recently, Kar-Yong Lim's doctoral dissertation attempted to find out the reason why Paul made the theme of suffering so essential to his argument in 2 Corinthians.[42] He has come up with many findings as he employed a narrative approach to the many passages in 2 Corinthians that speak of Paul's sufferings. His findings offer interesting insights, but his observation that Paul's suffering is intrinsically related to the story of Jesus is hardly anything new as it has been time and again pointed out that Paul's suffering is related closely to Jesus and his death. Indeed, for Paul, his identification with the suffering of Jesus was, as Stegman put it, the "linchpin to Paul's argument in 2 Corinthians."[43] Nevertheless, in order to understand the core issue of why the earthly suffering of Jesus was so important for Paul, one needs to find the origin of Paul's suffering. Paul did not simply narrate his suffering for the purpose of encouraging those who suffered as well. There was a cause behind his suffering and one can reveal it by analyzing the social dimension of his weakness from a disability perspective.

In 1988, John T. Fitzgerald worked towards making sense of this catalogue of suffering and the relationship between Paul and the ancient literary convention of compiling lists of sufferings.[44] His book highlights the many catalogues of hardships found in ancient documents, but ultimately the author employed what he considered the most important of the various types – the suffering Wiseman catalogued to study Paul and his lists of sufferings in 2 Corinthians. Fitzgerald contended, "'*peristaseis* catalogues' function as rhetorical and literary foils for the depiction and demonstration of the sages' various qualities as the ideal philosopher and . . . serve to legitimate

---

42. Lim, *Sufferings*.
43. Stegman, *Character of Jesus*, 1.
44. Fitzgerald, *Cracks*.

the claims made about a person and show him to be virtuous."⁴⁵ This seems to fit well with the apostle Paul here in 2 Corinthians as he articulated his θλίψις and ἀσθένεια in order to validate his office and calling. One of the main problems of Fitzgerald's method is the inability to explain Paul's "*peristaseis* catalogues" in chapter 11:23–29. Thus, it is not surprising to find that this portion is glaringly absent in his monograph because the nature of Paul's catalogue of hardship in 2 Corinthians 11:23–29 is very different from that of 2 Corinthians 4:8–9 and 6:8–10.

## 1.4.2 Important Literature Applying Disability Perspectives to Pauline Texts

Some of the literature discussed here is not directly concerned with Paul's suffering and weakness in 2 Corinthians. However, they are discussed here because they employ disability as a method of study. Hence, the purpose of this survey is to show the feasibility of employing a disability perspective in the theological and biblical world. At the same time, it will be apparent that there is not enough literature engaged with Pauline texts from a disability method or perspective.

Ever since the publication of *The Disabled God: Towards a Liberatory Theology of Disability* by Nancy Eiesland in 1994, the importance of studying biblical texts and undertaking theology from a disability perspective has come to the forefront.⁴⁶ Eiesland struggled with her own disability and found it difficult to believe in a perfect God because it did not make sense to her and to the many who are disabled.⁴⁷ Eiesland "argues that traditional images of God, especially those that lead to views of disability as either blessing or curse, are inadequate. Within the course of her own experience, she wondered whether such a God could even understand disability, let alone be meaningful to her."⁴⁸ Thus, she came up with "the disabled God" model, which would make sense of her own condition. While her attempts are laudable, at the same time they are not without their demerits. As Creamer rightly pointed out, "it leaves no

---

45. Fitzgerald, 203.
46. Eiesland, *Disabled God*.
47. Eiesland identifies herself as "a woman with disabilities, a sociologist of religion, and a professor at a seminary in the United States" (Eiesland, "Things Not Seen, 103").
48. Creamer, *Disability and Christian Theology*, 85.

room for individuals who might have an ambivalent or negative relationship with their own disability and Christian theology disability."[49]

In 2009, Deborah Beth Creamer developed her own disability model called a "limits model."[50] This model understands disability from three perspectives, namely: "the notion that limits are an *unsurprising* characteristic of humanity,"[51] "limits are an *intrinsic* aspect of human existence – part of what it means to be human,"[52] and "the limits perspective implies that limits are *good* or, at the very least, not evil."[53] This model implies that disability is a part of being human. Her works enable one to understand fully and sympathize with those whom one would consider "disabled," but the vertical notion of how a God would allow for their present limited state seems to be lacking in her models.

In her book, she briefly discusses the notion of Paul's thorn in the flesh (2 Cor 12:7) as disability from a social perspective. After arguing the many possible interpretations of this "thorn in the flesh," she believes that,

> The affliction bore directly on Paul's stature and authority before the Corinthians, and so had social consequences within the Corinthian community. If the thorn was a human opponent known to the Corinthians, then the challenge to Paul's authority was direct and obvious. If the thorn was a physical affliction, then the Corinthians may have been concerned that Paul was unable to heal himself.[54]

Here, Creamer points to the possibility of reading Paul's "thorn in the flesh" as something that was happening in his body. This is not something new in scholarly interpretation, but what is interesting is the way she argues in relation to Paul's infirmities and their social implications. However, as Creamer was most concerned with establishing the relationship of disability and Christian theology, it would be unfair to her to expect more insights on Pauline texts aside from this brief analysis of 2 Corinthians 12:9.

---

49. Creamer, 90.
50. Creamer, 94.
51. Creamer, 94.
52. Creamer, 94.
53. Creamer, 94–95.
54. Creamer, 73.

Another important work on the Corinthian text is done by Hans Ucko who took up 2 Corinthians 4:7 for a brief exegesis through a disability lens.[55] In his work, he believes that there is a wrong conception perpetrated by the church that those who are disabled are individually weak.[56] In order to rectify this misconception, he calls on the argument that Paul gave in 2 Corinthians 4:7, in which he believes that Paul thought, "Weakness is not a characteristic of an individual or a particular group, but of the entire church."[57] John Piper, in his book *Disability and the Sovereign Goodness of God*, finds comfort for the disabled in 2 Corinthians 12:9, where Paul wrote, "My grace is sufficient for you."[58] Piper's work on Paul is mainly theological in nature. The same goes with John Swinton's attempts to trace the possibility of inclusive social community from Galatians 3:28.[59] He believes that from this verse, one can find the possibilities of a disability theology that is inclusive.[60] The important contribution of these brief articles is the benefit that they bring to the argument that Pauline texts are ripe for analysis from a disability perspective.

In 2011, Candida Moss and Jeremy Schipper edited a book called *Disability Studies and Biblical Literature*.[61] This book's main purpose was to bring together the "two fields of disability and biblical studies," where the different biblical texts are analysed from a disability perspective. This important collection of work includes Adele Yarbro Collins's article "Paul's Disability: The Thorn in His Flesh," which talks about the possibility that Paul's thorn in the flesh might have been epilepsy.[62] Even though Collins's work mainly concentrates on a historical as well as literary investigation of the interpretation concerning Paul's thorn in the flesh, it is nonetheless very crucial from a disability perspective. This is because she brings together the hypothesis that Paul's thorn must be his disability in the form of epilepsy and that this epilepsy was very much a reason for someone to endure shame and suffer stigmatization. According to Collins, "The impact

---

55. Ucko, "Christian Perspective," 151.
56. Ucko, 150.
57. Ucko, 151.
58. Piper, *Disability*, 16.
59. Swinton, "Who Is the God," 307.
60. Swinton, 307.
61. Moss and Schipper, *Disability Studies*.
62. Collins, "Paul's Disability," 165–183.

of the hypothesis, when taken seriously, affects most immediately our construction of Paul's life, his biography, and autobiography. It also may clarify certain rhetorical and theological choices that Paul made."[63]

In 2018, *The Bible and Disability: A Commentary* (the first commentary of its kind), edited by Sarah Melcher, Mikeal Carl Parsons, and Amos Yong, came out. This publication marks a significant growth in the study of biblical texts from a disability perspective.[64] Included in this commentary is "Paul," an essay by Arthur J. Dewey and Anna C. Miller, in which they use a disability perspective to analyse the Pauline Epistles.[65] They are aware of imposing a modern understanding of the term disability, stating, "We aim to respect the differences in terminology and construction between modern and ancient understandings of disability, even as we interrogate the way that Paul's deployment of impairment impacts his theological formulations."[66] Their work is laudable for its effort to employ the social and cultural method to find the underlying disability insights offered by Paul's Letters, if there are any.[67] However, one must raise some issues concerning their work.

First, they start from the premise that Paul was not disabled, but he understood "human limitations," and thus, one can interpret his work from a disability perspective.[68] It is surprising, given the fact that although they mention using the social and cultural model of disability,[69] they seem to have failed to observe Paul as disabled. Second, because of their premise, they do not see evidence of physical disability in Galatians 4:14–15, contrary to Amos Yong's suggestion that these texts suggest Paul's disability.[70] For them, Paul mentioning his weakness is a rhetorical strategy "toward the realization of his ideal community."[71] One is not surprised to observe that they do not connect the socially disabling stigmatization of a rhetor with the contemptible

---

63. Collins, 176–178.
64. Melcher, Parsons, and Yong, *Bible and Disability*.
65. Dewey and Miller, "Paul," 379–425.
66. Dewey and Miller, 380.
67. Dewey and Miller, 380–381.
68. Dewey and Miller, 420–422.
69. See Dewey and Miller, 380.
70. Dewey and Miller, 390; Yong, *Bible*, 86.
71. Dewey and Miller, "Paul," 390

manner of speaking and weak appearance in 2 Corinthians 10:10.⁷² Finally, their treatment of 2 Corinthians shows that they are aware of Paul talking about his "human limitations" metaphorically.⁷³ In addition, even though they admit that "Paul speaks of a chronic disability" (2 Cor 2: 7–9) when he discusses his thorn in the flesh, their conclusion that a search for the origin of Paul's chronic disability "is rather beside the point" is quite unsatisfactory.⁷⁴

Close on the heel of this commentary, Anna Rebecca Solevåg published her work *Negotiating the Disabled Body: Representations of Disability in Early Christian Texts*.⁷⁵ In her work, "early Christian textual representation of bodies that are marked as non-normative or deviant are explored through the lens of disability studies."⁷⁶ She "suggests that insights from this interdisciplinary field can be helpful for understanding more fully how the disabled body is negotiated in early Christian texts."⁷⁷ In one of the chapters, she touches on the possibility that the Corinthian Christians considered Paul as having gone mad and that he was greatly stigmatized for this because madness was a form of disability in those days.⁷⁸ It is interesting that she clubbed together the narratives of Jesus and Paul, whom their respective opponents labelled as mad. According to her, "Jesus and Paul were attacked by opponents who tried to stigmatize them by accusing them of madness and demon possession."⁷⁹ Although she is interested in the impact of Paul's stigmatization by those who called him mad or accused him of demon possession in both 1 and 2 Corinthians,⁸⁰ her work certainly shows that the letter to the Corinthians can be analysed from a disability perspective.

Coming to the Asian subcontinent, one can find emerging important works on this subject.⁸¹ For this present study, Roji T. George's "'(Dis)abled Jesus': Reading Jesus, His Mission, and the Jesus' Community for a (Dis

---

72. Dewey and Miller, 401.
73. Dewey and Miller, 400–401.
74. Dewey and Miller, 402.
75. Solevåg, *Negotiating the Disabled Body*.
76. Solevåg, 1.
77. Solevåg, 1.
78. Solevåg, 95–116.
79. Solevåg, 115.
80. See Solevåg, 114.
81. See Longchar and Rajkumar, *Embracing*; Mathew, "Disability," 43; Longchar & Cowans, *Doing Theology*; Rajkumar, *Sprouts*; Mathew, "Jesus," 48.

ability Perspective" is insightful.[82] In his work, George proposes to undertake a reading of the biblical text from a (dis)ability perspective in non-essentialist terms. Taking into consideration the ambiguous nature of disability, George proposes a different but unique way of looking at disability and using it in a way to better understand the biblical texts that portray Jesus, his mission, and his community. In his analysis of 1 Corinthians 11:8, he also touches briefly on Paul and his problem of disability, especially as it connected to social ostracizing.[83] Concentrating on the Greek word *ektroma* (untimely born), and finding support in the Septuagint (Job 3:16; Num 12:12) and Philo's work (*Legum Allegoriae* 1:76), George feels that this word may have been used by Paul's opponents to insult him.[84] Besides this, he also analyses the evidence provided by the apocryphal work of *Acts of Paul and Thecla* that does not seem to give a favourable impression on the figure of Paul. George points to the possibility of hardship and suffering that Paul would have faced from his society's ridicule of physical deformity, deeming disabled people as unfit for temple services.[85] Even though his work is brief, it opens up the possibility and need for examining Paul's suffering and weakness in 2 Corinthians from a disability perspective.

In regard to analyzing 2 Corinthians from a disability perspective, one of the most important works done to date is Martin Albl's article "'For Whenever I Am Weak, Then I Am Strong': Disability in Paul's Epistles," in which he looks at Paul's weakness from a disability perspective.[86] Here, Albl specifically examined Galatians 4:13–14 and 2 Corinthians 12:1–10. After carefully analyzing these texts, Albl concludes that disability takes the reader to the very heart of Paul's gospel.[87] As has been previously mentioned, his premise that "Paul wrote in a bicultural context, and, in order to comprehend his thought, one must consider both the ancient Jewish and the ancient Hellenistic backgrounds"[88] is solid. One may go so far as to suggest that Albl's work paves the way for all who seek to employ a disability perspective

---

82. George, "(Dis)abled Jesus," 101–125.
83. George, 118.
84. George, 118.
85. George, 118.
86. Albl, "Whenever I Am Weak," 145–160.
87. Albl, 145–160.
88. Albl, 145.

to the study of Pauline texts. He has rightly pointed out the importance of acknowledging the social stigma attached to Paul's disability, from which he was defending himself in his letters. Moreover, he insists that one observes the dual aspects of disability in Paul: "(1) disability conceived as a kind of natural impairment or functional limitation (a biomedical condition) and (2) disability construed as the social stigma or limitations placed by a society on certain groups who are labelled as 'disabled.'"[89]

However, in spite of the well-structured arguments, his treatment of Paul's disability as caused by social stigmatization has left a gap that needs to be filled. His argument that "in 2 Corinthians Paul again is at pains to defend his authority as an apostle" needs augmenting with evidence from a disability perspective on Paul. One may also ask, what made Paul defend his authority as an apostle? It seems logical to reason that Paul could be defending himself and his apostolic mission in the light of the social stigma attached to his disability. Surely Albl's use of a disability perspective would have allowed him to unearth much deeper aspects of Paul's struggle than to just defend his apostolic authority without much substantiation. Moreover, one observes that there are hardly any background studies, whether historical or sociological, in his analysis of the Corinthians text compared to what he did on the Galatians text.[90] It is unfortunate that he did not bring to light the many social stigmatizations suffered by physically challenged persons in his study of the 2 Corinthians text.

However, to be fair to Albl, his work was just an article where he was mainly concerned with highlighting Paul's disability and the subsequent social stigmatization he might have endured for it. Besides, what is positive about his work is that it encourages one to conduct a deeper and more comprehensive examination of the social and historical aspects of disability among the Corinthians. It also necessitates the need to further study 2 Corinthians exhaustively, to examine the many passages in 2 Corinthians that abound with Paul's θλίψις and ἀσθένεια, such as 2 Corinthians 1:3–11, 4:1–18, 6:3–10, and 10:1–12:20. Most of all, his work is a confirmation that disability studies can contribute substantially to a deeper and more thorough understanding of Paul's suffering and weakness in 2 Corinthians.

---

89. Albl, 145.
90. See Albl, 153–155.

There are some important findings from the above surveys of important selected literature. The following points highlight these:

1. Paul's θλίψις and ἀσθένεια are very significant themes, as is evident from the many important New Testament scholars who have spent their time trying to understand them from a different perspective. There seems to be a broad consensus where scholars understand Paul's θλίψις and ἀσθενής as identifying or imitating Christ's suffering, which Paul linked intrinsically to his apostolic ministry. Nevertheless, what is true is that there are not enough works done to show the importance of Paul's disability, especially the social dimension of Paul's weakness and suffering, particularly in 2 Corinthians.

2. Another significant finding is that disability studies have started to become an integral part of biblical studies. Long before biblical texts were scrutinized from a disability perspective by biblical scholars, various theologians tried to develop their disability theology. As the church is often accused of not doing its fair share of accepting the disabled along with the able, it is encouraging to note that the importance of disability studies in Christianity as a whole has been gaining momentum.

3. When it comes to studying the biblical texts, parts of the Old Testament and New Testament (especially Jesus's ministry) have been analysed from a disability perspective with great success. However, concerning the Pauline texts, aside from Galatians 4:13–14, 1 Corinthians 11:8, and 2 Corinthians 12:1–10, not many of the Pauline letters have been analysed from a disability perspective. Given the fact that a disability perspective seems to offer a viable means of gaining insight into Paul's argument, particularly in 2 Corinthians, there is not enough work done as of this moment. In spite of the fact that discussing biblical texts, especially Pauline texts, through a disability perspective is building momentum slowly, it would be safe to assume that this is a new significant area of study for biblical students.

## 1.5 Research Questions

Significant questions arise as one contemplates analyzing Paul's suffering and weakness in 2 Corinthians by employing a disability hermeneutic.

### 1.5.1 The Primary Question

The main question of this present study is, "What is the significance of analyzing Paul's suffering and weakness in 2 Corinthians from a disability perspective?" In other words, "What deeper and more comprehensive role does disability play in the attempt to understand Paul's suffering and weakness in 2 Corinthians?"

### 1.5.2 Secondary Questions

This primary question directly spawns a set of secondary questions such as:

- How should this present study understand and define the term "disability"?
- How should this present study attempt to formulate a disability hermeneutic in order to objectively analyse the selected texts as far as possible?
- How pervasive was the problem of disability in antiquity?
- How did the Greeks, Romans, and Jews deal with the issues relating to disability in their societies during the time of Paul?
- How far can the analysis of these selected texts from a disability hermeneutic help in the understanding of Paul's suffering and weakness in 2 Corinthians?
- Lastly, one must ask, what would be the ramifications of a disability hermeneutic on Pauline studies in general, and what impact can a study of Paul's suffering and weakness in 2 Corinthians have on the church's treatment of its disabled members?

## 1.6 Scope and Limitations

There are lots of singular words and meanings describing the condition of physically challenged human beings in the New Testament. Words such as τυφλός (blind), παραλυτικός (lame, paralyzed), νόσος (sick), πυρετός (fever), ἄλαλος (mute), κωφός (deaf), and so on, describe a particular type of disability. They are found spread throughout the New Testament. However, it is not the contention of this thesis to look into these words and examine them to bring about valuable insights into the study of a biblical theology on disability. Rather, this thesis attempts to focus on the in-depth understanding of Paul's θλίψις (suffering) and ἀσθενής (weakness) from a disability perspective as it pertains to the Apostle Paul and his struggles with the Corinthian congregation. In other words, this thesis is not a discussion on disability as a subject per se; it is an analysis of Paul's struggle and the possibility that disability seems to play, or could play, an integral role in the overall understanding of his suffering and weakness in 2 Corinthians.

As such, it must be pointed out that the present study focuses particularly on analyzing Paul's suffering and weakness. The study argues, building on the work of those scholars who believe that Paul suffered from some sort of disability[91] to some degree. Therefore, in chapter 3, the present study will work towards validating the argument of Paul's disability before actually analyzing the selected texts.

In this way, whatever findings arise from the exegetical analysis of the selected texts will strengthen the argument that Paul's suffering was compounded by his disability.

The primary passages for analysis from a disability perspective will be 2 Corinthians 1:3–11, 4:1–18, 6:3–13, and 10–13. Because of limited space, only those texts that contain direct references to Paul's suffering and hardships have been included even though the whole of 2 Corinthians can be analysed from this disability perspective.

In terms of methodology, disability studies have their fair share of methods or models that scholars have introduced.[92] However, this thesis has formulated an alternate methodology that is eclectic in nature to deal with the biblical text exhaustively, keeping in mind the need to delve deep into the social, historical,

---

91. On some scholars who think Paul was disabled, please see section 3.4.1.3 of this present study.

92. Some models include "the accessible God" proposed by Block in *Copious Hosting*, 82; "the interdependent God" proposed by Black in *Healing Homiletic*, 37–38; "the disabled God" proposed by Eiesland in *Disabled God*; and "the limits model" proposed by Creamer in *Disability and Christian Theology*, 95.

cultural, and rhetorical context of the texts to be analysed.[93] Nevertheless, it acknowledges that this formulated methodology is not a fix for all methodology; it is possible that one can come up with another methodology to suit one's exegesis of certain texts. Yet, the hermeneutical key "disability" remains unchanged. The next chapter (chapter 2) attempts to define the term "disability" as well as formulate a disability hermeneutic that this present study will use to exegetically analyse the chosen texts.

Lastly, this present study recognizes that the use of a disability hermeneutic to analyse Paul's weakness and suffering is very much in its nascent stage. As such, it will take time for the whole argument to develop properly. However, these are exciting times to start a conversation that will influence the whole of Pauline studies.

## 1.7 Structure of the Thesis

This present study consists of seven chapters that include the introduction. A brief description of the overall structure of the thesis is as follows: chapter 1 contains the introduction as well as important literature reviews focusing on the present study. Chapter 2 concentrates on the formulation of an eclectic methodology that this study will be employing. The methodology consists of a disability perspective, as well as rhetorical and sociological criticism that are specifically designed to analyse Paul's suffering and weakness in 2 Corinthians from a disability perspective. Chapter 3 analyses the history, culture, and social and religious environment of the Greco-Roman and Jewish world for the presence of disability. This chapter also contains a discussion on the nature of Paul's disability by analyzing various historical evidence. Chapter 4 specifically analyses the socio-rhetorical context of 2 Corinthians from a disability perspective with the expectation that it will provide background insight into the major exegesis. Included in this chapter is a discussion on the literary unity of 2 Corinthians and the identity of Paul's opponents in Corinth. Chapter 5 contains the exegetical analysis of the selected texts – 2 Corinthians 1:3–11, 4:1–18, 6:3–13, and 10–13 – by using the disability methodology formulated in chapter 2. This present study focuses on these particular texts because they contain important catalogues of Paul's sufferings

---

93. See section 2.4 of this present study.

and hardships. Chapter 6 contains this present study's critique, which is a culmination of all the analytical findings of the previous chapters, especially that of the exegetical chapter. In other words, it presents the answers to the research questions. Chapter 7 is the conclusion or summarization of the present study and contains important implications.

CHAPTER 2

# Disability Hermeneutic

## 2.1 Introduction

Very recently, a group of scholars published the first commentary offering a disability reading of the Bible. Significantly, Melcher acknowledges, "At the time of this writing, there is no book that explores disability in the New Testament."[1] This is especially true when it comes to the study of Pauline texts. As such, an important question to ask is how one should formulate an effective hermeneutical tool that is capable of providing biblical insights from a disability perspective, while retaining a fair respect for the text. In connection to this, one must also ponder how far it is possible to trace a broad pattern of how disability models have been employed in analyzing biblical texts. Another pertinent question for the present study is how it should set forth its understanding of the term "disability." Was "disability" used as an umbrella term in the Bible to refer to physical deformities or, in other words, a person with a disability (hereafter PwD)? If not, then how does it speak of its disabled individuals? Can the term "disability" be justifiable for describing the disabled people of antiquity? If so, how should one define disability to employ it for analyzing 2 Corinthians? Thus, this chapter seeks to answer these important questions.

---

1. Melcher, "Introduction," 12.

## 2.2 The Term "Disability"
### 2.2.1 The Ambiguity of the Term "Disability"

Although the first use of the word "disability" was in 1545,[2] the comprehensive categorization of physically, mentally, and emotionally challenged individuals as "disabled" is of a recent origin.[3] In antiquity, there were many words used to describe the condition of physical disability. Generally, disability would refer to the kind of deformity affecting a particular organ, like being τυφλός (blind), παραλυτικός (lame, paralyzed), νόσος (sick), πυρετός (feverish ), ἄλαλος (mute), and κωφός (deaf) in antiquity.[4] However, the umbrella term "disability" is absent in the Bible. Albl thinks that "the closest ancient Greek parallel to the modern term 'disability' is the word ἀσθενής ('weak') and its correlates."[5] What could be the reason for the absence of an umbrella term such as "disability" in ancient society? According to Laes, one such reason for the absence of disability as an umbrella term is that "the focus lies on the body's physical and cognitive limitations."[6] This means, "the disabled persons are considered from their situation of weakness or from their appearances as cripples, bent, with distorted limbs, and, finally from the consequences of this situation, their hindrance to act or to move."[7] The society focused on the specific location of what makes an individual limited. This made it unnecessary for them to connect it with a broader and more inclusive term. It is rather an uncomplicated and precise way of depicting infirmities.

Because of this, Laes argues, "the term disability is simply unsuitable to describe concepts and conditions of people in the ancient world."[8] He proposes that an examination of infirmities in antiquity would be better served if one were to study them under the following categories: "1) Physical handicaps/mobility impairment 2) Sensory impairment (visual, auditory) 3) Speech disorder 4) Learning disorders or intellectual disabilities 5) Mental

---

2. *Merriam-Webster*, s.v. "disability," accessed September 5, 2018, https://www.merriam-webster.com/dictionary/disability.

3. Laes, introduction to *Disability in Antiquity*, 4.

4. See appendix 1 of this present study for various lists of infirmities recognized in antiquity.

5. Albl, "Whenever I Am Weak," 146.

6. Laes, introduction to *Disability in Antiquity*, 4.

7. Samama, "Greek Vocabulary of Disabilities," 134.

8. Laes, introduction to *Disability in Antiquity*, 6.

conditions and 6) Multiple impairments (often combinations of the above)."[9] Laes's proposal seems quite reasonable given the fact that the notion of applying the modern understanding of "disability" would mar one's investigation. The complexities and inclusivity that have become part of the modern understanding of disability may create an unnecessary obstacle to the unencumbered understanding of physical and cognitive deficiencies in antiquity.

It is interesting that in the modern era, in spite of the term "disability" covering all sorts of infirmities,[10] the World Health Organization (WHO) is inclined to specifically identify terms such as "impairments,"[11] "activity limitations,"[12] and "participation restrictions"[13] that were already covered under its definitions of disability. It may also be pointed out here that when it comes to defining the severity of a person's disability, the WHO has come up with a system of grading disability where the sum 0 becomes the lowest grade or least disabled and 12 is the maximum grade or the severest.[14] However, this system of grading disability has its drawbacks because it focuses on impairments where "impairments" are understood as "any loss or abnormality of psychological, physiological, or anatomical structure or function."[15] Since the term disability covers more than impairments, the grading system becomes problematic when it comes to assessing how much a societal attitude towards imperfection contributes to the overall severity of a person's disability.[16] The currently rejected model of disability study (the medical model) tends to do such gradation purely based on the observed physical or mental condition, overlooking the social dimension of associated stigmatization.[17] Hence, it is not helpful for the disability theologian to employ a gradation of disability level in their textual engagement. Moreover, it may also be pointed out here

---

9. Laes, 6.

10. WHO, "Disabilities."

11. WHO defines impairment as "a problem in body function or structure" ("Disabilities").

12. WHO understands activity limitation as "difficulty encountered by an individual in executing a task or action" ("Disabilities").

13. WHO defines it as "a problem experienced by an individual in involvement in life situations" ("Disabilities").

14. For more information on the WHO grading system, see Brandsma and Van Brakel, "WHO Disability Grading," 366–373

15. WHO, *International Classification*, 27.

16. See de Souza et al., "Is the WHO," 192.

17. See section 2.2.3 of this chapter.

that some disabled groups do not want to be clubbed together with other disabled groups. For instance, Davis noted, "many Deaf activists do not consider themselves disabled."[18] Instead, these activists are willing to identify themselves with linguistic minorities like those of Latin or Asian origin in the US.[19]

## 2.2.2 Justification for the Use of the Term "Disability"

Should one then discontinue using the term "disability" when investigating the ancient Greco-Roman and Jewish world? If one is to continue employing it, then what will be the justification for using it to analyse disability and its effect in the Bible? Without a doubt, Laes's argument brings to light the complexity of using the modern term "disability" in antiquity. Nevertheless, against this understanding, one may note that any discussion on human limitation invites complexity not just from the external evidence but more so from the intangible reality.[20] His proposal of breaking down and studying the different forms of infirmities in antiquity leaves out the crucial aspect of the societal attitude towards disabled people. The concept of disability in the ancient Greco-Roman and Jewish world is not just a systematized cataloguing of the terms of physical and cognitive limitations. Those "suffering" individuals are active members of society. As such, there is a need to study and analyse early cultural expectations and societal reactions to those people who exhibited these limitations.

Laes was critical of using the modern term "disability" to denote the problem of deformities because he questioned the possibility of the modern term "disability" standing for all the types of infirmities recorded in antiquity. However, if one can come up with a definition of disability that is able to encompass all of the phenomena, including the physical, emotional, mental, and social aspects associated with infirmities in antiquity, then this problem in terminology need not be a point of contention. Therefore, the study of ancient texts from a modern disability perspective would be justifiable if the term "disability" is to denote all the narrow and multiple ways of speaking about infirmities in antiquity. If so, then the argument that studying the phenomenon from a localized point of view is better just because the word "disability"

---

18. Davis, "Crips Strike Back," 503.
19. Davis, 503.
20. See Kaplan, "Definition of Disability," 352.

was absent in antiquity becomes unwarranted. It is also misleading to think that because the ancient society localized their infirmities, any form of social stigmatization for the PwD is non-existent. Disability, as is understood by Thomson, is not just a "self-evident physical condition."[21] Rather, it is much more complicated as it describes so much more than just a plain physical condition. Hence, it is hardly justifiable to think that the concept of human suffering was confined to physical deficiency during antiquity.

However, what is true is the need to redefine or reconfigure the term "disability" to cover all the nuances of infirmities in antiquity. The definition of "disability" ought to be viable from both ends, both in dealing with antiquity and in the modern sense. It must be comprehensive and informed by any previous attempts to define it.[22] Before an attempt is made to define such a term, as necessitated by the problem mentioned above, a quick look at the history of the definition and understanding of disability is in order.

## 2.2.3 Multiple Approaches of Defining the Term "Disability"

There have been multiple approaches to defining "disability" throughout history. First, the moral model defines disability as the direct result of sin. It is one of the oldest in the history of disability definition and understanding. This moral model has a direct affinity with the religious model.[23] This model identifies religious books and teachings, even beliefs, as the primary source for pointing out disability. It specifically allows one to study these sources and find the means to change how they are interpreted. One can also say that its strength is also its weakness because, in this model, disabled people feel guilty because they think that their disability originates from their sins or wrongdoings.[24] There are many who blame biblical teaching for nurturing this kind of explanation.[25] It can have an adverse effect on the family as a whole, not just the PwD.[26]

---

21. Thomson, *Extraordinary Bodies*, 6.
22. Interestingly enough, Rebecca Atkinson feels that she will continue to use the word "disability" precisely because there is no other better term yet (Atkinson, "Viewpoint.")
23. Zedda, "In The Loop."
24. David Pfeiffer, "The Disability Paradigm and Federal Policy Relating to Children with Disabilities," (PhD diss., University of Honolulu, 1998), quoted in Kaplan, "Definition of Disability," 353.
25. Clapton and Fitzgerald, "History of Disability."
26. Kaplan, "Definition of Disability," 353.

The second approach to defining disability is the medical model that defines disability as a defect or some kind of sickness that needs curing through medical intervention involving "management, repair, and maintenance of physical and cognitive capacity."[27] The advantage of this model is the attention it pays to the individual who suffers. Michael Oliver, the great English disability activist, termed this medical model as the "individual model" because it focuses so greatly on the individual.[28] Because people thought that an underlying medical condition caused such defects, no expense was too much in the effort to make the medically disabled individual better. However, the definition upholding this model's premise implies that "the disabled individual is viewed as innately, biologically different and inferior"[29] and fails to take into account the socially disabling attitude that the individual encounters in his/her daily life.

The third approach is the rehabilitation model that defines "disability as a deficiency that must be fixed by a rehabilitation professional or other helping professional."[30] This model is "an offshoot of the medical model" because the source of disability lies in/with the individual.[31] However, with the development in the understanding of disability, people started to become aware that the causes of disability could also be deeply psychological. This is especially true as one realizes that a perfectly normal person can suddenly become a victim to the condition of disability due to war or accident. For such a person, disability is not just physical but becomes much more psychological. Thus, the rehabilitation model becomes much more prominent after the end of World War 2 when persons without any visible disability went to war and came back disabled with cut-off limbs, blindness, or deafness.[32] Nonetheless, the social aspect still does not make it to the agenda.

The fourth approach is the social model of defining disability that came into being because of the weakness shown by the other approaches. People realized that the source of disability was much more complex than what has been understood before. As was previously noted above, the source of

---

27. Creamer, *Disability and Christian Theology*, 24.
28. Oliver, *Understanding Disability*, 30.
29. Crossley, "Disability Kaleidoscope," 649–650.
30. Kaplan, "Definition of Disability," 534.
31. Kaplan, 534.
32. Kaplan, 535.

disability is not just physical or mental, but disability can also arise from negative societal attitudes towards a person who may be different from others. As such, in 1974, UPIAS (Union of the Physically Impaired Against Segregation) defined disability as "the loss or limitation of opportunities to take part in the normal life of the community on an equal level with others due to physical and social barriers."[33] Building upon this, in 1988, C. H. Liachowitz clarified this definition further by stating that disability is "a continuous relationship between physically impaired individuals and their social environments, so that they are disabled at some times and under some conditions, but are able to function as ordinary citizens at other times and other conditions."[34]

This social model "was successfully launched in Western academia by Michael Oliver in 1990."[35] The social model is conscious of two important factors: (1) a person's physical or mental traits and (2) the surrounding environment, which is at least partly constructed by others.[36] In contrast to the previous models, this model sees disability as disadvantages flowing from social systems and structures more than a biological phenomenon.[37] This model is one of the better models to define disability, but it is not without its drawback. Tom Shakespeare, in writing of the weakness of this model, correctly postulates that this model is more like a slogan and political ideology rather than an academic account of disability.[38] Another major obstacle of this model is that it neglects individual experiences of impairment.[39]

The fifth approach is the cultural model that closely relates to the social model.[40] The interrelatedness of this model with the social model is very apparent; as Crossley states, "disability is constructed not only by barriers erected in the physical environment but also by the barriers embedded in

---

33. Bickenbach, Chatterji, Badley, and Ustun, "Models of Disablement," 1173–1186. UPIAS was founded in 1972 by Paul Hunt, who developed his ideas when he was living in an institution where he and others had been struggling with the authorities over the right of disabled people to control their own lives ("UPIAS Founding statement").
34. Liachowitz, *Social Construction of Disability*, 2.
35. Oliver, *Politics of Disablement*, 11.
36. Samaha, "What Good Is," 1.
37. Crossley, "Disability Kaleidoscope," 653.
38. Shakespeare, "Social Model of Disability," 199.
39. Shakespeare, 199.
40. Schipper, *Disability Studies*, 20.

social structures and societal attitudes."[41] This model defines disability as a cultural construct in which a given culture creates an atmosphere of exclusion for those who are different because of negligence or ignorance.[42] The outcome of such ignorance leads to people labelling "individuals with disabilities as freaks or dangerous monsters."[43] Crossley rightly notes, "These stereotyped depictions tend to perpetuate societal prejudice and to bolster nondisabled persons' fear of disabled people."[44]

From all these definitions or understanding of disability, one can relate to the problem that the PwD experiences in real life. What this means is that disability is altogether a complex phenomenon that comprehensively involves the individual's physical, mental, emotional, and most importantly, his/her social and cultural interactions. This brings to light the stark reality of the mountains of obstacles and the scope of barriers that persons with disability encounter in their societies.[45]

## 2.2.4 The Definition of the Term "Disability" for this Study

This present study then defines the term "disability" as indicating a person's bodily limitation(s) or *imperfections*, coupled with the negative social reaction to those bodily limitation(s) or *imperfections*. The bodily limitations or *imperfections* can be various sorts of physical defects or inferiority that cause much hardship; however, the important aspect to be considered is the negative or hurtful social impact of those defects. This is because the physical deformity or limitations of an individual becomes socially oppressive and mentally agonizing due to the social stigma attached to what society considers *imperfections*. At times, more challenging than the physical limitation experienced is the negative social mindset and derogatory caricature of a disabled individual in their socio-cultural and religious environment.

---

41. Crossley, "Disability Kaleidoscope," 655–656.
42. Crossley, 655.
43. Crossley, 655.
44. Crossley, 655.
45. Crossley, 654.

## 2.3 Trends of Disability Hermeneutics (DHs) in Current Biblical Studies

As has been previously noted, the analysis of biblical texts by applying a disability hermeneutic is of recent origin, although disability scholarship has made a passing and sometimes general reference to how the Bible plays a role in the culture and reception of disability.[46] For instance, Avalos, Melcher, and Schipper have noted, "Biblical scholars are just beginning to contribute to this growing body of scholarship."[47] Avalos, in particular, was involved in surveying the different ways scholars employed the disability perspective in their attempts to analyse biblical passages. He identified three basic approaches: (1) redemptionist, (2) rejectionist, and (3) historicist.[48] According to him, a scholar who employs the redemptionist approach "seeks to redeem the biblical text, despite any negative stance on disabilities, by re-contextualizing it for modern application."[49] The rejectionists "argue that the Bible has negative portrayals of disability that should be rejected in modern society."[50] The historicist examines disabilities in "the Bible and its subsequent interpretation, sometimes in comparison with neighbouring ancient cultures, without any overt interest in the consequences of the conclusions for modern application."[51] Even with this broad and inclusive identification of disability approaches, Avalos, Melcher, and Schipper acknowledge the need and possibility of combining disability perspectives with different critical tools to study the biblical texts.[52] The following sections provide a descriptive history of disability methods employed by different scholars and theologians, assessing their strengths and weaknesses.

---

46. It was only in the 1980s that serious academic work on the study of disability and its relationship with biblical texts was achieved (see Avalos, Melcher, and Schipper, *This Abled Body*, 2).
47. Avalos, Melcher, and Schipper, 2.
48. Avalos, "Redemptionism," 91–100.
49. Avalos, Melcher, and Schipper, introduction to *This Abled Body*, 4.
50. Avalos, Melcher, and Schipper, 5.
51. Avalos, Melcher, and Schipper, 5.
52. Avalos, Melcher, and Schipper, 4.

## 2.3.1 DH Focusing on a Medical Diagnostic Perspective

One of the earliest tools that disability scholars employed to study the Bible was to use the medical perspective of disability. This approach focuses on the correct diagnosis of what a particular biblical character suffered from. For instance, Harrison in his article "Lame," in *The Interpreter's Dictionary of the Bible,* tried to diagnose the man in Acts 3:2 as someone who suffered from "weakness of the astragalus and metatarsus bones of the foot."[53] This type of medical diagnosis is still prevalent even today, judging from the work of Jo Ann Scurlock and Burton R. Andersen, *Diagnoses in Assyrian and Babylonian Medicine: Ancient Sources, Translations, and Modern Medical Analyses.*[54] Here, they attempted to "provide a comprehensive review and analysis of all available ancient Mesopotamian texts dealing with medicinal diagnosis or prognosis."[55]

The problem of employing this type of disability hermeneutic is that it neglects the primarily social aspect of disability. Concentrating on finding out medical conditions alone is not enough to get the whole picture of how the disabled felt. For instance, when such a perspective is applied to the analysis of King Asa's disease (1 Kgs 15:23; 1 Chr 16:12), the focus tends to be solely on the "diagnosis of Asa's disease,"[56] and the "diagnoses include gout, dropsy, gangrene, peripheral obstructive vascular disease, and prostate cancer among others."[57] This highlights the interpreter's focus, which is on identifying the underlying cause of the sickness. However, the interpreter refrains from engaging the theological stance or the social implications of the disease. In other words, this approach does not seriously take into account the social, cultural, and historical situation of the biblical texts.[58]

Nevertheless, in the recent works of scholars like Mikeal C. Parsons, one sees an attempt to incorporate the sociological aspect of disability along with a medical perspective. In his work "His Feet and Ankles Were Made Strong: Signs of Character in the Man Lame from Birth,"[59] Parsons analyses the

---

53. Harrison, "Lame," 3:59–60.
54. Scurlock and Andersen, *Diagnoses.*
55. Scurlock and Andersen, introduction to *Diagnoses,* xvii.
56. Schipper "Embodying Deuteronomistic Theology," 81.
57. Schipper, 83; Rosner, *Medicine in the Bible,* 58–59; Sweeney, *1 and 2 Kings,* 195.
58. Moss and Schipper, introduction to *Disability Studies,* 3.
59. Parsons, "His Feet and Ankles," 151–164.

lame man in Acts 3–4 from a physiological perspective. He believes that the descriptions of infirmities pointing to the "feet and ankles" were particularly important to "the compilers of the physiognomic handbooks."[60] Parsons connects this interest in descriptions of the feet and ankles not just to a medical point of view but also to what the ancient writers thought of them as revealing the character of a person. He believes that people in antiquity despised and ostracized these disabled people.[61]

Likewise, Nicole Kelley's work "'The Punishment of the Devil Was Apparent in the Torment of the Human Body': Epilepsy in Ancient Christianity," explains the disease in general and describes the relationship between epilepsy and demonic possession.[62] She explores the occurrences of epilepsy "as it appears in the Synoptic Gospels, situating this episode within the larger context of the ancient Greco-Roman world's varied etiologies for epilepsy and its explanations of disease in general."[63] After which, she turned her attention "to several late-antique Christian texts."[64] She came to believe that the problem of epilepsy was far more serious than just a simple medical condition. Instead, epilepsy occasioned "disabling conditions" among the religious community in a society.[65]

## 2.3.2 DH Focusing on a Theological Perspective

This is one of the most common approaches employed in a disability study of the Bible. Among the more important works, mention may be made of Eiesland's groundbreaking work, *The Disabled God: Towards a Liberatory Theology of Disability*, which she published in 1994. In her work, Eiesland made use of a theological model, "the disabled God," where she portrayed God as "disabled."[66] She was trying to redeem the character of God, whom many thought to be someone holy and perfect. To her mind, such a God could scarcely sympathize with her or make much sense to her as she was

---

60. Parsons, 151–152.
61. See Parsons, 151.
62. Kelley, "Punishment of the Devil," 205–221.
63. Kelley, 206.
64. Kelley, 206.
65. Kelley, 206.
66. Eiesland, *Disabled God*, 89.

disabled.[67] It must be said that her attempts to develop a theology of disability were informed by the historical and sociological struggles that disabled people encounter, as well as her desire to liberate others from the traditional acceptance of a perfect God.[68]

Eiesland identified three important problems when it comes to the application of this particular hermeneutic. The first is the notion that disability occurs because of someone's sin.[69] Second, the problem has to do with the notion that many understand disability in terms of virtuous suffering.[70] This has created a distorted view of disability as it allows the possibility of further punishment, all for the sake of outward appearances. Third, the problem of interpreting disability as a charity case is another big obstacle to the overall emancipation of disabled people.[71] These traditional understandings of disability allow others to see the PwD as someone who needs help intrinsically. This contributes to a mental subjugation which results in a loss of motivation to rise above the PwD's current position and state of mind. Thus, she believes that a liberatory theological model would address these issues for the abled as well as the disabled, setting the field level for all concerned.[72]

Aside from her, Kathy Black proposed a theological hermeneutic called "theology of interdependence" that emphasized her understanding of Christian community as a place where all are called to "work interdependently with God to achieve well-being for ourselves and others."[73] Creamer also came up with what she termed a "limits model," in which she tried to understand disability as an intrinsic aspect of human existence.[74] Recently, Swinton and Brock have published their work *Disability in the Christian Tradition: A Reader*, in which key writers offered important theological

---

67. According to Douglas Martin, "By the time the theologian and sociologist Nancy Eiesland was 13 years old, she had had 11 operations for the congenital bone defect in her hips and realized pain was her lot in life" ("Nancy Eiesland Is Dead").

68. This is evident in chapters 1 through 3 of Eisland's book, before she eventually developed the liberatory theology of a disabled God (see Eiesland, *Disabled God*, 23, 31, 49–57).

69. Eiesland, 73–75.

70. Eiesland, 73–75.

71. Eiesland, 73–75.

72. See Eiesland, 105.

73. Black, *Healing Homiletic*, 37–38.

74. Creamer, *Disability and Christian Theology*, 95.

insights on the subject of disability.[75] Along with these, one may also mention Timothy J. Basselin's article that underscores the importance of this perspective. In his work, "Why Theology Needs Disability," he urges the church to develop a theology of disability.[76] Indeed, developing a liberatory disability model from a theological perspective is a step in the right direction of analyzing biblical texts.

## 2.3.3 DH Focusing on a Socio-Cultural Perspective

Avalos, Melcher, and Schipper pointed to 20 November 1995 as the landmark day when interest in applying disability hermeneutics from a social and cultural perspective to biblical studies saw light in the larger academic circle.[77] This marked the day when biblical scholars realized the importance of using the socio-scientific methodological tools that were within their grasp to study the biblical text from a disability perspective. This socio-cultural perspective understands the deep nature of the complexity of disability studies and its relationship with biblical texts. It sees disability not simply as "a set of biological conditions" but something that "emerges as a complex product of social, institutional, environmental and biological discourses," which opens "up the study of disability as a subject of critical inquiry."[78]

Among the important works that are under this approach, mention may be made of Hector Avalos, one of the first pioneers in this regard. His book *Illness and Health Care in the Ancient Near East*, published in 1995, was important as it focused on the social experience of disability and disease.[79] Then in 2006, Schipper employed cultural criticism to the study of disability in the Hebrew Bible, especially in the story of Miphibosheth.[80] Olyan and Raphael expanded Schipper's work from a literary-critical method.[81] The other important scholars who used cultural methods to study biblical texts

---

75. Swinton and Brock, *Disability*; see also Wilder, *Disability*, which takes into account the background history of disability and deals with the problem of disability.

76. Basselin, "Why Theology Needs Disability," 47–57.

77. According to them, the landmark session was the Religion and Disability Studies Consultation held at the American Academy of Religion/Society of Biblical Literature annual meeting in Philadelphia (Avalos, Melcher, and Schipper, introduction to *This Abled Body*, 3).

78. Snyder, Brueggemann, and Garland-Thomson, "Introduction," 3.

79. Avalos, *Illness and Health Care*.

80. Schipper, *Disability Studies*.

81. Olyan, *Disability*; Raphael, *Biblical Corpora*.

include Mitchell, Snyder, David, and Thomson.[82] Then in 2007, the Society of Biblical Literature (SBL) published *This Abled Body*, an important work that used various cultural and literary criticisms to interrogate "various literary and cultural poetics within ancient texts as well as various scholarly interpretative assumptions regarding disability within the academy."[83]

The scholarly interest in combining disability perspectives with a socio-scientific approach is a recent phenomenon. As such, it is not surprising to hear Moss and Schipper rightly acknowledging that the application of a socio-cultural perspective is mainly concentrated in the Hebrew Bible and that "currently, there are no books in print devoted to disability studies and the New Testament."[84] The book that comes closest to this is *The Bible and Disability: A Commentary*, edited by Sarah J. Melcher, Mikeal C. Parsons, and Amos Yong.[85] However, this interest is slowly gaining ground among biblical scholars. These are constructive times for biblical scholars to make their mark on wider academic scholarship, especially in the field of DHs.

Recently, building upon his earlier work,[86] George attempted to formulate a disability hermeneutic that takes the middle route where both the disabled and abled would benefit from encountering God in the biblical texts without polarization.[87] He argued that it is possible to formulate a disability hermeneutic "that defies bi-polarity while exhuming relevant insights from a text."[88] To this end, he proposed a disability hermeneutic called "(dis)ability hermeneutic" that is "contextual in nature" and that leans heavily on the principles of postmodern criticism as well as relying on the need to be culturally sensitive.[89] His proposal lends validity to this study's attempt to formulate a disability hermeneutic that would critically engage with the Pauline texts. This is because the principle of a hermeneutic of suspicion enables the researcher to call into question the validity of the concluding remarks drawn

---

82. See Moss and Shipper, *Disability Studies*, 5, for lists of scholars who used critical methods.

83. Avalos, Melcher, and Schipper, introduction to *This Abled Body*, 4.

84. Moss and Schipper, introduction to *Disability Studies*, 6.

85. Melcher, Parsons, and Yong, *Bible and Disability*.

86. See George, "(Dis)abled Jesus," 101–125.

87. George, "Towards a Hermeneutic, 155–173.

88. George, 156.

89. George, 159, 162–167.

by previous interpreters, while the hermeneutics of retrieval allows one to re-work through the text to "recover" the cultural elements of the biblical passages. George correctly observed the importance that culture plays on the interpretation of biblical texts, particularly when it comes to the problem of disability. As he rightly argued, it is possible to "unearth not only the ideological basis of the text . . . but highlight the liberative thrust of the Scripture."[90]

## 2.4 Developing a Viable Method of DHs

From the above discussions, it can be observed that various scholars have employed disability studies from different perspectives such as medical diagnostic, theological, and socio-literary perspectives. In such a situation, there is an opportunity for analyzing Paul's suffering and weakness in 2 Corinthians from a disability perspective. However, the question is how to go about integrating a disability perspective into the exegetical analyses of 2 Corinthians while adding depth to its interpretative and exegetical dimensions. As such, this section will formulate a DH for analyzing the selected 2 Corinthians texts.

What then is the proposed DH that this present study will use to analyse 2 Corinthians? To state the definition, this DH is a perspectival exegetical-interpretative engagement with the text, where one intentionally foregrounds the reality of disability and the associate socio-cultural elements to gain liberative insights for today. Perspectival reading means "consciousness of or the process of using different points of view" in reading biblical texts.[91] Here, the selected texts from 2 Corinthians will be consciously analysed from the perspective of disability. Way back in 1861, Jowett had argued, "The true use of interpretation is to get rid of interpretation, and leave us alone in the company of the author."[92] However positive the intention behind this kind of thinking, it is just not sustainable for the precise reason that no interpreters could be totally objective in their approach. This present study is aware of the pitfalls of subjectivity into which a perspectival reading may lead the researcher. Nevertheless, this DH attempts to be as analytical as possible in its approach.

---

90. George, 165.

91. *Merriam Webster*, s.v. "Perspectivism," accessed August 31, 2018, https://www.merriam-webster.com/dictionary/perspectivism.

92. Jowett, "On the Interpretation," 384.

Before proceeding further, there are important methodological principles or assumptions to consider. First, as with any other critical tools, DHs also calls into question the previous scholarly interpretations of Paul's suffering and weakness in 2 Corinthians. This is mainly because they did not think it important enough to take into account the fact or possibility of Paul as a PwD. If they had done so, then their interpretations of Paul's sufferings would have shown an affinity towards a disability reading, which seems to be central to the understanding of 2 Corinthians. Previous scholars held Paul in high esteem – so much so that it was difficult for them to identify Paul as a disabled man. In their eyes, the only greater person than Paul himself was Jesus Christ.[93] They find it difficult to see Paul as a disabled human being whom the Corinthian Christians and other opponents of Paul despised rather intensely. This present study does not hold Paul in less esteem, but any sort of interpretation that builds itself upon an inability to accept Paul as disabled or physically limited will result in a skewed exegesis that fails to get to the bottom of Paul's struggle. Thus, if one attempts to analyse Paul's text seriously from a disability perspective, the first step is to be "suspicious" of the many interpretations that preceded this present research.

Second, DHs are very much concerned with their exegetical dimensions. While working on the assumption that Paul's Second Letter to the Corinthians contains evidence of Paul's disability, this DH will employ different exegetical tools such as rhetorical criticism and a sociological approach. These two biblical critical tools have proven effective in analyzing the Pauline Letters. These critical tools will be explained further below; however, suffice it here to state that these components will work in tandem to reveal the complex texture of the text. They will also make known the cultural bias inherently embedded in the text's composition, as the DH aims to draw relevant biblical insights for understanding Paul's suffering and weakness in 2 Corinthians.

Third, this DH involves the pressing of a disability perspective into the reading of Paul's Second Letter to the Corinthians. This is partly because a DH assumes that Paul is disabled in some manner or degree. It also assumes that disabilities and the way they were treated are present in ancient literature including the biblical texts. As such, proper analyses of this literature involve a disability perspective, which can foreground and assist in the proper exegesis

---

93. See sections 1.4 and 1.5 of chapter 1 for the lack of scholarly work on Paul as a PwD.

of the biblical text. Therefore, a disability perspective is central to a DH and becomes the guiding principle for all subsequent exegesis of the chosen texts, along with the examination of historical materials and the reconstruction of socio-cultural elements of Paul's milieu. In short, a DH is a perspectival textual engagement with an eclectic combination of interdisciplinary methodological tools. The following sections further break down the details of the DH proposed for this present study.

## 2.4.1 Disability Hermeneutics: Rhetorical Criticism Explained

Kennedy defines rhetorical criticism as the attempt to read the biblical texts "as it would be read by an early Christian, by an inhabitant of the Greek-speaking world in which rhetoric was the core subject of formal education and in which even those without formal education necessarily developed cultural preconceptions about appropriate discourse."[94] It involves "the analysis of the macro-level patterns and various micro-level devices which compose a literary unit,"[95] where the macro-level patterns stand for the arrangement of the materials and the micro-level indicates the style that the rhetor used. The goal of rhetorical criticism, according to Hatfield, is to understand "how the macro-level patterns and micro-level devices help to convey the meaning of the author and how they help to persuade the reader."[96] In short, rhetorical criticism can stand for "the criticism of [any] rhetorical discourses."[97] For instance, according to Aristotle, "Rhetoric is the faculty (power) of discovering in the particular case what the available means of persuasion are."[98] As such, the immediate function of rhetorical criticism is to find out how the rhetor attempts to persuade the readers.

Wuellner believes that "Rhetorical criticism comes into focus primarily on one issue: The text's potential to persuade, to engage the imagination and

---

94. Kennedy, *New Testament Interpretation*, 5.
95. S. G. Hatfield, "The Rhetorical Function of Selected Vice/Virtue Lists in the Letters of Paul" (PhD diss., Southwestern Baptist Theological Seminary, 1987), 113, quoted in Bliss, "Rhetorical Analysis," 2–3.
96. Hatfield, "Rhetorical Function," 113.
97. Black, *Rhetorical Criticism*, 10.
98. From Lessing's translation of *Scriptorium Classicorum*, 1355:25; cf. Lessing, "Preaching," 395.

will, or the text's symbolic inducement."[99] Therefore, rhetorical criticism emphasizes "the optimum *ways* of achieving certain ends, studying and using the set of principles or prudential techniques by which humans sought to persuade each other."[100] Aristotle delineated "three kinds of rhetorical speeches, deliberative, forensic, and epideictic."[101] According to him,

> The deliberative kind is either hortatory or dissuasive; for both those who give advice in private and those who speak in the assembly invariably either exhort or dissuade. The forensic kind is either accusatory or defensive; for litigants must necessarily either accuse or defend. The epideictic kind has for its subject praise or blame.[102]

Persuasion, thus, plays an important function in rhetorical criticism as it concerns itself with prioritizing "the text's intentionality to 'move' the reader."[103]

### 2.4.1.1 Methods of rhetorical criticism

Among scholars, James Muilenberg was one of the first to consider seriously the use of rhetorical criticism as a supplement to the literary criticism in biblical studies.[104] Muilenberg urged scholars to "venture beyond the confines of form criticism into an inquiry into other literary features."[105] Subsequent biblical scholars have taken up his challenge to develop rhetorical criticism as a critical tool for biblical studies.[106] At present, rhetorical criticism has become one of the most important critical tools that scholars employ to analyse biblical passages, especially the Pauline Letters. However, it seems Kennedy was the first to develop a rhetorical criticism that can substantively interpret New Testament methodology.[107] He developed five important steps for studying biblical texts which scholars employ in their research. One may

---

99. Wuellner, "Rhetorical Criticism," 178.
100. Howard, "Rhetorical Criticism," 92.
101. Aristotle, *Rhetoric*, 1.3.
102. Aristotle, 1.3.
103. Wuellner, "Rhetorical Criticism," 178.
104. Lieu and Rogerson, "Rhetorical Criticism," 618.
105. Muilenburg, "Form Criticism," 4.
106. A brief history of this development tracing back to Muilenberg is found in Koptak, "Rhetorical Criticism," 26–32.
107. Kennedy, *New Testament*, 4.

mention here that even though Kennedy's method is one of the most logical sequencing of rhetorical criticism as formulated for biblical analysis, it is by no means the only method by which rhetorical criticism could be done.

The first step is the need to "determine the rhetorical unit" and whether or not the passage to be analysed has any noticeable unit.[108] According to Kennedy, "a rhetorical unit must have a beginning, a middle, and an end."[109] It is important to ascertain if the given passage has a beginning and an end, and whether or not there is an observable coherent theme holding this passage together.[110] As Bliss states,

> A rhetorical unit may consist of an entire discourse or of a smaller portion of a whole discourse. In the case of the latter, its distinctiveness as a unit is determined by the presence of its introductory and concluding parts, and its rhetorical interpretation is considered in view of the rhetoric of the entire work.[111]

If the epistle is short, "it is possible, to begin with, the whole letter as a unit."[112] However, it becomes trickier to establish a rhetorical unit from a longer epistle. In such a case Kennedy advocates one to "experiment by seeking signs of opening and closure (for which the term *inclusio* is sometimes used), of proem and epilogue."[113] It is important to identify the rhetorical unit that "has an identifiable introduction, body, and conclusion since these are the parts necessary for any complete development of a theme."[114]

Second, the next step involves finding out the rhetorical situation or exigence that prompts the rhetor to make such arguments or statements. Black highlights the need to identify the rhetorical situation as it refers "to the prevailing state of the audience's convictions, the reputation of the rhetor, the popularity and urgency of his subject."[115] Bitzer further defines Black's description of "situation" as "a complex of persons, events, objects, and relations

---

108. Kennedy, 33.
109. Kennedy, 33.
110. Kennedy, 34.
111. Bliss, "Rhetorical Analysis," 42.
112. Kennedy, *New Testament*, 33.
113. Kennedy, 33.
114. Bliss, "Rhetorical Analysis," 42.
115. Black, *Rhetorical Criticism*, 133.

presenting an actual or potential exigence which can be completely or partially removed if discourse, introduced into the situation, can so constrain human decision or action as to bring about the significant modification of the exigence."[116] Bitzer has extensively dealt with the concept of the rhetorical situation and has provided a framework for understanding it. He believes that three components essentially make up a rhetorical situation: (1) the exigence, (2) the audience, and (3) the constraints.[117]

According to Bitzer, an exigence "is an imperfection marked by urgency; it is a defect, an obstacle, something waiting to be done, a thing which is other than it should be."[118] He believes that "in any rhetorical situation there will be at least one controlling exigence which functions as the organizing principle: it specifies the audience to be addressed and the change to be effected."[119] Bitzer also understands "the audience" as "those persons who are capable of being influenced by discourse and of being mediators of change."[120] Finally, Bitzer believes that there are constraints like "beliefs, attitudes, documents, facts, traditions, images, interests, motives and the like" that "have the power to constrain decision and action needed to modify the exigence."[121] Hence, "these three constituents – exigence, audience, constraints – comprise everything relevant in a rhetorical situation."[122]

Kennedy further builds upon these understandings when he explains a rhetorical situation as that which "roughly corresponds to the *Sitz im leben* of form criticism."[123] Along with Bitzer, Kennedy understands a rhetorical situation as indicating "a situation under which an individual is called upon to make some response; the response made is conditioned by the situation and in turn has some possibility of affecting the situation or what follows from it."[124] Hansen suggests that in rhetorical situation one should "define

---

116. Bitzer, "Rhetorical Situation," 6.
117. Bitzer, 8.
118. Bitzer, 6.
119. Bitzer, 7.
120. Bitzer, 8.
121. Bitzer, 8.
122. Bitzer, 8.
123. Kennedy, *New Testament*, 34.
124. Kennedy, 35.

the *stasis*, or basic issue, of the case," [125] as well as setting forth the "genre of rhetoric to which the speech belongs – Judicial, Deliberative, and Epideictic."[126] Weima further explains these three genres as follows,

> Judicial (or forensic) rhetoric belongs to the setting of a courtroom where the audience functions as judges who must make a decision of guilt or innocence concerning some past event. Deliberative rhetoric belongs to the setting of a public assembly where the audience must make a decision about the best course of action concerning some future activity. Epideictic (or demonstrative) rhetoric belongs to the setting of the public marketplace or civic event where the audience, rather than making a judgment about some past or future activity, observes the skill of the orator as he seeks to persuade them to adopt or reaffirm some point of view in the present, whether it be the praise or blame of some person or quality.[127]

The third step is to ascertain the rhetorical problem of a given rhetorical unit. It is possible that in any given passage, some "overriding problem" which needs to be directly addressed by the rhetor is present. As Kennedy explains, the rhetor's "audience is perhaps already prejudiced against him and not disposed to listen to anything he may say; or the audience may not perceive him as having the authority to advance the claims he wishes to make."[128] It is important that the rhetor should discern the attitude of the audience, whether they are "kindly disposed, or hostile, or neither good nor bad" towards him.[129] Depending on the audience's attitude, the rhetor can then arrange his material to mount his own defence or attack. For instance, if the audience is "kindly disposed" or "neither good nor bad," then the rhetor does not have to do much, but if the audience is "hostile" then this presents a "difficult situation for an orator and it requires him to take a different approach."[130] Kennedy men-

---

125. Hansen, "Rhetorical Criticism," 824.
126. Weima, "What Does Aristotle," 460.
127. Weima, 460.
128. Kennedy, *New Testament*, 36.
129. Christian, "Insinuatio," 2.
130. Christian, 2.

tions that in such a case, the "classical rhetoricians" would resort to the use of a rhetorical "technique" called *insinuatio* to deal with the given problem.[131]

This rhetorical technique *insinuatio* can be very useful in identifying the overall nature of the rhetor's argument. One can broadly define *insinuatio* as "a method for securing goodwill."[132] According to Sandnes, "The *insinuatio* will in an indirect way attract the attention of this audience, if necessary even by applying concealment. This approach is not restricted to the introduction, but may influence the entire speech."[133] Witherington understands it as "a sort of emphatic throwing down the gauntlet . . . where one merely hints at the real bone of contention at the outset and reserves until much later dealing with it."[134] Therefore, in *insinuatio*, "The general idea, in fact, is to counter the audience's hostility by an indirect approach . . . preferably discrediting our opponent at the same time."[135] While the "Greco-Roman rhetorical handbooks discuss *insinuatio* within their discussions of the exordium,"[136] the discussion of *insinuatio* can be included in the discussion of the rhetorical situation as Kennedy indicates.[137]

There is a different way the Greeks and Romans went about discussing the *insinuatio* in their rhetorical discourses. Timothy J. Christian has observed that the "Greek rhetorical theory instructed orators to approach prejudice head-on at the beginning of the speech so that they could successfully make their case. So then, the placement of addressing prejudice was positioned at the beginning of the speech for the Greeks."[138] On the other hand, Roman *insinuatio* differed from that of the Greeks in that

> Roman rhetorical theory instructed orators to approach prejudice and scandalous cases in an indirect manner, saving the difficult topics for much later in the speech. This meant that the beginning and middle parts of the speech must avoid the

---

131. Kennedy, *New Testament*, 36.
132. See the definition of *insinuatio* in "Canons of Rhetoric."
133. Sandnes, "Paul and Socrates," 15–16.
134. Witherington, *New Testament Rhetoric*, 53.
135. Bower, "ΕΦΟΔΟΣ," 224.
136. Christian, "*Insinuatio*," 4.
137. Kennedy, *New Testament*, 36.
138. Christian, "*Insinuatio*," 6–7.

scandalous points and could even function as a buttering up of the audience.[139]

Aside from this, the "Roman rhetorical theory added two other categories for *insinuatio*, namely, (1) for an audience that has been won over by a previous orator, and (2) for a wearied, tired audience."[140] Thus, in a way one should understand *insinuatio* as "multifarious" and not "monolithic."[141]

The fourth step is the arrangement of materials. In this step, rhetorical critics analyse the text for "what subdivisions it falls into, what the persuasive effect of these parts seems to be, and how they work together – or fail to do so – to some unified purpose in meeting the rhetorical situation."[142] This step pays "attention to such things as the best sequence to use, or whether one should expand upon this or that point, or how best to develop a subtheme."[143] If it is possible, one should "identify not only the kinds of proofs used in the argument but also the relative proportions of the three types of internal proofs."[144] The "internal evidence proofs artistically created by the orator occurs in three persuasive modes."[145] The first mode is the *logos* that points to "the mode of inductive or deductive argument"; the second, *pathos*, is an "appeal to the listeners' emotions of fear and steadfastness in the face of dire adversity"; and the third, *ethos*, makes the rhetor "credible, authoritative, and enduring."[146]

According to Watson, "various components such as the *exordium* ('introduction'), *narratio* ('statement of facts'), *probatio* ('main body'), and *peroratio* ('conclusion')" make up this arrangement.[147] However, one should know that there are differences in how many components one might come across in the arrangement. This is because Aristotle, Cicero, Quintilian, and *Rhetorica ad Herennium* (Handbook of rhetoric) maintained different patterns of

---

139. Christian, 12.
140. Christian, 3.
141. Christian, 3.
142. Kennedy, *New Testament*, 37.
143. Moon, "Paul's Discourse," 55.
144. Weima, "What Does Aristotle," 462.
145. Black, "Rhetorical Criticism," 79.
146. Black, 80.
147. Watson, "Notes," 111.

arrangement.¹⁴⁸ The following chart represents the different traditions of arrangement:¹⁴⁹

| Arist. Rhet. 3.13 | Cic. Inven. 1.14 | Quint. Inst. 3.9.1 | Rhe. ad Her. 1.4 |
|---|---|---|---|
| Exordium | Exordium | Exordium | exordium |
| | narration | narration | narratio |
| probation | quaestioes (or argumentatio) | probatio refutatio | divisio confirmatio confutatio |
| | peroratio | peroratio | peroratio |

*Exordium* is "the introduction of a speech, where one announces the subject and purpose of the discourse, and where one usually employs the persuasive appeal of *ethos* in order to establish credibility with the audience."¹⁵⁰ *Narratio* is where the rhetor "provides a narrative account of what has happened and generally explains the nature of the case. Quintilian adds that the *narratio* is followed by the *propositio*, a kind of summary of the issues or a statement of the charge."¹⁵¹ The *confirmatio* is "the main body of the speech where one offers logical arguments as proof. The appeal to *logos* is emphasized here."¹⁵² The *refutatio* is devoted "to answering the counterarguments of one's opponent."¹⁵³ Hence, it is "the central and decisive part of the speech that helps to make the party's represented position plausible through several proofs."¹⁵⁴ Finally, the *peroratio* is "the conclusion of a speech that has two objectives: to refresh the memory and to influence the emotions. In the *peroratio*, the speaker should achieve the final affect, arousing the pity and sympathy of the audience, so he/she often uses pathos for a strong emotional appeal."¹⁵⁵

---

148. Aristotle, *Rhetoric*; "Quintilian, *Institutio Oratoria*, bk 3; Cicero, *Rhetorici libri*; [Cicero], *Rhetorica ad Herennium*.
149. See Moon, "Paul's Discourse," 55–56.
150. See the definition of *exordium* in "Canons of Rhetoric."
151. See the definition of *narratio* in "Canons of Rhetoric."
152. See the definition of *confirmatio* in "Canons of Rhetoric."
153. See the definition of *refutatio* in "Canons of Rhetoric."
154. Moon, "Paul's Discourse," 56.
155. Moon, 56.

The final step of the rhetorical method is the evaluation of the effectiveness of the rhetorical criticism.[156] Here, one can "look back over the entire process of analysis and review its success in meeting the rhetorical exigence and what its implication may be for the speaker or audience."[157] This step pays attention to the product and prompts the rhetorical critics to consider whether the "detailed analysis" of the unit obscured the larger picture of the text. This evaluation of the effectiveness of the process of rhetorical criticism points to the fact that it "can be a creative act" where the given text being analysed becomes "clearer," while at the same time allowing the text to communicate relevance beyond itself and speak to an "awareness of [the] human condition."[158]

There are other techniques developed aside from Kennedy that use rhetorical critical tools to study biblical texts. For instance, Hansen has described "five rhetorical techniques" to study Pauline texts. The first is an "argument by authority" through which the text is studied from the orator's authoritative point of view.[159] It is "an argument that depends upon the prestige, reputation or moral character of the orator."[160] Second, an "argument by definition" is employed which recognizes the passages' central theme by recognizing the different terms that are introduced along with it.[161] For example, in Paul's attempts to define the gospel in Galatians, he substantiates his argument by introducing key terms such as "promise, faith, Law and works of the Law."[162]

Third, an "argument by dissociation of ideas" analyses the texts for whether the argument in a given passage is "structured by the dissociation of ideas."[163] This means that an argument could be developed by using opposing ideas such as "curse/blessing, works/faith, flesh/spirit, Law/Christ, Law/Spirit, slavery/freedom."[164] Fourth, there is the "argument by the severance of the group and its members."[165] This analyses an argument for whether the text is struc-

---

156. Kennedy, *New Testament*, 37–38.
157. Kennedy, 38.
158. Kennedy, 38.
159. Hansen, "Rhetorical Criticism," 824.
160. Hansen, 824.
161. Hansen, 824.
162. Hansen, 824.
163. Hansen, 824.
164. Hansen, 824.
165. Hansen, 824.

tured in a way that brings division among a group of members.¹⁶⁶ Fifth, the "argument by sacrifice" points to the fact that the rhetor made an argument to persuade others by mentioning all the hardships and sufferings that the person had gone through for someone.¹⁶⁷

### 2.4.1.2 Rhetorical criticism in the study of the New Testament Epistles

The use of rhetorical analysis in general is not something new to the study of the New Testament.¹⁶⁸ Early church fathers, such as Basil the Great, Clement of Alexandria, Gregory of Nyssa, Origen, and Chrysostom, employed the technique of ancient rhetoric to the literary investigations of the Pauline texts.¹⁶⁹ Even Augustine found it proper to use rhetorical perspective to analyse 2 Corinthians and thought that it was "a *refutatio* aimed at charges of opponents."¹⁷⁰ The uses of rhetorical analysis by these church fathers indicate that the Pauline texts have some affinity with the theories of ancient rhetoric. Recently, scholarship on this particular subject also abounds with literature. In fact, Troy W. Martin found it quite challenging to survey all the work written, commenting, "Some may indict me on the charge of foolishness for attempting the formidable task of surveying the numerous rhetorical studies of Paul's letters that have 'increased exponentially' over the past thirty years."¹⁷¹

There are certain important assumptions and hypotheses to consider when one employs rhetorical criticism to the New Testament Epistles. For instance, the use of rhetorical criticism in studying the New Testament Epistles is predicated upon the assumption that "the NT authors adopted and adapted ancient rhetoric for their Christian purposes of communication."¹⁷² This means, "Rhetoric was widely used, at least potentially, by almost anyone in the ancient world."¹⁷³ According to Witherington, "the Roman Empire was a

---

166. Hansen, 824.
167. Hansen, 824.
168. Olbricht mentions, "Even in the first century CE, Philo was using rhetorical analysis in his remarks on the Hebrew Bible" ("Rhetorical Criticism," 12).
169. Olbricht, 12.
170. Watson, "Part 2," 102.
171. Martin, "Invention and Arrangement," 48.
172. Witherington, *New Testament Rhetoric*, 6.
173. Porter, "When It Was Clear," 534.

rhetoric-saturated realm. It was in the education, in public speeches, in the inscriptions, in the Imperial propaganda, and elsewhere."[174] Litfin has stated that the "popularity of oratory was very broad-based. It seemed to permeate the entire Greco-Roman world, from the emperors to the man in the street."[175] If this is the case, then "the NT authors must have been rhetoricians, some even of the first order," and "virtually the entire NT has at least the potential to become rhetoric and [is] in need of a rhetorical analysis."[176]

Another important assumption is the presumed "oral culture of [the] Greco-Roman world," with "educated leaders" heading the task of evangelizing the Gentiles.[177] Again, Witherington believes that "large portions of early Christianity, particularly the more Gentile portions, were led by several rather remarkably gifted and indeed well-educated persons – like Paul, Apollos, Luke, and others."[178] This was needed since the "culture was largely an oral culture, not a culture of texts."[179] If the evangelist were to persuade a largely Gentile audience saturated with rhetorical teachings, then the proclamation of the gospel would have relied on those evangelists having a decent educational background. The reason is that these people needed the "Greco-Roman rhetoric" to persuade them.[180] In such a situation, the educated leaders would send a letter that reflected their rhetorical skills.[181] Witherington believes that "most often this was done using an epistolary framework"[182] that contained "both epistolary features and rhetorical features."[183] This letter then would be "proclaimed orally when the messenger arrives with the document in hand, rolls it out, and dramatically delivers it."[184]

Having laid out these assumptions, rhetorical criticism has been applied to the study of the Pauline Epistles, particularly to 2 Corinthians, to find out

---

174. Witherington, "Almost Thou Persuadest Me," 69.
175. Litfin, *St. Paul's Theology*, 124.
176. Porter, "When It Was Clear," 534.
177. See Porter, "When It Was Clear," 534.
178. Witherington, "Almost Thou Persuadest Me," 69.
179. Witherington, 69.
180. Witherington, 69.
181. Witherington, *New Testament Rhetoric*, 19.
182. Witherington, 19.
183. Witherington, 19.
184. Witherington, 19.

what kinds of speech categories they fall into. Scholars like Young and Ford, Betz, and Kennedy think that Paul's rhetorical speech in 2 Corinthians is "forensic."[185] For instance, according to Moon, Betz thinks, "Paul employs a defence speech in the same way as a philosopher of the Socratic-Cynic tradition might employ it, in contrast to the style of self-defence of the rhetorician and sophist."[186] This means that Paul was having a dialogue with the Corinthians and not the instigators or his opponents themselves.[187] However, this position is narrow considering the possibility that some could influence the Corinthians to create a problem with Paul.[188] Yong and Ford argue that Paul wrote his letter as an "apology," in the manner of Demosthenes, which was a good "example of the standard form of forensic speech in epistolary form."[189] They believe that "2 Corinthians was self-consciously conceived as an apology according to the norms of the day."[190] Hence, Paul wrote 2 Corinthians to defend his apostleship.

However, although Witherington has acknowledged the centrality of forensic rhetoric to 2 Corinthians,[191] he also believes that one can observe a deliberative rhetoric.[192] In other words, he regards the whole of 2 Corinthians as forensic in nature; however, Witherington believes that the deliberative rhetoric can specifically be observed in 2 Corinthians 6:14–7:1 and 8:8.[193] Nonetheless, these deliberative speeches also ultimately "serve the larger forensic purpose."[194] Thus, one can state that he sees a "mixed type" of rhetorical speech in 2 Corinthians.[195] Peterson also believes that both forensic and deliberative rhetoric are discernible in 2 Corinthians.[196] This shows that

---

185. Betz, *2 Corinthians*, 13; Kennedy, *New Testament*, 86–87.
186. Moon, "Paul's Discourse," 27.
187. Betz, *Paul's Apology*, 2.
188. Moon, "Paul's Discourse," 28.
189. Young and Ford, *Meaning and Truth*, 38.
190. Young and Ford, 43.
191. Witherington, *Conflict & Community*, 333.
192. Witherington, 339.
193. Moon, "Paul's Discourse," 28
194. Moon, 28.
195. Witherington, *Conflict & Community*, 465.
196. Peterson, *Eloquence*, 141.

Paul's rhetoric in 2 Corinthians is quite difficult to pin down to one kind of rhetorical speech.[197]

### 2.4.1.3 Critical appraisal of rhetorical criticism

First, scholars like Weima have pointed out that "the use of rhetoric was so pervasive in the ancient world" that it affected every aspect of society.[198] For instance, Olbricht asserted that rhetoric "so permeated Hellenistic culture that it seems inconceivable for Paul to have escaped altogether rhetorical insight or, at a minimum, a familiarity with Greek literature so affected."[199] Longenecker also stated, "The forms of classical rhetoric were 'in the air,' and Paul seems to have used them almost unconsciously for his own purposes."[200] Recently, Witherington has been very vocal about the Greco-Roman society being "saturated" by rhetoric.[201]

However, this particular assumption has come in for sharp criticism by Porter who is especially critical of Witherington's claims that "the Roman Empire was a rhetoric-saturated realm."[202] Porter believes that during Paul's time there was hardly the presence of "rhetoric in the air" as Longenecker has stated.[203] According to Porter, this "rhetoric in the air hypothesis" is simply not viable, for it would require Paul and the other disciples, who wrote the New Testament text, to be good rhetoricians.[204] It also would indicate that the rabbinic literature that arose out of the Second Temple period had high concentrations of Greco-Roman rhetoric. However, Patrick and Scult have observed, "There is simply no manifestly rhetorical culture from which the Hebrews could have borrowed the idea of artfully casting their religious texts as persuasive discourse until the majority of the texts were composed and edited."[205] Philipps gave a more conservative criticism to this hypothesis by stating, "An implicit theory of rhetoric can be drawn from the Talmud," but

---

197. See McCant, *2 Corinthians*, 13.
198. Weima, "What Does Aristotle," 462.
199. Olbricht, "Aristotelian Rhetorical Analysis," 221.
200. Longenecker, *Galatians*, 112–113.
201. Witherington, "Almost Thou Persuadest Me," 69.
202. Witherington, 69.
203. Porter, "When It Was Clear," 535.
204. Porter, 535–537.
205. Patrick and Scult, *Rhetoric and Biblical Interpretation*, 30.

admitted, "It is likely that the rabbis were not even aware of the existence of an art of rhetoric in any other culture."[206]

Second, Porter is highly critical of Witherington's claim "that early Christianity was a group of illiterates [living] within an oral culture" who were all in some way acquainted with the techniques of rhetoric.[207] Putting this assumption into perspective, it would mean that when the educated evangelists sent letters using the latest rhetorical style, the audiences would know exactly what they intended to say. Contrary to this, Porter feels that "these documents were not necessarily rhetorical or literary but documentary, conveying the substance of day to day life, by means of easily accessible and cheap papyrus."[208] He believes that Witherington "fails to take into account the literate culture in which ancient society existed, in which written documents formed a written tapestry that united together daily life."[209] Besides, Steve Walton claims that the "classical rhetorical theory" is applicable only "for speeches, not for written letters."[210] Even if Porter's claim was possible that every letter written during early Christianity was documentary, without using any rhetorical devices or literary styles of writings, it would have been still doubtful for the many "illiterate" first-century Christians (see 1 Cor 1:26–30) to totally grasp the meaning of these discourses.

Third, the foundation for employing rhetorical criticism lies in the assumption that Paul would have some sort of proper training in rhetoric. Some scholars like E. A. Judge think highly of Paul as a rhetorician. According to him, "Whatever the circumstances of his upbringing and education, it is beyond doubt that Paul was, in practice at least, familiar with the rhetorical fashions of the time."[211] Judge clumps Paul together with the famous Sophist orators of the day, from "the Stoic Epictetus to the vagabond Cynic preachers, and the more religious teachers from the neo-Pythagorean sage Apollonius of Tyana to the charlatan Peregrinus."[212] The main reason he clumps these people together is because he believes that "they were all travellers, relying

---

206. Philipps, "Place of Rhetoric," 303; Philipps, "Practice of Rhetoric," 37–46.
207. Porter, "When It Was Clear," 534.
208. Porter, 534.
209. Porter, 534.
210. Walton, "Rhetorical Criticism," 6.
211. Judge, "Early Christians," 540.
212. Judge, 540.

upon the hospitality of their admirers, all expert talkers and persuaders, all dedicated to their mission and intolerant of criticism."²¹³ Not only him but others like Hock and Witherington also think highly of Paul's rhetorical skills. Hock believes that Paul should be included among the "very tiny elite" of the educated because of his "much greater educational achievement."²¹⁴ Likewise, Witherington also thinks, "Paul was in the upper 1–2 percent of well-educated people in his day."²¹⁵

On the other hand, those who have considered Paul to be an unskilled rhetorician, as he himself claimed in his letters (see 2 Cor 11:6), stretch all the way back to the early church historian Eusebius, who believed that Paul along with the other apostles of Jesus were not able "to present the Master's teaching with rhetorical skills."²¹⁶ Indeed, as Weima points out, "there is no concrete evidence that Paul knew or was ever trained in ancient rhetoric."²¹⁷ Among the recent interpreters of Paul, Vergeer must be one of the most vocal opponents of Paul's portrayal as a skilled rhetorician. He believes that Paul's "lack of rhetorical training is . . . something that stands out in all genuine letters of Paul."²¹⁸ He feels that Paul "ignores all the rhetorical rules" and "models," and his composition reflects "simplicity and roughness [that] would be unheard of in a skilled Attic orator."²¹⁹ However, Vergeer has conceded that Paul was skilful in "Jewish forms of exegesis."²²⁰ Nonetheless, he considers him a "semiliterate bumpkin" who does not "show any proficiency in Greek rhetoric."²²¹

One may never know for sure if Paul had trained himself in the art of rhetoric or attended any rhetorical schools. However, it seems there are enough examples of "figures of speech" and "rhetorical techniques" in Paul's Epistles to indicate that Paul was no stranger to the nuances of rhetorical ingenuity.²²² Moon has surmised, "As a writer, Paul who has oral performance

---

213. Judge, 540.
214. Hock, "Paul," 215.
215. Witherington, *Paul's Narrative Thought World*, 216.
216. Eusebius, *Church History*, 99.
217. Weima, "What Does Aristotle," 464.
218. Vergeer, *Letters*, 319.
219. Vergeer, 319.
220. Vergeer, 319.
221. Vergeer, 319.
222. For these examples, see Bullinger, *Figures of Speech*, 715–717, and also Tolmie, "Rhetorical Analysis."

in mind may structure the argumentation in a written text either simply or elaborately, depending on rhetorical training, experience, context, and many other factors."[223] In order to understand this dilemma better, there are two possibilities to consider here. First, it is possible that Paul was proficient in written rhetoric but unexceptional in his oratory skills. In that case, one might explain the accusation in 2 Corinthians 10:10 that his "letters are weighty", but his "speech is contemptible." Second, it is also possible that Paul was not good at the art of classical rhetoric either in writing or in speaking. If this was the case, then one can postulate that some friends who were proficient in rhetoric helped Paul to compose his letters. Loubser seems to advocate this idea, as he believes that it explains "the similarity between the Pauline Letters and 1 Peter, allegedly documented by Silvanus."[224] However, regardless of these possibilities, the rhetorical implication of Paul and his letters is real, and hence, rhetorical criticism has a role to play in the investigation of Paul's suffering and weakness in 2 Corinthians.

## 2.4.2 The Sociological Approach of DHs Explained

The sociological approach is defined as "that phase of the exegetical task which analyses the social and cultural dimension of the text and of its environmental contexts through the utilization of the perspectives, theory, models and research of the social sciences."[225] In a way, it offers a vast array of interpretative tools making it a flexible criticism under which comprehensive analysis of the given biblical text is accomplished.[226] According to Tate, a sociological approach "seeks to understand texts in their social, cultural, historical, and literary contexts in order to understand the social institutions, the cultural values, and the norms of a particular era."[227] As a tool for analyzing the biblical texts, it "analyses the social and cultural dimension of a text by clarifying the differences between historical conditions and social institutions with respect to the biblical accounts thereby providing a clearer comprehension for the reading and use of the Bible and biblical history."[228]

---

223. Moon, "Paul's Discourse," 52.
224. Loubser, "Reconciling Rhetorical Criticism," 100–101, esp. n25.
225. Elliott, *What Is*, 7.
226. See Horrell, "Social-Scientific Interpretation," 3.
227. Tate, *Biblical Interpretation*, 79.
228. Tate, 79.

The need for a sociological approach to be employed in the study of the biblical texts is predicated upon the assumptions that "the world of the modern reader is so far removed from the world of the biblical text" that the "meaning cannot be adequately determined without consideration of social aspects."[229] According to Meeks, there is an "air of unreality that pervades much of the recent scholarly literature about the New Testament and early Christianity" because the study of the New Testament was isolated from socio-historical studies.[230] The Bible is "culturally conditioned . . . written in a different place and time and in a different social location" and "only the original author and original hearer knew the totality of the social conditions."[231] By "culturally conditioned," one means the way that the "environment shapes [the] attitudes, expectations, values, and beliefs" of the people recorded in the Bible.[232] As such, there is a need to employ sociological criticism to gain deeper insights into the biblical texts.

One technique for utilizing a social-scientific model is to use knowledge gleaned from the study of "modern Mediterranean cultures" in the hope that they "have remained relatively unchanged for centuries."[233] This assumes that "the social structures of contemporary Mediterranean cultures supply social scientists with information resembling ancient biblical societies."[234] This information then is used in the examinations of various issues of "self-identity, social organization, kinship systems, patrilineal descent, economic implications or marriage, family, lineage, customs, economics, and political structures" that made up the value systems in the Bible.[235] Moreover, from this investigation, "the socio-scientific critic hopes to diminish the tendency of modern readers to project the structures of their own social locations into the systems of both Israelites and early Christian cultures."[236]

---

229. Tate, 79.
230. Meeks, *First Urban Christian*, 1.
231. Tate, *Biblical Interpretation*, 79.
232. Tate, 79.
233. Tate, 79.
234. Tate, 79.
235. Tate, 79.
236. Tate, 79–80.

## 2.4.2.1 Methods of a sociological approach

As a critical tool, a sociological approach "utilizes the resources that social sciences have to offer, thereby enabling a fuller and better appreciation of the biblical texts and communities with their historical, social and cultural setting."[237] However, because of the vastness of the area covered, as well as the multi-dimensional nature of its area of interest, it is difficult to describe specific methods or approaches. Hence, Malherbe writes, "Personal interests, if not always competence, have naturally influenced selection of the topics, as well as the way in which they were approached."[238] As such, depending on the scholars and the areas they want to investigate, the uses of a sociological approach can be very general or very specific.

For instance, Theissen's sociological approach is to "rely on analytic methods, that is, inferences drawn from historical events, social norms, or religious symbols."[239] Theissen believes that there are instances where one can refer to the historical record of the Bible to gain some insights. For example, he concludes that Jesus and his disciples made the rural district their home by inferring from the many times Jesus talked about cities without actually entering them (Mark 5:2; 7:24, 31; 8:27). Alongside historical events, Theissen believes one can also draw inferences from the norms and symbols of the society.[240] Another important method he utilizes is called "comparative procedures" which compares "primitive Christianity by analyzing the differences (or similarity) . . . with the surrounding cultures."[241] Thus, Theissen combines a creative and eclectic use of sociological perspectives with a careful analysis of historical evidence in order to study early Christianity.

Another example is Abraham Malherbe's "social-historical" method, which he employs in his various works.[242] He believes that for one to be sensitive and in tune with the social dimensions of early Christianity, one must closely investigate the written sources. According to him, the purpose is to examine the character and intention of the documents "in order to discern

---

237. Horrell, "Social-Scientific Interpretation," 3.
238. Malherbe, *Social Aspects*, ix.
239. Theissen, *Social Setting*, 180.
240. Theissen, 182.
241. Theissen, 192.
242. See Malherbe, *Paul and the Thessalonians*; Malherbe, *Paul and the Popular Philosophers*, 2006.

how they functioned in relation to the communities with which they were associated."[243] For instance, in his book *Paul and the Popular Philosophers*, he looks at the influence that the Platonists, Peripatetics, Cynics, Stoics, Epicureans, and Pythagoreans must have had on the life of Paul. He believes that they contributed to a view of a syncretistic philosophical *Koine*, of which Stoicism was of greatest importance.[244]

Then there is the cultural anthropological method employed by Malina in his book *The New Testament World: Insights From Cultural Anthropology*.[245] His main aim was "to present, from the area of cultural anthropology, some useful models that might aid in fathoming the social-system context of the behaviour of the people present in the New Testament."[246] According to Malina, he used this model "precisely" because it helps to "hear the meaning of the documents in terms of the social systems in which they were originally proclaimed."[247] Through employing cultural anthropological models, Malina proposes that "the central features and values of that culture were honour and shame, dyadic rather than individual personality, the perception of limited good, distinctive norms of kinship and marriage, and a set of purity rules to distinguish clean and unclean."[248] Along with this, mention may be made of Segovia's two paradigms of "cultural criticism and cultural studies" which foreground "culture" as central to understanding and interpreting biblical texts.[249] Another model worthwhile mentioning is the cultural cartography that calls for the importance of listening to a variety of voices and speaking multiple languages across diverse terrains.[250]

Because of these diverse opinions on methods, some scholars have attempted "to classify this varied and ongoing work according to the method employed and the scope of the investigation."[251] One such scholar is Elliot

---

243. Malherbe, *Social Aspect*, 20.
244. Malherbe, *Paul and the Popular Philosophers*, 5.
245. Malina, *New Testament World*.
246. Malina, xi.
247. Malina, xi.
248. Horrell, "Social Sciences."
249. Tolbert, "Writing History," 21.
250. Smith, "Drawing New Maps," 120. See also Giroux, *Pedagogy*; Smith, "Drawing New Maps," 117–144.
251. Horell, "Social Sciences Studying," 9.

who has differentiated these diverse approaches into five categories. The first category is the "investigation of social realia (groups, occupations, institutions, and the like)."[252] According to Elliot, this first category is "generally to illustrate some feature or features of ancient society but with no concern for analyzing, synthesizing, and explaining these social facts in social-scientific fashion."[253] The second category describes a construction of "a social history of a particular period or movement or group,"[254] avoiding the conscious use "of social theory and models."[255] The third category involves studying "the social organisation of early Christianity," in addition to "the social forces leading to its emergence and its social institutions."[256] This third category includes "the deliberate use of social theory and models."[257] The fourth category focuses on "the social and cultural scripts influencing and constraining social interaction" in the "cultural environment of the New Testament."[258] The last category uses "the research, theory, and models of the social sciences . . . in the analysis of biblical texts."[259]

Besides Elliot, mention may be made of Tate who grouped these various approaches into four categories. He called the first category "the Social description approach" which "evaluates information gathered from the New Testament literature and archaeology, i.e. Art, coins, inscriptions, etc.[260] The second category is "the Social history approach" which "examines the social developments and movements of the early Christians within the Greco-Roman world."[261] The third is the "Sociology of knowledge" which "looks at particular cultural groups and how they organise and interpret experiences within society."[262] Finally, "Models from the Social Sciences involves the study of a number of similar cultures in order to create a grid or model that allows

---

252. Elliott, *What Is*, 18.
253. Elliott, 18–20.
254. Elliott, 18–20.
255. Elliott, 18–20.
256. Elliott, 18–20.
257. Elliott, 18–20.
258. Elliott, 18–20.
259. Elliott, 18–20.
260. Tate, *Biblical Interpretation*, 80.
261. Tate, 80.
262. Tate, 80.

anthropologists to map the 'dynamics' of cultures and to describe certain phenomena that occurs in many cultures."²⁶³

Recently, Horrell has attempted to distinguish various sociological approaches into three main categories. He grouped the first category under "Cultural anthropology and the Context Group."²⁶⁴ Scholars like Malina, Neyrey, Esler, and Rohrbaugh draw on the "studies of the Mediterranean, both ancient and modern, and using models developed by anthropologists, they have consistently developed and applied a range of reading strategies to illuminate the foreign world of the early Christians."²⁶⁵ The strength of this group of scholars and their method is their ability to come up with a "clear and explicit set of models" with which they "illuminate the strikingly different social dynamics at work in the biblical texts."²⁶⁶

The second category is the "Historical sociology/social history" approach. Horrell believes that this approach stands in close proximity to the "historical-critical study."²⁶⁷ The incorporation of sociological elements enables those utilizing the historical-critical method to better understand "the social context, dynamics and impact of the texts."²⁶⁸ Scholars such as Theissen, Meeks, Kee, Watson, and Barclay have adopted this approach, and they have generally regarded "themselves primarily as social historians, or have used social theory to develop a theoretical or research framework, but have rejected a specifically model-based approach."²⁶⁹

Horrell distinguishes the third category as "Radical social history and emancipatory theologies."²⁷⁰ This group consists of scholars like Fiorenza and Schottroff who have attempted to integrate political and sociological approaches in the study of "early Christianity, often allied to the concerns of some form of emancipatory or liberation theology."²⁷¹

---

263. Tate, 80.
264. Horrell, "Social Sciences," 11.
265. Horrell, 12.
266. Horrell, 13.
267. Horrell, 15.
268. Horrell, 15.
269. Horrell, 16.
270. Horrell, 17.
271. Horrell, 17.

### 2.4.2.2 Critical appraisal of a sociological approach

A sociological approach in the study of the New Testament is "now widespread and firmly established."[272] According to Horrell, a sociological approach "enables a fuller and better appreciation of the biblical texts and communities within their historical, social, and cultural settings."[273] It helps the researcher dig into "the social context behind a text" and assess "the ideology and impact of the text itself."[274] In this way, it becomes almost indispensable to the study of biblical texts. And as it "complement[s] both the already established and the newly developing methods of biblical criticism," it "offer[s] tools to enrich the historical study of the social context within which such theology was formed."[275] Indeed, the analysis of biblical texts has much to gain from sociological criticism. For instance, according to Tolbert, even though "the sources for historical writing about early Christianity are scarce and difficult to use for a variety of reasons," a sociological approach can "fill the gaps among the fragmentary sources we have and ... provide a fuller picture than the sources themselves alone would allow."[276]

Sociological criticism "address[es] issues of group prejudices, where groups' reasoning and behaviours are influenced and distorted at a larger scale and through complex mechanisms, including the construction of shared values."[277] It "questions the past by asking how people at the time perceived and interpreted themselves, what material, mental, and social motivations respectively influenced theory forms or perceptions and production of sense, and the effects such forms produced."[278] It not only takes a keen interest in the collation of the history of the people that it studies, but it also takes into consideration their cultural and anthropological concerns. As Tolbert has stated, "Indeed, one of the lasting benefits of the development of sociological and anthropological approaches to New Testament history writing has been the opening up of the wider world of Greco-Roman sources and studies for

---

272. Horrell, 26.
273. Horrell, 3.
274. Horrell, 26.
275. Horrell, 26.
276. Tolbert, "Writing History," 22.
277. Punt, "Others' in Galatians," 46.
278. Ute Daniel, *Kompendium Kulturgeschichte: Theorien, Praxis, Schlüsselwörter* (Germany: Suhrkamp, 2001), 19, quoted in Arcangeli, in *Cultural History*, 9.

use in understanding New Testament texts. Early Christianity was very much conditioned by this."[279]

Though a sociological approach has many advantages, there are some pertinent concerns as well. There are those who doubt whether "the ancient sources yield adequate data of a kind suitable for sociological analysis (compared with the contemporary opportunities for interviews, observation, etc.)."[280] For instance, Cyril S. Rodd believes that "it is a cardinal error to move promiscuously between the two" – between the world of the researcher and the world being researched.[281] This is often referred to as the problem of "anachronism," which is basically the use of "sociological models and methods which have taken shape in the analysis of modern organizations, groups or societies and using them as tools of analysis for the interpretation of groups and societies in Mediterranean antiquity."[282] As such, one must be aware of this possible pitfall and take caution when applying modern understandings to the study of biblical texts.

Another concern is the possibility of "reductionism," which is "the idea that social-scientific theories will 'explain' religious phenomena purely in terms of social or economic forces."[283] One can claim too much for what sociological criticism can achieve when applied to the exegesis of a text. Barton points out, "functionalist sociology is especially open to this problem."[284] According to Cookson and Sadovnik, "functionalist sociologists begin with a picture of society that stresses the interdependence of the social system."[285] Functionalist sociology believes "that there must be a common bond to unite groups."[286] With this, the functionalist will "examine the social processes necessary to the establishment and maintenance of social order."[287] One can observe this when Meeks explains Paul's early converts "as a function of members' experiences

---

279. Tolbert, "Writing History," 22–23.
280. Horell, "Social Sciences," 17.
281. Rodd, "On Applying," 105.
282. Barton, "Social-Scientific," 893.
283. Horrell, "Social Sciences," 18.
284. Barton, "Social-Scientific," 893.
285. Cookson and Sadovnik, "Functionalist Theories," 271.
286. Cookson and Sadovnik, 267.
287. Cookson and Sadovnik, 267.

of status inconsistency in the wider world."²⁸⁸ Paul's gospel appealed to those people to whom he preached because they found solace and an answer to what they were currently going through. This functional model of "status inconsistency" allows one to see "the possible influence of hidden psychosocial and socio-economic forces on converts to Christianity."²⁸⁹ However, what functionalist sociology fails to take into account is the personal choices or feelings involving "the intellectual, spiritual/mystical and emotional dimensions of the transformation (cf. 1 Thess 1:9–10; Gal 1:6–17; Phil 3:2–11)."²⁹⁰

### 2.4.2.3 *The significance of a sociological approach in the interpretation of the Pauline Epistles*

Sociological approaches have come to play an important role in analyzing the Pauline Epistles, judging from the many works that have been done by different scholars.²⁹¹ This is because the letters written by Paul, the people he preached to and interacted with, and the places in which he lived and travelled to, all influenced his life and work in a very significant manner. Tidball is right to think, "The churches founded by Paul were not abstract theological entities formed in a social vacuum but real life community of men and women who inhabited particular social settings."²⁹² Indeed, "early Christianity was shaped by and in turn, helped to shape the values and structures of the societies and cultures in which it took root and grew."²⁹³ The possibility of "using social theories and cultural methods drawn from other cultures, for which more information, more evidence might be available [is a] sensible way to fill the gaps among the fragmentary sources . . . and to provide a fuller picture than the sources themselves alone would allow."²⁹⁴

One can appreciate the impact on Paul's Epistles, as scholars like Barton analyse them in the context of Mediterranean social values like the "ethic of holiness" drawn from the Jewish concept of holiness. According to Barton,

---

288. Meeks, *First Urban Christians*.
289. Barton, "Social-Scientific," 894.
290. Barton, 894.
291. See Horell, "Social Sciences," 1–28, for the comprehensive lists of scholars and their works.
292. Tidball, "Social Setting," 883.
293. Barton, "Social Values and Structures," 1127.
294. Tolbert, "Writing History," 22.

"the basic presupposition is the holiness of the temple where temple is extended metaphorically to stand for the community of God's people."[295] This social value concept illuminates the teaching of Paul, especially in 1 Corinthians 3:16–17 where he equates the believers to the temple of God. A socio-economic model also greatly helps in identifying the class distinction as well as the possibility of social mobility among the early Christians and their respective societies.[296] Meeks has pointed out that social movement from the bottom layer to the upper layer was possible, stating that "the most fundamental change of status for a person of the lower classes was that from slavery to freedom" and that "slaves worked hard to obtain their manumission and often did."[297]

Sociological models also greatly contribute to the study of the Pauline Epistles. Some of these models include the following: honor and shame, patronage and clientage,[298] and child-parent relationship.[299] Malina has defined "models" as "abstract, simplified representations of more complex, real-world objects and interactions. Like abstract thought, the purpose of models is to enable and facilitate understating."[300] Malina has also delineated the process of how a person can develop a "scientific method" using social values and models of interpretation. According to him, the first step consists of postulating "a model (or theory or paradigm)," and the second step involves the testing of this "model against the real-world experience it relates to."[301] The final step is to "modify the model in terms of the outcome of the test to reduce the misfit by detecting errors of omission and commission."[302]

For instance, Peter Balla has worked extensively on the relationship between a child and his/her parents in the New Testament texts by employing the child-parent relationship model. What this model seeks to achieve is to help in understanding the different characteristics of a child-parent relationship in the Bible with the help of external sources for comparison purposes.

---

295. Barton, "Social Values and Structures," 1128.
296. Boardman, Griffin, and Murray, *Oxford Illustrated History*, 355.
297. Meeks, *First Urban Christians*, 20.
298. Rohrbaugh, *Social Sciences*, 19, 144, 159.
299. See Balla, *Child-Parent Relationship*, 1–4.
300. Malina, *New Testament World*, 18.
301. Malina, 18.
302. Malina, 18.

According to Balla, this model aims "to find out what is shared by the first Christian generations with their non-Christian neighbours, Jewish and pagan, and what may be called Christian characteristics in which they differed from their surrounding world (if in fact they differ)."[303] This model is particularly significant given the fact that Paul considered the Corinthians as his children in a number of places (see 2 Cor 6:11–13; 11:2).

In another instance, Malina proposes the social value of honour and shame as a viable model for interpreting the biblical texts. Malina defines honour as "the positive value of a person in his/her social group."[304] While "shame," when used in conjunction with honour, derives a positive dimension because it indicates "sensitivity about one's own reputation."[305] However, "a shameless person or group is one who does not recognise the rules of human interaction, who does not recognize social boundaries."[306] To put this into perspective, this "honour and shame" paradigm would offer insights into the rivalries of the Corinthian congregation (see 1 Cor 1:10–17). It is possible that the rivalry among the Corinthian Christians was because of the competition for "honour" with each other.[307]

When it comes to patronage and clientage, one cannot be certain it will play a significant role in relation to this present study's discussion of Paul's suffering and weakness in 2 Corinthians. However, many scholars feel that this model best explains the relationship (or its breakdown) existing between Paul and the Corinthian congregation.[308] What is this patronage and clientage model? Elliot explains it as follows:

> In general, the relation is one of personal loyalty and commitment (*fides*) of some duration entered into voluntarily by two or more individuals of unequal status. It is based on differences in social roles and access to power, and involves the reciprocal exchange of different kinds of goods and services of value

---

303. Balla, *Child-Parent Relationship*, 3.
304. Malina and Neyrey, "Honor and Shame," 25–26.
305. Malina, *New Testament World*, 49.
306. Malina, 18.
307. Barton, "Social Values and Structures," 1129.
308. See Rice, *Paul and Patronage*, 155, and Chow, *Patronage and Power*, 189. Briones argues in his monograph that patronage does not play a part in their breakdown of relationship (*Paul's Financial Policy*, 177–179).

to each partner. In this relationship of binding and long-range character designed to advance the interests of both partners, a "patron" (*patronus, patrona*) is one who uses his or her influence to protect and assist some other person who becomes the patron's "client" (*cliens*). In return, this client provides to the patron certain valued services.[309]

The meaning is certainly clear from the above explanation. The question is, how does this model work in understanding the biblical texts? What is the frame of reference that one should have in order to compare the type of relationships that one finds in the New Testament? In other words, is there any significant external literary evidence that one can examine to form an educated opinion? The answer fortunately is that there are external sources from roughly the period of the New Testament with records of such a type of relationship existing between a patron and a client. One can say that in such a relationship, there is a give and take between the two parties, but the patron holds the upper hand because of their wealth and influence. For instance, there is a record of a message from Pliny to Emperor Trajan, where Pliny petitioned the emperor as follows:

> Gaius Pliny to the Emperor Trajan. Valerius Paulinus, sir, has left a will which passes over his son Paulinus and names me a patron of his Latin freedmen. On this occasion I pray you to grant full Roman citizenship to three of them only; it would be unreasonable, I fear, to petition you to favour all alike, and I must be all the more careful not to abuse your generosity when I have enjoyed it on so many previous occasions.[310]

A sociological approach assists in the proper understanding of the Pauline congregations. For instance, many have thought that Paul's congregation was mainly from the lower strata of the Greco-Roman society. According to Deissmann, the New Testament "was not a product of the colourless refinement of an upper class that had nothing left to hope for. . . . It was, humanly speaking, a product of the force that came unimpaired, and strengthened

---

309. Elliot, "Patronage and Clientage," 148–149.
310. Pliny, *Epistles* 10.104, quoted in Elliot, "Patronage and Clientage," 144.

by the Divine Presence, from the lower class."³¹¹ The critical passage that substantiates this insight is 1 Corinthians 1:26–29. However, Theissen, by employing his sociological method in analyzing the same text from which Deissmann drew his conclusion (i.e. "those who are wise, those who are powerful, and those who are of noble birth") yet managed to arrive at an altogether different conclusion.³¹² This is because Theissen made use of the "wealth of background material from non-Christian sources" and showed, perhaps convincingly, that "some, at least, of the Christians at Corinth were probably quite well-to-do and of a relatively high social standing."³¹³

Therefore, the sociological approach as an interpretative tool has made its mark on the Pauline texts in particular, as well as the whole New Testament. Horrell is correct to point out that,

> Whether in the study of the social context in which a text was written, the ideology and impact of a text itself, the character and expansion of the early Christian communities, or indeed of the social location and interests of contemporary interpreters, the social sciences have shown that they offer rich resources to complement both the already established and the newly developing methods of biblical criticism.³¹⁴

Understandably, one has to be aware that some materials may not always withstand the intense scrutiny of scholars,³¹⁵ but the lasting benefits of the development of socio-historical and cultural-anthropological approaches to the writing of New Testament history are undeniable. It has and will continue to open up the wider world of Greco-Roman sources for use in the understanding of New Testament texts.³¹⁶ It will also continue to "address issues of group prejudice, where groups' reasoning and behavior are influenced and distorted at a larger scale and through complex mechanisms, including the construction of shared social values."³¹⁷ Indeed, the analysis of the Pauline

---

311. Deissmann, *Light*, 144.
312. Theissen, *Social Setting*, 70.
313. Tuckett, *Reading the New Testament*, 137.
314. Horrell, "Social Sciences," 28.
315. Tolbert, "Writing History," 22.
316. Tolbert, 22–23.
317. Punt, "Others' in Galatians," 46.

Epistles and the biblical text as a whole has much to benefit from employing a sociological approach.

## 2.5 A DH Pressed into the Reading of 2 Corinthians

As a critical tool, the use of a DH to study Pauline texts is still in its infancy. As has been previously noted, while some have employed disability as a critical tool in tandem with other biblical criticism or theological models, so far there has been the lack of a systematic definition of disability as an interpretative tool.[318] However, the present research offers the opportunity to come up with one's own DH as an analytical tool for studying the biblical text. It is hoped that DHs will open up the selected passages of 2 Corinthians (1:3–11; 4:1–18; 6:1–13; and 10–13) to find the reason Paul describes his sufferings and weaknesses here much more than in any of his other epistles. The previous section formulated a viable DH comprised primarily of rhetorical criticism and a sociological approach as its analytical tools, and a disability perspective as the lens through which these tools operate. In what follows, this section will briefly analyse how this DH is going to help one understand Paul's suffering and weakness in 2 Corinthians.

This present research acknowledges the need for reinvestigating the social world of Paul thoroughly with disability in mind. This is because of the glaring truth that there is a lack of concern for investigating the place of disability in Paul's social milieu or even the fact that Paul was suffering the consequences of his disability. In order to establish a proper foundation for the exegesis of the chosen texts, it becomes necessary to re-discover and reconstruct the socio-cultural history of Paul's time with a particular focus on the pervading societal attitude towards a PwD during Paul's time. Therefore, in what will become the background chapter (chapter 3), a historical description of the society from a disability perspective will be done by analyzing the available literature.

Not just the biblical text, but any relevant texts from ancient writers will be analysed from a disability perspective. This will reveal the place of disability

---

318. See Avalos, "Redemptionism, Rejectionism," 91–100; Schipper, *Disability Studies*; Raphael, *Biblical Corpora*; Black, *Healing Homiletic*, 37–38; Creamer, *Disability and Christian Theology*, 95.

in Paul's social milieu. It will also reveal the extent of the attitude (most likely a negative attitude) that the so-called "normal" people of that society had towards their disabled members. At the same time, since this study is predicated upon the belief that Paul is disabled in some manner an examination of the historical literature will also be done with a view to establish the condition of Paul's disability. As was noted in the definition of "disability,"[319] the focus of this attempt will not just be to identify the physical disability of Paul but will pull heavily on the social aspect of disability as well.

The DH will also examine the socio-rhetorical context of 2 Corinthians as a whole. One expects that this present study will reveal the obscured nature of the place of disability within the inner layers of ancient society which has resulted from the failure to study 2 Corinthians from a disability perspective. Judge has rightly stated that modern readers should "know not only who they [Corinthian believers including PwD] were and what relation they had as a group to the social structure of their own communities, but what they existed for as a group, what activities they engaged in, and what their contemporaries would have made of them."[320] Thus, by employing a sociological approach, a DH will also investigate disability in the Corinthian context. A socio-historical analysis will assist in reconstructing the Corinthian society as well as inferring the make-up of the Corinthian congregation.

According to Tate, a socio-historical approach "examines the social developments and movements of the early Christians within the Greco-Roman world."[321] This will help in restructuring and evaluating the history of the city of Corinth with disability in mind, along the way providing an answer to the presence or absence of disability in its midst. Scholars like Garland and Martin have noted that Corinthian society was unique and open to new ideas, with an appreciation for symmetrical bodies and oratorical skills.[322] If this were the case, then Paul, who was weak in appearance and lacking in oratorical skill, would have had a difficult time avoiding the negative attitude directed towards his shortcomings. Therefore, a DH will reinvestigate Paul's letter anew to offer insights into Paul's sufferings and weaknesses in 2 Corinthians.

---

319. See chapter 2, section 2.2.4, of this present study.
320. Chow, *Patronage and Power*, 18.
321. Tate, *Biblical Interpretation*, 80.
322. See Garland, *2 Corinthians*, 24; Martin, *Corinthian Body*, 35.

Then again, if Paul was disabled, the next logical thing to do is to exegete Paul's rhetoric in 2 Corinthians with disability central to the discussion. While there is ambiguity to the extent of Paul's knowledge of ancient Greco-Roman rhetoric,[323] the overall inclination of scholars is that even though Paul may not have attended any rhetorical school, the presence of many rhetorical devices and figures in 2 Corinthians suggests the possibility of him being knowledgeable about the finer points of rhetoric as a discipline.[324] As such, one can observe Paul's Second Letter to the Corinthians as rhetorical in character. Therefore, the rhetorical criticism components of this DH will investigate 2 Corinthians to reveal evidence of his disability however subtle it may be. In this manner, this DH will examine the nuances of Paul's argument in 2 Corinthians to show that he was defending himself from the attacks of his opponents and the Corinthians on account of his disability.

Recently, scholars such as Witherington have identified the forensic nature of Paul's rhetoric in 2 Corinthians.[325] If this is right, then it points to the fact that there was something deeply unsettling about the attack on Paul. The first step to analyzing Paul's defence would be to figure out and identify the rhetorical unit of the chosen passage. The rhetorical unit is "an argumentative unit affecting the reader's reasoning or the reader's imagination."[326] It also recognizes the "line of thought that runs throughout the section."[327] After the examination, one hopes to ascertain that these passages are a unit in themselves and at the same time, work for a greater "persuasive purpose" in the whole argument of 2 Corinthians.[328]

Witherington has identified the rhetorical arrangement of the whole of 2 Corinthians as "*Exordium*: 1:3–7. *Narratio*: 1:8–2:16. *Propositio*: 2:17. *Probatio* (*refutatio*): 3:1–13:4. Argument I: 3:1–6:13. Argument II: Digression (*Egressio*): 6:14–7:1. Argument III (with *Amplificatio*): 7:2–16. Argument IV: Chapters 8–9. Argument V: 10:1–13:4. *Peroratio*: 13:5–10. Closing Epistolary

---

323. See chapter 2, section 2.4.2.2.
324. See Bullinger, *Figures of Speech*, 715–717.
325. Betz, *2 Corinthians*, 13; Kennedy, *New Testament*, 86–87; Young and Ford, *Meaning and Truth*, 37–40; Witherington, *Conflict & Community*, 333, 339, 465; Peterson, *Eloquence*, 141; McCant, *2 Corinthians*, 13.
326. Wuellner, "Where Is Rhetorical Criticism," 455.
327. Moon, "Paul's Discourse," 52.
328. Moon, 52.

Greetings and Remarks: 13:11–13."[329] One should note here that there are no fixed rules as to what should make up the parts of rhetorical speech. For instance, while Aristotle recognized mainly the *exordium* (statement of facts) and the *probatio* (the proofs), others like Cicero, Quintilian, and the *Rhetorica ad Herennium* (Handbook of rhetoric) recognize different parts of speech besides those two.[330]

This study will examine 2 Corinthians 1:3–11 as the *exordium* which, according to Aristotle, "is the beginning of a speech . . . paving the way for what follows."[331] The *exordium* will show that Paul's rhetoric points towards an exigence or a rhetorical situation that requires further investigations. Aristotle identified many methods that a rhetor could use in his *exordium*; however, all these methods involved the removal of "prejudice" that was cast upon the rhetor by the accuser.[332] As such, the *exordium* will reveal the rhetorical situation as well as explain the problem that Paul faced (perhaps, in this case, the accusation against his disability could be the reason behind Paul's suffering).

The subsequent passages (4:1–18; 6:1–11; and 10–13) then make up the *probatio* of Paul's defence from this accusation. *Probatio* consists of "the main body of the speech where one offers logical arguments as proof."[333] According to Aristotle, "proofs should be demonstrative", and the "demonstration should bear upon the particular point disputed."[334] Here, the *probatio* will "identify not only the kinds of proofs used in the argument, but also the relative proportions of the three types of internal proofs, those of *ethos*, *pathos*, and *logos*."[335] As such, *probatio* then becomes "the central and decisive part" of Paul's proof made in defence of his disability.[336]

The chosen texts, all informed by a disability perspective, will be thoroughly analysed as to which one takes into consideration the social, historical, and cultural aspects. The sociological dimension of the DH will aid the rhetorical dimension of the DH. The various aspects of the components of

---

329. See Witherington, *Conflict & Community*, the table of contents.
330. See chapter 2, section 2.4.1.1, for the explanation of this point.
331. Aristotle, *Rhetoric*, 3.14.
332. Aristotle, *Rhetoric*, 3.15.
333. See the definition of *confirmatio* in "Canons of Rhetoric."
334. Aristotle, *Rhetoric*, 3.17.
335. Weima, "What Does Aristotle," 462.
336. Moon, "Paul's Discourse," 56.

a sociological approach that are deemed useful and relevant for revealing further insights into the disability-related Corinthian value system will be judiciously employed. As one continues to employ a DH further into the study of these chosen passages – 2 Corinthians 1:3–11, 4:1–18, 6:3–13, and 10–13 – it is hoped that better and more comprehensive insights into Paul's arguments in 2 Corinthians, where his disability lies at the root of his suffering and weakness, will be revealed.

## 2.6 Summarization

This chapter focuses on the term "disability" and its definition. The definition formulated in this chapter focuses on the social aspect of how one should understand disability as intricately connected to physical limitations, or *imperfections*, and the far-reaching consequences on those who experience them. This study is very much aware that disability is also a cultural product residing in the social environment, which is partly responsible for its formation. This chapter also traces the different disability tools employed by scholars in biblical studies. It finds that all these lack, in one way or another, comprehensive analysis of Paul's Second Letter to the Corinthians. Thus, this chapter formulates a viable critical tool called a disability hermeneutic (DH). This DH is a perspectival exegetical-interpretative tool that will engage with the selected texts of 2 Corinthians critically, with disability as its primary focus, aware that in the multifaceted society of antiquity, the disabled are regarded as social outcasts, and their voices are often silenced.

CHAPTER 3

# Disability in the Greco-Roman, Jewish World

## 3.1 Introduction

Chapter 3 will focus mainly on the issue of how the ancient Greco-Roman and Jewish societies dealt with disability. In his introduction to *Disability in Antiquity*, Christian Laes has correctly pointed out that "for many periods and regions, disability studies in the ancient world are only at the very beginning phase."[1] However, within a short span of time, one observes a rapid progress, particularly in the field of ancient disability history,[2] and in this chapter, three important issues will be specifically dealt with. The first issue deals in general with the question of the nature and place of disabled people in the ancient Greco-Roman and Jewish world. Was disability a problem to these people from the first century, and if so, how did these ancient societies treat disability? The second issue involves the question of how disability relates particularly to Corinthian society. How far can an analysis of the Corinthian society and its history, culture, social and religious environment reveal the status of the PwD? In addition, can one substantiate further the issue of disability as it pertains to the Apostle Paul himself? This is because, when it

---

1. Laes, introduction to *Disability in Antiquity*, 2.

2. Laes has traced important works concerning ancient disability (see Laes, introduction to *Disability in Antiquity*, 7 onwards).

comes to Paul, one can say that there are two camps – one that maintains that Paul was not disabled and the other that argues that Paul suffered disability.

## 3.2 General Attitudes towards Disability among Greeks, Romans, and Jews

In the previous chapter, it was observed that there is ambiguity in the use of the term "disability" to label those who were physically challenged in antiquity.[3] One recollects the reason given by Laes as to why "disability" as an umbrella term was absent in antiquity.[4] According to him, in ancient society "the focus lies on the body's physical and cognitive limitations."[5] For instance, if an individual could not walk, the obvious choice for describing that individual was to call them lame, and if someone could not see, then they were simply a blind person. That is why there were so many individual words for disability.[6] However, as was previously mentioned, under the definition of the term "disability" for this present study, all these individuals' limitations, along with the societal attitudes which make them more disabled, can be subsumed.[7] Having established that understanding, this section will focus on the general understanding of how the Greco-Roman and Jewish societies treated their PwDs and what kind of attitude was prevalent during those days.

The history on disabilities is quite limited. According to Laes, "what is left of the literary record of the period before 500 BCE is almost completely silent on the matter."[8] In fact, Homer, the earliest classical historian, has "hardly any disabled war veterans . . . except for Philoctetes who due to his war wounds was suffering from exile, isolation and pain on the island of Lemnos."[9] It seems that "the lyric poets of the 6th century BCE do not pay any attention to disablement whatsoever; although they lament the harsh sorrows of old age."[10] However, there is a good number of materials pertaining to the Roman

---

3. See chapter 2, section 2.2.1, of this present study.
4. Laes, introduction to *Disability in Antiquity*, 6.
5. Laes, 4.
6. See appendix 1 of this present study for such lists.
7. See chapter 2, section 2.2.2, of this present study.
8. Laes, introduction to *Disability in Antiquity*, 11.
9. Edwards, "Philoctetes," 55–69.
10. Laes, introduction to *Disability in Antiquity*, 11.

Empire, where "a large collection of data in written sources in both Latin and Greek, as well as archaeological and osteological records" are available and can shed considerable light to the general understanding of disability within first-century Palestinian societies.[11]

For instance, Grmek has observed that "about 10 percent of the skeletons found in the Greek world showed at least one fracture *in vitam (when alive)*."[12] Additionally, consider the work of fifth-century Greek grammarian and lexicographer Hesychius of Alexandria, *Collection of All Words*, which listed "many words [indicating disability] that are found in surviving texts of the Greek literature."[13] This led Samama to surmise correctly that the evidence points to "the widespread existence of disabled people."[14] She went to a great length to list vocabularies that pertain to the word deformity or limited physicality.[15] Some of the more obvious words include *battalos*, meaning "stammerer," and *cholos*, which means "lame, paralysed or limping."[16]

### 3.2.1 Disability and Ancient Greek Society and Culture

Jenkins and Turner have examined scores of sculptures and arts from the Greco-Roman period. In their preface to *The Greek Body*, they wrote that

> more than any other civilization in antiquity, ancient Greece is remarkable for the central place it gave to the sculpture of the human body. It could be said that the Greeks invented the body in art or, at least, the idealized male body conceived as a thing of beauty and bearer of meaning.[17]

Indeed, one would think that their obsession with beauty and perfection would imply a society full of human beings who showed no signs of physical deformities or any kind of disabilities. The truth seems far contrary to this assumption. The following section will briefly examine the historical evidence

---

11. Laes, 11.
12. Mirko D. Grmek, *Les Maladies `a l'aube de la Civilisation Occidentale* (Paris, 1994), 93, quoted in Samama, "Greek Vocabulary," 121.
13. Samama, "Greek Vocabulary," 121.
14. Samama, 121.
15. See appendix 1 of this present study for this collection of disability vocabulary.
16. Samama, "Greek Vocabulary," 123.
17. Jenkins and Turner, preface to *Greek Body*.

to observe the presence of disabled people and the attitude of Greek society towards them.

### 3.2.1.1 Insights into the attitude of Greek society towards the PwD

There were disabled people present in ancient Greek society. Now the next thing to consider is how they fared in such a society and how the society treated them. Martha Lynn Rose's observations prove critical at this point. According to her, "the criteria of ability and disability rested not on one's ability to function as an individual, but on one's functional ability within the community."[18] In other words, it is possible for a person to get a fuller picture of the relationship between disability and the ancient community only if one gets to see the interaction between them (i.e. the society and the PwD). There is, fortunately, quite a significant amount of literature from which one can draw valuable insights into the inner workings of how society treated those with disabilities. Robert Garland drew insight on the subject of disability from the writings of Sophocles, Euripides, and Aristophanes. According to Garland, "Both Greek tragedy and comedy have provided us with some memorable characters afflicted with a disability, notably those who are blind, lame, and temporarily insane."[19] In order to shed further light on this issue, various examples of ancient literature are analysed in what follows.

First, Rose studied the remarkable case of disability in Lysias's *On the Refusal of a Pension to the Invalid*.[20] What is noteworthy about this case is that the defendant Lysias was handicapped, and it caused him pain and prevented him from travelling a long distance.[21] Because of his *adunatos* (inability or "the affliction of his body"),[22] he drew a pension from the Athenian government. However, he could take care of himself and even had the capability to earn a livelihood. And this caused some to envy him and file a case against him so that he may not draw his pension anymore. Nevertheless, Lysias defended himself saying that his "father left him nothing," and that he had "an aged mother whom he had to support and the lack of children to support him

---

18. Rose, "Ability and Disability," 151.
19. Garland, "Disabilities," 154.
20. Lysias, *On the Refusal*, 24.6; see Rose, "Ability and Disability," 141.
21. See Lysias, *On the Refusal*, 24.13.
22. Rose, "Ability and Disability," 141.

when he reached old age."²³ What is significant for this present study is the comment made by Lysias that he would become "able" if they removed him from receiving a pension, and if he was "able," then he would be "eligible to serve as *archon* or chief magistrate."²⁴ From his comment, one can draw a connection between the word "able" and "eligible" for higher offices in that period. In other words, what this indicates is that only an "able" person could serve as chief magistrate or hold important official posts. Dasen's study on ancient Egyptian and Greek dwarfs seems to confirm this assessment.²⁵

Second, another story is from Sophocles's work *Oedipus the King*. In the story, King Oedipus had a mutilation that greatly shamed him.²⁶ The king held the seer Teiresias responsible for his disability and sought out ways to humiliate him by taunting the seer's blindness, which made Teiresias feel very shameful.²⁷ In fact, Garland interpreted the shame as an "indication of the stigma that he has borne throughout his life."²⁸ In the same manner, Sophocles's narration of the lame but skilled archer Philoctetes, who was socially an outcast because of his affliction, also supports this interpretation. A snake bit Philoctetes and this caused him to be afflicted with sores that could not heal, and which became "repulsive" to others. Because of this, he had to fend for himself, a social outcast, and was left to die alone on Lemnos Island.²⁹ However, as fate would have it, in the Trojan War, the seer Calchas predicted that they needed Philoctetes to win the war. Only then did Odysseus and his young companion Neoptolemus seek him out without expressing "the least iota of compassion towards him."³⁰

Third, Herodotus, the famous Greek historian, in his work *The Histories* narrates the story of Croesus, who was a powerful king of the Lydian with two sons, "one blasted by a natural defect, being deaf and dumb; the other, distinguished far above all his co-mates in every pursuit."³¹ Again, what is significant

---

23. Lysias, *On the Refusal*, 24.6; Rose, "Ability and Disability," 141.
24. Lysias, *On the Refusal*, 24.13; Rose, "Ability and Disability," 141.
25. See Dasen, *Dwarfs*, 212.
26. Sophocles, *Oedipus*, 1035.
27. Sophocles, *Oedipus*, 372, 412.
28. Garland, "Disabilities," 155.
29. Sophocles, *Philoctetes*.
30. Garland, "Disabilities," 156.
31. Herodotus, *History*, 1.34.

for the present study is the way Croesus committed injustice against his disabled son by not acknowledging his existence and not counting him as his son. In the story, Croesus said to his able son that "thou art the one and only son that I possess; the other, whose hearing is destroyed, I regard as if he were not."[32] One can only surmise how painful it must have been to the disabled son to hear of his father's rejection. Moreover, if a king could show such disdain for his son, one shudders to think of the domino effect it would have on the broader society and culture of that time.

### 3.2.1.2 Greek societal attitudes towards rhetors with disabilities

It seems that ancient Greek society was harsh upon rhetors having some sort of disability no matter how skilful they may have been. For instance, consider the case of Demosthenes who struggled against societal bias and ridicule because of his speech problem and bodily weakness before he could achieve fame. According to Plutarch, Demosthenes "was lean and sickly, and his opprobrious surname of Batalus is said to have been given him by the boys in mockery of his physique."[33] The first time Demosthenes spoke in front of the people, "he was interrupted by their clamours and [they] laughed at *his* weakness of voice and indistinctness of speech and shortness of breath which disturbed the sense of what he said by disjoining his sentences."[34]

The attitude of ancient Greek society was truly unforgiving and ruthless towards someone who spoke in public and did not have good physical features. This becomes much clearer when we see another public figure, Alcibiades, suffering from lisping, yet enduring no ridicule or harmful attitude from the audience. What seems to have set Alcibiades apart from Demosthenes is the fact that Alcibiades possessed "excellent natural parts. Even the lisp that he had became his speech, they say, and made his talk persuasive and full of charm."[35] Why was there such an attitude and expectation among the people? What gave them the right to judge people like that? It is possible to find some connection to the teaching of Aristotle, who believed that the most important

---

32. Herodotus, *History*, 1.38.
33. Plutarch, *Demosthenes*, 4.3.
34. Plutarch 6.3."
35. Plutarch, *Alcibiades*, 1.4.

part of rhetoric was the "moral character of the speaker."[36] That is, instead of the content of the speech and the ability to move the audience, the speaker's bodily presence and reputation was the aspect that people first judged.

### 3.2.1.3 Insights from "honour and shame" culture

Laes believes that when abled people during Paul's time confronted deformity in others, it evoked certain attitudes like "shame, mockery, fascination, pity and fear,"[37] and that these attitudes as an instant reaction were, according to Laes, "almost interlocked in the ancient Greek world."[38] The need to mock and deride those who were seen as different seems to make sense when viewed from the honour and shame model of cultural anthropology that scholars like Bruce Malina have made use of in their studies of the New Testament world.[39] According to Malina, "honor means a person's (or group's) feeling of self-worth and the public, social acknowledgement of that worth," while shame refers to "sensitivity about one's own reputation, sensitivity to the opinion of others."[40]

To put this into perspective when it comes to the notion of disability, it becomes clear that in a culture that praised mental and bodily perfection, a case of deformity was an absurdity that they could do without, as it would add shame to themselves as well as to their family. Maybe this is why "mentally disabled individuals were by custom kept inside and Plato in his ideal state would have a law that these were definitely to be kept inside by their relatives, and not allowed to wander the streets."[41] Dillon points out that "in shame-culture, i.e. based on honour, shaming the other was important as ensuring one's physical and intellectual integrity."[42] Disability then becomes a reflection of the imperfection one does not possess; therefore, "when we mock someone we do so because they are different or act differently from the rest

---

36. "Aristotle, *Rhetoric*, 1.2.3.
37. Christian Laes, *Beperkt? Gehandicapten in het Romeinse Rijk* (Leuven: Davidfonds Uitgeverij, 2014), 197–201, quoted in Mitchell, "Hellenistic Turn," 193.
38. Laes, *Beperkt?*, 197–201, quoted in Mitchell, "Hellenistic Turn," 193.
39. See Malina, *New Testament World*.
40. Malina, 49.
41. Dillon, "Legal," 167.
42. Mitchell, "Hellenistic Turn," 193.

of the main group."[43] From all the examples seen from the above, one can say that ancient Greek society was not that welcoming to the less fortunate PwD.

## 3.2.2 Disability and Ancient Roman Society and Culture

The many sculptors and other art that have survived wars and disasters reflect the Romans' admirations of physical perfection. Trentin has mentioned that there were hardly any representations of disability in "the entire repertoire of Roman art."[44] For instance, the famously disabled god Hephaestus who was "crook-footed" or with "feet turned backwards" in Homer's *Iliad*[45] was "never portrayed as overtly disabled in the visual tradition; his lameness, when represented, is always discreet."[46] Even Emperor Claudius, whom Suetonius claimed had a speech disability and probably was also physically lame, was never portrayed as someone who was physically challenged.[47] According to Suetonius, Claudius's

> knees were feeble, and failed him in walking . . . his gait was ungainly, both when he assumed state, and when he was taking a diversion. He was outrageous in his laughter, and still more so in his wrath, for then he foamed at the mouth and discharged from his nostrils. He also stammered in his speech, and had a tremulous motion of the head at all times, but particularly when he was engaged in any business, however trifling.[48]

Although the satirist mocked him, when it came to outward appearances, it seems superficiality and public image were more important than portraying the reality. However, the problem with this is that in reality, disability did not really have any place in Roman society. The following sections look at some of the problems faced by the PwD in Roman society.

---

43. Mitchell, 193; see also Bergson, *Laughter*, 9–11.
44. Trentin, "'Other' Romans: Deformed Bodies in the Visual Arts of Rome," 233.
45. Homer, *Iliad*, 1:607.
46. Trentin, "'Other' Romans," 233.
47. Trentin, 233.
48. Suetonius, *Claudius*, ch. 30.

## 3.2.2.1 Practice of exposing children

The practice of child exposing seems to have been prevalent in ancient Roman society. According to Gracie Joy, "Children with birth defects or handicaps were usually subject to exposure and infanticide."[49] Exposing means the tradition of keeping or leaving outside to die any children showing some form of physical or mental defects. It is believed that this practice can be traced back even to the founders of Rome, the twins Romulus and Remus, who were supposedly exposed as infants. Legend has it that they were exposed and left to die, but fortunately, a she-wolf and a woodpecker took care of them until they were in the care of Faustulus the herdsman.[50] Dionysius of Halicarnassus described a law supposedly coming from Romulus that "required the citizens to bring up all their male children and the first-born female child, and not to kill any children under the age of three except those that were deformed."[51] In the writing of Seneca the Elder, one observes explicit evidence of the practice of exposing infants. According to him, "Many fathers are in the habit of exposing offspring who are no good. Some, right from birth damaged in some part of their bodies, weak and hopeless. Their parents throw them out, rather than expose them."[52] Therefore, one can infer that infant exposing was a cultural practice in Roman society.

Why was such a seemingly cruel practice prevalent during those times? What made it a valid practice even to the point of necessity that parents would willingly leave their children to die out in the open? Littell believes that there are multiple reasons like "economic," "birth defects," "illegitimacy," "evil omens," and "gender" which perpetrated the practice of infant exposing.[53] The younger Seneca explained this practice in his book *De Ira*.[54] According to him, "Unnatural prodigy we destroy; we drown even children who at birth are weakly and abnormal. Yet it is not anger, but the reason that separates the harmful from the sound."[55] To be fair, it is understandable that without the

---

49. Joy, "Obstetrics and Gynaecology," article 7.
50. "Romulus and Remus."
51. Harris, "Child-Exposure," 5.
52. Seneca, Controversiae, 10.4.16, translated by M. Winterbottom, quoted in Laes, "Learning from Silence," 94.
53. Littell, "Why Were?"
54. Seneca, *De Ira*, 1.15.2.
55. Trans. by J. W. Basore, as quoted in Laes, "Learning from Silence," 94.

advances in modern medical equipment and knowledge, infants born during those days had a serious disadvantage. To let an infant with a birth defect live would have been a difficult choice for the parents to make. However, the fact that Roman society was partial to its healthy babies over ones with defects is undeniable. Ancient Roman society killed those they considered deformed, such as "androgyns, malformed babies, precocious babies, monsters half human-half beast, and multiple births," mainly because such children did not have a place in the society.[56]

### 3.2.2.2 Disability and the Stoics' teachings

The Stoics were not known to make the physical body important; for them, virtue was all that mattered, so in terms of a general philosophical understanding among the Stoics, they tended not to laugh at the disabled.[57] However, people know that Cicero "encourage[d] mocking physical flaws as a strategy in juridical speeches."[58] Plutarch recorded Cicero making fun of Vatinius, whose neck swelled, as a "tumid orator."[59] Seneca tried to justify this mocking and derision by saying that "if he could do this thanks to the harshness of his speaking – his continuous insulting had made him forget the shame."[60] What this means simply is that indeed it is shameful to possess such deformity, but if you allow people to make fun of you and do not take it to heart, soon you will make them forget wanting to shame you. This, according to Seneca "is a sort of vengeance to ruin the pleasure of someone who has insulted you."[61] Did Seneca have this mindset when he made fun of Emperor Claudius's speech impediment and ridiculed him? It is something that one cannot be certain of. However, even if the end justifies the means, to make fun of disability can hardly be positive to the one at the receiving end.

---

56. See Laes, "Learning from Silence," 95.
57. Gevaert, "Perfect Roman Bodies," 216.
58. Cicero, *De Oratore*, 239, 245–246, 249.
59. Plutarch, *Cicero*, 26.2.
60. Seneca, *De Constantia*, 17.3–4. Born Lucius Annaeus Seneca, his date of birth is not certain, some say 4 BC while others in 1 BC. However, his death date is certain (AD 65). He was born in Cordoba (Spain) and educated in rhetoric and philosophy in Rome (Vogt, "Seneca").
61. Seneca, *De Constantia*, 17.3–4.

### 3.2.2.3 Insights into the attitude of Roman society towards the PwD

It has been noted that Romans valued bodily perfection, that disability did not seem to have a place in their arts, and at the same time, disabled people were mocked and made fun of in their literature, particularly their satirical literature. Even in the rare cases where their arts represented dwarfs, hunchbacks, and pygmies, they functioned as comparative pointers to the differences between the viewers and the disabled.[62] In terms of affirming the viewers' "privileged health, wealth and social standing," what this artistic representation of the disabled did was to "serve as a stark and explicit validation of everything that the viewer is not."[63]

The making fun of the disabled, even though they may have been powerful, seems to have been the norm for the satirist in those days. The attitude of Cicero was disheartening, for he believed that it was clearly his job as an orator to raise laughter no matter the cause.[64] According to Laes, "Mockery and disdain were almost certainly part of the lives of the disabled."[65] Bond and Gellar-Goad are on point when they remark that the "Romans' satirists take advantage of pervasive social norms that deprecated and disempowered those with bodily differences – norms of healthy and unhealthy, sane and insane, whole and unwhole, strong and weak – in order to pursue their own poetic and moralistic agendas."[66] Thus, it is clear that the satirist reflected what the public wanted, and this reveals the deeper insights into the relationship between disabled people and their society.

So, why would the Romans have such disregard for the disabled members of their society? Vlahogiannis believes that the influence of religion was at the heart of the Romans' attitude in regards to the disabled.[67] According to him, "Disabilities – the destruction of limbs through paralysis or injury, loss of the use of senses, personal appearance, sanity, impotence – became

---

62. See Trintin, "'Other' Romans," 236–243, for the depiction of these deformities according to the Romans.
63. Trentin, 245.
64. Cicero, *De Oratore*, 236.
65. Laes, "Learning from Silence," 114.
66. Bond and Gellar-Goad, "Foul and Fair," 231.
67. Plutarch, *Quaestiones Romanae*, 73, quoted in Vlahogiannis, "Disabling Bodies," 18–19.

intertwined with punishment for violations of the divine and moral order."⁶⁸ Suetonius also mentioned how Emperor Augustus thought of the dwarfs "as *lususnatura* ('nature's abortions'), and of evil omen."⁶⁹ In short, disability according to the Romans was the result of a curse by the gods, and as such, it hardly had any place in their society.

## 3.2.3 Disability and Ancient Jewish Society and Culture

In a certain manner, doing disability research among the ancient Israelites is knotty due to limited resources. Kellenberger recognizes this problem when he states, "The few excavated Hebrew (and Aramaic) texts do not mention disabilities; we are, therefore, restricted to the limited corpus of the Old Testament."⁷⁰ What this indicates is that studying disability in Israelite culture and society is hard but not entirely impossible. The Hebrew Bible remains the best primary source of information concerning how Jews viewed disability.

### *3.2.3.1 Hebrew terminology for disability*

When it comes to examining disability in the Hebrew Bible, Kellenberger has studied the noun patterns present in the Mesopotamian language. He realized that just as in "Akkadian, many disability designations follow the noun pattern *PuRRUSU*. . . . In Hebrew *also*, the pattern *PaRRiS* (also with doubling the middle consonant) designates common variations in seeing, hearing and walking."⁷¹ Besides this noun pattern, a bit more limited is "the Hebrew conceptual term 'blemish' ('*mum*'), which is used to designate some physical anomalies."⁷² Even though the etymology is not clear, the "LXX translate the term as μωμος which is used to indicate 'blame' or 'disgrace' in non-Jewish Greek literature."⁷³

Again according to Kellenberger, the criterion for whether impairments count as *mum* or not is clear. Often it concerns the aesthetic ideal of symmetrical body halves; for example, a knocked-out tooth is considered a blemish

---

68. Vlahogiannis, "Disabling Bodies," 29.
69. Suetonius, *Augustus*, ch. 81.
70. Kellenberger, "Mesopotamia and Israel," 47.
71. Kellenberger, 48.
72. Kellenberger, 49.
73. Kellenberger, 49.

(Lev 24:20).[74] The bodies of sacrificial animals and of the priest had to be without blemish (Lev 22:18–25; 21:17–23). However, other impairments like deafness, muteness, psychic and mental disorders, as well as polluting phenomena like skin diseases, seminal discharges, and menstruation, do not appear under the term "blemish."[75] The "most frequent word pairs are 'blind and lame' and 'deaf and blind.'"[76] Then there are others like the "widows, orphans and strangers . . . pregnant women and women in labour who are vulnerable socially and belonged to the margins of society (Ps 113:7–9; Job 24:21; Isa 56:3–7)."[77]

### 3.2.3.2 The cause of disability

When one closely examines the causes of disability in the Hebrew Bible, one can see that there is a close connection between disability and punishment by God. This is most obvious in Deuteronomy 28:28–29 where it says that their disobedience will result in them being made blind and mad, among other things, by the Lord. Claasens seems to be correct in her interpretation that this was "probably (the) most disturbing . . . way in which disability is used as a curse in the biblical traditions."[78] Take, for instance, the condition of Saul and his madness: one could infer from this that it was literally "an evil spirit from the Lord [that] came upon Saul" (1 Sam 19:9). Aside from these, one also finds in Exodus 4:11 that God is the one "who makes a person mute or deaf or seeing or blind."[79] Likewise, some important figures like Jacob are recorded with a limp in the Hebrew Bible because of the direct action of God (Gen 32:25).

### 3.2.3.3 Close relation between the Hittites' practice and the Hebrews

According to Kellenberger, "Extrapolating information about Mesopotamia to Israel is often plausible but always risky."[80] Indeed, it is possible to get some

---

74. See Samuel, "Person with Disability," 131–133.
75. Kellenberger, "Mesopotamia and Israel," 49.
76. Kellenberger, 50.
77. Kellenberger, 50.
78. Claasens, "Job, Theology and Disability," 56.
79. See the third paragraph of section 3.2.3.4 in this study for further thoughts.
80. Kellenberger, "Mesopotamia and Israel," 47.

insights from the Hittite texts dealing with disability but with caution because reading into a given culture from another is complex and often runs the risks of subjective impositions. One of the most striking cases of disability that one can gain insight into from the Hittite practices is the blindness of Samson. Judges 16:21 narrates how his enemies captured Samson and had his eyes gouged out. This punishment makes sense if seen from the Hittite background because "a Middle Hittite treaty stipulates blinding" as a form of punishment.[81] For instance, "a letter from Sarpa in Sapinuwa to the governor in Tapigga recorded that 'Blind men have fled from the mill house.'"[82] This is very similar to the condition of Samson who, after being blinded, was working in a mill, grinding.

Besides this, the axiom, "eye for an eye, tooth for tooth, hand for hand, foot for foot," in Exodus 21:24, is very much similar to that of the Hittite cultural practices. For example, an "edict in the Middle Hittite period rules that 'if a slave steals and (the injured party) holds him for theft, if he has been blinded, they shall hand him over.'"[83] This indicates that the injured party could blind slaves as a form of payback, and no further action would be taken as long as they handed the slave back to the authority.

### 3.2.3.4 Insights into the attitude of Jewish society towards the PwD

The concern in this section is to understand how Jewish cultures and society treated, accepted, or rejected the PwD. Is it possible to make a case of mistreatment or injustice? How far was their disability a factor in the social hierarchy? Schipper's studies of Mephibosheth do not offer a conclusive sense of how society treated him. However, his understanding of Mephibosheth's "paralysis as an obstacle for becoming king" indicates a negative attitude of the ancient Jewish society in regard to disability.[84] This seems clear from the text indicating how Mephibosheth considered himself "a dead dog" (2 Sam 9:8b), which could be taken as an implication of his personal struggle against the societal attitude towards his disability. Indeed, his servant Ziba

---

81. Beal, "Disabilities from Head," 38.
82. Hoffner, *Letters*, 210.
83. Beal, "Disabilities from Head," 38.
84. Kellenberger, "Mesopotamia and Israel," 53.

took advantage of his disability and won the sympathy of David when he was fleeing for his life (see 2 Sam 16:3).

The instruction in Leviticus 21:17–23 is clear; no one who has a defect can come to the Lord for offering worship.[85] This "ministry of sacrifice was forbidden to blemished priests, though such persons kept all other priestly rights (Lev 21:21–22): he shall eat the bread of his God (both of the holiest, and of the holy), this allowed a sort of social security in the case of later acquired impairment."[86] Yet there are places in Leviticus itself where harming or disparaging the deaf and blind are condemned (Lev 19:14); indeed, such behaviour is seen as deserving of the curses of Deuteronomy 27. As such, the irony of this instruction does not escape one's attention. Thus, it seems better to understand the Levitical instruction as rules governing what was permitted or forbidden for priests depending on deeper cultural and theological reasons to do with purity and wholeness – similar to the way it could only be unblemished animals that should be sacrificed.

For a case in point, Moses's rejection of God's initial calling to go back to Egypt and deliver the Israelites from their bondage could be seen as a response to cultural hindrances for a disabled man to be the leader of a nation. In Exodus 4:10, one reads, "Moses said to the LORD, 'Pardon your servant, Lord. I have never been eloquent, neither in the past nor since you have spoken to your servant. I am slow of speech and tongue." (NIV) Terrence E. Fretheim is of the mind that Moses is "likely" suffering from a "speech impediment."[87] However, Fretheim is quick to point out that this disability is not from God, even though the rhetoric in Exodus 4:11 seems to suggest it. Instead, Fretheim rightly understands God's reply to Moses as "a general statement that the world is so created by God that such things will happen."[88] In fact, the focus of the texts is God's acceptance of a disabled man to be the leader of a nation! As such, Moses's hesitancy must be personal, arising from the culturally constructed inability to see a speech impediment as a characteristic of a leader figure.

---

85. See Schipper, "Disability."
86. Kellenberger, "Mesopotamia and Israel," 49.
87. Fretheim, *Exodus*, 71.
88. Fretheim, 71.

## 3.3 Disability in Corinthian Society

The previous sections have looked into the problem of disability in a wider scope among the Greco-Roman and Jewish societies. This section will briefly focus one's attention on the PwD in the Corinthian city. Was disability prevalent in the city of Corinth? If so, how did Corinthian society treat them? In addition, what kind of attitude did the majority of the Corinthians have towards disabled people? Tracing disability among the Corinthians or any kind of examination or analysis is still at an infant stage, so the problem of limited resources exists. However, the materials one can access are enough to set this research on the right course and to get specific insights into the problem of disability among the Corinthians.

### 3.3.1 A Brief History of the City of Corinth

Pausanias, an ancient Greek traveller, "reputedly born in Lydia," wrote numerous accounts of the places he visited between "143 CE (and) 161 CE."[89] According to him, "The Corinthian land is a portion of the Argive, and is named after Corinthus."[90] The city of Corinth was a thriving city way back before Paul had ever stepped foot in the city. Pausanias, in his book, described the beauty of the ancient city of Corinth and what went on inside, in detail.[91] The main reason why it was such a thriving city was due to its strategic location. Corinth lay on "the isthmus which formed the gateway to the Peloponnesian peninsula. Corinth's two ports, Lechaeum and Cenchreae facilitated and handled a large volume of trade."[92] Its strategic location also served well in terms of military. Therefore, Hodge stated, "Corinth becomes the chief city of Greece, not only in authority, but in wealth, magnificence, literature, the arts, and in luxury."[93]

Bruce also mentions that the city of "Corinth survived many crises in Greek history."[94] However, the inhabitants of Corinth brought about their demise at the hands of the Romans when they decided to join the Achaean

---

89. Pausanias, *Corinth*.
90. Pausanias, 2.1.1.
91. Pausanias.
92. Horrell, *Social Ethos*, 64; see also Strabo, *Geography*, 8.6.20–23; Pausanias, *Description of Greece*, 2.1.2.
93. Hodge, *Commentary*, vii.
94. Bruce, *1 and 2 Corinthians*, 18.

League who revolted against the mighty Roman control.[95] In 164 BC, the Roman general L. Mummius sacked the ancient city of Corinth and brought to ruins its walls and city. According to David E. Garland, "when the Roman consul Lucius Mummius destroyed Corinth in 164 BC, he killed most of the Greek male population and sold the women and children into slavery."[96] It can be safe to surmise that there would have been no room for the disabled because they would just prove to be a liability, and it would have been easier to dispose of them than to care for them. Nevertheless, after lying in ruins and desolation for a long time, finally in 44 BC, Julius Caesar realized the strategic location of the ancient city and started rebuilding it to enhance the military as well as the economic might of the Roman Empire.[97] When Julius Caesar decided to rebuild the city, he repopulated the city with "freedmen and women, urban plebs and army veterans."[98] Thus, when Paul visited Corinth, the city was already thriving again.

### 3.3.2 Evidence of Disability in Corinth

With a fluid social mobility, the social structure of Corinth was unlike any of the cities in the Roman Empire. However, were there disabled people among the Corinthians? If so, how did the Corinthians treat them? The first re-settlers were mainly the Roman armies. Meeusen states, "Considering the long list of wars and battles in Greco-Roman times . . . the theme of wounded generals and soldiers is a recurrent motif in several Plutarchan writings."[99] As such, the possibility of finding PwDs among them is rather strong.[100] It does not require much of an imagination to think that army veterans without limbs or an eye would be among the re-settlers. Another important thing to consider is the rise in commerce as the seaports were working again and the occurrence of the Isthmian Games that brought in scores of people from everywhere in the Roman Empire.

It is highly likely that the new city of Corinth would have attracted countless people because of the endless opportunity for survival that the

---

95. Pausanias, *Corinth*, 2.1.1–2.
96. Garland, *2 Corinthians*, 21.
97. Hodge, *Commentary*, viii.
98. Horrell, *Social Ethos*, 65; see also Strabo, *Geography*, 8.6.23
99. Meeusen, "Plutarch's 'Philosophy,'" 204.
100. See Meeusen, 204.

city provided.¹⁰¹ Among them, the lame and blind, beggars, and the destitute would have been present. This influx of people would cause overcrowding and therefore unhygienic living conditions, which no doubt "encouraged the spread of water-borne diseases,"¹⁰² leading to some health problems. Amidst this, Stambaugh and Balch have pointed out that some of "the strategy by which a poor man could survive was to beg, steal or be under a patronage."¹⁰³ Where there were opportunities for plenty of work, it is sensible to think that one would come across disabled people begging for a living. Thus, in this kind of unique social structure, one can assume strongly that there would have been disabled people in all spectra of the society.

### 3.3.3 The Attitude of Corinthian Society towards the PwD

When it comes to analyzing the societal attitude towards disabled persons, particularly in the Corinthian matrix, there is one important factor that one must consider as the guiding principle, and that is wealth. The effect of wealth on Corinthian society is particularly evident, as wealth was the one influencer of a successful social mobility. There was a vast social and cultural gap between wealthy and poor inhabitants. For instance, Alciphorn vividly described this disparity in his *Epistles*, "For I soon discovered, the disgusting manners of its rich men, and the misery of its poor. After most of them had been to the bath, when it was midday, I saw . . . others picked up pieces of bread, which had fallen on the ground and been trodden underfoot, and greedily gulped them down."¹⁰⁴ It seems that how much wealth a person had (or lacked), and in what ways this wealth could be flaunted, was one of the most important aspects that the Corinthians considered. For example, Lucian observed, "It is not so much being rich that they like as being congratulated on it. The fact is, of course, that the man who lives in a fine house gets no good of it, nor of his ivory and gold either unless someone admires it all."¹⁰⁵ The more wealth a person has, the more he or she can display, and vice versa, but one ought to know the cultural effect this would have had on the Corinthians.

---

101. Barnett, *Second Epistle*, 3.
102. Pudsey, "Disability and Infirmitas," 32.
103. Stambaugh and Balch, *New Testament*, 112.
104. Alciphron, *Epistles*, 3.60, in *Alciphron*, 95–207, 219–227.
105. Harmon, *Lucian Works*, 123.

So, what does this have to do with the Corinthian attitude towards the PwD? There are three things to consider. First, since wealth was the main marker of the status of a person, it was possible that a PwD could have been wealthy. In other words, others would not ridicule a wealthy limping man or stammering person. In fact, wealthy PwDs would have enjoyed the amenities that society provided, as well as the begrudging respect of the populace. Thus, as long as the PwD was rich, he or she would be free from social stigmatization. Second, if the PwD happened to be poor, then, as Savage pointedly remarked, "The poor and the delinquent were less fortunate and their miseries brought instant scorn."[106] Therefore, if a society estimates a person's worth in terms of their wealth, then one should know that a poor PwD would get a two-layered stigmatization, first because he is poor, and second because he is disabled.

Third, the stark division of classes that was evident in Corinthian society made it worse for the lower classes that were poor and in want, particularly the portions who were disabled and could not but beg for their livelihood or do some derogatory work for the amusement of the wealthier class. As has been observed by Alciphron, the wealthier class had so much leisure time on their hands that when the sun was at its peak, they went to relax in the public bath while the poor scourged the street for leftovers. This resulted in the poor and the disabled needing to constantly find work and not having any leisure time. We know from Plato's writing that "multitude of pretenders unfit by nature, whose souls are bowed and mutilated by their vulgar occupations" cannot comprehend the art of philosophy.[107] Such teachings would influence the wealthier class to adopt a superior mentality and an unbearable attitude towards the disabled as well as those who worked hard for their livelihood.

## 3.4 Paul and Disability

When it comes to Paul and disability, some believe that Paul showed signs of disability while others are not so sure or are disinterested in whether or not Paul was disabled. To the latter, it seems unlikely that one of the most important pillars of Christianity could have been disabled. However, some

---

106. Savage, *Power though Weakness*, 23.
107. Plato, *Republic*, 6.495d.

historical witnesses offer us insights into the physical conditions of Paul. What are these, and how far can they shed light on the issue of Paul and disability? How reliable are they? With these questions in mind, this section will examine these historical witnesses to support Paul's disability.

### 3.4.1 Paul's Own Testimony

The earliest evidence one can bring to light on Paul's disability is his own testimony, sparsely scattered in his letters to the different churches that he established. The following sections briefly analyse some of the more important texts of Paul.

#### 3.4.1.1 "ἐκτρώματι" in 1 Corinthians 15:8

The first to be examined is found in 1 Corinthians 15:8, where Paul called himself an ἐκτρώματι ("untimely born" or "abnormally born") when he described himself as among the people to whom the risen Christ appeared. The researcher is well aware that Paul uses the subordinate conjunction ὡσπερεὶ (like, as though) in describing the event that the risen Christ appeared to him. Even though this ὡσπερεὶ makes it difficult to interpret ἐκτρώματι as an actual physical condition, it nonetheless leaves room for an interpretation that could shed light on how Paul feels about his condition as well as the way others might think of him. As such, the following analyses the different points of view.

According to Munck, "the term ἔκτρομα in 1 Corinthians 15:8 is difficult to interpret. This is the sole appearance in the NT, and the context gives no clear indication of its significance."[108] Munck has covered the different scholarly opinions of this particular Greek word. However, he could not make a conclusive remark except that one should "try to discover the ideas connected with birth and miscarriage."[109] In spite of his objectiveness, he declined to believe or be swayed by the arguments that Paul might be talking about his limited condition.[110] Even the Reformers gave no indication that one can connect Paul's word with his disability. According to Luther, "Paul compared

---

108. Munck, "Paulus Tanquam Abortivus," 180.
109. Munck, 192.
110. See Munck, 192–196.

himself with a dead child . . . a decayed fruit . . . reborn by Christ."[111] Calvin also interpreted this word along the lines of Paul receiving God's grace.[112] Thus, the tone of interpretations set by the Reformers influenced subsequent interpreters. For instance, Hodge believed that Paul used this word in "self-abasement" because of the "unmerited favours" given by Christ.[113]

However, there are scholars who feel that Paul here was talking about his physical deficiency. For instance, George gives three supports to consider that this word, ἐκτρώματι (*ektromati*) points to some sort of disability. First, he looks at the etymology of this word from *A Greek-English Lexicon of the New Testament*, which indicates that this word refers to "a birth that violates the normal period of gestation . . . *and* in any case the point related to some deficiency in the infant."[114] Second, he finds support from the Septuagint in which this word ἐκτρώματι, "refers to [the] 'ugliness' of [the] 'monstrous' nature of such a birth (Job 3:16; Eccl 6:3; and Num 12:12)."[115] Third, he also finds support in the work of Philo whom he believes "use[d] the term in contrast to a perfect being capable to live."[116] In *Legum Allegoriae*, Philo wrote, "For the soul of the worthless man is not calculated by nature to bring anything to perfection which is likely to live. But everything which it appears to bring forth is found to be abortive and immature."[117]

George argues that before Paul uses this term to his "advantage," his opponents used it to hurl insult at him.[118] Likewise, Bjorck also amply supported these assumptions because, after examining the word and tracing its history, he remarked, "It is in my opinion that not only is the significance 'freak,' 'monster' that which fits the Pauline text best, but that it is also the only one that would occur to a Greek of his period."[119] Moreover, in line with these interpretations, Weiss and Parry think that some in Corinth could have taken

---

111. Luther, *Commentaries*, 83.
112. Calvin, *First Epistle*, 315.
113. Hodge, *Commentary*, 316–317.
114. Bauer et al., *Greek-English Lexicon*, 733; George, "(Dis)abled Jesus," 118, emphasis original.
115. George, "(Dis)abled Jesus," 118.
116. George, 118.
117. Philo, *Legum Allegoriae*, 1:76, in *Works of Philo: Complete and Unabridged*, trans. By C. D. Yonge (USA: Hendrickson, 1993), quoted in George, "(Dis)abled Jesus," 118.
118. George, 118.
119. Björck, "Nochmals Paulus Abortivus," 3–8.

this term and used it to abuse Paul as they probably compared him with Peter and Apollos.[120] This study also concurs with these scholarly interpretations when it comes to the deeper insights of why Paul calls himself ἐκτρώματι.

### 3.4.1.2 "ἀσθένεια τῆς σαρκός" in Galatians 4:13–14

The second testimony is from Galatians 4:13–14: "You know it was because of a bodily ailment that I preached the gospel to you at first, and though my condition was a trial to you, you did not scorn or despise me, but received me as an angel of God, as Christ Jesus" (RSV). According to Betz, Paul reminds the Galatians of "how they first met and of the Galatians' initial deep affection for him."[121] Here, Paul explained to the Galatians that the reason for him to preach the good news to them in the first place was his "bodily ailment," which in Greek is ἀσθένεια τῆς σαρκός. One recollects that this word ἀσθένεια means "weakness or powerlessness of various kinds," be it "literally, of bodily ailment, weak, ill, sick, and of physical or intellectual inability, inadequate," or "figuratively, of what is less effective weak, feeble, not strong."[122] On the other hand, σαρκός can have a range of meaning such as "*flesh*, all the solid part of the body," "the substance (material) of the body," "*humanity* as such, without any necessary connotation of frailty," and "fleshly (physical) weakness, helplessness."[123]

Paul wrote in verse 14 that his ailment was a trial (πειρασμόν) and that they did not scorn or despise (ἐξουθενήσατε οὐδὲ ἐξεπύσατε) him, but received him as not just like an "angel of God," but even as Christ Jesus himself. Why was it a trial to them? To answer this question, some interpreters think that Paul showed signs of "repulsive physical appearance,"[124] while there are some who feel that the Galatians thought Paul was a sinful man or that he was possessed by the devil because of his physical ailment, therefore he was a threat to the Galatians.[125] Albl has strongly remarked that we are "dealing with a

---

120. Johannes Weiss, *Der erste Korintherbrief,* 351–352, quoted in Harris, "Child-Exposure," 5; Parry, *First Epistle,* 218.
121. Betz, *Galatians,* 220 quoted by Albl, in "For Whenever," 153.
122. Zmijewski, "ἀσθένεια," 170.
123. Souter, *Pocket Lexicon,* s.v. "σάρξ," 231–232.
124. Wilkinson, *Bible and Healing,* 212.
125. Betz, *Galatians,* 225; see also Martyn, *Galatians,* 21.

negative social definition placed on a disabling condition."[126] He associates "this πειρασμός with the temptation to attach a social stigma to Paul's disability," and he believes that Paul had in some degree "expected social stigma" from the Galatians.[127]

An interesting observation was made by Longenecker and recently picked up by Albl as they attempted to understand what Paul meant by the Greek word ἐκπτύω in combination with ἐξουθενέω in Galatians 4:14.[128] They both believe that the phrase οὐκ ἐξουθενήσατε οὐδὲ ἐξεπτύσατε could hold the key to further insights on what ailed Paul. The literal meaning of ἐκπτύω is to "spit out,"[129] "both as a gesture of disrespect and as a means of protection against the evil eye or demons."[130] However, what is remarkable is the fact that ἐκπτύω and ἐξουθενέω become so "synonymous . . . that P[46] omits the latter here, evidently believing it to be redundant." Drawing on this "literal understanding of ἐκπτύω (to spit) for support," one can perhaps identify Paul's problem as "epilepsy."[131]

It is a common thing to connect epilepsy with that of spitting out or drooling in the Greco-Roman and the Jewish world. While Plautus "describes epilepsy as the disease that is spat upon (*morbusquiinsputatur*),"[132] Pliny wrote that epilepsy was an illness in which a person spits on it.[133] The idea behind this spitting was to "throw back infection (*contagia*) . . . [and] . . . ward off witchcraft and bad luck."[134] One can see that Pliny connected epilepsy with "witchcraft and bad luck," thereby indicating that this type of disability comes with a cultural judgement. In the Hebrew Bible, one could make a comparison from 2 Samuel 21:13 where David pretended to be mad, spitting out his saliva and letting it run down his beard. Because of this display, King Achish regarded David as a "madman." What is more remarkable is that the LXX rendered this Hebrew word שָׁגַע (see 1 Kgs 9:11) as ἐπιλήμπτων (1 Sam 21:15)

---

126. Albl, "For Whenever," 154.
127. Albl, 154.
128. Longenecker, *Galatians*, 191; Albl, "For Whenever," 154.
129. Gingrich, "ἐκπτύω," in *Shorter Lexicon*, 61.
130. Longenecker, *Galatians*, 91.
131. Thomas, *Devil*, 58.
132. Plautus, *Captivi*, 3.4..
133. Pliny, *Natural History*, 28.7.
134. Pliny, 28.7.

or "suffering from epilepsy." Therefore, one can surmise that Paul in Galatians 4:14 was probably referring to epilepsy that was disabling him.

### 3.4.1.3 "παρουσια του σωματος" and "ὁ λόγος ἐξουθενημένος" in 2 Corinthians 10:10

The text of 2 Corinthians 10:10 reads: "His letters are weighty and strong, but his bodily presence is weak, and his speech of no account" (ESV). Paul supposedly quoted this remark that the Corinthians or his opponents had made of him. Many contemporary interpreters seem hesitant to connect Paul's weakness with disability in this verse. For instance, Hodge clearly felt that "the phrase ἡ παρουσια του σωματος probably refers not to his personal appearance, but to his deportment which was the representation of his enemies; the truth of which, however, the apostle denies."[135] Kistemaker is very firm in his understanding that "the presence of his body" is to be understood as neither Paul's physical arrival in Corinth nor his outward appearance but as "a man without stamina or eloquence."[136] Bruce Winter thinks that Paul was a skilled rhetorician whose strategy was not to act as one but to point out his weakness so that the "Corinthian congregation may benefit" from it.[137]

On the other hand, some scholars have acknowledged that Paul had a disability. For instance, Ironside stated,

> I judge Paul's physical appearance was not that of a great statesman or a great leader. The Greek particularly admired splendid physique, as we may see from the many magnificent statues they have left behind. The name "Paul" means "little one," and people naturally received names in those days that intimated what they were. His outward appearance was weak and his speech contemptible. . . . So they despised him because of physical infirmities.[138]

Likewise, McGee's position is also clear, when he says that Paul "must have been a weak-looking vessel."[139] According to Martin, the Corinthians'

---

135. Hodge, *Commentary*, 617.
136. Kistemaker, *Exploration*, 345.
137. Winter, *Philo*, 212.
138. Ironside, *Addresses*, 220.
139. McGee, *2 Corinthians*, 118.

"verdict is damningly positive," and "in their ears, Paul's rhetorical ability was non-existent and his public presentations of the message moved them to contempt and scorn."[140] Thus, "Paul cannot disguise his weakness and . . . his enemies . . . branded his artless preaching as being unworthy of the attention of educated Greeks!"[141]

What is remarkable about this accusation is that when Paul replied, he did not deny the problem but rather acknowledged in 2 Corinthians 11:6 that he was an ἰδιώτης, "unskilled" when it came to speaking.[142] The word ἰδιώτης can mean, first, "a person who is relatively unskilled or inexperienced in some activity or field of knowledge," and second, "one who is not knowledgeable about some particular group's experience, one not in the know, [and] an outsider."[143] In this particular case, the use of ἰδιώτης by Paul about himself seems to be indicating that he was "unskilled in speaking."[144] Thus, one can say with certainty that this text clearly reveals Paul's limitations.

### 3.4.1.4 "σκόλοψ τῇ σαρκί" in 2 Corinthians 12:7

The text of 2 Corinthians 12:7b reads, "There was given me a thorn in my flesh, a messenger of Satan, to torment me" (NIV). Among the earliest interpretations, Latin church father Tertullian and "the majority of interpreters, [took] the thorn to be some form of physical illness."[145] They related this physical illness with a variety of illnesses ranging from "epilepsy, malarial fever, eyesight problems, speech difficulties, [and] psychosomatic disorders."[146] While "the Greek fathers, on the other hand, held that the thorn was persecution,"[147] with some identifying "the thorn as Alexander the coppersmith, the 'ministers

---

140. Martin, *2 Corinthians*, 312.
141. Wilson, *2 Corinthians*, 128.
142. See Becker, *Letter Hermeneutics*, 116.
143. Arndt, Danker, and Bauer, "ἰδιώτης," 468.
144. Arndt, Danker, and Bauer, 468.
145. Twelftree, "Healing, Illness," 379.
146. See Plummer, *Second Epistle*, 351; Lightfoot, *Epistle*, 186–191; Benard, *Second Epistle*, 110–111; Ramsay, *St. Paul*, 94–97; Bultmann, *Second Letter*, 224; Barrett, *Second Epistle*, 315; Nisbet, "Thorn in the Flesh," 126; Minn, *Thorn*, 23–31; Marshall, "Metaphor," 315–316; Hughes, *Paul's Second Epistle*, 442–448; Furnish, *2 Corinthians*, 549–550; Martin, *2 Corinthians*, 414.
147. Russell, "Redemptive Suffering," 556.

of Satan' at Corinth, or the Corinthian congregation itself."[148] Then, in the middle ages, a new "interpretative tradition arose when the thorn was associated with sensual temptations or spiritual trials."[149] For instance, the Vulgate translated the "thorn in the flesh" as "*stimulus carnis*,"[150] and this no doubt influenced some interpreters who were interested in monastic traditions.[151]

Recent interpreters think that this spiritual struggle is "caused by demonic visitations or the pricking of the apostle's arrogance."[152] Among the recent interpreters, the work of Adele Yarbro on "Paul's Disability: The Thorn in His Flesh" contains an excellent assessment concerning this particular Pauline text.[153] She is inclined to believe that Paul was talking about epilepsy when he wrote about his "thorn in the flesh," taking support from Galatians 4.[154] She believes that "this shameful character would explain why he considered the disease to be a sort of counterweight to his vision and revelations."[155] Further, it makes sense to connect Paul's problem here with the one found in Galatians as it clearly talks about social stigma. Kierkegaard has remarked, "2 Cor 12:7–9 had allowed for all sorts of ingenuity and foolishness to surface as interpretation and offered everyone the opportunity to become an interpreter."[156] Indeed, interpreters throughout the ages have had their share of "ingenuity" as well as "foolishness" leading to interesting interpretations nonetheless. However, what seems to be the fact about all the interpreters of this particular "thorn in the flesh" is that they all point to some sort of malady that Paul suffered from, physically, mentally, and spiritually. Creamer also observes the connection between Paul's thorn in the flesh and its disabling relationship with the Corinthians. She believes that this thorn in the flesh "bore directly on Paul's stature and authority before the Corinthians, and so

---

148. See Mullins, "Paul's Thorn," 299–303; O'Collins, "Power Made Perfect," 216–227; McCant, "Paul's Thorn," 550–572.

149. Russell, "Redemptive Suffering," 556.

150. "Epistula Ad Corinthios 2 – Chapter 12," Vulgate.org, accessed January 15, 2018, http://vulgate.org/nt/epistle/2corinthians_12.htm.

151. Russell, "Redemptive Suffering," 556

152. See Tasker, *Second Epistle*, 175; Price, "Punished in Paradise," 33–40.

153. See Collins, "Paul's Disability," 165–183.

154. See section 3.4.1.2 for a discussion on Paul and epilepsy.

155. Collins, "Paul's Disability," 174.

156. Kierkegaard, *Edifying Discourses*, 2:164.

had social consequences within the Corinthian community."¹⁵⁷ As such, this study also interprets this ailment of Paul in 2 Corinthians 12:7 as indicative of Paul's disability.

### 3.4.2 Evidence from the *Acts of Paul and Thecla* (*APT*)

*APT* is one of the earliest of the apocryphal acts of the apostles.¹⁵⁸ Traditionally it was in circulation as a part of a larger book called the *Acts of Paul*. However, scholars believe that *APT* was "also handed down separately."¹⁵⁹ The larger section of the *Acts of Paul* contains the narrative of Paul, who seems to picture him as a divine and human being. According to Peter Wallace Dunn, *Acts of Paul* describes Paul as "a wandering missionary and a wonder-worker who creates disturbances everywhere he goes, though he always manages to convert not a few and escape, until his martyrdom at the hands of Nero."¹⁶⁰ Inside this *Acts of Paul*, one finds the section titled *APT*, which according to Goodspeed is a "religious romance,"¹⁶¹ or rather, a narrative about how teaching on celibacy by Paul managed to influence the virgin Thecla, fiancée of Thamyris, "to embrace Christianity and chastity."¹⁶²

What piques one's interest about this work is that, at the start of the story, "there is a description of Paul that seems to have no parallel in early Christian literature."¹⁶³ The original Greek reads, "ειδεν δε τον Παύλον ἐρχόμενον, ανδρα μικρόν τω μεγέθει, ψιλόν τη κεφαλή, ἀγκύλον ταις κνήμαις, εὐεκτικόν, σύνοφρυν, μικρῶς ἐπίρρινον, χάριτος πλήρη ποτε μεν γὰρ ἐφαίνετο ὡς ἄνθρωπος, ποτὲ δέ ἀγγέλου πρόσωπον ειχεν."¹⁶⁴ When translated, it reads, "And he saw Paul coming, a man small of stature, with a bald head and crooked legs, in a good state of body, with eyebrows meeting and nose somewhat hooked, full of friendliness; for now he appeared like a man and now he had the face of

---

157. Creamer, *Disability*, 73.
158. Klijn "Apocryphal Acts," 195.
159. See Elliott, *Apocryphal New Testament*, 350–357.
160. Dunn, "Acts of Paul," 4.
161. Goodspeed, "Acts of Paul," 185.
162. Dunn, "Acts of Paul," 4.
163. Grant, "Description of Paul," 1.
164. Lipsius, "Acta Pauli et Theclae."

an angel."[165] These lines are the earliest and most vivid description of Paul's physical appearance by someone who obviously had a deep respect for Paul.

### 3.4.2.1 Dating of APT

James Dunn believes that this work can be "dated with some confidence to the second half or the late decades of the second century (AD 170–180) since Tertullian almost certainly referred to such a writing at the turn of the second/third centuries (Tertullian, *de Bapt.* 1.17)."[166] Tertullian, in his work "Concerning Baptism", commented about this book,

> But if they claim writings which are wrongly inscribed with Paul's name – I mean the example of Thecla – in support of women's freedom to teach and baptize, let them know that a presbyter in Asia, who put together that book, heaping up a narrative as it were from his own materials under Paul's name, when after conviction he confessed that he had done it from love of Paul, resigned his position.[167]

Souter also believes that "the work was composed in Greek, possibly at Smyrna, about A.D. 160."[168] However, Ramsay believes this work to be a first-century document.[169] Moreover, Peter Dunn, who in his doctoral dissertation carefully investigated the opinions of many scholars and church fathers, concluded that the most probable date for this work is between AD 120–200.[170]

This present study agrees with Peter Dunn's assessment that this work must have been in circulation in the first part of the second century. Not only is this possible, but an early dating also seriously considers this work as a historical witness. Late dating evidently causes scholars to gloss this work over as not historically viable. This is starkly evident when Barrett completely disregards it in his work "Pauline Controversies in the Post-Pauline Period," and M. C. de Boer also conveniently omits it in his "Images of Paul in the

---

165. Schneemelcher, *New Testament*, 2:239.
166. Dunn, *Neither*, 163.
167. Tertullian, "Concerning Baptism," par. 17.
168. Tertullian, par. 17.
169. Ramsay, *Church*, 381.
170. Dunn, "Acts of Paul," 9.

Post-Apostolic period."[171] As the next section will make clear, this kind of prejudicial attitude on the part of scholars is simply wrong.

### 3.4.2.2 *The* APT *and canon*

The early church historian Eusebius commented, "Among the books which are not genuine must be reckoned the Acts of Paul, the work entitled The Shepherd, The Apocalypse of Peter, and in addition to them the letter called of Barnabas and the so-called Teachings of the Apostles ... [and] the Revelation of John, if this view prevails."[172] It is clear that Eusebius considered *APT* as not genuine enough to be included in the canon. However, one observes that the book of Revelation is also among the unaccepted works by Eusebius. One has to question the validity of Eusebius's selections because aside from *APT* and Revelation, most modern New Testament scholars consider all the other works mentioned by him as important to the study of the New Testament.[173]

In another instance, Schneemelcher, who edited the *New Testament Apocrypha*, wrote, "In the canon catalogue of the Codex Claromontanus the seven 'catholic' epistles and the Apocalypse are reckoned to the canon, but not Hebrews. It is striking that *Hermas*, the *Acts of Paul* and the *Apocalypse of Peter* are named in this catalogue – and probably as recognized writings."[174] Indeed, it is startling that the *Acts of Paul* made it to the list while the book of Hebrews did not make it. From this revelation, it is obvious that the *Acts of Paul* can be dated quite early as all these lists included by Eusebius and Codex Claromontanus are from an early date.[175] Lastly, Malherbe's assessment in relation to the *APT* and canon is noteworthy. According to him,

> The author of the Acts knew the canonical Acts and other NT writings, as well as current legendary tradition, all of which he used to construct a work intended for edification. In doing so, he was more concerned with current conceptions of Paul than the Paul of the NT, although he used the NT material freely.

---

171. Barrett, "Pauline Controversies," 229–245; Boer, "Images of Paul," 359–380.
172. "Eusebius, *Ecclesiastical History*, 1:257.
173. See "Literature, Early Christian," in Freedman, *Anchor Bible Dictionary*, 4:341–345; Hannah, *Kregel Pictorial Guide*, 7.
174. Schneemelcher, "On the History," in *New Testament*, 30.
175. Dunn has rightly surmised, "the value of the *ActPl* for understanding the early Pauline legacy depends partly upon its date" ("Acts of Paul," 8).

Yet there are hints in Paul's letters that he was not an outstandingly robust physical specimen (e.g., 2 Cor 10:10; 13:7–12; Gal 4:13–16), which do not make the description in the Acts incongruous.[176]

While every scholarly opinion has its own merits, one must be careful not to totally disregard the witness of *APT* just because early church fathers classified it as apocryphal. Rather, from the above information, one ought not to take the *Acts of Paul* tradition lightly as it is an important document for understanding what Paul looked like.

### 3.4.2.3 Scholars' interpretations of Paul's description in APT

One of the main concerns of scholars is the vivid description of Paul. One wonders if one should consider it real or a distortion of the real image of Paul that one infers from the Pauline Letters. Martin Luther's comment, "I believe Paul was a despicable person, a poor one,"[177] concerning the image portrait here in *APT* is still followed by many, particularly among German scholars. For instance, according to Zahn, Paul's image was "unflattering,"[178] while others like Findlay,[179] MacDonald,[180] and Tajra[181] are gracious enough to think that Paul's portrait in *APT* is a "distortion conforming more to the tastes of second-century readers than to the Paul of the epistles."[182]

There is a growing trend among recent scholars to interpret this description of Paul in a positive light. Among them, Grant has been one of the first to employ physiognomy to the study of Paul's description in *APT*, and he interpreted it as that of a "general."[183] Grant found support from the passage of the poet Archilochus who stated, "I love not a tall general nor one long-shanked, nor with splendid curls or partly sheared. Let me have one who is

---

176. Malherbe, "Physical Description," 171.
177. Luther, *Werke: Tischreden* (Weimar: Herrmann Böhlaus, 1913), 2 no. 1245, quoted in Malherbe, "Physical Description," 171.
178. Zahn, "Paulus der Apostel," 70.
179. Findlay, *Byways*, 263.
180. MacDonald, "Apocryphal," 57–58.
181. Tajra, *Martyrdom*, 126
182. Dunn, "Acts of Paul," 145.
183. Grant, "Description of Paul," 4.

short and bow-legged, firm on his feet, full of heart."[184] Because of this, Grant argued, "the description of Paul comes ultimately from Greek poetry perhaps by the way of Greek rhetoric. It owes nothing to Paul."[185] Likewise, Malherbe also thinks that this portrayal is not negative during the time of its writing. According to Malherbe, "It is clear by now that Paul's hooked nose, bowed legs, and meeting eyebrows were not unflattering features in the context in which the Acts was written."[186] Moreover, Omerzu concluded his research by commenting, "With regard to the *Acts of Paul and Thecla,* ancient physiognomic ideals, as well as the broader storyline, suggest that Paul's description in *Acts of Paul and Thecla* is not derogatory but rather favourable."[187]

However, is it really a favourable impression of Paul? Will it make more sense if one were to assume that the actual physical imperfection of Paul might have been a concern initially and that the description of Paul in *APT* was tinged with some positive vibes? For someone who admired and loved Paul such as the supposed author of the *APT* seemed to have, it is likely that the author might have toned down the image of Paul because they wanted the reader to focus on the endearing and angelic qualities of Paul rather than his bodily limitations. The description of Paul in *APT*, when taken at face value without any idealistic inclination, reveals a man who is short, crooked-legged and bald, with eyebrows meeting in the centre and a hooked nose. Because the actual date of writing and the supposed death of Paul is just about half a century apart, it is highly likely that the oral traditions of what Paul might have looked like would have survived without much distortion. To sum up, this kind of physical figure hardly evokes confidence to garner respect from a society obsessed with superficial qualities.

### 3.4.3 Establishing Paul as a PwD

An examination and careful analysis of different evidence strongly suggests that Paul suffered disability though it is difficult to describe the exact kinds of disability that he suffered. He himself acknowledged that he was a "weak" man, "different" from the other apostles, that he was not trained in "rhetoric,"

---

184. Grant, 2.
185. Grant, 2–3.
186. Malherbe, "Physical Description," 174.
187. Omerzu, "Portrayal," 268.

and that his overall physical stature was not something he would boast about to anyone. Indeed, the image of Paul as a short man, with a balding head and crooked legs, points to a man who was physically weak. It is highly possible that in a society where an unimpressive disposition was a thing of disdain, Paul was very much a disabled man.

At times, more than the physical limitation experienced, the social mindset and derogatory caricature conjured up is a much more effective way of disabling a person. George's assessment of Paul's description in the *APT* is right on point. According to him, "his unimpressive physical appearance was used as a point to discredit him of his apostolic status."[188] It is like a vicious cycle wherein a man with weak physical disposition, suddenly having bouts of epilepsy and stammering when speaking in public, is judged on account of his weakness because the culture and social practices of that time did not accept leaders exhibiting these kinds of limitations. This further stigmatizes him as someone who is from the "outside" and is unacceptable to them.

Putting these findings alongside the disability definition that this study has put forward in the previous chapter,[189] one can argue strongly that Paul was disabled. It is true that one cannot stress enough the importance of the "services which were rendered to Christianity by Paul of Tarsus."[190] However, the wisdom of Chrysostom, "For if he was a Paul, he also was a man,"[191] must be relevant when it comes to an objective examination of the evidence of disability related to Paul. F. W. Farrar wisely stated, "If we look at his actions as though it were irreverence to suppose that they ever fell short of his own ideal – we not only describe an impossible character, but we contradict his own reiterated testimonies."[192] Thus, one can say with a degree of certainty that Paul was suffering from a disability.

---

188. George, "(Dis) ability," 118.
189. See chapter 2, section 2.2.4, of this present study.
190. Farrar, *Life and Work*, 2.
191. Quoted in Farrar, *Life and Work*, 6.
192. Farrar, 6.

## 3.5 Summarization

This chapter has described three important points in relation to the study of disability. First, it examines and analyses, in general, the Greco-Roman and Jewish society in relation to disability. This present study finds the possibility of the presence of PwDs in their midst and the likelihood that they were not treated fairly enough. Garland could not have described the condition better as he stated, "People with congenital deformities and disabilities experienced widespread stigma and discrimination because they exhibited physical and aesthetic deviations from the able-bodied norm . . . *which* inspired negative reactions, and sometimes even outright odium, among the able-bodied population."[193] Second, although disability studies among the Corinthians or any kind of examinations or analyses are still at the beginning, there are enough materials to offer the researcher specific insights into the problem of disability present among the Corinthians. Third, to the issue of disability and the Apostle Paul, this present study is leaning towards the possibility that the Apostle Paul had some form of disability for which he suffered stigmatization.

---

193. Garland, *Eye of the Beholder*, 11.

CHAPTER 4

# The Socio-Rhetorical Context of Paul's Second Letter to the Corinthians

## 4.1 Introduction

Studying the socio-historical context of Corinth for a better understanding of Paul's words to the Corinthians is important. From the time of E. A. Judges, there have been steady streams of scholarly articles and books published at regular intervals.[1] One must concur with Mitchell's advice that one ought to analyse Paul's letter "in the light of the Greco-Roman rhetorical tradition which was operative and pervasive at the time of the letter's composition."[2] However, Schellengberg seems cautious as he states, "The rhetorical exemplars that have been reserved represent but a minute fragment of the rhetoric discourse of the ancient world. . . . We simply do not have the data we should need to construct a full taxonomy of ancient rhetorical practice."[3]

While one is aware of this problem, the concern of this chapter, however, is to search for "Paul's voice" in relation to "his social location."[4] How can one understand the socio-rhetorical contexts of 2 Corinthians to get a better perspective of Paul's argument with the Corinthian Christians? Therefore, in

---

1. Judge, "Paul's Boasting," 37–50; Judge, *Social Pattern*; "Early Christians," 4–15; Judge, "Paul," 191–203. One can also find an extensive list of scholarly works in Witherington, *Conflict & Community*, 61–67.
2. Mitchell, *Paul*, 6.
3. Schellenberg, *Rethinking*, 8.
4. Schellenberg, 13.

what follows, this study will take a closer look at the various aspects of the socio-rhetorical context of 2 Corinthians from a disability perspective.[5] In order to read 2 Corinthians from a disability perspective, this section will map out the socio-rhetorical overview of this particular letter, including its background studies, literary issues, and the opponents of Paul.

## 4.2 Authorship and Date

When it comes to the authorship of 2 Corinthians, there is not much to discuss, as there exists an agreement with the knowledge that "the authenticity of 2 Corinthians is thoroughly Pauline in form, style, and content."[6] Because of this, no one in general challenges today the fact that Paul authored both 1 and 2 Corinthians.[7] However, concerning its external attestation, unlike 1 Corinthians, which the early church fathers such as Clement, Ignatius, and Polycarp had attested to, it was only at the time of Marcion that others came to know of the existence of 2 Corinthians.[8] Knowing the historical stability of Paul as the author of 2 Corinthians emboldens one to define what kind of a man Paul was from a socio-rhetorical perspective. In other words, what kind of a man was the author Paul from the perspective of the Corinthians as one reads his letter? From a cursory reading of 2 Corinthians, it is clear that there is something in Paul's "outward" appearances that they did not like or endorse (2 Cor 10:7, 10). Paul must have felt insulted by their behaviour, judging from the intense emotional arguments he makes. Carson states, "His language is frequently passionate, his rhetorical questions emotive, his sequence of thought compressed, his syntax broken (as a glance at the various translations of, say, 2 Cor 13:2 readily suggest!)."[9] Indeed, this Second Letter to the Corinthians was quite personal to Paul.

As to the date of Paul sending his second letter, it seems proper to trace his itinerary first for it will go a long way in establishing the timing of this letter. Veerbrugge correctly states, "The date of Paul's missionary stay in the

---

5. See Albl, "For Whenever," 145–160.
6. Furnish, *2 Corinthians*, 30.
7. Veerbrugge, "1 Corinthians," 248.
8. Moffatt, *Introduction*, 114.
9. Carson, *Model*, 13–14.

city of Corinth is one of the most certain in NT chronology."[10] This is mainly because of the incident recorded in Acts 18:12–17 where Paul has to stand trial "before the proconsul Gallio." According to Thiselton, "the discovery of the Delphic letter of Claudius which relates to Lucius Junius Gallio" allows one to state with a high degree of certainty the timing of Paul's stay in Corinth.[11] This "Delphic letter" is the official report to Emperor Claudius who reigned from AD 41–54.[12] Scholars agree that the dating of this letter is either "April or May AD 52."[13] Now, "since it deals with a report" of what had happened in different parts of the Roman Empire, it begs to be stated that "the proconsulship of Gallio at Corinth must have run" earlier than AD 52.[14] That is why scholars generally think Paul's missionary activities in Corinth must have happened in between AD 50–51.[15]

In Acts 18, Luke tells the reader that Paul came to Corinth from Athens. After spending "a year and six months" there, Paul took Priscilla and Aquila, who came to Corinth from Rome because of the expulsion of the Jews by Claudius (Acts 18:2), and journeyed on to Cenchrea all the way to Ephesus. From Ephesus, he went to Caesarea and Antioch to greet the church (Acts 18:22). After this, he passed "through the Galatian region and Phrygia" (Acts 18:23) and then found himself at Ephesus (Acts 19:1). Now, comparing these records with that of Paul himself in 1 Corinthians 16:2–8 and 2 Corinthians 1:15–16, the difference in Paul's travelling itinerary becomes apparent.[16] In 1 Corinthians 16:8, Paul told the Corinthians that he was in Ephesus spending Pentecost with the congregation there. Then in 1 Corinthians 16:5, he told the Corinthians that he would visit them as he passes "through Macedonia." Likewise, in 2 Corinthians 1:16, Paul reiterated his initial plan to visit them once he passed through Macedonia, on his way to Judea. However, from Luke's record, one observes that Paul did not fulfil his intention to visit them, and this is what might have caused the Corinthians to label Paul as "fickle minded" (see 2 Cor 1:17).

---

10. Veerbrugge, "1 Corinthians," 247.
11. Thiselton, *First Epistles*, 29.
12. Lightfoot, "Roman Empire."
13. Thiselton, *First Epistles*, 29.
14. Thiselton, 29.
15. Thiselton, 28; see also Kistemaker, *Exposition*, 3.
16. See Harris, *Second Epistle*, 60.

From a disability perspective, this is very significant, for in Greco-Roman worldview a man is as good as his words were. In the words of Marincola, "It would be difficult to over-emphasize the importance of speech in Greek and Roman life.... Already in Homer, the heroes are 'speakers of words and doers of deeds' (*Il.* 9.443).... With words one gave advice to friends, allies, fellow-citizens or even kings and despots."[17] The same holds true for the Jewish people also, for "in Old Testament times ... once a word was uttered, it could not be flippantly recalled or cancelled"[18] (see Josh 9:8–9, 16, 18–19). In an interesting comment on the value of giving one's word in the Old Testament, House stated, "One's words flow from one's character."[19] Given the sacredness involved in the societal attitude towards giving one's word and not fulfilling it, it is probable to think that since Paul did not visit Corinth as he promised, the Corinthians just labelled him as someone who was not trustworthy.

Harris, Barnett, and Hall are certain that Paul sent this second letter while he was in Macedonia (see 2 Cor 9–10).[20] Luke's records show that during his third missionary journey, Paul went to Macedonia and, right after he went to Greece, he came back to Macedonia where they set sail to Philippi on their way to Jerusalem (see Acts 20:1–21:15). The question here is to ascertain as best as possible when Paul came to visit Macedonia. However, before that, one needs to trace the date of Paul's writing his first letter to the Corinthians. In 1 Corinthians 16:8, Paul told the Corinthians that he would stay at Ephesus until Pentecost, which was the Jewish "feast of harvest" festival (see Lev. 23:9–16).[21] Now, if Paul was to have left Corinth in AD 52, he would have gone straight to Cenchreae and then to Ephesus and all the way to Judea (Acts 18:22). It seems the first time he stopped at Ephesus was so brief that Luke made a passing remark about it (Acts 18:21). However, after he started again from Antioch in what was supposed to be his third missionary journey, he came to Ephesus, and this time he was there for quite some time. Even Luke devoted a whole chapter to Paul's stay in Ephesus this time (Acts 19).

---

17. Marincola, "Speech," 118.
18. Kaiser et al., *Hard Sayings*, 186.
19. House, *Old Testament Theology*, 163.
20. See Harris, *Second Epistle*, 65; Barnett, *Second Epistle*, 11–12; Hall, *Unity*, 248.
21. Kistemaker and Hendriksen, *Exposition*, 600.

From this information, it seems unlikely that Paul would have sent his first letter during his first stop at Ephesus (Acts 18:22). That leaves the option to suggest that the second time Paul came to visit Ephesus was probably around "A.D. 53 or 54."[22] If this is the case, then Paul sent his letter in AD 53 or 54, probably along with Timothy whom Paul recommended highly to the Corinthians (1 Cor 4:17; 16:10).[23] One is uncertain how long Timothy stayed in Corinth before finally re-joining Paul again, but it is obvious that he must have reported to Paul the things he had heard and experienced while he was in Corinth. This would have no doubt prompted Paul to write a second letter to the Corinthians; therefore, considering all these factors, it is possible that Paul would have written his second letter in between AD 54–55.

## 4.3 Occasion and Purpose of Paul

After Paul came back to Ephesus, important developments had taken place in Corinth that would require Paul to address them through a second and more passionate letter. These developments had seriously dampened the once cordial relationship of Paul and the Corinthians. From a disability point of view, some major problems would have occasioned for Paul to send them a letter defending his position. First, the problem of weak physical appearances and contemptible speech that Paul mentions in 2 Corinthians 10:10 sheds some light on why the Corinthians would have closed their hearts and affections for Paul (2 Cor 6:12–13). In the previous chapter, from the comparison of the public receptions of Demosthenes, who was weak but a good orator, and Alcibiades, who had a good physique but was lisping (a form of speech defect), one understands the depth of social stigmatization attached to weak and unimpressive physical bodies. It seems Paul was neither physically well built nor a gifted orator.

The problem of Paul would have been compounded by the coming of Apollos who was well gifted in speaking (Acts 18:24). According to Barnett, Apollos's "coming to Corinth must have demonstrated to the Corinthians that Paul's was not the only expression of the gospel and that some, at least,

---

22. Witherington, *Conflict & Community*, 351–352.
23. Barnett, *Second Epistle*, 11.

probably regarded it as inferior to Apollos."[24] From a disability perspective, this is particularly significant because the Corinthians were specifically targeting his rhetorical abilities or the lack of them in combination with his physical appearances (2 Cor 10:10). As such, one of the main incidents that occasioned Paul sending his second letter was because the Corinthian congregation needed "radical reorientation."[25] Dutch believes that it was not fair for Paul because these people "transfer the cultural values of *paideia* learnt in the gymnasium with its intellectual and physical conflict, set within their religious tradition, to their new faith."[26]

Second, Paul talks about his near-death experience while he was in Asia (2 Cor 1:8). There are those who have argued that Paul's sickness was the result of his chronic illness.[27] Barrett in particular stated, "Physical illness, the shadow of death, the failure of his work in Corinth, were among the causes that led to the breaking down of a man who, if any had ground for confidence in the flesh, had more (Phil 3:4; cf. 2 Cor 11:22)."[28] In the previous chapter, it has been pointed out that Paul was probably suffering from epilepsy.[29] If this were true, then the social ramifications of such a physical illness would have been obvious considering the ancient Greco-Roman world's attitude towards sickness. For instance, Kelly observed how the "ancient texts" show epilepsy as a "physiological condition . . . having demonic origins."[30] If so, then the Corinthians would have considered Paul not fit to be their apostle anymore. In connection to this, Paul saw fit to talk about the origin of his "thorn in the flesh," which the Corinthians or his opponents seemed to have taken issue with in 2 Corinthians 12:7–10. It seems this "disability" was taken as an excuse that Paul was not fit to be their apostle, thus furthering the necessity to clarify his ability to be their apostle in his letter.[31]

---

24. Barnett, 10.
25. Dutch, *Educated Elite*, 302.
26. Dutch, 302.
27. Harris, *Second Epistle*, 170–172; Barrett, *Second Corinthians*, 64; Harvey, *Renewal through Suffering*, 20.
28. Barrett, *Second Corinthians*, 64.
29. See chapter 3, sections 3.4.1.2 and 3.4.1.4, of this present study.
30. Kelley, "Punishment," 206.
31. This argument will become clearer in the exegetical chapter (chapter 5).

In addition, the influence of Cephas in Corinth had probably cast a darker shadow on the way the Corinthian Christians regarded Paul. Barnett deduced, "the coming of Cephas prompted the even more fundamental question that would cloud all subsequent relationships with the Corinthians, namely, was Paul truly qualified to be an apostle?"[32] However, scholars are not sure if Peter had come to Corinth or if he had sent men to Corinth to disturb Paul at all.[33] Still, one cannot rule out outside influences that would make the Corinthian Christians ask or worry about the credentials of Paul as an apostle. Indeed, one of the main points that occasioned this letter was the Corinthians' disregard for Paul's authority, as well as comparison of his apostolic standing with that of the other "super-apostles" (2 Cor 11:5). They even went so far as to question whether Christ was really speaking through him (2 Cor 13:30). All these socio-rhetorical issues thus became an occasion for Paul to respond quite emotionally to the Corinthians a second time.

Third, since this present study argues that disability also arises from social stigmatization, the problem of Paul mixing up manual labour and public oration would have caused social ostracization since Paul insisted on supporting himself by working manually. One knows from Bruce W. Winter that there were plenty of sophist orators "such as Dio Chrysostom, Aristides, Favorinus, and Philostratus" during Paul's time.[34] It seems these rhetoricians were "thoroughly preoccupied with honour (φιλοτιμία) and glory (δόξα), received wealth and fame in public life (πολιτεία), education (παιδεία), and the courts on arriving at various cities."[35] This brings up the problem of the sponsorship or patronage system that was prevalent in those days. Unlike these orators who vied for sponsorship among the Corinthians, Paul did not wish to make himself a burden financially, but this move on his part seems to have backfired (2 Cor 11:6–9) and caused more division between them.[36] The Corinthians could have been thinking that Paul did not consider them important enough to want their help (2 Cor 12:13), thereby driving a further wedge into their relationship and their view of Paul. Witherington was right

---

32. Barnett, *Second Epistle*, 10.
33. McClelland, "Super-Apostles," 83.
34. Winter, "Entries and Ethics," 55–74; see also Briones, "Paul's Financial Policy," 247n159.
35. Briones, "Paul's Financial Policy, 247n159.
36. Winter, "Entries and Ethics," 74; see also Judge, "Social Identity," 214.

on point when he suggested, "the opponents seem to have convinced some Corinthians that Paul saw them as an inferior *ekklesia* since he took money from the Philippians but not from them."[37]

Since the negative attitude towards Paul's disability occasioned him to send his letter, what would then be the rhetorical nature of Paul's argument in this Second Letter to the Corinthians? Lim stated,

> Paul's occasional letters written to various Christ-communities are primarily meant to persuade, correct, and shape the thinking and behaviour of his audience so that they are rooted in his understanding of the gospel. To achieve this goal, he uses a variety of means including rhetorical strategy, emotional appeals, and references to Scripture in his letters.[38]

So, was Paul's tone judicial, or deliberative, or epideictic, or was it a combination of these three in his Second Letter to the Corinthians? According to Aristotle,

> The deliberative kind is either hortatory or dissuasive; for both those who give advice in private and those who speak in the assembly invariably either exhort or dissuade. The forensic kind is either accusatory or defensive; for litigants must necessarily either accuse or defend. The epideictic kind has for its subject praise or blame (Arist., *Rh.* 1.3.3).[39]

Scholars have tried to pin down the nature of Paul's argument in the past years.[40] Some of these scholars like Young and Ford, Betz, and Kennedy think that Paul's rhetorical speech in 2 Corinthians is "forensic" in nature.[41] However, although others such as Witherington acknowledge elements of a forensic approach are definitely present in 2 Corinthians,[42] yet they also

---

37. Witherington, *Conflict & Community*, 418n20.
38. Lim, *Metaphors*, xv.
39. Aristotle, *Rhetoric*."
40. Stegman, *Character of Jesus*, 46.
41. Young and Ford, *Meaning and Truth*, 37–40; Betz, *2 Corinthians*, 13; Kennedy, *New Testament*, 86–87.
42. Witherington, *Conflict & Community*, 333.

believe that deliberative arguments are in 2 Corinthians.[43] Witherington sees a "mixed type" of rhetorical speech in 2 Corinthians.[44]

This study believes that Paul's main purpose for sending his Second Letter to the Corinthians was to reclaim his authority despite the negative attitude towards his disability and win their trust back. As such, it sees this second letter is mainly forensic in nature. In other words, "Paul must resort to defense and attack in regard to his own ministry to the Corinthians."[45] Then there is that rhetorical technique called *insinuatio*, which this study understands as "a sort of emphatic throwing down the gauntlet . . . where one merely hints at the real bone of contention at the outset and reserves until much later dealing with it."[46] A rhetor can apply *insinuatio* to his arguments in two ways, either the Greek way or the Roman way. According to Christian, the Greek way is "to approach prejudice head-on at the beginning of the speech so that they could successfully make their case."[47] However, the Roman way is "to approach prejudice and scandalous cases in an indirect manner, saving the difficult topics for much later in the speech."[48] A cursory reading of the developments of Paul's argument in 2 Corinthians shows a Roman pattern of the rhetorical technique *insinuatio*, where 2 Corinthians 1–9 is quite mild compared to the more explosive last four chapters (2 Cor 10–13).

## 4.4 The Social Matrix of the Corinthian Congregation

From the summarization of Chow,[49] it is evident that scholars have drawn certain insights into the social context of Paul and his letters. They do not "dispute that the church at Corinth was made up of both rich and poor people" even though the "social identity of these Christians . . . continues to be a matter of debate."[50] Scholars also understand that there is a "conflict in the

---

43. Witherington, 339.
44. Witherington, 465.
45. Witherington, 328.
46. Witherington, *New Testament Rhetoric*, 53.
47. Christian, "*Insinuatio*," 6–7.
48. Christian, 12.
49. Chow, *Patronage and Power*, 12–25.
50. Chow, 26.

church between the rich and the poor ... between Paul and some of the Corinthians quite firmly in the convention of friendship and the exchange of gifts,"[51] that is, in accordance with the patronage system prevailing that time.[52] It is estimated that during the time of Paul, the new city of Corinth had a population of about "seventy to eighty thousand inhabitants."[53] If this is the case, then the probability of finding Greeks, Romans, and Jews making up a percentage of the Corinthian congregation runs high.[54] However, the question one must ask here is the possibility of disabled people being present among the Corinthian Christians.

In the previous chapter, one has observed that in the vibrant city of Corinth, Paul was involved with a repopulation of freedmen, armies, and many other people all over the Roman Empire by Julius Caesar.[55] According to Liftin, in the course of time, these inhabitants became "more Greek than Rome, more Roman than Athens [and] if any city of the first-century world deserves the hyphenated designation 'Greco-Roman' it was Corinth."[56] What caused this unique assimilation of cultures between the Greeks and the Romans? Horsley explained this phenomenon as follows,

> Corinth was initially Roman and not a restoration of a Greek city, but by the second century ... it was said that Corinth, though Roman, had become thoroughly Hellenized. Under Hadrian, in the early second century, the official language was finally changed from Latin to Greek. Despite the predominance of Latin inscriptions in the middle of the first century, the time during which Paul founded the Corinthians assembly, Hellenistic culture must have already been dominant among those of

---

51. Chow, 27; see also Marshall, *Enmity in Corinth*, 145.

52. MacGillivray defines patronage "as a voluntary, though often exploitative, reciprocal relationship that pervaded Roman society, whereby a gift from a superior obligated an exchange, usually of intangible commodities such as political support or public laud of the patron's munificence. The client's exchange would in turn be requited to restore the debt and a reciprocal cycle would ensue" ("Re-Evaluating Patronage," 38).

53. See Witherington, *Conflict & Community*, 18.

54. See Barrett, *Commentary*, 2.

55. See section 3.3.1 of this present study.

56. Litfin, *St. Pauls Theology of Proclamation*, 142.

indigenous Corinthian stock, those from elsewhere in Greece itself, and those from the rest of the eastern Mediterranean.[57]

From this, one can deduce that the new city of Corinth had a different and unique vibe. It shows that in the new city of Corinth, there was no culture or tradition that was dominant except for the Greek culture that took precedence over the others. Maybe because of its relative newness, it is possible that the Corinthian society was more flexible and porous, with social mobility more fluid than in other cities.[58] Prior to their coming into Corinth, the new inhabitants would have made up the lower half of the social hierarchy in the Roman Empire, but in the new Corinth they had the chance to be on the top of the social hierarchy. Thus, we see a breakdown of the strict hierarchy based on groups or families or legacy towards a focus on individuality.[59] Savage observed this change in Corinth by pointing out that, "No longer was corporate solidarity the ideal. Instead, people cultivated a rigorous self-sufficiency. Consequently, people began to focus on themselves and in particular on cultivating their self-worth."[60]

Theissen, in his examination of the social matrix of the Corinthian congregation, concluded that there were poor and rich people, but mainly the poor making up the majority of the congregation.[61] Likewise, Meeks also agreed that the Corinthian congregation paints a "picture in which people of several social levels are brought together."[62] Again, in the previous chapter, this study has argued that since the army veterans repopulated the new city of Corinth, there was a high probability of there being people with disability among them. Moreover, with the trade and commerce picking up soon after and with the strategic location of a seaport, the probability of poor and disabled people begging to keep themselves alive was also present.[63] When it comes to postulating the presence of disabled people in the Corinthian congregation, one does not have hard evidence. Yet, it is not altogether impossible

---

57. Horsley, *1 Corinthians*, 25.
58. See Garland, *2 Corinthians*, 24.
59. Cf. Horrell, *Social Ethos*, 65–73, and Meeks, *Moral World*, 32–64.
60. Savage, *Power though Weakness*, 19.
61. Theissen, *Social Setting*, 55–57, 145–174.
62. Meeks, *First Urban Christian*, 55–63.
63. See section 3.3.2 of this present study.

to logically deduce that if the majority of the congregation were from the poorer section of society (as Deissmann suggests),[64] or there were army veterans, the likelihood is that there were people with disabilities, even if only a small percentage.

Where would Paul fit into this seemingly unique social matrix of the Corinthian congregation? Paul seems to be an "itinerant preacher,"[65] but his vocation would seem to provide an answer to his social status and how the Corinthians thought of him. Luke recorded that Paul was a "tent maker" (Acts 18:3), and as such, the Corinthians would have considered him a manual worker. Hock has examined Paul's vocation from the Greco-Roman artisan perspective and the effects it must have had on the Corinthians.[66] Hock believes that since Paul stated he "worked night and day" in 2 Corinthians 11:2, it portrays him to be "like any artisan."[67] The problem this would create for Paul is the stigma attached to the artisan's work as they "were regarded as slavish."[68] Moreover, there seems to have been a cultural prejudice against the artisan's vocation because the society thought, "Artisans [are] incapable of achieving virtue."[69] As such, it is possible that they regarded "tent-making" as "unnecessary," "useful only to those who lived for luxury and extravagance."[70] According to Fredrick J. Long, "we cannot ignore the fact that Paul was criticized also for his . . . lowly manual labor."[71] Stowers went so far as to confidently remark, "it is doubtful that he could have overcome the stigma of these roles even if he had sought to do so."[72] Therefore, from this discussion, what is starkly evident is that Paul would have been further disabled by the social stigmatization he faced because of his vocation.

---

64. Deissmann, *Light*, 144.
65. Theissen, *Social Setting*, 71.
66. Hock, *Social Context*, 37.
67. Hock, 35.
68. Hock, 35.
69. Hock, 35.
70. Hock, 36.
71. Long, *Ancient Rhetoric*, 121.
72. Stowers, "Social Status," 74.

## 4.5 The Corinthians' Attitude towards Rhetoricians and Disability

Stambaugh and Balch have pointed out, "There are indications in the New Testament that Paul and other early Christian leaders were judged on their rhetorical abilities and that some of their audiences were comparing them as if they were engaged in an oratorical competition."[73] They seem to be on the right track as 2 Corinthians 10:10 states, "For they say, 'His letters are weighty and strong, but his personal presence is unimpressive and his speech contemptible'" (NASB). Stambaugh and Balch also believe that the way Paul fought is "a ringing sarcasm to show that he too knew how to play the game of rhetorical vituperation (2 Cor 10-13)."[74] Indeed, a cursory reading of Paul's letter to the Corinthians, as well as other letters, points to the fact that there was a high regard for rhetorical skills among ancient Greco-Roman society. It would seem that "the ancient world placed a premium on rhetorical skills"[75] and that "there was a great demand for orators to speak well and strong in public."[76] According to Witherington, "Early in the first century A.D. rhetoric became the primary discipline in Roman higher educations."[77] Likewise, Peterson wrote,

> In Hellenistic society, the practice and expectations of rhetorical eloquence were pervasive. Not only were political leaders expected to speak persuasively and eloquently, but also those who claimed authority in philosophy and religion. Among such people, there was a great competition, and success depended upon one's ability to express the power of the divine in his or her performances – not only through miracles, but also through rhetorical performances.[78]

If Stambaugh and Balch's claim that "rhetorical technique was the chief content of higher education" is true,[79] it would not be surprising to find that

---

73. Stambaugh and Balch, *New Testament*, 122.
74. Stambaugh and Balch, 122.
75. Garland, *1 Corinthians*, 33.
76. Meeks, *Moral World*, 63.
77. Witherington, *Conflict & Community*, 40.
78. Peterson, *Eloquence*, 59.
79. Stambaugh and Balch, *New Testament*, 122.

the general populace had interest in this kind of technique. Tacitus offered an interesting insight into the cultural adaptation in regards to how the public perceived rhetoricians by comparing the attitude of the public then and now.[80] According to him, "The people of the past, ignorant and uncultured as they were, patiently endured the length of a very confused speech."[81] By contrast, Tacitus wrote of his own day, "there is scarce a bystander in the throng who, if not fully instructed, has not at least been initiated into the rudiments of culture."[82] Therefore, a culture of judgment, where the audience acted as the judge on whether or not a rhetor performed well would indeed have been intimidating. In addition, since orators normally spoke in public, their physical countenances and the ability to command their voices would have needed to be impressive for the audience to appreciate it.[83]

In the case of Paul, Long is on point when he states, "The Corinthians felt they had the right to judge Paul and his message and were evaluating him by the same criteria by which popular orators and teachers were judged."[84] Witherington correctly indicates the power that the Corinthian congregation had when he states, "In a culture where public reputation was of great importance a crowd could make or break the career of an orator."[85] Moreover, given the fact that Paul was disabled, it is not surprising that the Corinthians would judge his oratory skill even more because of it. Jong also believes that "his various afflictions and weakness caused serious doubts about Paul and the power of the Spirit in him."[86] In the previous chapter, this study has shown that when it came to judging rhetorical skills, the crux of the matter was that the rhetor needed to be both skilled as well as physically admirable.[87] Thus, in a society where even the emperor could not escape the social stigmatization of disability and the inability to speak eloquently,[88] Paul, who was suffering from disability, would have undoubtedly faced social stigmatization.

---

80. Tacitus, *Dialogue on Oratory*.
81. Tacitus, ch. 19.
82. Tacitus, ch. 19.
83. Stambaugh and Balch, *New Testament*, 122.
84. Long, *Ancient Rhetoric*, 121.
85. Witherington, *Conflict & Community*, 47.
86. Long, *Ancient Rhetoric*, 121.
87. See section 3.2.1.2 of this present study.
88. Laes, "Silent History?," 164–165.

What this indicates is that the debate of whether Paul was skilful in the art of rhetoric does not matter if he was physically weak.[89] Schellenberg is right on point with his statement that "Paul cannot rely on the persuasive power of calm and dignified self-possession. His voice comes from a more tenuous place. His is a rhetoric that arises from vulnerability, desperation, and defiance."[90] Indeed, in a society where "rhetoricians, in particular, strove to improve their own physical appearance in order to enhance the power of their speeches [the ancient Greco-Roman world would] . . . point out the weakness of their opponents' bodies as proof of their weakness of character."[91] If this were true, Paul's detractors would compare his appearance with that of "slaves" and "women" because of his apparently weak body.[92] As such, the Corinthians would consider him unfit to be a "leader."[93]

## 4.6 Literary Unity of 2 Corinthians Correspondence

When it comes to 2 Corinthians, one of the biggest issues is the question of its unity that has surfaced in the academic world "ever since Johann S. Semler's commentary on 2 Corinthians in 1776."[94] He first proposed that 2 Corinthians contains different sets of letters.[95] This is because Semler observed the similarity in subject matter when he discussed chapters 8 and 9, especially when it came to the matter of collecting the offering.[96] Ever since, there has been abundant, well-documented scholarly debate over this literary unity problem.[97] The following section is a brief account of the different hypotheses of scholars.

---

89. See Martin, *Corinthian Body*, 35.
90. Schellenberg, *Rethinking*, 311.
91. Albl, "For Whenever," 156; see also Martin, *Corinthian Body*, 35.
92. See Fortenbaugh, *Aristotle's Practical Side*, 245.
93. See Harrill, *Slaves*, 36.
94. Long, *Ancient Rhetoric*, 1.
95. See Semler, *Paraphrasis 2*.
96. See Thrall, *2 Corinthians*, 4.
97. See Maschmeier, "2 Corinthians," 152–153.

### 4.6.1 The Letter Is a Compilation

As observed above, in 1776, Semler in his commentary on 2 Corinthians "proposed for the first time the hypothesis that Paul's Second Epistle to the Corinthians is composed of several distinct fragments."[98] Soon after, this argument gained momentum in the scholarly fields, especially among those who were interested in the unity of 2 Corinthians. Betz metaphorically described the effect of Semler's contribution as a broken dam, "releasing a mighty flood which swept scholars of all persuasions and schools into the debate on partition theories of 2 Corinthians and other Pauline Letters for the next two hundred years."[99] The partition theory is still not a settled matter. Duff, an old student of Betz, observed, "Although a few voices still insist that canonical Second Corinthians represents only one letter, the majority agree that it represents a collection of letters."[100] The following section makes a survey of the various hypotheses of the compilations of 2 Corinthians.

#### 4.6.1.1 Compilation of two letters

In this particular hypothesis, Paul's letter to 2 Corinthians contains two distinct letters, chapters 1–9 and chapters 10–13. The reason for this is the sharp tonal differences noticeable even to the superficial reader between chapters 1–9 and 10–13. Under this hypothesis, it is also important to know that there are different scholars who believe that the arrangement and placing of the two blocks of chapters also matter.[101] For instance, scholars like Hausrath, Schmeidel, J. H. Kennedy, Plummer, and Watson would argue that chapters 10–13 are earlier than chapters 1–9 because it does not make sense to praise them then suddenly scold them harshly.[102] On the other hand, there are important scholars like Pherigo, Barrett, Bruce, Furnish, and Somney who think that there is nothing wrong with the fact that chapters 1–9 should be earlier

---

98. Betz, *2 Corinthians*, 4.
99. Betz, 4.
100. Duff, "Paul's Elusive Opponents," 40n12.
101. See Thrall, *Corinthians 1–7*, 47–49.
102. Von A. Hausrath, *Der Vier-Capitel-Brief des Paulus an die Korinther* (Verlagsort: Heidelberg/Erscheinungsjahr, 1870), quoted in Thrall, *Corinthians 1–7*, 49; W. Schmithals, "Die Korintherbriefe als Briefsammlung," *ZNW* 64 (1973): 263–288, quoted in Thrall, 49; Kennedy, *Second*, 95; Plummer, *Critical and Exegetical*; Watson, "2 Cor," 324–346.

than 10–13.¹⁰³ However, whatever the position may be, these scholars are in agreement over the notion that 2 Corinthians is a composite letter of chapters 1–9 and 10–13.

### 4.6.1.2 Compilation of three or more letters

Some others believe that 2 Corinthians is composed of not just two but three or more letters combined. First, important scholars like Semler, Windisch, and Martin think that 2 Corinthians contains three separate letters where chapters 1–8 make up one, then chapter 9 the second, while chapters 10–13 make up the third letter.¹⁰⁴ The reason for this hypothesis is mainly that since chapters 8 and 9 contain many similarities, they must have been a separate letter each. A slightly different analysis but with the same three-letter hypothesis is given by Lang who feels that Paul first sent chapters 10–13, then sent chapters 1–8 to reconcile with them, and lastly sent chapter 9 for collecting money.¹⁰⁵

Second, there are those groups of scholars like Bornkamm, Georgi, Suhl, Marxsen, Schenke and Fisher, and Vielhauer who all assume that Paul's Second Letter to the Corinthians is a combination of four or five different letters.¹⁰⁶ According to these scholars (except for Vielhauer who believes that chapters 2:14–7:4 belong to chapters 10–13), 2 Corinthians 2:14–7:4 is a compact separate letter that is different from chapter 10–13 as well as

---

103. Pherigo, "Paul," 341–351; Barrett, *Commentary*, 10–12; Bruce, *1 and 2 Corinthians*, 170; Furnish, *2 Corinthians*, 26–29; Sumney, *Identifying Paul's Opponents*, 125–126.

104. Semler, *Paraphrasis 2: Epistolae ad Corinthias*, 238, quoted in Thrall, *Corinthians 1–7*, 4; H. Windisch, *Der zweite Korintherbrief*, KEK 6 (Gottingen: Vanden- hoeck & Ruprecht, [1924] 1970), quoted in Thrall, *Corinthians 1–7*, 48; Martin, *2 Corinthians*, xlvi.

105. F. Lang, *Die Briefe an die Korinther*, NTD 7 (Gottingen: Vandenhoeck & Ruprecht, 1986), quoted in Thrall, *Corinthians 1–7*, 48.

106. See Bornkamm, "History," 258–264; Georgi, *Opponents of Paul*, 14–17; A. Suhl, *Paulus und Seine Briefe: Ein Beitrag Zur Paulinischen Chronologie*, vol. 11, SZNT (Gütersloher Verlagshaus Mohn, 1975), quoted in Thrall, *Corinthians 1–7*, 48; Marxsen, *Introduction*; H. M. Schenke and K. M. Fisher, *Einleitung in die Schriften des Neuen Testamnts I: Die Briefe des Paulus und die Schriften des Paulinismus* (Berlin, 1978), quoted in Thrall, *Corinthians 1–7*, 48; P. Vielhauer, *Geschichte der Urchristlichen Literatur* (Berlin, 1975), quoted in Thrall, *Corinthians 1–7*, 48.

According to Bornkamm, 2 Corinthians can be differentiated into five letters: "2:14–7:4; 10–13 (painful letter); 1:1–2:13 with 7:5–16 and perhaps with letter 8 (letter of reconciliation); 9" (quoted in Thrall, *Corinthians 1–7*, 48). According to Suhl, the division is as follows: "2:14–7:4; 10–13 (painful letter); 1:1–2:13 with 7:5–8:24 (letter of reconciliation); 9" (quoted in Thrall, *Corinthians 1–7*, 48).

chapters 1:1–2:13.¹⁰⁷ Finally, mention may also be made of the six-letter hypothesis of J. Weiss and the nine-letter hypothesis of Schmithals.¹⁰⁸ The interesting thing about these hypotheses is that both the scholars believe 1 Corinthians can also be included in 2 Corinthians. For instance, Weiss is convinced that "the old church tradition has collected in these two documents the remains of more than two letters and that these letters originated at different stages of the dispute."¹⁰⁹ Thus for him, the first letter contains "I Cor 10:1–23, 6:12–20, 11:2–34, 16:7 (?), 8f; perhaps 16:20f; II Cor 6: 14–7:1."¹¹⁰

## 4.6.2 The Letter Is Not a Compilation

Traditionally, it has always been the conviction of church fathers and scholars alike that 2 Corinthians is a unified letter. It was only after the introduction of critical studies of the New Testament that scholars such as Semler started to investigate the composition of 2 Corinthians. It gained so much ground within the academic circle that to say or believe that 2 Corinthians is a unified letter is to put oneself in an awkward position. However, when it comes to defending the unity of 2 Corinthians, one of the strongest allies on the side of those scholars who would argue for unity is the fact that "there is no textual evidence for partition theories, and the epistle was always treated as a unity."¹¹¹ Black also wrote convincingly, "The integrity of the transmitted letter has the unquestioned support of the entire textual tradition, a fact that cannot be set aside gratuitously."¹¹²

Young and Ford are correct to believe that "so strong has been the attack on unity that the burden of proof appears to be on those who would defend it."¹¹³ These two scholars believe that Corinthians is a unified letter. According to them, "For all its mood-changes, we suggest that this text is to be read as a whole, that the cross-references to Titus, to other letters and visits, are all consistent with this reading and that even in the final words

---

107. Thrall, *Corinthians 1–7*, 48–49.

108. Weiss, *Earliest Christianity*, 356–357; W. Schmithals, "Die Korintherbriefe als Briefsammlung," *ZNW* 64 (1973): 263–288, quoted in Thrall, *Corinthians 1–7*, 48.

109. Weiss, *Earliest Christianity*, 324.

110. Weiss, 356.

111. Young and Ford, *Meaning and Truth*, 28.

112. Black, *Paul*, 57.

113. Young and Ford, *Meaning and Truth*, 29.

the anguish of Paul's love and concern for his rebellious children coheres with all that has gone before."[114] As such, scholars like Denney, Bachmann, Menzies, Lietzmann, Kummel, Stephenson, and Bates, to name a few, have given their own support and explanation of the seemingly contrasting tone and redundant words and subjects in 2 Corinthians.[115]

### 4.6.3 The Integrity of 2 Corinthians from a Disability Perspective

This study also maintains the literary integrity of 2 Corinthians. It argues that the subject of disability holds the letter together and can explain the seeming contradictions of the letter's contents. For instance, disability words or indicators abound in 2 Corinthians. Case in point, the Greek word θλιψις that can refer to "harassment, affliction, or oppression" is scattered in 2 Corinthians 1:4, 2:4, 4:17, 6:4, 7:4, 8:2 and 13.[116] Similarly, its cognate θλιβω is present in different places like 2 Corinthians 1:6, 4:8, and 7:5. Besides this, Greek words like θανατος (2 Cor 1:9, 10; 2:16; 3:7; 4:11, 12; 7:10; 11:23), παθημα meaning "suffering" (2 Cor 1:5, 6, 7), κοπω meaning "trouble, difficulty" (2 Cor 6:5; 10:15; 11:23, 27) are all spread throughout 2 Corinthians.[117] All these words indicate to a certain degree a sense of desperation, most probably brought on by Paul's struggle with his infirmities and the subsequent social stigmatization.

Barrett correctly pointed out (though he was not in support of the literary unity of the text) that 2 Corinthians is where Paul "wears his heart on his sleeve and speaks without constraint, [without] hiding his affection, nor his anger, nor his agony."[118] Indeed, from the first chapter (see 1:5) to the last (2 Cor 10–13), one reads of the distress and hardship and problems brought about by his limited physical conditions. Seen from this perspective, one is not surprised if there are fluctuations in tones and straying of thoughts, for

---

114. Young and Ford, 26.
115. Denney, *Second Epistle*; P. Bachmann, *Der zweite Brief des Paulus an die Korinther*, Kommentar zum Neun Testament 8 (Leipzig, 1909), quoted in Thrall, *Corinthians 1–7*, 49; Menzies, *Second Epistle*; H. Leitzmann, *An Die Korinther 1–2*, HNT 9 (Tubingen, 1909), quoted in Thrall, *Corinthians 1–7*, 49; Kummel, *Introduction*; Stephenson, "Defence," 82–97; Bates, "Integrity," 56–69.
116. Schlier, "*thlíbō* (to press, afflict)," in *TDNT* abridged in one volume, 334.
117. All Greek words and meaning taken from BibleWorks 8, 2009.
118. Barrett, *Commentary*, 32.

Paul did not write any other letter that reveals his emotional roller coaster more than 2 Corinthians. According to Voorwinde,

> Specific references to Paul's emotions are found no less than thirty-five times, and twenty different Greek words are used. No less impressive is the range of emotions expressed. He despairs (1:8), experiences sorrow (2:1, 3; 6:10), is glad (2:2; 12:9, 15), rejoices (2:3; 6:10; 7:4, 7, 9, 13, 16; 13:9), feels anguish of heart (2:4), sheds tears (2:4), loves (2:4; 5:14; 6:6; 11:11; 12:15), is perplexed (4:8), groans (5:2, 4), has regrets (7:8), is afraid (7:5; 11:3; 12:20) and jealous (11:2), mourns (12:21) and burns with distress (11:29).[119]

The resultant distributions of Paul's emotions across the letter connect directly to the subject of literary unity. As Wallace acknowledges, "one would be hard-pressed to see a difference in tone" if one puts chapters 1–9 and 10–13 parallel with each other.[120] Therefore, from a disability perspective, one can argue that one ought to read and consider 2 Corinthians as a whole letter.

## 4.7 Opponents of Paul in Corinth: Identities and Hypothesis

New Testament scholars, as well as the early church fathers, knew that Paul was beset with problems from people who did not want him to succeed.[121] However, when it comes to a serious scholarly discussion on his opponents, Ellis has stated, "Baur was the first to make Paul's opponents a decisive key to the whole of the Apostle's writings."[122] So far, Witherington identifies "at least fourteen different proposals about Paul's opponents in 2 Corinthians."[123] However, in the following, this study will briefly discuss the "four basic

---

119. Voorwinde, "Paul's Emotions," 86.
120. Wallace, "8. 2 Corinthians."
121. Porter, "Introduction," 1. He correctly points out, "It has long been recognised in critical scholarship that Paul was faced with situations in which there was some opposition to this work" (1).
122. Ellis, "Paul," 271–272.
123. Witherington, *Conflict & Community*, 343.

groups: Judaizers, Gnostics, Divine Men, and Pneumatics,"[124] along with the "Sophists,"[125] as the chief opponents of Paul.

## 4.7.1 Judaizers

According to Baur, Paul's opponents were the Judaizers attaching themselves to Peter as opposed to the Gentile Christians who were loyal to Paul (see 1 Cor 1:12).[126] Baur believes that Judaizers were "Jewish Christians who demand continuing observance of the Law of Moses. They contend that one is not saved by Paul's gospel and that the first step to Christian salvation must be circumcision."[127] However, Baur knows that hardly anything in 1 and 2 Corinthians "suggests the presence of Judaizers" except for 2 Corinthians 3, where one can assume that Paul was talking about the Judaizers.[128] As such, in order to maintain his hypothesis, Baur suggests, "that in Corinth the opponents' main point has shifted from circumcision to the notion of apostolic authority."[129] This means that they are still Judaizers, but they have evolved their narrative depending on the situation. Sumney thinks that Baur was able to come up with this hypothesis by leaning on the insights gained from the "Pseudo-Clementine Homilies" which recount "an argument between Peter and Simon Magnus over apostolic authority."[130] From this, Baur established that one could become an apostle only by becoming "a disciple of earthly Jesus."[131] Therefore, Baur simply presumes that since Paul was not a disciple of the earthly Jesus, hence his opponents, that is, the Jewish Christians belonging to Peter, claim that Paul is not among the "super-apostles" (see 2 Cor 11:5).

Along with Baur, scholars such as Oostendorp, Barrett, Gunther, and Lüdemann "conclude that the opponents of Paul in 2 Corinthians are Judaizers,"[132] albeit a slight modification from what Baur proposed. For

---

124. Sumney, *Identifying Paul's Opponents*, 15.
125. See Moon, "Paul's Discourse," 21.
126. Sumney, *Identifying Paul's Opponents*, 16.
127. Quoted in Sumney, 15.
128. Duff believes that 2 Corinthians 3 does not talk about Judaizers ("Paul's Elusive Opponents," 37–59). This is because there was no circumcision issue like the one found in Galatians.
129. Sumney, *Identifying Paul's Opponents*, 18.
130. Sumney, 16.
131. Sumney, 16.
132. Sumney, 15.

instance, Oostendorp believes that "the opponents are Judaizers who are interested in the righteousness of the law" and "the driving force behind the opponents at Corinth was their own understanding of the eschatological prophecies of the Old Testament."[133] Mention may be made of Barrett who thinks that the main reason behind this change had to do with the "Corinth . . . environment in which Gentiles were exercising a fundamental Gentile judgment in apostolic claimants."[134] This caused the Judaizers to adopt "Hellenistic criteria" and use it on Paul, whom they criticized as not belonging to the super-apostle category.[135]

There are important things to consider here. First, Baur's premise that Peter was the frontman of the Judaizers is not entirely correct. A socio-cultural study of Peter's missionary activities to the Gentiles shows that he was sympathetic to spreading the gospel to the Gentiles, albeit with the Spirit prompting him (see Acts 10:1–20; 11:1–48; 15:7; Gal. 2:1–8). In fact, Peter's position was neither James-centric nor Paul-centric, but he was in the centre himself. As Dunn would say, "The bridge-man who did more than any other to hold together the diversity of first-century Christianity."[136] Second, as Georgi has pointed out, "all past and present advocates of the 'Judaizers' hypothesis had difficulty in explaining Paul's polemic against libertinistic tendencies, the disputes about sophia and gnosis . . . as found in 2 Cor."[137] If for a moment, one could consider these Judaizers coming from James in Jerusalem, then it obviously means that the motives of these Judaizers would be to disturb Paul just because he dared to mingle with the Gentiles and even shared table-fellowship with them.[138] For if these people from James could hound Peter while he was at Antioch (Gal 2:11–14), they would have had no qualm to hunt down Paul and disturb him wherever he went. Moreover, there is a possibility that these Judaizers could have come from Jerusalem with their credentials from James and not Peter, which they would have used without hesitation to discredit Paul.

---

133. Oostendorp, *Another Jesus*, 2, 84.
134. Barrett, *Commentary*, 30.
135. Barrett, 30.
136. Dunn, *Unity and Diversity*, 385.
137. Georgi, *Opponents of Paul*, 4.
138. Esler points out, "as a general rule Jews did refrain from eating with gentiles" (*Galatians*, 95).

## 4.7.2 Gnostics

Among the scholars who believe Paul's opponents in 2 Corinthians were the gnostics, "Schmithals presents the most developed case for this position."[139] Other scholars include the likes of Lütgeret and Schlatter, with Bultmann being the "last serious" scholar who attempted "to argue that Paul's opponents in 2 Corinthians were Gnostics."[140] A gnostic was one who practiced "Gnosticism," and according to Schmithals, "Gnosticism" stood for a "religious movement which teaches man to understand himself as a piece of divine substance. Although he has fallen, through a disastrous fate, into captivity to an alien world and its demonic rulers, he may be certain of liberation from that captivity because he possesses the awareness of his inalienable divine being."[141] After a careful examination of First and Second Corinthians, Schmithals is of the opinion that regardless of what 1 Corinthians 1:12 records about the many opponents Paul faced in Corinth, "the results can be related to only one group,"[142] and that is Gnosticism "of Jewish origin (cf. 2 Cor 11:22)."[143] He thinks that the gnostics had introduced "the anthropological Christ myth" (see 2 Cor 12:1–10) among the Corinthian Christians and that they believed "every apostle must be a pneumatic in the Gnostic sense" (see 2 Cor 4:2–5).[144]

Therefore, according to Schmithals, the gnostic Corinthian Christians were expecting Paul to show signs of Gnosticism,[145] that is, he must demonstrate "that Christ is actually ... speaking in him (2 Cor 13:3)."[146] However, there are scholars such as Pascuzzi and Wilson who argue that Schimthals's position is not sustainable because of "the lack of evidence in 1 Cor for any extraneous mediators of gnostic ideas in the community."[147] Moreover, according to Horrell and Adams, "The collapse in scholarly confidence in the concept of pre-Christian Gnosticism meant that it could no longer be invoked

---

139. Moon, "Paul's Discourse," 20.
140. Hafemann, *Paul's Message*, 5.
141. Schmithals, *Gnosticism in Corinth*, 30.
142. Schmithals, 115.
143. Schmithals, 155.
144. Schmithals, 209, 183.
145. See Schütz, *Paul*, 254.
146. Schmithals, *Paul*, 31n46.
147. Pascuzzi, *Ethic*, 52; see also Wilson, "Gnosis at Corinth," 102–119.

as a possible source for Corinthian belief and action."[148] Therefore, while Schmithals's proposal is attractive, the fact that he also left out the possibility of Paul's disability or weakness as the root cause of the Corinthians' reluctance to treat Paul as their leader or someone with apostolic authority is problematic. Even Schmithals seems to have struggled with how to interpret 2 Corinthians 10:10, as he stated, "As for the physical weakness, it is hardly conceivable that anyone could make it an accusation against Paul at all."[149] Yet, right from 2 Corinthians 1:8 until the last three chapters, Paul was focusing much of his letter and argument on his bodily weakness.

### 4.7.3 Θειος ἀνηρ (Divine Men)

Not satisfied with the above two explanations on the identities of Paul's opponents in 2 Corinthians, "a number of interpreters, led by Georgi, argue that the opponents of 2 Corinthians were 'divine men.'"[150] According to Georgi, these θειος ἀνηρ were "migrant preacher[s] of Jewish origin" who had "come from the world of Hellenistic-Jewish Apologetics."[151] They preached "Jesus as an extraordinary pneumatic, as a θειος ἀνηρ," and they compared the earthly Jesus to Moses whom they also considered θειος ἀνηρ.[152] Georgi feels strongly that "Paul sees his very existence threatened by these intruders for they attacked his function as a missionary, the center of his life."[153] Therefore, Paul, in his letter, especially in "2 Cor 2:14–7:4 and 2 Cor 10–13 attacked the activity" of these divine men.[154]

However, some scholars are cautious of Georgi's assumptions of these divine men with their theology, especially their Christology.[155] For instance, Sumney, along with Holladay, thinks, "such connections with a reconstruction are an insufficient basis for importing the 'divine man' theological scheme into the theology of the Corinthian opponents."[156] Kee also wrote, "But in

---

148. Horrell and Adams, "Scholarly Quest," 16.
149. Schmithals, *Gnosticism in Corinth*, 176.
150. Sumney, "Studying Paul's Opponents," 16.
151. Georgi, *Opponents of Paul*, 315.
152. Georgi, 274.
153. Georgi, 316.
154. Georgi, 315.
155. See Conway, *Behold the Man*, 35.
156. Sumney, "Studying Paul's Opponents," 16; see also Holladay, *Theios Aner*.

truth, except for a widespread fondness for apotheosis of great men, there is no set type or model of *theios aner*."[157] What is also difficult to accept is Georgi's position that Paul felt threatened by the comparison between Moses and Jesus as divine men. If one looks at Paul's arguments in 2 Corinthians 3-4, it is apparent that he considered Mosaic law a relic of the past, especially pertaining to the rules and regulations that can be interpreted to exclude a segment of Jewish society. It seems Paul was much more bothered by the eschatological implication, or rather its failure to deliver a comprehensive eschatological deliverance, since he described Mosaic law as a ministry of "death" and "condemnation" (2 Cor 3:7, 8).

### 4.7.4 Pneumatics

Käsemann "argues that the opponents of 2 Corinthians are travelling preachers who have a different understanding of apostleship that Paul does."[158] Käsemann labelled them as "pneumatics" because these people believed that "the benchmark of apostolic dignity was their ability to free speech (either in tongues or otherwise), along with the power to perform miracles and experience ecstatic journeys into the upper world through visions or auditions."[159] In addition, these pneumatics came from "Jerusalem Church, carrying 'letters of recommendation' (2 Cor 3.1) to prove their official status."[160] According to the pneumatics, all the signs pointing to someone who was pneumatic is "absent from Paul's life," thereby pronouncing him as "a spiritual simpleton."[161] For instance, in 2 Corinthians 10:10 and 11:6, Paul talks about his weakness, which confirms the pneumatics' criticism of Paul.[162] Sumney thinks that Käsemann came closest to the identification of Paul's opponents in 2 Corinthians.[163] Nevertheless, he feels that "there is far too little justification for Käsemann's claim that they are related to the Jerusalem church."[164] Besides,

---

157. Kee, *Jesus in History*, 152.
158. E. Käsemann, "Die Legitimität des Apostels," *ZNW* 41 (1942): 33–71, quoted in Sumney, "Studying Paul's Opponents," 16–17.
159. Guenther, "Gnosticism in Corinth?," 49.
160. Guenther, 50.
161. Guenther, 49.
162. See Guenther, 49.
163. Sumney, *Identifying Paul's Opponents*, 177, 179.
164. Sumney, "Studying Paul's Opponents," 17. See also Sumney, *Identifying Paul's Opponents*, 127–191; McClelland, "'Super-Apostles,'" 79–133.

"whatever other theological, soteriological or christological differences there may be between Paul and these teachers . . . the only theological point about which Paul finds it necessary to argue with them is that of the image of the apostle/minister."[165]

One can state that Paul's arguments in 2 Corinthians 1–13 are mainly along the lines of defending his reputation as an apostle, as well as his ministry. According to Sumney, because of the Spirit's manifestation in the pneumatics' lives, "it makes them powerful speakers, and personalities who must be obeyed by the congregation."[166] One of the means by which "they exercise this spiritual power" is to accept the Corinthians' "financial support."[167] However, it seems that Paul's weak physical appearances and his inability to speak well in public (see 10:10) allowed these pneumatics to accuse Paul of not being a real apostle. Besides, Paul's refusal to accept financial support from the Corinthians was more damning to his claim of being in their rank (see 2 Cor 11:9, 20–21). Still, it does not really make sense to think that Paul was not showing signs of the Spirit, for he clearly stated in 1 Corinthians 2:4 that he came to minister to them "not in persuasive words of wisdom, but in demonstration of the Spirit and of power" (NASB).[168]

### 4.7.5 Sophists

Winter argues, "Paul deliberately adopts an anti-sophistic stance and thus defends his church-planting activities in Corinth against the background of sophistic conventions, perceptions and categories."[169] Winter built upon the foundation laid out by Munck who postulated that Paul had encountered a sophist when he came to Corinth.[170] In addition, Marshall also suggests that the works of the sophists influenced the opponents of Paul in Corinth.[171] Accordingly, who were these sophists? Bowerstock defines them as "virtuoso rhetor with big reputation,"[172] which means that a sophist was a master class

---

165. Sumney, "Studying Paul's Opponents," 17.
166. Sumney, 17
167. Sumney, 17.
168. See Guenther, "Gnosticism in Corinth?," 49
169. Winter, *Philo and Paul*, 145.
170. Munck, *Paul*, 153.
171. Marshall, *Enmity in Corinth*, 180–181.
172. Bowerstock, *Greek Sophists*, 13.

public speaker with a great deal of magnetic power over others. According to Philodemus, sophists thought "their art (τεχνη) was the mother of all other arts and sciences" and that their "art" dealt "with the three branches of rhetoric, namely Judicial, deliberative and epideictic oratory."[173]

Philo wrote, "A vast number of those who are called sophists, being admired in their respective cities . . . attracted almost all the world to look upon them with honour, on account of their definitions and their excessive cleverness in inventions."[174] The problem with these sophist teachings was the need to look well both in outside adornment and physical stature. For instance, Philostratus commented on the case of Alexander of Seleucia when he came to visit Athens, "the Athenians thought his appearance and costume so exquisite that before he speaks a word a low buzz of approval went round as a tribute to his perfect elegance."[175] In another case, Epictetus described a "young rhetorician coming to him with his hair too elaborately ornamented, and his dress very fine,"[176] who was clearly influenced by the "bodily presence . . . immensely important during" this time.[177]

Winter again claims that the sophist opponents of Paul in 2 Corinthians were "Jewish in origin . . . well trained in Greek rhetoric. As Hellenophiles, they would have propounded the view that such elitist training was the ideal or even an essential prerequisite for the high teaching or preaching office of the church, especially in Gentile areas."[178] Some of the main issues these sophists had with Paul include "'unpresentable' in appearance as a public speaker . . . [and] 'inarticulate,'" as is evident from 2 Corinthians 10:10. They also contended that Paul "was only a layman on oratory (11:6) who used underhand methods to obtain financial support for his ministry (12.14–18)."[179] As far as this suggestion of Paul's opponents explains Paul's failure to meet the rhetorical criteria in Corinth, it is possible that one can say they were the sophists of his time. However, as the previous study on the attitude towards disability in Greco-Roman and Jewish society has shown, it will be incomplete

---

173. Philodemus, *Rhet.*, 1.195, xiv, as quoted in Winter, *Philo and Paul*, 5.
174. Philo, "Treatise on Tilling of the Earth by Noah," 32, in *Works of Philo Judaeus*, 407.
175. Philistratus, *Philostratus and Eunapius*, 195.
176. Epictetus, *Discourses*, trans. Higginson, bk 3.
177. Epictetus, bk 3.
178. Winter, *Philo and Paul*, 235.
179. Winter, 204.

to simply state that Paul's opponents were sophists. One may grant that the sophists greatly influenced the Corinthian congregation to a certain extent, but they were really instigators who turned sour the Corinthians' loyalty to Paul.

## 4.7.6 The Opponents from a Disability Perspective

While Paul's rhetorical inabilities compounded by his weak physical appearance may support Winter's arguments as to the identity of Paul's opponents, one must remain open-minded. Why should one remain open-minded? This is because of the possibility that Paul might have had multiple opponents attacking him simultaneously. Indeed, from a disability perspective, a cursory reading of 2 Corinthians sustains the reading that Paul's opponents were attacking him and his ministry from different angles. For instance, if the sophist opponents were attacking Paul's rhetoric as well as pointing out his weak physical appearance, somewhere else the Judaizers could have pointed out Paul's lack of credentials (coming, perhaps, from James rather than Peter). At the same time, the "divine men" could also have accused Paul and his ministry by comparing it with that of Moses.

The previous scholarly hypotheses about Paul's opponents in 2 Corinthians show that each of these suggestions in their own right have some positive points as well as some inconsistencies. As such, will it not be better to suggest that Paul was fighting with multiple opponents who saw Paul as the common enemy to be rid of? Moreover, one must also equally cast the blame on the Corinthian congregation. In fact, McClelland claims, "the true opponents of Paul in Corinth are the misguided church members themselves."[180] McClelland has a point because one can argue that the Corinthian Christians' broken relationship with Paul originates either from them or from Paul's opponents who could have instigated them. Regardless, as long as they questioned his authority or continued to do the bidding of their instigators, they were also Paul's opponents.

Therefore, Paul could have multiple opponents in relation to 2 Corinthians instead of just one. While it is unlikely that one may get to know the full identifications of these opponents, what is knowable is that the Corinthian

---

180. McClelland, "Super-Apostles," 85.

congregation was part of those opponents.[181] In sum, it must have been a blow to Paul's ego as the Corinthian Christians seemed to accept readily the "super-apostles" who came "preaching" (ἐκηρύξαμεν) "a different gospel other than the one they received" from Paul (2 Cor 11:4).[182]

## 4.8 Summarization

This chapter has discussed and analysed the socio-rhetorical context of 2 Corinthians. One can sum up the findings of this chapter as follows:

First, Paul was the author of this particular letter, and as to the date of when he sent his letter, this study believes with other scholars that it might be around AD 53–54 when Paul visited Ephesus on his third missionary trip.[183]

Second, as to the occasion and purpose of this letter, the relationship between Paul and the Corinthian congregation broke down drastically. Due to some reasons, possibly because of Paul's disability and ancient societal negative attitudes towards disabled people, the Corinthian Christians were distancing themselves from Paul and his ministry. In such a scenario, Paul composed a forensic letter in the Roman style of *insinuatio*.

Third, this study sees the possibility of Paul as a rhetorician to some extent but not educated in a Roman rhetorical school. During Paul's days, it was not enough to know only the technique of rhetoric; one must also be physically pleasing to others. In that regard, Paul failed, for he was weak in his physical appearance (see 2 Cor 10:10).

Fourth, the social matrix of the city of Corinth was unique because they were "more Greek than Rome, more Roman than Athens."[184] In the rebuilt city of Corinth, Julius Caesar repopulated the new city with freedmen and war veterans, among which the likelihood of disabled persons being included is very high. Unlike other cities under the Roman Empire, Corinth was relatively porous in terms of social mobility. Yet class distinction between the poor and

---

181. Chapter 5, the exegetical chapter, hopes to shed further light on this point.

182. According to Gingrich, "κηρύσσω" is the technical Greek word used "most often in reference to God's saving action Mt 10:27; Mk 13:10; Lk 24:47; Acts 15:21; Rom 2:21; 1 Cor 9:27; 2 Cor 4:5; Gal 2:2; 1 Thess 2:9; 2 Tim 4:2; Rev 5:2" (*Shorter Lexicon*, 108).

183. Witherington, *Conflict & Community*, 351–352.

184. Litfin, *St. Pauls Theology of Proclamation*, 142.

the rich was stark. In such a society, there was a good chance that they would have looked down upon Paul if he did not have a good support system.

Fifth, to the question of the letter's unity, this study thinks that Paul's Second Letter to the Corinthians was likely one whole letter and not a compilation of some other letters.

Finally, as to the identification of Paul's opponents in 2 Corinthians, it is possible that Paul was fighting multiple opponents during his ministry at Corinth, with the Corinthian congregation themselves taking an active part.

CHAPTER 5

# Excavating Insights for Disability Theology in 2 Corinthians: An Exegetical Exploration of the Selected Passages

## 5.1 Introduction

The preceding chapters have given this present research a platform from where it can further launch an investigation into the notion that Paul's disability could be the source of Paul's narration of his weakness and suffering in 2 Corinthians. Chapter 2 witnesses the development of a DH that allows the researcher to analyse biblical texts in their socio-cultural and historical contexts with disability specifically in mind. Chapter 3 shows that the socio-historical context of Paul was oppressive to the disabled. It also argues that Paul was a disabled individual. Chapter 4 analyses the Corinthians' negative attitude towards disability. It also reveals just how easily they could have given a hard time to Paul who was disabled. This chapter seeks to analyse Paul's record of his struggle with the Corinthians, his narration of weakness and sufferings, from a disability perspective.

What was the role of Paul's disability, and how far did it influence his experiences with the Corinthians and their instigators, that is, his opponents?[1]

---

1. Here, the term "opponents" and "instigators" are interchangeably used.

Is it possible to point out from the text that the Corinthians themselves were socially stigmatizing Paul because of his weakness (i.e. disability)? Will one be in a better position to understand Paul's ἀσθένεια if one looks at his struggle from a disability perspective? How far can the infusion of insights gained from a conscientious exploration of his social and cultural context – that is, his Jewish and Greco-Roman context – through a disability perspective aid in the search of Paul's suffering and weakness in 2 Corinthians?[2] With these preliminary questions, this chapter will analyse the selected texts of 2 Corinthians – namely, 1:3–11, 4:1–18, 6:3–13, and 10–13 – from a disability perspective, as mentioned earlier.[3]

## 5.2 Applying a DH to the Exegetical Analysis of 2 Corinthians 1:3–11

The following section will analyse Paul's arguments in response to the situation that he was facing. The Corinthians and their instigators were taking advantage of Paul's disability, for which he suffered intensely in Asia. However, Paul fought back against his detractors instead of just accepting their criticism. Witherington and others have taken 1:3–11 as the *exordium* of the entire 2 Corinthians.[4] This exegetical analysis will also follow the same pattern of classification and consider 2 Corinthians 1:3–11 as the *exordium* of 2 Corinthians. The *exordium*, as had been explained, is "the introduction of a speech, where one announces the subject and purpose of the discourse."[5] Hence, the exegetical analysis of this section from a disability perspective will bring to light Paul's statements concerning his intentions to persuade the Corinthians to abandon their antagonistic view of his person and ministry due to his disability.

---

2. See Albl, "For Whenever," 145–146.
3. See chapter 2, section 2.5, of this present study.
4. Witherington, *Conflict & Community*, 87; Aune, *NT*, 186.
5. See the definition of *exordium* in "Canons of Rhetoric."

## 5.2.1 Establishing the Rhetorical Unit: Paul's Self Defence of His Disability

The first step of analyzing a text from a DH perspective requires that one identify the chosen text and whether or not it rhetorically comprises one unit. The chosen text must have "a decided introduction, body, and conclusion, and may either comprise an entire work or be a part of a larger one."[6] Despite some, like Belleville, Garland, and McCant, arguing otherwise,[7] 2 Corinthians 1:3–11 constitutes "a coherent unit."[8] The difference in opinion is mainly on how to interpret the function of verse 1:8 – whether or not it "indicates the beginning of the letter's body."[9] However, in favour of 2 Corinthians 1:3–11 as a coherent unit, one may argue that "the conjunction (γαρ) clearly indicates that 1:8 is closely connected to the preceding section."[10]

Second Corinthians 1:3, "Εὐλογητὸς ὁ θεὸς καὶ πατὴρ τοῦ κυρίου ἡμῶν Ἰησοῦ Χριστοῦ, ὁ πατὴρ τῶν οἰκτιρμῶν καὶ θεὸς πάσης παρακλήσεως," acts as the opening part of this unit, and it is clear that Paul was making a statement to the Corinthians that God is the one who blesses him and comforts him. Subsequently, one finds in the body of this rhetorical unit the "twin realities of his sufferings (θλίψεις . . . παθήματα), and God's comfort (παράκλησις) . . . elements in tandem that will repeat" in 4:8–9, 6:7–13, and 10–13.[11] As one observes the structure of this rhetorical unit, it becomes evident that Paul employs a rhetorical device called an anaphora which is "the repetition of the same word at the beginning of successive sentences.[12] This is evident in his consistent use of the Greek words for consolation such as "compassion" (οἰκτιρμῶν), found in verse 3, and "comfort" (παρακλήσεως), found five times in this unit (see vv. 3, 4, 6 [two times], and 7).

In the same way, one observes Greek words for suffering and hardships, such as θλίψει, which appears three times both in vv. 4 and 8, παθήματα and πάσχομεν, which appear three times in vv. 5, 6, and 7, and even "death"

---

6. Watson, *Invention*, 8.
7. Belleville, "Letter," 142–163; Witherington, *Conflict & Community*, 335; Garland, *2 Corinthians*, 72; McCant, *2 Corinthians*, 30.
8. Lim, *Sufferings*, 41.
9. Lim, 41.
10. Lim, 41; Thrall, *Corinthians 1–7*, 100; Furnish, *2 Corinthians*, 122.
11. Barnett, *Second Epistle*, 66.
12. Bullinger, *Figures*, 199–205.

(θάνατος), found two times in vv. 9 and 10. Undoubtedly, there is a "high concentration of suffering-and-consolation-words,"[13] so much so that McCant likened it to "a series of hammer blows."[14] Actually, this strategy of bombarding the *exordium* with these words is a reflection of Aristotle's rhetorical strategy where the rhetor arranges his materials for the maximum effect.[15] Paul's disability was most likely the reason for his near-death experience in Asia (vv. 8–9). Hence, Paul defends and explains the nuances of his suffering (vv. 8–10), assuring the Corinthians that his sufferings directly benefited them and enabled them to experience God's comfort (vv. 3–7).

In what is the closing of this unit (v. 11, "συνυπουργούντων καὶ ὑμῶν ὑπὲρ ἡμῶν τῇ δεήσει, ἵνα ἐκ πολλῶν προσώπων τὸ εἰς ἡμᾶς χάρισμα διὰ πολλῶν εὐχαριστηθῇ ὑπὲρ ἡμῶν"), Paul continues to carry on the flow of his persuasive strategy from the opening verse (v. 3) where he refrained from giving thanks to the Corinthians. Even though the "thanksgiving" (εὐχαριστηθῇ) formula made its presence here, Paul could not bring himself to thank the Corinthians. The construction of this verse (v. 11) is not easy to render because of its genitive construct, which Barnett rightly referred to as "syntactically awkward."[16] For instance, how does one translate the genitive absolute (συνυπουργούντων καὶ ὑμῶν ὑπὲρ ἡμῶν) present at the beginning of the sentence of verse 11? Should one understand this as "you also must help us" (RSV), or "as you help us" (NIV), or "if you help us"?[17] Looking at Paul's argument so far, where the Corinthian congregation are playing the supportive role, these translations are acceptable. The subsequent conditional clause introduced by the ἵνα reiterates Paul's statement that "thanks will be given by his readers for him"[18] and not the other way around. In short, the Corinthians owed their allegiance to him in spite of their problem with his disability. The next section will further elucidate the situation that prompted Paul to take such stands.

---

13. Wan, *Power in Weakness*, 35.
14. McCant, *2 Corinthians*, 31.
15. Aristotle, *Rhetoric*, 2.1.2.
16. Barnett, *Second Epistle*, 89.
17. Martin, *2 Corinthians*, 14.
18. Thrall, *Corinthians 1–7*, 128.

## 5.2.2 The Rhetorical Problem: The Issue of Disability

This section deals with the rhetorical situation and problem that caused Paul to write his defence. Rhetorical situation involves the delineation of "a situation under which an individual is called upon to make some response."[19] In a rhetorical problem, one must find the "overriding problem" that a rhetor had to deal with.[20] The preliminary observations so far strongly indicate that Paul was experiencing a strained relationship with the Corinthians. The rhetorical unit reveals instances of negative reactions to Paul's disability. Paul informs the Corinthians that God is the one who comforts him in all his suffering. Moreover, in the process of informing them of this, he issues a veiled threat that if he were not comforted then the Corinthians would also fail to get God's comfort and even their salvation. As such, this section will analyse in detail "the problem or issue that needs to be corrected or addressed."[21]

The key to finding the exigence or the rhetorical problem of the *exordium* lies in verses 8–10 where Paul narrates the near-death experience that he suffered in Asia.[22] In these few verses, Paul indicates that he suffered from affliction (θλίψεως) that caused him intense suffering. This particular Greek word θλίψεως and its cognates are present four times in this rhetorical unit alone (vv. 4, 6, and 8; see also 2:4; 4:17; 7:5; and 8:13). The secular Greek usage of this word can have a different connotation depending on the context of its usage. While in its "literal sense" this word can be used for "pressure in the physical sense," "to squash," or "hem in," it can also be used figuratively to mean "afflict," "oppress," "harass," or "to discomfort."[23] One also finds the medical use of this word in the surviving fragment of the writings of the Greek physician Oribasius Latinus where he mentioned θλιψις στομαχου (affliction of the stomach).[24] Soranus also wrote of "ὑστερικας . . . θλιψεις" (hysteria trouble) in his work *Gynaecia*.[25] Accordingly, what was the "affliction" or disability that caused Paul to "intensely suffer" to the point of being dead (vv. 9–10)?

---

19. Kennedy, *New Testament*, 35.
20. See Kennedy, 36.
21. Weima, "What Does," 460.
22. Barnett, *Second Epistle*, 83.
23. Schlier, "θλιβω, θλιψις," in *TDNT*, 2:139.
24. Schlier, "θλιβω, θλιψις," in *TDNT*, 2:139. See Oribasius Latinus (fragments).
25. Sorani, *De signis fracturarum*, 6.1.42.

### *5.2.2.1 Paul suffers from chronic illness*

Scholars such as Harris, Barrett, and Harvey support the view that Paul's sufferings could stem from his chronic illness.[26] Barrett was among the first to have proposed Paul's severe illness as the "natural" explanation of his distress in Asia.[27] According to him, "Physical illness, the shadow of death, the failure of his work in Corinth, were among the causes that led to the breaking down of a man who, if any had ground for confidence in the flesh, had more (Phil 3:4; cf. 2 Cor 11:22)."[28] However, Oropeza has recently objected to this interpretation because he felt that the plural "we" in 1:8 (θέλομεν, ἐβαρήθημεν, ἡμῶν) "makes it unfeasible."[29] Nevertheless, Paul's use of "we" or "our" does not necessarily indicate plurality; it is just as possible that he may be talking about himself, for he was even known to speak of himself in the third person (see 2 Cor 12:2–4).[30]

Paul describes the effect of his affliction as καθ' ὑπερβολὴν (beyond measure), which is "particularly characteristic of 2 Corinthians (cf. 1.8, 3:10, 4:7, 17, 9:14, 11, 23, 12:7)."[31] Besides this, Paul's use of the infinite ἐξαπορηθῆναι (be in great difficulty) is a "colourful compound verb . . . [that] . . . points to the total (ἐξ-) unavailability (-α-) of an exit (πόρος, 'passage') from oppressive circumstances, a situation prompting not so much acute embarrassment as unnerving despair."[32] Again, the use of the perfect ἐσχήκαμεν to indicate how he compared his illness to "sentence of death" is revealing in itself. The meaning of "the Greek perfect tense describes the present state which is the

---

26. Harris, *Second Epistle*, 170–172; Barrett, *Second Corinthians*, 64; Harvey, *Renewal through Suffering*, 20.

27. Barrett, *Second Corinthians*, 64.

28. Barrett, 64.

29. Orpeza, *Exploring Second Corinthians*, 84.

30. Thrall has worked on the question of whether or not Paul employed "the literary plural, i.e., the convention whereby 'we' is used for the singular 'I'" in 2 Corinthians. She believes that since both instances are present in Paul, "each has to be judged on its individual merits, in relation to the context in which it occurs" (*Corinthians 1–7*, 107). Moreover, Scott Hafemann has pointed out, "In the light of 1 Cor 1:17; 2:1–5; 3:6, 10; 4:14–16; 9:1–2; 15:1–3 and 2 Cor 7:14; 10:13f.; 11:2–4 . . . Paul considered himself alone to be the founder of the Corinthian community" (*Suffering*, 16). Hence, in this context, Paul's uses of "we" are an indication of himself as "I."

31. Barrett, *Second Corinthians*, 64. Indeed, it is a language that befits him (See Rom 7:13; 2 Cor 1:8, 12: 31; Gal 1:13).

32. Harris, *Second Epistle*, 154.

result of a past action."³³ Paul could probably have used an aorist if he wanted to focus solely on what had happened in Asia.³⁴ However, Paul's use of the perfect tense to put emphasis on "the present state that exists because of a past action is most natural if the [affliction] was illness."³⁵ The implication being that Paul had an affliction in the past and this was manifesting again intensely when he was in Asia. Hence, it may have been an "incurable malady, which had at one point almost killed him,"³⁶ and was somehow recurring again. The constant use of the present tense "comfort" in vv. 4–6 (four times), "the perfective implications of ἐσχήκαμεν (v. 9)," and the middle future "ῥύσεται in 1:10,"³⁷ which is repeated twice, all support this interpretation.

It is interesting to note that the first middle future ῥύσεται in verse 10 from the root ῥύομαι has a history of textual problems.³⁸ First, manuscripts such as P⁴⁶, Codex Sinaiticus, and Codex Vaticanus record the future tense.³⁹ Second, the present tense ῥύεται is recorded in the second corrected version of Codex Claromontanus, the Byzantine manuscripts, as well as a fragment of a Greek citation prepared by the early church father Origen.⁴⁰ Third, textual witnesses such as Codex Alexandrinus and the original version of Codex Claromontanus omit the word altogether.⁴¹ Martin felt that this change was "an attempt to 'improve' the meaning"⁴² of Paul describing himself as undergoing deliverance in Asia, instead of the future tense where Paul hoped to be delivered again. In the case of the Byzantine text, one observes a logical flow to the thrice-repeated ῥύομαι in verse 10. First, by using ἐρρύσατο (an aorist indicative middle of ῥύομαι), Paul talked about his deliverance from his affliction in the past; second, by using the present indicative middle ῥύεται, God is delivering him in the present; and third, by using the future indicative middle "ῥύσεται," God will deliver him again in the future.

---

33. Penner, *Guide*, 56.
34. Barrett, *Second Corinthians*, 64.
35. Barrett, 66.
36. Stanley, *Boasting*, 71–72.
37. Harris, *Second Epistle*, 171.
38. See Aland et al., "2 Corinthians 1:10," in *Greek New Testament*, 611.
39. Aland et al., 611n3.
40. Aland et al., 611n3.
41. Aland et al., 611n3.
42. Martin, *2 Corinthians*, 13.

However, if the first textual reading is correct, there are just the aorists, and the twice-repeated future tense of ῥύομαι in verse 10, intensifying the meaning more, which might as well explain the severity of Paul's descriptions. Paul, in the present state, did not find the deliverance he had hoped to find from his affliction as he had in the past, but this did not cause him to lose hope but to continue to hope for future deliverance. His use of the perfect ἠλπίκαμεν again is informative as it tells the reader that his hope was not an idle hope but rested on the reality of past fulfiled promises.[43] Thus, one is inclined to think with Dodd that Paul was suffering "from some physical disability which from time to time checked his efficiency and hindered his work" but for which he did not give up hope for future deliverance.[44]

### 5.2.2.2 *The nature of the disability/affliction Paul suffered in Asia*

If Paul was suffering from "some physical disability," then is it possible to identify what kind of disability he was suffering from? From the examination of Paul's testimony, this study has previously argued that he was suffering from some sort of physical disability.[45] In Galatians 4:13–14, Paul told the Galatians that it was because of his ἀσθένεια τῆς σαρκός (affliction of the flesh) that he preached the good news to them. What is revealing about Paul's illness is his remark that the Galatians did not scorn (ἐξουθενήσατε, which is indicative aorist active of ἐξουθενέω) or despise (οὐδὲ ἐξεπύσατε, which is indicative aorist active of ἐκπτύω) him even though it was a trial (πειρασμόν) to them. This weakness or affliction of the flesh made its appearance, albeit with a bit of modification, in 2 Corinthians 10:10, where Paul quoted his instigators as saying, παρουσία τοῦ σώματος ἀσθενὴς καὶ ὁ λόγος ἐξουθενημένος (the appearance of his body is weak/afflicted and his speech contemptible). It must be more than a coincidence that the exact verb ἐξουθενημένος (the participle perfect passive of ἐξουθενέω) also made its appearance here in 2 Corinthians as well as in Galatians (see Gal 4:14). In the previous chapter, a detailed analysis was done on Galatians 4:14, particularly to the examinations of the Greek words ἐξουθενήσατε οὐδὲ ἐξεπύσατε.[46] Once again, for the sake of clarity, one

---

43. See Harris, *Second Epistle*.
44. Dodd, *New Testament Studies*, 68.
45. See chapter 3, section 3.4, of this present study.
46. Please see Chapter 3, particularly section 3.4.2.

reiterates here that the literal meaning of ἐξεπύσατε as to spit upon supports the hypothesis that Paul was suffering from the disabling effect of epilepsy which made its presence felt while he was in Asia. This would have caused him not just physical pain but intense socially disabling scrutiny that resulted in him being ostracized by the society. The following section analyses the effect of such affliction in the society.

### 5.2.2.3 The Corinthians' attitude towards Paul's affliction in Asia

It has been suggested by Barnett that the "Corinthians have not heard this 'affliction' from Paul" directly, but it must have been reported to the Corinthians by "the Ephesian Christians" or "by Titus and the Macedonians bearers of 2 Corinthians."[47] He believes "Paul is here emphasizing the intensity rather than the fact of the 'affliction.'"[48] Similarly, Harris also points out that "the absence of detail concerning its precise nature and its exact location suggests that the Corinthians lacked information about the severity of the particular incident or sequence of events although they had knowledge of its occurrence."[49] Indeed, it seems more likely that Paul wanted the Corinthians to focus on the intensity of his sufferings rather than the identification of his affliction. Paul's rhetoric in verses 3–7, where Paul uses the present tense verbs consecutively in his discussion on his suffering and comfort, seems to indicate that the Corinthian congregation were well aware of the identification of his malady. Even when he talks of his Asian distress in verse 8, Paul uses the present indicative active θέλομεν (desire/wishes) and the infinitive present ἀγνοεῖν (to know). Thus, Οὐ γὰρ θέλομεν ὑμᾶς ἀγνοεῖν (1:8) specifies that they were "not able to understand," or they "disregard[ed]," the despair of Paul's sufferings.[50]

How did they disregard his sufferings, and what could be the nature of their attitude? Thrall has questioned the logic behind why the Corinthians and their instigators brought Paul's rhetorical inability to light in 10:10.[51] This,

---

47. Barnett, *Second Epistle*, 83.
48. Barnett, 83n11.
49. Harris, *Second Epistle*, 153.
50. The Greek word ἀγνοεῖν can also mean "not to understand (cf. Mark 9:32)," "sin in ignorance (cf. Heb 5:2)," or to "disregard (cf. 1 Cor 14:38)"; Gingrich, "ἀγνοέω," in *Shorter Lexicon*, 3). See Harris, *Second Epistle*, 153; Thrall, *Corinthians 1–7*, 15.
51. Thrall, *Corinthians 1–7*, 633.

if not anything else, seems to point towards an attempt to belittle Paul and find an opportunity to put him down. When Paul first came to Corinth, he made it a point to tell the Corinthians that it was with the power of the Spirit that he preached the gospel to them (1 Cor 2:4). However, now that he was unable to get healing from this affliction, it provided the perfect opportunity for his opponents to further their agenda of creating problems for Paul. If he had the power of the Spirit, why could he not heal himself (see 2 Cor 13:3; 12:8)? Thus, the adage "Physician, heal yourself" (Luke 4:23) would be an apt retort to Paul by his detractors.

Whether Paul's affliction was epilepsy or any other form of sickness, the Greco-Roman and Jewish cultures did not leave much room for an objective interpretation of any kind of illness. Take for instance the case of leprosy in the Hebrew Bible: one can agree that the most disconcerting consequence about this disease was not on the leprous person's wellbeing, but rather the effects their leprosy had on society.[52] In the case of epilepsy, Kelly believes that the "ancient texts" showed epilepsy as a "physiological condition . . . having demonic origins."[53] It was a common thing to connect epilepsy with that of spitting out or drooling in the Greco-Roman and the Jewish world. In the previous section, it has been pointed out that in antiquity, the practice of spitting and epilepsy went hand in hand.[54] This was because they thought epilepsy to be the devil's work and that by spitting on it, they would prevent others from getting epilepsy.[55] However, by equating afflictions like epilepsy with the devil, the people of antiquity connected this type of disability with a cultural judgment.

It would not be too far-fetched to think that the instigators knew Paul's affliction would cause a further complication between the Corinthians and Paul. This is because of the societal attitude that was prevalent towards any physical irregularities that deviated from the standard norms of the day. Just as they anticipated, the Corinthians allowed their "superstition and prejudice" to overcome their respect for Paul.[56] Therefore, Paul suffered comprehensively

---

52. See Pilch, *Healing*, 59; cf. Glessner, "Ethnomedical Anthropology," 25.

53. Kelley, "Punishment of the Devil," 206.

54. Plautus, *Captivi*, 3.4; cf. "Pliny, *Natural History*."

55. Pliny, *Natural History*.

56. According to Betz, "2 Cor 12:7–10 shows illness was likely to be interpreted by common people as demon possession" (*Galatians*, 225).

not just from the "chronic, incurable, physical affliction that caused acute, intense, disabling, sudden pain,"[57] but more so from the negative attitude of the Corinthians towards his affliction.

### 5.2.3 Paul's Statements in Defence of His Disability

As has been pointed out, this rhetorical unit is the *exordium* of the complete 2 Corinthians. One recollects that *exordium* is "the introduction of a speech, where one announces the subject and purpose of the discourse, and where one usually employs the persuasive appeal of ethos in order to establish credibility with the audience."[58] As a rule, the *exordium* reveals the rhetorical situation as well as explaining the problem that a rhetor is facing. In this case, Paul faced an uphill task of defending himself while persuading the Corinthians to correct their flawed view of his person and ministry. What are the main points of Paul's argument in his *exordium*?

#### 5.2.3.1 Statement 1: Paul directly appeals to God for comfort in his affliction (vv. 1-4, 8-10)

Paul's opening statement in verses 3-4 is rather revealing:

> Εὐλογητὸς ὁ θεὸς καὶ πατὴρ τοῦ κυρίου ἡμῶν Ἰησοῦ Χριστοῦ, ὁ πατὴρ τῶν οἰκτιρμῶν καὶ θεὸς πάσης παρακλήσεως, ὁ παρακαλῶν ἡμᾶς ἐπὶ πάσῃ τῇ θλίψει ἡμῶν εἰς τὸ δύνασθαι ἡμᾶς παρακαλεῖν τοὺς ἐν πάσῃ θλίψει διὰ τῆς παρακλήσεως ἧς παρακαλούμεθα αὐτοὶ ὑπὸ τοῦ θεοῦ. ("Blessed be the God and Father of our Lord Jesus Christ, the Father of mercies and God of all comfort, who comforts us in all our affliction to enable us to comfort [those who are] in any affliction through the comfort which we ourselves are comforted by God").[59]

If one takes a closer look at the way Paul developed his opening statement, one sees a resemblance of the rhetorical device known as "Anadiplosis."[60] In

---

57. Nash, "Paul's 'Thorn,'" 33.
58. See the definition of *exordium* in "Canons of Rhetoric."
59. Translation is the author's own, with the help of Greek lexicons, unless otherwise indicated.
60. Robert A. Harris defines *anadiplosis* as a rhetorical device that "repeats the last word of one phrase, clause, or sentence at or very near the beginning of the next. It can be generated in series for the sake of beauty or to give a sense of logical progression" (*A Handbook of Rhetorical*

addition, a "logical progression" of thoughts continues to build up by a repetition of the particular word "comfort" in this *exordium*. Thus, one observes the foundation of Paul's argument here, which is the anchoring of God as the father of all mercies and comfort. God is the one who comforts him in his affliction so that he may be able to comfort others in their afflictions, just as God comforts him. In this short and succinct opening statement, Paul manages to encapsulate the core of his defence against the Corinthians and their instigators' accusations against his disability. McCant concisely states, "Paul believes that only God is his judge, as he affirms in 1 Cor 4:4 and repeats at 2 Cor 12:19."[61] Hence, in one sweeping blow, it seems Paul's "defence robs the Corinthians of their rank as jurors. Their opinions have no bearing on Paul's apostolic status."[62]

Indeed, Paul pointed out to the Corinthians that God is the source of his comfort in his affliction. He intentionally used Εὐλογητὸς (blessing) right at the beginning of verse 3, instead of the usual "thanksgiving" (Εὐχαριστῶ) that he employed in his opening statement elsewhere (see Rom 1:21; 1 Cor 1:4; Col 1:3; 1 Thess 1:2).[63] This sets the tone that his argument is *forensic* in nature. It may be pointed out here that there is such a thing as a rhetorical device called *benedicto*, which is related to "Eullogia and is classically seen as a form of Antisogoge – a device meant for the beginning of the oration."[64] Here, by employing this rhetorical device, Paul's appeal to God as the judge is evident. Garland agreed that Paul's use of Εὐλογητὸς is reminiscent of "a classical Jewish liturgical formula"[65] (see Gen 24:26–27; 1 Kgs 8:15; Pss 41:13; 72:18–19; 89:52; 106:48; 2 Macc 1:17). Even in the rabbinical literature, the biblical passages seemed to be interpreted according to an appeal to God's attributes. For instance, "in Genesis Rabbah, one of the oldest collections of Midrashim," Rabbi Aha had "developed a Midrash in which Abraham, in his pleading for Sodom, specifically reminds God of his oath after the Flood."[66]

---

*Devices*, 2, quoted in *VirtualSalt.Com*, last modified January 5, 2010, https://www.virtualsalt.com/rhetoric2.htm#Parallelism).

61. McCant, *2 Corinthians*, 31.
62. McCant, 31.
63. Garland, *2 Corinthians*, NAC, 53.
64. Howards, *Dictionary of Rhetorical Terms*, 56.
65. Garland, *2 Corinthians*, 58.
66. Segal, *Joseph's Bones*, 323.

Rabbi Aha's interpretation points to Abraham as referring "to God as 'Judge of all the earth.'"[67] Segal thinks that Rabbi Aha's interpretation of Abraham's rhetoric was "not so much an appeal to reason and logic as it is an appeal to psychology."[68]

Can Paul's appeal to God as the judge point not only to a rhetorical argument that he made to the Corinthian Christians but also to his own psychological state of being? It certainly would not be far-fetched to think so. If one carefully observes the logic of Paul's argument in these verses, it is clear that the object of the nominative Εὐλογητὸς ὁ θεὸς (blessed be God) in verse 3 is made clear in verse 4, ὁ παρακαλῶν ἡμᾶς, where the accusative pronoun ἡμᾶς clearly stands for Paul and not the Corinthians.[69] This indicates that by this "jubilant thanksgiving to God" Paul was making an emphatic statement to the Corinthians to let them know that God is primarily the one who comforts Paul and not the Corinthians.[70] Garland is correct to point out that by the use of this particular word Paul "focuses on himself, not his addressees."[71] In analyzing this stylistic switch, Witherington acknowledges that there is a "hint . . . that all is not well between Paul and his converts," causing Paul to fully turn his focus on God.[72]

It is significant that Paul deliberately describes God as the Father of Jesus Christ in his defence. While one realizes that there are finer theological points to discuss, as Belleville correctly argues, "Paul's concern at this point is not with theological precision but with personal experience."[73] Hence, when Paul calls God the Father of Christ, from a disability perspective one understands that Paul is pointing to God as the source of everything for Christ as well. This is important for Paul if he was to identify and find meaning for his sufferings in the sufferings of Christ (2 Cor 1:5). If God did not abandon Jesus

---

67. Segal, 324.
68. Segal, 324.
69. Barnett, *Second Epistle*, 66. Please see footnote @@894 for an explanation of how Paul's uses of "we" can be understood as "I."
70. Martin, *2 Corinthians*, 8.
71. Garland, *2 Corinthians*, 53.
72. Witherington, *Conflict and Community*, 356. Witherington attributes this ill spirit as caused by outsiders who were "peddler[s] of God's word" and a bad influence on the Corinthians. However, this premise needs further rectification as the Corinthians themselves were equally to be blamed (*Conflict and Community*, 357n1 and n87). See also Fitzgerald, *Crack*, 156.
73. Belleville, *2 Corinthians*, 56–57.

but raised him from the dead, ultimately Paul could also put his trust in God (see Acts 9:5; 1 Cor 15:8; 2 Cor 12:3–4). This understanding is brought to light in vv. 8–10 where Paul narrates the hardship that he experienced in Asia that almost left him for dead. Paul believes that through the suffering he endured, he learned to trust in God rather than in himself (v. 9).

The grammatical construction of verse 9b, ἵνα μὴ πεποιθότες ὦμεν ἐφ' ἑαυτοῖς ἀλλ' ἐπὶ τῷ θεῷ τῷ ἐγείροντι τοὺς νεκρούς, is a purpose clause introduced by ἵνα and negated by μὴ together meaning "in order not to." Generally, the following participle πεποιθότες is rendered as "rely" (see NIV, RSV, NRSV) or "trust" (see ESV, KJV, NASB, and NET) by various translators. It is interesting that while the literal meaning is "convince or persuade," if the tense happens to be perfect or pluperfect then "rely or trust" can be used (see Matt 27:43; Luke 11:22).[74] This translation is not, however, rigid, for in some cases where the tense is perfect, the word would still be rendered as "convincing" (see Rom 2:19; Phil 1:6).[75] The purpose of this grammatical comment is to draw attention to Paul's condition, which made him learn to trust in God when he was experiencing sufferings. As the perfect particle πεποιθότες indicates, Paul might have relied on himself in the past, but now he is convinced not to rely on himself, but upon God who raises the dead (ἀλλ' ἐπὶ τῷ θεῷ τῷ ἐγείροντι τοὺς νεκρούς).[76]

This new understanding of God's action in raising the dead (that is, Jesus Christ) is crucial to Paul's argument for his defence. It enables him to see his disability in a new light, and even though he suffered intensely for it, ultimately God will comfort him just as God comforted Christ. Therefore, Paul realizes that even in the past, it was God who rescued him (as the aorist ἐρρύσατο indicates in 2 Cor 1:10), therefore he hopes (the perfect ἠλπίκαμεν again indicates that this is not a vain hope but that it actually happened in the past) that he will be rescued in the future (cf. the middle future ῥύσεται, 1:10) from this suffering. Thus, his trust in God is made absolute through Christ.

---

74. Gingrich, "πείθω," in *Shorter Lexicon*, 154.

75. "πέποιθάς verb indicative perfect active 2nd person singular from πείθω" in Rom 2:19 is rendered as "convincing" by NIV and NET.

76. Harris is hard-pressed to find the reason Paul uses the Greek word ἐγείροντι to describe the action of God when Paul "did not die as a result of the θλῖψις," (*Second Epistle*, 158).

### 5.2.3.2 Statement 2: Paul abundantly identifies his disability with the sufferings of Christ (2 Cor 1:5)

Paul succinctly states that his sufferings are intrinsically related to the sufferings of Christ, and through that connection he found new meaning and understanding to his sufferings. In 2 Corinthians 1:5 Paul writes, καθὼς περισσεύει τὰ παθήματα τοῦ Χριστοῦ εἰς ἡμᾶς, οὕτως διὰ τοῦ Χριστοῦ περισσεύει καὶ ἡ παράκλησις ἡμῶν. This informs the reader that Paul richly (περισσεύει – "rich," "abound," "abundance") identifies with the sufferings of Christ and at the same time, he finds comfort through the suffering of Christ. The word πάθημα generally describes "suffering" or "misfortune" that a person undergoes or even "an inward experience of an affective nature."[77] Similarly, πάσχω also indicates "an unfavourable sense" or to "endure" suffering.[78] In antiquity, the frequent use of πασχω implied various meanings such as, "'to suffer,' 'to undergo,' 'to experience' . . . misfortune, blows of fate, disfavour of men and gods."[79] For instance, "πασχω, used from Homer on, means basically 'to experience something' which comes from without and which has to be suffered," particularly that of "evil."[80] Josephus, the Jewish historian in his book *Antiquities of the Jews*, used this word πασχω alone to mean, "To suffer punishment" before "death."[81]

Although Paul's usages of πάθημα and πάσχω are pregnant with theological supposition, Hafemann's choice to overlook the "experiential" side in his explanation of Paul's suffering as suffering for his apostolic ministry amounts to ignoring Paul's physical disability.[82] Some pertinent issues need explanation as one addresses Paul's persuasive rhetoric further. First, what was the nature or substance of Christ's suffering? Second, why was Christ's suffering so important to Paul that he would find comfort from his suffering in Christ's suffering (2 Cor 1:5)? However, before proceeding to answer these questions, a brief discussion of scholars' interpretations of the genitive τὰ παθήματα τοῦ Χριστοῦ is in order.

---

77. Bauer et al., *Greek-English Lexicon*, s.v. πάθημα, 747–748.
78. Bauer et al., s.v. "πάσχω," 785.
79. Michaelis, "πασχω," in *TDNT*, 5:905.
80. Michaelis, 904.
81. Michaelis, "LXX and Judaism," in *TDNT*, 5:910.
82. Hafemann, "Suffering," 919.

According to Garland, broadly speaking, there are four different views taken by scholars of the genitive construct of the παθήματα τοῦ Χριστοῦ (suffering of Christ) in 2 Corinthians 1:5. The first view suggests that Paul is talking about "suffering on account of Christ." In addition, very closely related to this is the second view, which sees Paul as referring "to suffering ordained by Christ for believers."[83] The first view indicates that when writing about the sufferings of Christ, "Paul refers to the suffering that comes to him as a loyal apostle to Christ who preaches a message that sparks violent reactions from those who remain savagely hostile to God in this world (cf. 4:10–12)."[84] In the latter view, Paul is referring to the larger body of believers who suffer for the sake of Christ. For instance, Harris believes that "the genitive is relational, 'the sufferings associated with Christ,' or possibly subjective 'the sufferings imposed (on his followers) by Christ' (cf. Acts 9:15–16)."[85] Elsewhere, Kistemaker and Hendriksen state, "In this view, these are the sufferings that Christ's followers undergo for his church and kingdom,"[86] for it was Christ who ordained that his followers suffer for his sake.

However, the soundness of these interpretations comes into question from the relational use of the genitive.[87] According to Proudfoot, since there are many uses of the genitive case, "such as source, quality, subject, possession,"[88] one needs to be careful of one's interpretation. One must understand the crucial role that Jesus Christ played in the life of Paul. The book of 2 Corinthians (see 1:3–11; 2:14–16; 4:7–12; 6:1–10; 11:23–12:10; 13:4) abounds with "Paul's presentation of his sufferings, the mediatory role of his apostolic mission [which] *are all* grounded in the story of Jesus."[89] As discussed previously, Paul points to God as his ultimate judge and the source of his sufferings and comforts. In this sense, the genitive Χριστοῦ in verse 5 becomes a repeat of the same genitive in verse 3 (Χριστοῦ); hence, Paul is here repeating the fact that he is anchoring the suffering of Christ in God. This is consistent with the way Paul argues with the Corinthians as it indicates the trajectory of his

---

83. Garland, *2 Corinthians*, 65.
84. Garland, 65.
85. Harris, *Second Epistle*, 146.
86. Kistemaker and Hendriksen, *Exposition*, 43; MacArthur, *2 Corinthians*, 24.
87. Thrall, *Corinthians 1–7*, 108. Garland, *2 Corinthians*, 65.
88. Proudfoot, "Imitation," 144.
89. Lim, *Sufferings*, 38.

argument, where God becomes the central source of comfort, first for Christ and subsequently for Paul as well.

The third view, which suggests that Paul had the thought of a "Messianic suffering" in mind when he wrote about this, is also an unlikely explanation for this context.[90] The proponent of this view believes that "Paul may have in mind the birth pangs of the Messiah that God's people must undergo prior to the coming of the kingdom."[91] Granted, the gospel account of Jesus's ministry is not free from these kinds of expectations. For instance, "In Matt 24:8 (Mark 13:8) Jesus assumes Messianic sufferings to happen but applies it to the persecution of believers that will occur in the interim period before his Second Coming."[92] This led Baker to think that Paul was also influenced by the thought of Messianic suffering when he wrote about the sufferings of Christ.[93] However, some scholars suggest that the theological development of the Jewish concept of the suffering Messiah happened only during Rabbinical Judaism after the gospel account had been put into words.[94] According to Michaelis, even the Old Testament "offers no special word for suffering,"[95] and because of this, the concept of a suffering messiah hardly made any sense to the Jews (see 1 Cor 1:23).[96] For Paul, what made sense was not the messianic sufferings endured by Christ, but as Smith has pointed out, "the experiential elements" of his suffering that made so much sense to Paul's own sufferings.[97]

Finally, "the fourth view understands Paul to be referring to the suffering Christ himself endured."[98] This fourth view, according to Garland, is the most probable understanding of Christ's suffering according to Paul.[99] Barnett remarks, "Just as Christ suffered in his ministry and death from forces hostile to God, so, too, the apostle, in continuity with Christ, suffered in the course

---

90. Garland, *2 Corinthians*, 66.
91. Garland, 66.
92. Baker, *2 Corinthians*, 66.
93. Baker, 66.
94. See Wicher, "Ancient Jewish Views," 320.
95. Michaelis, "LXX and Judaism," in *TDNT*, 5:911.
96. Harold Louis Ginsberg, "Messiah," *Jewish Virtual Library*, accessed June 13, 2018, http://www.jewishvirtuallibrary.org/messiah.
97. Smith, "Reason," 89.
98. Garland, *2 Corinthians*, 66.
99. According to Garland, "this interpretation best fits the way the expression is used in 1 Pet 1:11; 4:13 and 5:1" (*2 Corinthians*, 66n68).

of his ministry and proclamation."[100] This means that when Paul wrote that he was carrying in his body "the dying of Jesus" (2 Cor 4:10–11), he actually was referring to the fact "that his apostolic ministry extends Christ's earthly ministry, which included suffering and hardship."[101] Paul fought "the same evil forces that sentenced Christ to the cross so that in his suffering he joins in the suffering and death of Christ."[102] Thus, Lim contends, "Paul most likely interprets the phrase τὰ παθήματα τοῦ Χριστοῦ εἰς ἡμᾶς as the sufferings he experienced in his apostolic ministry for Christ."[103]

While these scholars' interpretations are not without their merits, they seem to fail to penetrate the real reason for Paul wanting to identify his sufferings with that of Christ's. One can fully comprehend the purpose of Christ's sufferings for Paul only through the disability perspective. Paul was suffering from the negative impact of his disability brought upon him by the Corinthians as well as their instigators. For Paul, to readily identify and find meaning and a sense of purpose to his life, it is only logical to think that Jesus must have suffered the same, if not a more intense form of hostility from his enemies.

It has become normative to speak of the floggings and crucifixion of Christ as the extreme sufferings that Christ endured while on earth. However, recently, scholars have begun to look at the life of Jesus from a disability point of view and to realize that Jesus had to endure so many social stigmatizations that it made him virtually a disabled man in his own society. For instance, George has studied Jesus's life and mission from a disability perspective and has come up with insights that make one understand more clearly why Paul identified with the suffering of Christ.[104] George points to the humiliating experience of the "incarnation" of Jesus Christ as a helpless infant (see John 1:14). According to him, Jesus's incarnation "is a radically subversive theological proposition which, unlike Jewish or Greek understanding, affirms the 'able-bodied' eternal God taking over the human limitation, weakness and

---

100. Barnett, *Second Epistle*, 75.
101. Garland, *2 Corinthians*, 67; cf. Belleville, *2 Corinthians*, 56–57.
102. Garland, 67.
103. Lim, *Sufferings of Christ*, 63.
104. See George, "'(Dis)abled Jesus," 111–116.

disabilities in multiple respects upon Himself by the process of enfleshment."[105] Indeed, Paul identified this self-abasement of Christ in Philippians 2:7–8.[106]

Jesus according to all social norms was born as an "illegitimate." Matthew 1:19 shows that πνεύματος ἁγίου (the Holy Spirit) caused Mary to be with a child before she had any sexual relationship with her fiancé. When Joseph hears this, he "wishes to secretly release her" (ἐβουλήθη λάθρᾳ ἀπολῦσαι αὐτήν, Matt 1:19) from her pledge, but he is told not to do so in a dream (Matt 1:19). The possibility of "having a child outside of marriage"[107] being perceived as a scandal in antiquity must not be overlooked if one is to critically study the biblical text. In the case of Jesus, Bockmuehl believes that "the New Testament gospels notoriously fail to resolve a problem at the heart of their genealogies of Jesus."[108] The problem of dissimilar genealogies found in Matthew (1:16) and Luke (3:23) can be taken as an indirect confirmation of this evidence. One way to explain this dissimilarity is to say that it was the Jewish custom to trace ancestors either from the mother's side or the father's side. However, as Levin claims, the explanation of "the vast majority of commentators [who] simply refer to 'Jewish custom' or 'Jewish Law'" is not sustainable when there is "no Jewish precedence or proof of such evidence" to support this explanation.[109] On the other hand, McDougall has stated, "Children born to a union not recognised as legitimate, according to Jewish law (Deut 23:2), faced considerable disabilities in Ancient Israel at least in principle."[110] Therefore, one can posit with Robinson that Christ "is deliberately making himself about as outcast as possible" even from the start.[111]

If Paul's disability caused him to be socially awkward or stigmatized, the knowledge that Jesus started his life on earth as part of the extreme spectrum of society where shame, social discrimination, and prejudice were a part of his life must have been comforting to Paul. Moreover, Jesus's eventual death by hanging on a tree, which is a reminder of how a cursed man died in the Old Testament (Deut 21:23), is paradoxically a welcome notion to Paul. In

---

105. George, 111.
106. See George, 111.
107. Robinson, "Birth of Jesus."
108. Bockmuehl, "Scriptural Completion," 192.
109. Levin, "Jesus," 422.
110. McDougall, *Royal Bastard*, 25.
111. Robinson, "Birth of Jesus."

his mind, he may be connecting the dots between Jesus, who endured social stigmatization and was glorified by God, and himself, who was also greatly stigmatized because of his disability. According to Wan, Paul's sufferings because of his "lack of extravagant prowess and elegant presence compared to the super-apostles – are the points at which he identified with the suffering and death of Christ."[112] In other words, Paul's sufferings, because of his disability, become the source of his identification with the sufferings of Jesus Christ, who suffered the shame and social stigmatization of his people to the same degree if not much more.

### 5.2.3.3 Statement 3: Paul suffering from disability is important for the Corinthians (1:6–7)

In the preceding sections, Paul points out that God is the one who comforts him, and that he finds meaning and validation from the suffering of Christ. In the final point he makes to the Corinthians, Paul is pointing out the fact that his suffering is for the purpose of their "comforts and salvation" (1:6). It is interesting to find here that Paul is equating his sufferings, which resulted from his disability, as instrumental to the salvation of the Corinthians. Since he suffered because of his disability, he occupied a unique position as an intermediary between God, Christ, and the Corinthians. The conditional clause in verse 6 (introduced by εἴτε followed by the indicative present θλιβόμεθα in the protasis) shows that the assumptions that Paul makes in verses 6 and 7 are based on truth. Paul was really convinced that his sufferings benefited the Corinthians (ὑπὲρ τῆς ὑμῶν παρακλήσεως καὶ σωτηρίας). How so? Thrall correctly states, "'Salvation' for Paul, is an eschatological concept, consisting in the deliverance from God's wrath, and the restoration to man of his lost divine glory, which will take place at the Parousia" (see Rom 5:9; 13:11; 1 Cor 3:15; 5:5; Phil 1:28; 2:12).[113] Precisely because Paul suffered, he could gain deeper insights into the saving grace of God as well as the salvific work of Christ through his sufferings.

A person gaining better insight through experiencing suffering was not uncommon in antiquity.[114] For instance, suffering "according to Hesodius (*Opera et Dies*: 218) can and should increase experience and give a better

---

112. Wan, *Power in Weakness*, 14.
113. Thrall, *Corinthians 1–7*, 110; Cranfield, *Critical and Exegetical*, 88–89.
114. See Michaelis, "πασχω," in *TDNT*, 5:906.

insight into things."¹¹⁵ Aeschylus, in his work *Agamemnon*, also wrote, "Justice inclines her scales so that wisdom comes at the price of suffering."¹¹⁶ Thus, it is acceptable to say that because Paul suffered, he was able to gain deep insights, which otherwise he would have missed if he were not disabled. Thus, one could contend that Paul desired the Corinthians to understand his "disability" as not an end in itself but as a means to "experience the comfort of God . . . so he might be able to comfort others (2 Cor 1:3–7)."¹¹⁷ Therefore, his disability should be important for them: if the Corinthians suffered humiliation because they accepted Paul, who was spiteful in the eyes of other apostles or leaders, then their suffering would not be without its merits. Ultimately, since they shared in his suffering and shame, they would enjoy his rewards as well, which were comfort and salvation in the days to come.

Paul felt it necessary that the Corinthians should know they have everything to lose if they stopped sharing in his suffering. Paul was the connecting link between Christ and them. Garland's comment that "they should not look upon his suffering with such a jaundiced eye" for "if they do not share his sufferings, then they will not share his consolation" sums up well what the Corinthians' attitude should be towards Paul's disability.¹¹⁸ Various translators have rendered the genitive construction of τῶν παθημάτων in verse 7 as "our sufferings" (see NIV, ESV, NET, NASB, RSV), which leaves the question of who suffers ambiguous. Harris points out that this genitive construction is "probably anaphoric," thus better rendered as "these sufferings."¹¹⁹ However, this still does not clear up the identity of the sufferer. It could be just Paul himself,¹²⁰ or it could be Christ,¹²¹ or better still, it could be Paul identifying himself and Christ.¹²² If one connects Paul's use of the genitive phrase παθήμα-

---

115. Michaelis, "πασχω," 5:906. Hesiod "was the son of an immigrant from Aeolian Kyme (Cyme) in Asia Minor. He was among the earliest poets and teachers . . . before Orpheus and Mousaios and . . . homer," (Athanassakis, *Hesiod*, ix).

116. Aeschylus, *Agamemnon*, 250. Aeschylus (c. 500 BC) was one of the earliest "successful playwright[s] and one of the most respected citizens of the Greek city-state Athens" (Bailey, *Ancient Civilization*, 8.

117. Kruse, "Afflictions," 20.

118. See Garland, *2 Corinthians*, 70.

119. Harris, *Second Epistle*," 150.

120. Harris, 150.

121. Garland, *2 Corinthians*, 69.

122. As Wallace has pointed out, even though the "use of the genitive is fairly common," it is "largely misunderstood" (*Greek Grammar*, 95).

τα τοῦ Χριστοῦ in verse 5, it is possible to identify the τῶν παθημάτων as Paul and Christ himself. Regardless of how one wants to interpret it, the overriding sense of Paul's argument is not affected; Paul wanted the Corinthians to share (with Christ) in his sufferings.

From the perspective of a sociological approach, there is a strong undercurrent of the cultural anthropological models of "honour and shame" resonating in the *exordium* that very much sheds light on Paul's defence of his disability.[123] According to Pitt-Rivers, "Honour is the value of a person in his own eyes, but also in the eyes of his society. It is his estimation of his own worth, his claim to pride, but it is also the acknowledgement of that claim, his excellence recognised by society, his right to pride."[124] "On the other hand," as Malina explains, "people get shamed when they aspire to a certain status and this status is denied them by public opinion."[125] Witherington recognizes how much "honour and shame" permeated the Corinthians culture when he states, "public recognition was often more important than facts" and "the worst thing that could happen was for one's reputation to be publicly tarnished."[126] In Paul's *exordium*, one sees that Paul refuses to thank the Corinthians in his second epistle to them as he usually did in his other epistles. Instead, he redirects his gratitude to God who gives him comfort. At the same time, he informs them that he is the conduit to their comfort and salvation, which means he is important to them. From these, one sees that Paul is winning back his honour, which they tarnished even as they failed to comfort him in his sufferings.

To sum up the discussion in this section, there is nothing in the *exordium* to indicate that Paul wanted to thank the Corinthians for any reasons whatsoever. Instead, Paul presented himself as the middleman through which the Corinthians benefitted from his suffering. Thus, it is not surprising to find Paul directly appealing to God as it served his rhetorical purpose. In forensic rhetoric, it is the custom to address the judge directly.[127] Likewise, Paul, who had to defend himself from the Corinthians and the instigators, was directly

---

123. This model will resonate more as one exegetically analyses the substance of his defence from the other chosen passages (i.e. 4:1–18; 6:1–13, and 10–13).

124. Pitt-Rivers, "Honour," 21.

125. Malina, *New Testament World*, 52.

126. Witherington, *Conflict & Community*, 8.

127. Witherington, 356.

appealing to God as the judge. For Paul, the Corinthian Christians were the secondary recipients of whatever comforts and salvation (1:6) they were entitled to receive. In other words, the Corinthian Christians were dependent on Paul for their comfort. Therefore, Paul had every right to defend his person and his claim as their rightful leader in spite of the rejection and sufferings he met at the hands of the Corinthians because of his disability/affliction.

## 5.3 Applying a DH to the Exegetical Analysis of 2 Corinthians 4:1–18

In this unit, one sees Paul confronting the Corinthians by asserting his self-respect and defending his ministry. Lindgård considered this section to be an offering of an "implicit polemical section where Paul criticizes the Corinthians for not knowing him well enough."[128] Various scholars who have dealt with the rhetorical analysis of 2 Corinthians agree that this passage (4:1–18) falls under Paul's argument or defence of his apostolic ministry.[129] While these scholars offer no specificity with the rhetorical terms, however, Witherington mentions that this passage falls under the *probatio* or *refutatio* of Paul's argument.[130] Previously, this study understands that *probatio* (or *refutatio*) describes "the main body of the speech where one offers logical arguments as proof."[131] The *probatio* is devoted "to answering the counter arguments of one's opponent."[132] "Proofs" in rhetorical criticism "should be demonstrative" and they "should bear upon the particular point disputed."[133] One reiterates here again that this study advocates the unity of 2 Corinthians along with various scholars like Young and Ford, Witherington, Long, Hester, and Amador.[134] As such, the

---

128. Lindgård, *Paul's Line*, 220.

129. Long, *Ancient Rhetoric*, 233; Roetzel, *2 Corinthians*, 53; Amador, "Revisiting 2 Corinthians," 98–99; Kennedy, *New Testament Interpretation*, 87–91; Hughes, "Rhetorical Criticism," 343.

130. Witherington, *Conflict & Community*, 335. He specifically includes this passage under "Argument 1, Division 2" of the *probatio* (385).

131. See the definition of *confirmatio* in "Canons of Rhetoric."

132. See the definition of *refutatio* in "Canons of Rhetoric."

133. Aristotle, *Rhetoric*, 3.17.

134. Young and Ford, *Meaning and Truth*, 36; Witherington, *Community & Conflict*, 335–336; Long, *Ancient Rhetoric*, 230–236; Hester, "Unity," 411–432; Amador, "Revisiting 2 Corinthians," 92–111.

rhetorical situation or problem established previously in the *exordium* acts as the foundation of Paul's *probatio* in 4:1–18.

Moreover, in the previous section,[135] this study argues that the rhetorical situation or problem was the Corinthians' accusation that Paul's disability prevented him from being an effective apostle and that was the main reason why Paul defended his ministry and his person. Harris points out that Paul was "dealing with the effects of the proclamation of the gospel against the backdrop of the activity of [his] adversaries."[136] In addition to this, his opponents were questioning his weak and fragile body in relation to his ministry. Bultmann believes that the main problem Paul dealt with in his letter to the Corinthians was the "content of the apostolic preaching,"[137] which he needed to clarify. Additionally, one must note the intricacies of the content of Paul's gospel along with his person. Witherington noticed the close connection between the two when he pointed out how Paul "had been forced to commend himself because his integrity and ministry had been questioned and jeopardized."[138] As such, Paul's opponents questioning his body's weakened state in relation to his ministry is clearly valid. A cursory reading of the passage reveals how much struggle Paul had to endure and put up with because of his disability. In this particular *probatio*, Paul explains to them the substance of his ministry. He also elaborates rather eloquently on his willingness to sacrifice for it. In addition, he also explains the hope and reason why Paul held on to this ministry.

In what is the first *probatio* that this study is dealing with, this section analyses the proof of Paul's argument as to why he considered his "ministry" so valuable, so much so that it made him endure public shame and ridicule. However, before that, one must ascertain that this first *probatio* is in fact a rhetorical unit where one finds a compact and clarity of Paul's argument. To this end, the next section identifies this passage (4:1–18) as a rhetorical unit.

---

135. See section 5.3.2 of this chapter.
136. Harris, *Second Epistle*, 320.
137. Bultmann, *Second Letter*, 111.
138. Witherington, *Conflict & Community*, 385.

## 5.3.1 Rhetorical Unity of 2 Corinthians 4:1–18

The passage (4:1–18) serves as a rhetorical unit where one finds the passage containing an "introduction, body, and conclusion."[139] The main contention of scholars in regards to the place of 4:1–18 is that this passage must belong to a bigger passage where the beginning of 4:1 (διὰ τοῦτο) connects with 2:14–17 or 3:7–18. For instance, Thrall thinks that 4:1 connects with 2:14–17,[140] while Harris seems to think that 4:1 connects with 3:7–18.[141] On the Greek word διακονίαν (ministry) present in 4:1, Thrall comments, "Paul is speaking about the διακονία he has described in 2:14–3:13.75."[142] Moreover, Thrall also observes, "the ἔχω-formulae occur in 4:7, 13, as well as in 3:4, 12, and 4:1."[143] Martin is not so sure if 4:1 connects with 2:14 or 3:7, but ultimately chooses to conclude that Paul "closes his elaborate discussion opened at 2:14."[144] Thus, according to these scholars, 4:1–7 belongs to its preceding passages (2:12–3:18). They are not wrong to think so, for instance, there are many structural similarities, especially between 4:1–7 and chapter 3. Harris points out these similarities as follows:[145]

| 4:1–6 | 3:7–18 |
| --- | --- |
| v. 1 τὴν διακονίαν ταύτην | v. 8 ἡ διακονία τοῦ πνεύματος<br>v. 9 ἡ διακονία τῆς δικαιοσύνης |
| v. 3 κεκαλυμμένον (twice) | vv. 13–16 κάλυμμα<br>v. 18 ἀνακεκαλυμμένῳ |
| v. 4 ἐτύφλωσεν τὰ νοήματα τῶν ἀπίστων | v. 14 ἐπωρώθη τὰ νοήματα αὐτῶν |
| v. 4 τὸ μὴ αὐγάσαι | v. 7 μὴ δύνασθαι ἀτενίσαι<br>v. 13 τὸ μὴ ἀτενίσαι |
| vv. 4, 6 τῆς δόξης | vv. 7–11, 18 δόξα |

---

139. Watson, *Inventio*, 8.
140. Thrall, *Corinthians 1–7*, 298.
141. Harris, *Second Epistle*, 322.
142. Thrall, *Corinthians 1–7*, 298.
143. Thrall, 298.
144. Martin, *2 Corinthians*, 76.
145. Harris, *Second Epistle*, 320.

While the structural similarities between these are undeniable, Kistemaker and Hendriksen's suggestion that this introduction (4:1–7) is different from the rest of chapter 4 (i.e. vv. 7–18) is unwarranted.¹⁴⁶ Especially seen from a disability point of view, this section will discuss the strong thematic unity and a coherent progression of thoughts that runs right through 4:1–18. As such, the preceding passages (i.e. 2:14–3:1–18) serve to provide the foundation for understanding why Paul suffered much for this ministry, which he discusses in 4:1–18. Thus, the διὰ τοῦτο in 4:1 serves as the culmination of the preceding discussion on his ministry as well as the introduction to the rest of what Paul argues for in this passage (4:1–18).¹⁴⁷

In 4:1–7, Paul acknowledges that he has a ministry by God's mercy that makes him and his companions not "lose heart" (ἐγκακέω can also mean "become weary, tired, lose heart or despair"¹⁴⁸) in spite of all the sufferings and hardships. After he introduces his ministry, Paul refutes the charges that he and his companions were using "deceptions" and fraudulent means to spread their "gospel" (v. 2). He then sets the record straight by pointing out that they were plainly "setting forth the truth" and that their conscience "was clear" in the sight of God, and if there were some who did fail to comprehend Paul's gospel, the fault lay with them [the Corinthians] (vv. 2–3). It is likely that Paul was defending his gospel and at the same time attacking his opponents.¹⁴⁹ As one analyses the nuances of his ministry further below, the interrelatedness of his disability and his ministry will become clear. Suffice it here to note that just as he discussed in his *exordium*, the reciprocal relationship between God, Jesus, and Paul is evident again in his *probatio*. He takes great effort to point out that Jesus is the one they preached and that they were not commending themselves. Verse 7 then becomes the sum total of his ministry, where Paul rightfully acknowledges the source of the power that was evident in his ministry, and that is God.

In 4:8–12, Paul clarifies further the sacrifice he had to make for his ministry. He highlights the extent of what he was willing to suffer as well as the nature of his past and present sufferings on account of his ministry which

---

146. Kistemaker and Hendriksen, *Exposition*, 146.
147. See Thrall, *Corinthians 1–7*, 298.
148. Gingrich, "ἐγκακέω" in *Shorter Lexicon*, 54.
149. Harris, *Second Epistle*, 324.

was intrinsically related to his disability. This will also become clear as one further breaks down Paul's argument below. Here also, one finds the story of Jesus, which according to Stageman, is "the linchpin to Paul's argument in 2 Corinthians."[150] Indeed, the story of Jesus is essential to Paul's ministry. In fact, one can so far state that without Jesus, Paul's gospel would not have seen the light of day. This is because, as was previously highlighted before in the *exordium*, Paul identified intrinsically with Jesus's sufferings at the hands of his people. Furthermore, in 4:13–18, Paul made clear the hope for future glory that he saw in the risen Christ. Thus, one finds Paul's defence tinged with eschatology where God will make whole his disabled body (vv. 14, 16–18).

As Martin makes clear, Paul in his *probatio* responded, "to another line of criticism brought against his Gospel and his ministry.... It is as though his hearers were groping in darkness, and his preaching cannot help them because it lacks the demonstrable signs of power to convince them of its authenticity" (see 13:3).[151] Indeed, "Paul has every reason to be discouraged since his person is marked by weakness and his message is ineffectual (cf. 10:10)" according to the Corinthians and their instigators.[152] Thus, in this rhetorical unit, Paul wrestles with this accusation and attempts to persuade the Corinthians of the truth of his struggles.

## 5.3.2 *Probatio*: Paul Defends His Apostolic Ministry

*Probatio* is where the rhetor makes his point and argues for it further so that he may persuade the reader to side with him. From the preceding sections, it is clear that there is a thematic unity to Paul's argument where Jesus Christ is the centre that holds it together. Besides, Paul's arguments here specifically point to the close correlation between his sufferings and his ministry. The following sections deal with these arguments in detail.

### 5.3.2.1 Paul's ministry: Making sense of it from disability perspective

In 4:1, Paul tells the Corinthians that he is in "possession of this ministry" (ἔχοντες τὴν διακονίαν ταύτην). In order to be better acquainted with what

---

150. Stegman, *Character of Jesus*, 146, 249–257.
151. Martin, *2 Corinthians*, 76.
152. Martin, 76.

this ministry is, one has to see the preceding chapter 3.[153] Wright correctly observes that Paul had "not been side-tracked from the discussion of his ministry," which he started in the preceding chapter.[154] In chapter 3, Paul revealed that the Corinthian congregation were well aware of his ministry (3:2), however, he seemed to be reiterating that this ministry was from God (3:4) and that it was more spiritual in its origin (3:5) compared to the ministry of Moses, which was more physical in nature (3:7). From a disability point of view, Paul's description of his ministry in comparison to that of Moses is quite revealing. Paul considered his ministry better, and he was negative and critical of Moses's ministry which he called a "ministry of death," "a ministry of condemnation," a ministry that was written in letter (by a human rather than the Spirit) and that which kills even though there is glory in it (3:7, 9). Paul also blamed Moses directly because in his opinion the Israelites had a hard time understanding what Moses wrote because Moses was hiding the glory of his ministry by putting a veil over his face, which had been made glorious by his meeting with God at Sinai (2 Cor 3:13; see Exod 19:20–24; 34:29–33).

In contrast, Paul explained to them that although both ministries were glorious, Moses's ministry was no match for the ministry that Paul was advocating because there was "liberty" in his ministry (3:17). Paul considered his ministry far better than the ministry of Moses because he believed that the content of his ministry was Jesus Christ who was the very "image" (εἰκών) of God (4:4). The theological implication of εἰκών in relation to Jesus and God is not the purview of this study, so suffice it to say that by using this word εἰκών, Paul showed the deeply entrenched similarity between God and Jesus that was embedded in his mind (see Col 1:15; 1:19; 2:9; Phil 2:6).[155] Why was he against the ministry perpetrated by Moses who had been the Israelites' moral guardian and foundation since they first came out of Egypt? Why did he consider the ministry of Moses as restrictive and his as more liberating (see Gal 3:28; 2 Cor 3:17)? Why did Paul consider his ministry more "righteous"

---

153. See Martin, *2 Corinthians*, 76; Thrall, *Corinthians 1–7*, 298; Harris, *Second Epistle*, 322.

154. Wright, *Climax*, 189.

155. According to Harris, "τοῦ θεοῦ may be classified broadly as a genitive of relationship or more narrowly as a genitive of possession ('the image of God' is the image God has), but it could also be viewed as an objective genitive (that is, Jesus 'images' God)," (*Second Epistle*, 331).

than that of Moses (2 Cor 3:9)? Ultimately, as with Savage, one asks, "What was it about the law that engendered such hostility?"[156]

There has been a lot of scholarly discussion on the topic of how Paul related to Mosaic law, which is fundamentally Moses's ministry.[157] Some scholars believe that Paul was angry with Moses's ministry because he could not fulfil the law.[158] On the other hand, others would argue that Paul disregarded Moses's ministry in the light of the coming of the Messiah.[159] Some argue that Paul uses Jeremiah 31 as the origin for his new teaching on the law,[160] while others believe that Paul was "an interpreter and exponent of the teachings of Jesus" about the law.[161] Still, some scholars think that the "Hellenistic" teaching on law was influencing Paul.[162] For instance, Räisänen sees Paul's missionary experience among the Gentiles, and his loggerhead with the "Judaizers" who did not wish to contextualize, as the origin of his view on the law.[163] Then there are those scholars who would locate Paul's struggle with the law in his Christology.[164] While all these proposals in some way shed some light on the reason Paul cast Moses in a negative light as he described his ministry to the Corinthians, it fails to grasp the root cause of Paul's problem with Moses's law.

In what is an interesting hypothesis, Murphy-O'Connor thinks that Paul contrasted himself with Moses because the "Spirit-people were comparing Paul unfavourably with Moses" in Corinth.[165] Some in the Gentile community seemed to think highly of Moses. He was a revered figure in both Greco-Roman and Jewish antiquity. For instance, Strabo considered Moses worthy

---

156. Savage, *Power through Weakness*, 131.

157. Parkes, *Jesus*, 140; Räisänen, *Paul and the Law*, 6–161; Wright, *Paul*, contains an excellent historical survey of scholarly hypotheses on Paul's relationship with the law.

158. See Deissmann, *St. Paul*, 94; Weinel, *St. Paul*, 71–72; Andrews, *Ethical of Paul*, 29.

159. Schweitzer, *Mysticism of Paul*, 64; Stendhal, *Paul*, 84–86.

160. Roetzel, *2 Corinthians*, 65.

161. Branscomb, *Jesus*, 279; Longenecker, *Paul*, 128.

162. Knox, *St. Paul*, 11; Kim, *Origin*, 45.

163. Räisänen, *Paul and the Law*, 252–263. Räisänen's stand has been challenged exhaustively by Van Spanje in his work *Inconsistency in Paul?* He feels that Räisänen gets it wrong because he fails to "make sufficient use of hermeneutical rules appropriate to the interpretations of Paul's letters" (249).

164. According to Sanders, "What went wrong with the law is that it is not Christ" (*Paul and Palestinian Judaism*, 551, 552). He also believes that "Paul's exclusivist soteriology compelled him to reject the Law" (*Paul, the Law*, 17–64); Savage believes that Paul was discontent with the law because of "its failure to reveal Christ" (*Power through Weakness*, 134).

165. Murphy-O'Connor, *Theology*, 34.

enough to include him among the many "prophets [who] received so much honour as to be thought worthy even of thrones."[166] Pompeius Trogus, a historian during the time of Emperor Augustine, also praised Moses as having inherited "his father's knowledge [and] the comeliness of his person (36. 2.11)."[167] This hypothesis, although shedding some light on the reason why Paul would portray Moses in a negative way to the Corinthians, seems too ambitious a reading. While it is not "ill-suited to a predominantly Gentile audience" for Paul to compare and contrast his ministry with that of Moses,[168] to think Paul was angry at Moses because the Corinthians held Moses in higher regard than they did him is to not understand the depth of Paul's struggle with the effects of Moses's law in his life.

Paul identifies the problem with Moses's ministry ultimately to be that it led to death (see διακονία τοῦ θανάτου in 3:7) and that the glory was fading (3:7–11), clearly suggests that Moses's ministry, in Paul's understanding, lacked a comprehensive eschatological perspective. In this regard, Meyer's suggestion is on the right track because he sees Paul's problem with the "Mosaic (old) covenant" being that it is "fundamentally non-eschatological."[169] For instance, Paul talked much about his hope for the eschatological culmination of his weakened body in ultimate glorification (see 1:9–10; 3:18; 4:16–18; 5:1–5; 13:4). One can so far suggest that this hope for a glorified eschatological body is indicative of the suffering and struggle Paul endured because of his weakness.

Paul also describes Moses's ministry as διακονίᾳ τῆς κατακρίσεως while he terms his ministry as διακονία τῆς δικαιοσύνης (2 Cor 3:9). This is significant because Paul indicates that Moses's ministry brought about "condemnation" (κατακρίσεως), which in a way was him telling the Corinthian congregation that the main issue with Moses's ministry was that it condemned him as a human being. Thus, by extension, anyone who based his or her knowledge or argument from the law of Moses would ultimately condemn him as unfit, and his ministry as not worthwhile to consider. Now the crux of the matter is to find the reason Paul would think that Moses's ministry was condemning him.

---

166. Strabo, *Geography*, 16.2.39.
167. Justinus, *Epitome*, 36.2.11.
168. Savage, *Power through Weakness*, 109.
169. Meyer, *End of the Law*, 1.

This is where reading the text from a disability perspective helps in providing answers to the development of his ministry, which the Corinthians and their instigators were currently undermining.

In 4:7, Paul describes himself as "earthenware" in which his ministry was stored. The Greek word that Paul uses in this verse is ὀστράκινος, which literally means "made of earth/clay," and when used with σκευος, it indicates a vessel made from earth or clay.[170] Witherington is of the opinion that the "earthenware vessels may be a reference to the cheap pottery lamps made in Corinth and used for walking about at night."[171] While this suggestion has some merit, Paul might mean an actual clay vessel in which someone keeps his or her valuables. If he had meant a "clay lamp," then he would have used λύχνος, which is "the specific word for lamp, in combination with ὀστράκινος."[172] Instead, Paul used σκευος, which is "the general word [for] vessel," thereby indicating the use of keeping valuables in a clay jar.[173] According to Young, "Clay pots were used to store all sorts of things in the ancient world – grain, oil, money, even books."[174] Wilson narrates his experience about visiting the Cyprus National Museum in Nicosia where among the displays was "a clay pot lying on its side with a bunch of coins spilling out of its mouth" dating back to "the first century CE."[175]

Thus, one can surmise Paul is informing the Corinthians that the gospel he called "treasure" (θησαυρός) was stored in the weak and fragile yet endurable vessel that was his body. Thrall is on the right track when she states that Paul uses this metaphor because he "does not only wish to stress the unimpressive and vulnerable nature of his apostolic life. He also wants to indicate that despite all this he is the bearer of something glorious, comparable to actual treasure."[176] By comparing his body with earthenware, cheap and easily available, fragile, and not impressive, Paul is acknowledging his disabled condition. In connection to this, Harvey comments that earthenware vessels "in themselves [were] neither durable nor valuable . . . if they became contaminated

---

170. Bauer et al., *Greek-English Lexicon*, s.v "ὀστράκινος," 730.
171. Witherington, *Conflicts & Community*, 377.
172. Wilson, "Treasures in Clay Jars."
173. Wilson.
174. Young, *Brokenness and Blessing*, 75.
175. Wilson, "Treasures in Clay Jars."
176. Thrall, *Corinthians 1–7*, 324.

or ritually impure . . . they were to be smashed (Lev 6:28)."[177] This also is indicative of the prejudicial attitude that others were directing towards his weak bodily appearances (2 Cor 10:10). However, how does knowing Paul's disability help in explaining the formulation of his ministry that he set firmly against the ministry of Moses?

There are two important clues in the text that could explain this conundrum. First, Paul describes the ministry of Moses as a ministry of condemnation in 2 Corinthians 3:9. Paul, in his own testimony, talks about how he was a "Hebrew of Hebrews; in regard to the law, a Pharisee [and] for legalistic righteousness, faultless" (Phil 3:5–6). However, was it by choice that he chose to adhere to the sect of Pharisees? Most probably Paul was a Pharisee because his father was also one (Acts 23:6). The Pharisees, according to Paul, were the strictest sect in Judaism when it came to keeping and observing the laws (Acts 26:5). He confessed that he was ἄμεμπτος ("blameless," "faultless") in matters concerning the religious requirements of the law (Phil 3:6). His loyalty towards the law seems unchallenged at this point. Paul's talk about how advanced he was in Judaism beyond anyone else (Gal 1:14) indicates his sound mental faculty. Nevertheless, why would an intelligent and motivated young man confess to the Corinthians that the ministry of Moses, the bedrock of their traditional beliefs, was condemning him?

If one carefully observes the law of Moses in regard to how it deals with those who are disabled, it becomes clear that indeed the ministry of Moses was intrinsically condemning Paul since he was disabled. The Mosaic law's concept of God's holiness clearly alienated certain sections of the Jewish people, notably the disabled section. This is evident as one observes the rules in matters relating to temple worship. In Leviticus 21:16–23, one finds strict rules that any priest "who is blind or lame, disfigured or deformed, . . . with a crippled foot or hand, or who is a hunchback or a dwarf, or who has any eye defect, or who has festering or running sores or damaged testicles" must not "come near to offer the food of his God" (NIV). The only underlying reason that they could not come to offer (προσφέρω, LXX) "gifts" (δῶρον, LXX) was because they had a "defect" (מום, Lev 21:21). It is in this context that the comments of Schipper ring true. Schipper states, "One begins to see some of the cultural and ideological significance encoded in disability in the ancient

---

177. Harvey, *Renewal through Suffering*, 55.

Near East when one examines certain contexts."[178] Beyond just a prohibition relating to temple service, the authors of the Hebrew Bible also have quite negative attitudes towards any "symbol" of disability. For instance, Raphael observes, "The rhetorical use of disability imaginary refers rarely to people with disabilities, but rather often refers to the able-bodied. Quite a lot of it refers to people whose eyes and ears and limbs work quite well."[179] As a case in point, one observes Deuteronomy 28:29, where a "simile involving blindness" is used which is quite a negative depiction of "blindness."[180]

However, what does this have to do with Paul, who was not a priest from the tribe of Levi, but a Benjamite, as he himself claimed (see Phil 3: 5)? It is true that Paul was not a priest and as such, these restrictions should not have caused him personal distress. Nevertheless, during the time of Paul, the fault seems to lie with the Pharisees who held absolute authority. Their interpretations and observations of the law's requirements were absolute.[181] This is not surprising because from the time Queen Alexandra took the throne from her husband Alexander Janneus in 76 BC until Titus destroyed the temple in AD 70, the religious power, including the temple rites and Mosaic interpretation, belonged to the Pharisees.[182] They were so powerful that even the Sadducees had to consult them about almost everything. Josephus explained that the Pharisees were able to exercise much power because they had the support of the people.[183] For instance, in the Babylonian Talmud the whole chapter of Tractate Yoma discussed the Pharisees' interpretation of Mosaic law for the rules that the high priest must observe "for the Service of the Day of Atonement."[184] Not only this, but according to Kohler, "the same sanctity that the priests in the Temple claimed for their meals, at which they gathered with the recitation of benedictions (I Sam 9:13) and after ablutions, the Pharisees established for their meals, which were partaken of in holy assemblies after

---

178. Schipper, *Disability Studies*, 67.
179. Raphael, "Images of Disability," 4. See also Raphael, *Biblical Corpora*.
180. Schipper, *Disability Studies*, 68.
181. Edersheim, *Life and Times*, 1466; Sanders, *Judaism*, 403, 412; Deines, "Pharisees," 495–496.
182. *Jewish Encyclopedia*, "Pharisees," by Kaufmann Kohler.
183. Josephus, *Antiquities of the Jews*, 18.1.4, 572.
184. "Tractate Yoma: Chapter 1."

purifications and amidst benedictions."[185] As such, for a devoted Pharisee like Paul not to be able to participate fully in the religious functions because of the strict observance of rituals would clearly be a cause of concern.[186] Therefore, one can claim that Paul, disabled but mentally perceptive, no doubt would have felt the power of how the Pharisees' interpretations of Mosaic law imposed upon him.

Second, the restrictions of the eschatological glory under the ministry of Moses could have been the most important factor that motivated Paul to search for an alternate ministry. It is quite significant to observe that there was no room for the PwD in the eschatological kingdom according to some of the teaching of the literature during Second Temple Judaism. According to Schipper, "the War Scroll states that . . . 'Anyone who is lame (פסח) or blind (עור) or crippled (הגר) or a man with an eternal blemish (מום) in his flesh or a man stricken by an uncleanness of his flesh – all of these may not go with them [to war] (1QM 7:4–5a).'"[187] Moreover, "The Rule of the Congregation" talked about the expectation of what would happen to Israel in those days. For instance,

> [The] rule [of] Israel in the final days states that: everyone who is defiled in his flesh, paralysed in his feet or 6 in his hands, lame, blind, deaf, dumb or defiled in his flesh with a blemish visible to the eyes, or the tottering old man who cannot keep upright in the midst of the assembly, these shall not enter to take their place among the congregation of famous men . . . when [God] begets the Messiah with them (1QS$^a$ 2.5–12).[188]

One finds this kind of teaching also in Yadin's translation of 4Q Florilegium 1:3b–4: "The Sanctuary of the Lord thy hands have established. The Lord shall reign forever and ever. That is the house where there shall not enter anyone in whose flesh there is a permanent blemish and an Ammonite and a

---

185. *Jewish Encyclopedia*, "Pharisees," by Kaufmann Kohler; see also Edersheim, *Sketches*, 115.

186. There are grounds to think that Paul was a member of the Sanhedrin (see Acts 26:10); however, as Murphy-O'Connor puts it, it is possible that Luke may have "exaggerated" Paul's testimony since his letters are silent in regards to this (*Paul*, 66).

187. Schipper, *Disability Studies*, 67.

188. Martinez, *Dead Sea Scrolls*, 127.

Moabite and a bastard and an alien for ever and ever."[189] The problem with this teaching is that disabled people cannot be a part of the Messianic kingdom. Thus, Baumgarten is right to point out that "the Qumran law, by analogy to the disqualifications for the priesthood in Leviticus 21, is broadened to apply to all permanent physical disfigurations."[190] Scholars like Gordon Fee have commented that "eschatological yearning should not be interpreted as an 'existential dilemma,' since [Paul] has none."[191] However, this line of interpretation is just not sustainable given the fact that Paul wrote much about the eschatological yearning in 2 Corinthians (see 2 Cor 1:10; 3:18; 4:16–18; 5:1–10). Because of such teachings and interpretations, there was hardly any room for him under the ministry of Mosaic law (other than condemnation). Ultimately, a disability perspective allows one to gain a better understanding of why Paul would have considered his ministry an upgrade to that of Moses'.

### 5.3.2.2 *The centrality of Jesus to Paul's sufferings*

The previous section explains that the strict interpretations and observations of Mosiac law especially for the PwD during Paul's time were at the root of his antagonistic attitude towards Moses's ministry. This is because, in spite of devoting his whole life to Mosiac law, it may have restricted Paul from having a fully functioning part in Jewish rituals as well as excluding him from enjoying eschatological glory. The resultant simmering resentment may allow one to suggest that Paul's desire for eschatological liberation and the need to belong without condemnation became two important factors for why Paul embraced Jesus whom he considered central to his ministry. In 2 Corinthians 4:4–6, Paul clearly describes to the Corinthians that his ministry is all about Jesus and the revelation of his glory that he received. Right from the *exordium* (see 2 Cor 1:3, 5), one is already aware of the centrality of Jesus in Paul's defence. In the *exordium*, one sees that the reason Jesus was so central to Paul's theology was that Paul felt a close affinity to the stigmatized yet glorified Jesus, and considered Jesus as the ultimate solution to his existential dilemma. Here, in this section, Paul once again argues that his ministry is to preach the lordship of Christ (2 Cor 4:5). Paul describes

---

189. Yadin, "Midrash," 95–96.
190. Baumgarten, *Studies in Qumran Law*, 76.
191. Fee, *Paul's Letter*, 148n38.

his willingness to undergo suffering for the sake of his ministry (4:8–10). He clearly states that his suffering, and motivation to suffer more for his ministry, is because he believes in the future glory of his disabled body (4:13–18). His faith is not a vain one but is firmly rooted in the risen Christ (4:14). However, since Paul founded his ministry on the centrality of Jesus, one must ask if Paul knew the real historical Jesus or if his knowledge was based on hearsay. If so, what made him shift his allegiance to the one whom he hardly knew and had persecuted via his followers?

There are differing opinions on whether or not Paul knew the real historical Jesus.[192] According to Patterson, Paul "pays so little attention to the historical figure Jesus of Nazareth that, paradoxically, one has been forced to conclude that Paul really did not know much about Jesus, or perhaps even that Paul simply was not interested in the historical person Jesus."[193] While some scholars like Tabor would state convincingly "Paul never met Jesus,"[194] others like Barnett think that there could have been a point of contact between Paul and the historical Jesus.[195] For instance, "when Jesus first came up to Jerusalem as a public figure, Paul had been living in the city for more than a decade [and] could hardly have been unaware of the current of thoughts in the Holy City."[196] It is true that from the evidence of the text, Paul barely concerned himself with the historicity of Jesus's life except to narrate what must have been the earliest creeds of his followers: that, according to the scriptures, Jesus died and rose again on the third day (1 Cor 15:3–4).[197] The aorist παρέλαβον in 1 Corinthians 15:3 shows that Paul received this knowledge from someone else.[198]

Nevertheless, Paul's argument in this rhetorical unit suggests strongly that Paul knew of the death and suffering of the historical Christ on the cross (2 Cor 4:10; 1 Cor 2:2) and a first-hand experience of the resurrected Christ (1 Cor 15:8; 2 Cor 4:14; 12:4–9; cf. Acts 9:5). Thus, the turning point

---

192. See Fraser, *Jesus and Paul*, 11–32; Dungan, *Sayings of Jesus*, xviii–xxix; Wilson, "From Jesus to Paul," 1–21.

193. Patterson, "Paul," 23.

194. Tabor, *Paul and Jesus*, 1.

195. Barnett, *Paul*, 16.

196. Barnett, 15.

197. Kistemaker and Hendriksen, *Exposition*, 528.

198. See Thiselton, *First Epistle*, 1186.

in Paul's life seems to have been the realization that suffering because of his disability was not an end in itself but an opportunity for something much more glorious in the future. In other words, for Paul, his disability was the focal point through which the historical Jesus's suffering, dying, and rising from death made absolute sense.[199]

As such, one is not surprised to find that some in Corinth were unresponsive to Paul's ministry (see 2 Cor 4:3), a ministry that he formulated out of his disability.[200] They failed to grasp the significance of his ministry, which was a means by which they could come to understand and be partakers of the glory of God (see 2 Cor 1:11; 4:15). As Savage points out, some of them could be asking, if Paul's "ministry is superior to that of Moses, then why is it so dark and uninspiring?"[201] Indeed, "where is the glory of his new covenant ministry that he so boldly announced (cf. 2 Cor 3)?"[202] The underlying reason for such an attitude, as has been pointed out, was that Paul formulated his ministry from a point of weakness, that is, his identification of his disability with the crucified Christ and his weakened condition (see 1 Cor 2:3). Because of this, Paul had a difficult time making converts, especially of the Jews in Corinth (see Acts 18:6), and this could have acted as proof to the rest of the Corinthian congregation that Paul's ministry lacked power.[203] Paul explained to them that the glory of Christ in the gospel he proclaimed was hidden only to those who were perishing (2 Cor 4:3).

However, was he making a veiled threat to the Corinthians by stating this? Was Paul insinuating to them that if they were against his gospel, then they were in danger of perishing? Scholars such as Thrall think that when Paul uses the Greek word ἀπολλυμένοις (perishing), he could not have had the Corinthian Christians in mind.[204] However, in some of the other Pauline texts where ἀπόλλυμι and its cognates occur, such as in "1 Cor 8:11, 10:9–10, 15:18 and in Phil. 1:28; 3:19," the context suggests strongly that Paul used

---

199. See George, "Resurrected," 313.
200. See Thrall, *Corinthians 1–7*, 304.
201. Savage, *Power through Weakness*, 111.
202. Matera is right to point out that "what [Paul] writes here is applicable to all members of the new covenant community" (*2 Corinthians*, 114).
203. Hughes, *Paul's Second Epistle*, 124–125.
204. Thrall, *Corinthians 1–7*, 305.

this Greek word to the believers themselves.[205] For instance, if one takes the case of 1 Corinthians 15:18, it is clear that the context indicates a rebuke to the Corinthian congregation, indicating that if they fail to believe Christ rose from death, then they are indeed "perishing."

In this rhetorical unit, Paul told the Corinthians that if they failed to see the significance of his ministry, which he called a "treasure," and concentrated only on his weak body (4:7), then they failed to grasp his gospel which was but a proclamation of the lordship of Jesus (4:5) and the glory of the risen Christ (4:4). They failed to grasp that his disabled body was the vessel of this glorious eschatological opportunity and the means by which they might also share in that future glory (4:15) because a veil was obstructing their understanding. Martin's comment at this point is informative,

> We know that a major debating point at Corinth was precisely the issue: Where is the real φανέρωσις, the true manifestation, of divine strength (cf. 4:2, 5:10, 11)? Paul's opponents appealed to their charismatic presence and signs (12:12). Paul himself saw the power of God in his weakness (12:1–10) because there he identified with him who was "crucified in weakness" (13:3).[206]

Paul writes to them in 4:10, πάντοτε τὴν νέκρωσιν τοῦ Ἰησοῦ ἐν τῷ σώματι περιφέροντες, ἵνα καὶ ἡ ζωὴ τοῦ Ἰησοῦ ἐν τῷ σώματι ἡμῶν φανερωθῇ (Paul again repeats the exact thoughts in the next verse, 4:11). The conditional clause introduced by ἵνα in the second colon clearly informs the reason Paul equates his weakened body as carrying the νέκρωσιν (death) of Jesus. Just as he identified (περιφέροντες) his disabled body with the death of Jesus continually (the adverb πάντοτε indicating continuity), he also hopes that he might manifest the life of Jesus in his body. His disability must have caused him much suffering, but he found strength in identifying his weak and "unpresentable body" with that of the "dying" (νέκρωσις) Jesus, for he experienced Jesus's glorious transformation when he encountered him on his way to Damascus (Acts 9:5).

However, can one ascertain the nature of this νέκρωσις, and in the process gauge the severity of Paul's sufferings as he identifies with the νέκρωσις

---

205. Thrall, 305.
206. Martin, *2 Corinthians*, 88.

of Jesus?²⁰⁷ Dunn is correct to point out that by saying this, Paul "reflects in his person the weakness and humility of Christ and so must endure the same – if not exactly in substance at least in principle – sort of ridicule and scorn, and even physical abuse, which Jesus himself experienced in his dying on the cross."²⁰⁸ Nevertheless, as was pointed out previously, he would have endured "ridicule and scorn" even before he ever met the risen Christ Jesus on the road to Damascus. The interpretations of Mosaic regulations against disability had done him an injustice and had created in him an existential anxiety that only made sense when he met the risen Christ. Thus, Paul's identification of the νέκρωσις of Jesus takes on an added significance when seen from a disability perspective.

A further analysis of the Greek word νέκρωσις (in 4:10) from a disability perspective reveals three significant insights that deepen the understanding of why Paul employs this word. First, the word is "used by ancient Greeks predominantly in reference to dead and/or dying tissue" which could be extremely painful.²⁰⁹ According to Coenen, when νέκρωσις sets in, "The body increasingly slumps, shivers, and swells, death grows more imminent . . . being eaten away and its decomposition renders one both weak and noxious. The post-mortem period only continues and intensifies the processes and breakdowns that precede death."²¹⁰ As such, "When Paul employs the word [νέκρωσις], then, he is using one of the starkest words at his disposal."²¹¹ Paul is right to use this word if he wanted to highlight the intensity of his suffering before them by implying the suffering of the historical Jesus.²¹²

Second, by using νέκρωσις Paul draws attention to the social stigmatization caused by the Mosaic regulations regarding the handling of dead bodies (see Lev 21:11; Num. 9: 6–10, 11, 16). According to Coenen, "The Mosaic Law draws an absolute boundary between the sphere of death and that of life. He who comes directly or indirectly in contact with the dead is unclean,

---

207. See Dunn, *Jesus and the Spirit*, 335.
208. Dunn, 335.
209. Fitzgerald, *Crack*, 177.
210. Coenen, "νεκρός," in *New International Dictionary*, 443.
211. Coenen, "νεκρός," 443.
212. Some scholars do not think that Paul was talking about the νέκρωσις of the historical Jesus (see Kramer, *Christ*, 200); cf. Gorman's comments, "Majority of scholars today do not believe Paul is narrating his own pre-conversion Jewish experience" (*Apostle*, 436).

i.e., separated from Yahweh."[213] By pointing to the similarity of the "dying of Jesus" with the "decaying of his outer body" (ἔξω ἡμῶν ἄνθρωπος διαφθείρεται, 4:16), Paul seems to be implying that Jesus also underwent the same prejudicial attitude from the people. The present indicative passive of διαφθείρεται indicates that the suffering of Paul was an ongoing process.

Third, νέκρωσις seems to have developed a new dimension in the New Testament's usages of this word. No longer is the word "used literally of people who are in the state of death (cf. Gen 23:3ff; 2 Kings 19:35; Deut 18:11)."[214] In addition, the hopelessness of dying or the morbid attitude towards those who are dead was no longer the focal point. For instance, in the Old Testament, the psalmist morosely stated that the "dead do not praise the LORD" (Ps 115:17 ESV), and the Teacher cynically stated, "But whoever is among the living has hope; a live dog is better than a dead lion" (Eccl 9:4 NET). This gives way to a more hope-filled attitude. Statistically, in the New Testament, "in no less than 75 places *nekros* is the object of *ereiro*, to awaken, or anastasis (resurrection), or their cognate words. In addition to this, there are a number of similar combinations, such as with *zoopoieo*, to make alive (Rom 4:17; Col 2:13)."[215] What this indicates is that νέκρωσις is not the end of a person's earthly life. It is no longer the "dismal" and "hopeless" situation of humanity. Rather, it is the end of suffering, a means of glorious transformation of ones "temporal" and decaying body (4:18, 16) "when viewed in the light of the resurrection of Jesus" (see 1 Cor 15:51–55).[216]

Ultimately, for Paul, the treasure that was his ministry was the proclamation of the lordship of Christ (4:5), who is the very image of God (4:4b).[217] Paul believed (4:13) in the same Jesus who suffered and died a shameful death on the cross (4:10), whom God raised gloriously from the dead (4:14), and who now acts as a beacon of hope for all those who seek eternal glory (4:17).[218] He believed that just as God raised Jesus from the dead, God will also make his disabled and suffering body whole again with Jesus, and

---

213. Coenen, "νεκρος," in *New International Dictionary*, 444.
214. Coenen, 444.
215. Coenen, 445.
216. Coenen, 445.
217. See Witherington, *Conflict & Community*, 386.
218. See Jervis, "God's Obedient Messiah," 22–23.

together they will be with God (4:14).[219] As the present indicative of the verb πιστεύομεν (from the root πιστεύω, 2 Cor 4:13) suggests, for Paul, the act of believing was an ongoing process. Believing involved knowing what had happened before and trusting that the one who let it happen will once again make it happen.

That is why his personal experience of the risen Christ on the road to Damascus was so crucial to his life. It provided him with an anchor to face the future challenges that the spreading of his gospel will bring about, quite notably a negative focus on his disability. Since he had received such a life-changing revelation in Christ, Paul did not mind suffering in his disabled, mortal body, for he knew "that the one who raised the Lord Jesus from the dead will also raise [Paul] with Jesus" (4:14). His "outwardly" disabled body thus took on a new meaning with such powerful revelations. All the injustice he suffered was just "temporary" (4:17). No longer did he see it as a disadvantage, but it became for him a catalyst to make him identify more with Jesus so that he might be able to achieve "an eternal glory that far outweighs them all" (4:17–18).

Therefore, he did not "lose heart" (4:16) but ploughed on ahead. In 4:8–9, Paul eloquently describes his suffering for the sake of his gospel. Witherington correctly points out that these verses "consist of eight present tense middle or passive participles in four contrasting pairs linked by *all' ouk* ('but not')."[220] One recollects that in the preceding verse (4:7), Paul informed the reader of the "treasure" that he kept inside his disabled body. Here, in 4:8–9, Paul enlightened the Corinthians that this disabled body was no pushover, but very resilient. However, "Paul adds that in his case his frailty ought to make obvious the power is coming from God and not from himself" (see 4:7b).[221] Indeed, a closer analysis of 4:8–9 shows that there is definitely an underlying "antithetical" thought between Paul's weaknesses and God's empowerment, as shown below.[222]

 ἐν παντὶ θλιβόμενοι (being oppressed in everything)
  ἀλλ' οὐ στενοχωρούμενοι (but not restricted [cf. 6:2]),

---

219. Matera, *2 Corinthians*, 116.
220. Witherington, *Conflict & Community*, 387.
221. Witherington, 387.
222. Roetzel, *2 Corinthians*, 78.

ἀπορούμενοι (perplexed)
ἀλλ' οὐκ ἐξαπορούμενοι (but not despairing),[223]
διωκόμενοι (being persecuted)
ἀλλ' οὐκ ἐγκαταλειπόμενοι (but not forsaken),
καταβαλλόμενοι (being struck down)
ἀλλ' οὐκ ἀπολλύμενοι, (but not dying)

How does one explain this seemingly excellent example of "rhetorical skill" that Paul shows in these verses?[224] According to Fitzgerald, this is the first instance where one finds "Paul's *peristasis* catalogues in 2 Corinthians."[225] Fitzgerald uses the term "*Peristasis* catalogue" to describe a "catalogue of circumstances [which] may be either 'good' or 'bad' or both."[226] According to him, "The term *peristasis* was well-established in rhetorical circles by the first century, in both Greek and Latin,"[227] and as such, "lists of suffering were commonplace in antiquity, especially in Cynic-Stoic diatribe."[228] For instance, Plutarch, Plato, and Seneca had employed this type of rhetoric.[229] Furthermore, in Epictetus's *Discourses*, one reads a similar *peristasis* catalogue: "Show me one who is sick, and happy; in danger, and happy; dying, and happy; exiled, and happy; disgraced, and happy."[230] Witherington notes, "Epictetus and the NT share the conviction that *peristasis* or 'tribulation' is sent by God and is an opportunity to demonstrate moral character."[231] If so, Paul could have employed this type of *peristasis* to "create empathy for his case."[232] In other words, "the rhetorical function of this material is that they are part of the attempt to establish Paul's ethos or character and the credibility of his ministry in the eyes" of the Corinthian congregation. Indeed, it has

---

223. Harris writes that the "colorful compound verb *exaporeomai* means 'be in extreme difficulty or doubt.' Its components point to the total (*ex*-) unavailability (-α-) of an exit (*poros*, 'passage') from oppressive circumstances" (*Second Epistle*, 154).

224. See Witherington, *Conflict & Community*, 387.

225. Fitzgerald, *Crack*, 166.

226. Fitzgerald, 45.

227. Fitzgerald, 37.

228. Fitzgerald, 169.

229. See Fitzgerald, 169–171.

230. Epictetus, *Discourses*, trans. Higginson, bk 2.

231. Witherington, *Conflict & Community*, 388.

232. Witherington, 388.

been established previously that Paul's "character or ethos was very much in doubt in Corinth."²³³

Now, with this concise yet eloquent construction of his sufferings, Paul tells the Corinthians that his character is without blemish. Though he may be weak and not measure up to their expectations, he more than made up for his deficiency in the hardships and struggles he underwent because he cared deeply for them. In spite of the similarity of Paul's rhetoric in 4:8–9 to the Stoic or Cynic sages, there are also differences. Whereas Seneca's sage "knows his own strength and is full of self-confidence, Paul knows God's strength and is full of confidence in him."²³⁴ Wan also observes that unlike the Stoics who thought a person showed his or her superiority by summoning their "internal psychic resources [to] become indifferent to all adversities under whatever circumstance, Paul, however, is advocating precisely the opposite."²³⁵

As such, Roetzel's observation that "more than a simple list of hardships, Paul's catalogue in 4:8–9 is a series of contrasts" by which Paul informs them that he does "not [want] to live above suffering, but to embrace it as a necessary part of his calling."²³⁶ Indeed, as his description in the first part of each clause shows, his weak and disabled body is a cause of concern. However, the second part of each clause shows that God is the one who gives him the strength and the power to go on. Ultimately, Paul argues that all his sufferings are for the benefit of the Corinthians (4:15), so that someday they will share in the "glory far beyond all comparison" (4:17).

## 5.4 Applying a DH to the Exegetical Analysis of 2 Corinthians 6:3–13

2 Corinthians 6:3–13 also comes under the *probatio* where Paul "offers logical arguments as proof" of his ability.²³⁷ It contains one of Paul's most "elegant" rhetorical constructions as he appeals his case to the Corinthians and shares how much he values his ministry (6:3–13). In 5:20–6:1–2, Paul implored the

---

233. Witherington, 388.
234. Fitzgerald, *Crack*, 166.
235. Wan, *Power in Weakness*, 79.
236. Roetzel, *2 Corinthians*, 71, 73.
237. See the definition of *confirmatio* in "Canons of Rhetoric"; Witherington, *Community & Conflict*, 398–401.

Corinthians to be reconciled to God and accept him as one who spoke for Christ. Then in what follows, "Paul explains what is involved in the exercise of that ministry (6:3–10)."[238] Paul's appeal is genuine and, at the same time, heart-wrenching. He wishes that the Corinthians would not "discredit" (6:3) his ministry just because they have something against him. Paul has suffered so much for this ministry in the hope that they may also benefit from it. In this passage, Paul "validate[s] his credentials as an ambassador for Christ (5:20), as a suffering and therefore true apostle."[239]

As was pointed out previously, Paul had to defend himself from the accusation that his ministry was not effective because it stemmed from his disability. Martin correctly points out that "Paul's ministry [was] under a cloud of suspicion."[240] Although the rhetorical situation clearly has to do with Paul's person in relation to his ministry once again, at this point Paul's argument is focussing on proving his personal integrity. The reason for this seems to be the fact that Paul wants "to present his ministry as pure" and irreproachable (6:3–4).[241] As Witherington points out, "indeed, the whole function of this letter is to remove such obstacles or *exigences*, saying whatever it takes within the bounds of personal integrity to produce that result."[242]

However, it seems unwarranted for Witherington to state specifically that Paul's defence is a "defense of his apostleship" and "not defense of himself."[243] It is illogical to think that one can dichotomize his ministry (or his apostleship) with that of his person. The two are intrinsically related, and if Paul could not defend his personal integrity, then he would fail to defend his apostleship and by extension his ministry. As one examines this passage more closely through a DH, this section will show that Paul once again appeals to the Corinthians that his personal integrity is beyond reproach, and thus, they should accept him and his ministry.

---

238. Harris, *Second Epistle*, 464.
239. Harris, 464.
240. Martin, *2 Corinthians*, 170.
241. Martin, 171.
242. Witherington, *Community & Conflict*, 398.
243. Witherington, 398.

## 5.4.1 Rhetorical Unit of 2 Corinthians 6:3–13

Although 2 Corinthians 6:3–13 is a continuation of Paul's argument concerning his ministry and the desire for the Corinthians to accept him, just like the other passages being discussed (2 Cor 1:3–11 and 4:1–18), this passage also presents itself as a rhetorical unit. One recollects that for a passage to be considered a rhetorical unit, there should be an identifiable "introduction, body, and conclusion, and may either comprise an entire work or be a part of a larger one."[244] In this unit, 6:3–4 is the introduction where Paul commends himself as a "servant of God" and describes his personal integrity as "unblemished," so that no one may speak ill of his ministry. Paul is "resorting once again to a rhetorical tactic to provide evidence of ethos or character" in these introductory verses.[245] In 6:5–10, the main body of this rhetorical unit, Paul lists out "a series of hardships," and, as "Fitzgerald demonstrates, this hardship catalog presupposes the earlier list in 4:8–10 and supplements or completes it."[246] Then, 6:11–13 closes this unit with an emotional appeal to the Corinthians to not shut him out from their lives (6:11–12) but to "open wide their hearts" for him (6:13).

The question raised with 6:3–13 as a rhetorical unit is what happened to the first two verses of chapter 6? A good deal of scholarly works recognize that there is a "break" between 6:2 and 6:3.[247] For instance, according to Martin, "This break alerts us to the fact that Paul is presently to diverge from his theme of reconciliation to a new theme of commending himself to the Corinthians as one worthy of God's ministry and worthy of their love."[248] Martin continues his discussion by suggesting, "6:2 appears as a parenthesis breaking Paul's train of thought."[249] At this point, Martin observes this "parenthesis" as "another example of how Paul's dictation did not produce a flowing discussion."[250] However, this observation seems overtly critical of Paul. For instance, Harris

---

244. Watson, *Invention*, 8.
245. Witherington, *Community & Conflict*, 398.
246. Witherington, 398; Fitzgerald, *Cracks*, 191.
247. Shillington, *2 Corinthians*, 136; Kistemaker and Hendriksen, *Exposition*, 206; Barton and Osborne, *1 & 2 Corinthians*, 361.
248. Martin, *2 Corinthians*, 160.
249. Martin, 160.
250. Martin, 160.

admits that even though there is "an abrupt transition at v. 3,"[251] this is not too "awkward" if one is to "recognize that the overall theme of this section is the essence and exercise of the apostolic ministry."[252] This makes sense because from chapter 3 onwards, Paul has been specifically arguing for and defending his ministry, which he takes up again in 6:3–13. However, from 6:3, as scholars rightly notice, Paul changes his tactic: he is focusing his defence of his apostolic ministry on a defence of his personal integrity, which is part of the overall argument being made in favour of the validity of his ministry.

As with Baker, "It seems best to view 6:1–2 as the practical capstone to his entire discussion begun at 5:11, with the quotation of Isaiah 49:8 in 6:2 functioning as the exclamation point, not only of his appeal to the Corinthians but of his entire ministry."[253] Since Paul shifts the focus of his argument by pointing to his personal integrity, one can say that "a separate section begins here,"[254] at 6:3, where "the participle of 6:3 (διδόντες)" becomes the "first of an extraordinary series extending to verse 10."[255] As such, scholars rightly consider 6:3–13 to fall within the "self-contained unit" of Paul's ministry defence that he stated specifically in chapter 3.[256] Now in a compact rhetorical unit (6:3–13), Paul presents his "catalogue of suffering" to prove that his disabled body is no pushover, but very resilient and worthy of their admiration.[257] Paul goes to great lengths to describe his suffering for the ministry (6:4b–10) and appeal to their "hearts" to accept him and his ministry (6:11–13).[258] Therefore, 6:3–13 is definitely a rhetorical unit where one observes a unity of thought, a procession of arguments that finally ends in a passionate appeal for them to "open wide" their hearts (see 6:11–13).[259]

---

251. Harris, *Second Epistle*, 464.
252. Harris, 464.
253. Baker, *2 Corinthians*, 243; Furnish, *2 Corinthians*, 341; Barnett, *Second Epistle*, 315; Harris, *Second Epistle*, 355.
254. Thrall, *Corinthians 1–7*, 455.
255. Barrett, *Second Epistle*, 184; see also Martin, *2 Corinthians*, 170.
256. Lim, *Sufferings of Christ*, 123.
257. Lim, 124.
258. Harris, *Second Epistle*, 464.
259. Martin, *2 Corinthians*, 164.

## 5.4.2 *Probatio*: Paul Defends Himself to the Corinthians

In this rhetorical unit, Paul argues to the Corinthians that though disabled, his physical toughness is unmatched and his personal integrity, irreproachable. As such, his disability must not be a factor in the rejection of his ministry. Witherington puts this particular *probatio* rather poignantly: "6:3–13 will be the last salvo in Paul's first major argument for his defense, ending in a final appeal for reconciliation before the digression in 6:14–7:1."[260] Indeed, a cursory reading of 6:3–13 shows that the development of his argument can be traced, wherein 6:3–4a introduces the focal point that Paul is making here. The subsequent verses (i.e. vv. 4b–10) describe his hardships and sufferings and why the Corinthians should consider his physical body beyond reproach. The last three verses (i.e. vv. 11–13) are an emotional appeal to the Corinthians not to withhold their love for Paul. This section will further analyse his arguments in detail.

### 5.4.2.1 Paul commends himself to the Corinthians

In 2 Corinthians 6:3–4a, one finds Paul picking up the theme "ministry" (διακονία) which he introduced back in 2 Corinthians 3:4. Here, Paul appeals to the Corinthians that his ministry is beyond reproach. Contrary to the "standard view that the passage is totally apologetic," Fitzgerald correctly sees this passage as an "exhortation" in nature, tone, and substance.[261] Paul writes to the Corinthians that "in no way have they [Paul and his friends] given a cause for offence" (μηδεμίαν ἐν μηδενὶ διδόντες προσκοπήν, 6:3a) when it comes to the proclamation of their gospel. In addition, "this ministry is without blemish" (μὴ μωμηθῇ ἡ διακονία, 6:3b). Paul's use of "alliteration" is noticeable here: μηδεμίαν ἐν μηδενὶ . . . μὴ μωμηθῇ (in no way has anyone . . . no blemish). Alliteration is "a stylistic device in which a number of words, having the same first consonant sound, occur close together in a series."[262] This is very much parallel to that of Plato's work: μηδεὶς μηδέποτε ἐάσῃ μηδαμοῦ θηρεῦσαι ("no one shall ever allow [a trapper] to hunt anywhere").[263] The μὴ

---

260. Witherington, *Conflict & Community*, 398.
261. By "exhortation" he meant "the centrality of character" which is "a vital part of persuasion" long recognised by the time of Paul (Fitzgerald, *Crack*, 185–186).
262. "Alliteration," Literary Devices, accessed November 12, 2018, https://literarydevices.net/alliteration/.
263. Pla., *Leg.*, 7, 824 B, quoted in Thrall, *Corinthians 1–7*, 455.

μωμηθῇ ἡ διακονία (especially the ministry) in 6:3b is immediately picked up again in 6:4a, but Paul tweaks the feminine nominative (διακονία) to masculine nominative διάκονοι (cf. 3:6), indicating that he was the "minister" of this "ministry" which is of God.[264]

Why did Paul use the particular Greek word προσκοπήν (6:3a) in his appeal to the Corinthians? This probably underscores the distance that had crept between the Corinthians and Paul. The Greek word προσκοπήν literally means "stumbling" and is used to indicate "taking offence," "aversion," or "irritation."[265] According to Stählin, the Stoics used this word technically to mean "a sick aversion which arises through antipathy as a result of an offence and is directed against things which should not be spurned as if they ought to be."[266] Stählin further explained that "the context" of 6:3 points to "προσκοπήν [as] an act which makes reproach possible."[267] Certainly, the Corinthians and anyone who opposed Paul might develop an aversion to his ministry and to Paul himself, who as a PwD did open up his ministry to lots of criticism (cf. μωμηθῇ, 6:3a).

Paul's use of the Greek "subjunctive aorist passive μωμηθῇ" (6:3b) after the "purpose ἵνα clause" is to clarify why Paul put "no obstacle in anyone's way."[268] While this grammatical construction does not necessarily "imply any doubt," from the context of how Paul uses it here, one cannot help escape from the element of doubt, a negative connotation that this subjunctive μωμηθῇ brings to the whole interpretation of how the Corinthians thought of his ministry.[269] His "commending" (συνίστημι) himself by extensively listing out his struggle and hardship in the following passage surely must support the idea that his ministry was seriously being slandered in connection to what was perceived as his "unimpressive body" (cf. 2 Cor 10:10b). This in turn makes one search for an answer not just for the content of the ministry itself, but also as to the one who ministered it. What will a further investigation on the Greek word μωμηθῇ yield to Paul's defence of his person?

---

264. Martin, *2 Corinthians*, 172.
265. Stählin, "προσκοπη," in *TDNT*, 6:747.
266. Stählin, 6:747.
267. Stählin, 6:754.
268. See Wenham, *Elements*, 161–162.
269. For the meaning and use of "ἵνα+Subjunctive," see Wallace, *Greek Grammar*, 472.

The basic meaning of the word μωμηθῇ or the root word μῶμος "is the 'censure' which derives from ill-will towards another, whether on the ground of his deficiency or of one's own censoriousness."[270] According to Hauck, the "LXX used it in the classic sense of 'reproach' [or] 'ignominy' (Sir 11:33, 18:15, 20:24, 47:20) often with reference to physical blemishes (Lev 24:20; Num.19:2; Dan 1:4; Cant 4:7)."[271] This Greek word is also affinitive with "Momus . . . the Greek god of mockery and ridicule."[272] It is possible that "Paul was concerned with more than simple finger pointing, for his message *was* inalienably offensive (1 Cor 1:23; Gal. 5:11)."[273] Moreover, at the same time Paul, by using μῶμος might "be thinking of the insults offered to him" by his detractors.[274] There certainly is a negative implication to Paul's disabled body here.

Paul, therefore, starts to "commend" (συνιστάντες, v. 4a) himself as just as capable as any abled-body person, and there is no reason for anyone to have a negative attitude towards his ministry. According to Kasch, "Paul uses the transitive σθνιστημι primarily in the good classical sense 'to commend.'"[275] Consequently, it is not surprising that Paul's uses of συνιστάντες have often been compared to the "self-praise" of the Cynics or the Stoics when they had to defend their character from those who wished to malign them.[276] Fitzgerald identifies Paul's "self-praise" or "commending" as "the victory over hardship [which is] a mixture of human effort and divine benevolence."[277] Furthermore, "Isocrates says that the most powerful way to be persuasive is to argue from one's own life."[278] Therefore, Paul's commendation of himself here is "to prove" or "to show" the Corinthians that his disabled body is more than capable of withstanding the extreme sufferings and hardships that anyone can imagine.[279]

---

270. Hauck, "μῶμος," in *TDNT*, 4:829.

271. Hauck, 4:830.

272. Hughes, *Paul's Second Epistle*, 221.

273. Martin, *2 Corinthians*, 170.

274. Plummer, *Critical and Exegetical*, 192.

275. Kasch, "σγνιστημι," in *TDNT*, 7:897.

276. Laertius mentions that Epicurus "will pay just so much regard to his reputation as not to be looked down upon" (*Lives of Eminent Philosophers*; see also Hawtrone, *Paul's Letter*, 191).

277. Fitzgerald, *Crack*, 114, 206–207.

278. Witherington, *Conflict & Community*, 398.

279. Kasch, "σγνιστημι," in *TDNT*, 7:898.

### *5.4.2.2 Disabled yet resilient: Paul lists his sufferings*

In what must be "one of the most lyrical passages in the Pauline corpus,"[280] Paul commends himself to the Corinthians by weaving complex lists of what his disabled body could take (6:4b–10). A number of scholars have appreciated the complexity of Paul's literary composition and rightly so, because his arrangements and construction of words in 6:4b–10 is highly "sophisticated,"[281] as the rhetorical device called "anaphora embroiders the lyrical quality."[282] Some have even gone to the extent of calling it "beautiful."[283] Indeed, it is "one of the high peaks of the Pauline epistles" that seems to mark him as an adequate and qualified rhetorician, however much his disability might have prevented him from fully achieving this distinction in the eyes of the Corinthians (see 2 Cor 10:10).[284]

Scholars agree that concerning its structure, there are four smaller sections derivable from Paul's lists of sufferings in vv. 4b–10.[285] According to Thrall, "there is a general agreement that this passage displays a formal structure created with conscious care, and all but complete agreement upon its internal division into smaller units."[286] The first two verses (4b–5) contain a list of "hardships" that is made up of "three triads of ἐν-phrases."[287] The second smaller unit (vv. 6–7a) contains a list of "virtues" introduced again by "ἐν-phrases," while the third smaller unit (vv. 7b–8a) contains a list of vagaries or variations of life's fortunes that are introduced by "διa-phrases." Finally, the fourth smaller unit (vv. 8b–10) contains "a series of antitheses,"[288] all beginning with ὡς, in which "five of these [are] introduced with και and in two

---

280. McCant, *2 Corinthians*, 56–57.
281. Harris, *Second Epistle*, 464.
282. McCant, *2 Corinthians*, 56–57.
283. Bullinger, *Figures of Speech*, 717.
284. Hughes, *Paul's Second Epistle*, 238.
285. See Bultmann, *Second Letter*, 169; Martin, *2 Corinthians*, 161; Thrall, *Corinthians 1–7*, 454; Harris, *Second Epistle*, 466; McCant, *2 Corinthians*, 56–57; Matera, *2 Corinthians*, 151. Wan, *Power in Weakness*, 93.
286. Thrall, *Corinthians 1–7*, 452.
287. Thrall, 454.
288. Bullinger describes "antithesis" as "a figure by which two thoughts, ideas, or phrases, are set over one against the other, in order to make the contrast more striking, and thus to emphasize it" (*Figures of Speech*, 715).

with δε."²⁸⁹ The representation of the structure below allows one to appreciate better Paul's compositions here:²⁹⁰

| LISTS OF HARDSHIPS (vv. 4b-5) | | |
|---|---|---|
| ἐν θλίψεσιν | ἐν ἀνάγκαις | ἐν στενοχωρίαις |
| ἐν πληγαῖς | ἐν φυλακαῖς | ἐν ἀκαταστασίαις |
| ἐν κόποις | ἐν ἀγρυπνίαις | ἐν νηστείαις |
| **LISTS OF VIRTUES (vv. 6-7)** | | |
| ἐν ἁγνότητι | ἐν γνώσει | ἐν μακροθυμίᾳ |
| ἐν χρηστότητι | ἐν πνεύματι ἁγίῳ | ἐν ἀγάπῃ ἀνυποκρίτῳ |
| ἐν λόγῳ ἀληθείας | ἐν δυνάμει θεου | |
| **LISTS OF VAGARIES OF LIFE'S FORTUNE (vv. 7b-8a)** | | |
| διὰ τῶν ὅπλων τῆς δικαιοσύνης | | |
| διὰ δόξης καὶ ἀτιμίας | | |
| διὰ δυσφημίας καὶ εὐφημίας | | |
| **LISTS OF ANTITHESES (vv. 8b-10)** | | |
| ὡς πλάνοι | καὶ | ἀληθεῖς |
| ὡς ἀγνοούμενοι | καὶ | ἐπιγινωσκόμενοι |
| ὡς ἀποθνῄσκοντες | καὶ | ἰδοὺ ζῶμεν |
| ὡς παιδευόμενοι | καὶ | μὴ θανατούμενοι |
| ὡς λυπούμενοι ἀεὶ | δὲ | χαίροντες |
| ὡς πτωχοὶ πολλοὺς | δὲ | πλουτίζοντες |
| ὡς μηδὲν ἔχοντες | καὶ | πάντα κατέχοντες |

This particular passage must be one of the few instances in his letters where one witnesses his skill in composition. Aside from this example, one can consider "1 Cor 13:1–13, Rom 8:28–39 and Col 1:15–20" as Paul's finest moments in rhetorical composition.²⁹¹ One gets to appreciate Paul's composite structuring of several themes into one flowing exhortation to the Corinthians. According to Bullinger, verse "4 is an oxymoronic usage by Paul," which

---

289. Thrall, *Corinthians 1-7*, 454.

290. For something similar, see McCant *2 Corinthians*, 56–57; and also Bullinger, *Figures of Speech*, 717..

291. Harris, *Second Epistle*, 466. Martin has also rightly compared the "lyrically attractive readings of" this passage with that 1 Corinthians 13:1–13 (*2 Corinthians*, 163).

indicates a "smart saying which unites words whose literal meanings appear to be incongruous, if not contradictory; but they are so cleverly and wisely joined together as to enhance the real sense of the words."[292] Therefore, when Paul wrote in quick succession, "the three words, *afflictions, hardships, and calamities*" sounded "synonyms."[293] However, one must realize the weight of Paul's struggle that is carried by each word. Take for instance the first word, "affliction" (θλῖψις). The previous section has clarified that it can mean "oppression, harassment or discomfort" both in a physical and emotional sense.[294] This interpretation finds support from the socio-rhetorical usages of the word in antiquity. It is worth repeating here that the Greek physician Oribasius Latinus used it in a medical sense to mean θλιψις στομαχου (affliction of the stomach).[295] Just as well, Soranus used this word to indicate the emotional and mental state of a person in his work *Gynaecia* as "ὑστερικας . . . θλιψεις" (hysteria trouble).[296]

The same applies to the second word, "hardships" (ἀνάγκη). The Greek word's root meaning is "compulsion and the means of compulsion or oppression."[297] The Old Testament employed this word to mean "constraint" by which "afflictions and oppressions are divinely caused and interpreted as divine visitations" (see Job 7:11; Jer 9:14).[298] However, Grundman believes that in apocalyptical and Rabbinical literature, this word means "messianic tribulations consisting of commotion and war, pestilence and hunger, famine, apostasy from God."[299] Thus, when Paul uses this word, it seems not too far-fetched to think that he perceived his disability, which was oppressive to him, as divinely sanctioned. However, in hindsight, it made sense to him only when he met the risen Christ. Now he is under divine "distress" to proclaim this gospel (see 1 Cor 9:16).

The third word, "calamities" (στενοχωρία), that Paul employs is rather revealing of his present condition. Figuratively, this Greek word can also

---

292. Bullinger, *Figures of Speech*, 817.
293. Omanson and Ellington, *Handbook*, 112.
294. See section 5.2.2 of this present study.
295. See Schlier, "θλιβω, θλιψις," in *TDNT*, 2:139.
296. Sorani, *De signis fracturarum*, 6.1.42.
297. Grundmann, "ἀνάγκ-outside the NT," in *TDNT*, 1:345.
298. Grundmann, 1:345.
299. Grundmann, 1:346.

mean "distress, difficulty, anguish, trouble" (Rom 2:9, 8:35; 2 Cor 6:4, 12:10).[300] According to Bertram, Paul's use of the noun here also indicates "narrow," "thin," "poor," and a "narrow place."[301] However, Bertram also notes that outside of Paul, the "noun στενοχωρία is rare" and is found "in connection with threats of punishment in Isa 8:22, 30:6."[302] It is interesting to note that Paul uses the verb στενοχωρέω later in 6:12 when he complains of the Corinthians withholding their "hearts" from him. When Paul paints his present situation as στενοχωρία, he is not exaggerating. Barclay argues that Paul was probably reasonable to "label" himself as an "apostate" in the minds of his fellow diaspora Jews. He writes, "Jewish hostility and synagogue beatings probably indicate that Paul was consistently repudiated as an 'apostate,' despite his continuing loyalties to the Jewish people."[303] In addition, this study has pointed out that the law of Moses alienated Paul as he was disabled,[304] and now the Corinthian congregation was seriously questioning his credentials as well as his ministry because of his weakness. Truly, Paul was becoming isolated from his own people and those he was ministering to.

In 6:5, one comes across another list of hardships, probably connected to Paul's proclamation of his gospel.[305] Paul was "beaten" (ἐν πληγαῖς) and "put in prison" (ἐν φυλακαῖς, see Acts 14:19; 16:22–23) and experienced "riots and disturbance" (ἐν ἀκαταστασίαις, see Acts 13:50 19:23).[306] He also went "without food" (νηστεία), possibly because of a conscious choice rather than not having the means to buy it. For instance, in Acts 9:9, right after Paul receives his revelation, he goes without eating or drinking.[307] Once again, all these sufferings serve to show how resilient the disabled Paul is when it comes to enduring pain.

---

300. Gingrich, "στενοχωρία, ας, ἡ," in *Shorter Lexicon*, 185.
301. Bertram, "στενοχωρία-A. Profane Usage," in *TDNT*, 7:604.
302. Bertram, 7:605.
303. Barclay, "Paul," 120.
304. See section 5.3.2.1 of this present study.
305. Matera, *2 Corinthians*, 152.
306. Matera, 152.
307. Was Paul fasting or unable to eat food in this verse? Bock thinks it is "implied" that Paul "probably" fasted as he thought of what had happened (*Acts*, 358). However, Bruce thinks Paul was unable to eat "probably [as] the result of shock" (*Book of Acts*, 185). Nevertheless, if one connects it with Paul's testimony about being taken up in third heaven (2 Cor 12:2-4), then it is reasonable to explain that Paul's intense experience makes him forego eating.

In 6:6, Paul changes his focus from drawing attention to what his disabled body can take to the virtuous side of his disabled character. Paul tells them that he has lived a "morally pure and blameless" (ἁγνότης) life, and as such, the Corinthians should find no fault in him, and by extension, his ministry.[308] In "knowledge" (γνῶσις), in "patience" (μακροθυμία),[309] in "goodness" (χρηστότητι), in "Holy Spirit" (πνεύματι ἁγίῳ),[310] in "sincere love" (ἀγάπῃ ἀνυποκρίτῳ), in "truthful word" (λόγῳ ἀληθείας), and by the "power of God" (δυνάμει θεοῦ), Paul invites the Corinthians to see that his disabled body is virtuous and, thus, his ministry borne out of this disability must be virtuous as well.

How does one make sense of Paul's uses of "weapons of righteousness" (ὅπλων τῆς δικαιοσύνης) in 6:7? Some scholars interpret this phrase as "violence imagery" or "military metaphor" on the part of Paul.[311] Yet, Harris points out that "Paul's use of military metaphors is no indication of a special interest in the art of warfare."[312] Harris opts for a "subjective" interpretation, where God provides "weapons of righteousness."[313] Nonetheless, he lacks clarity in his position because, while he thinks this is not a "metaphor," he fails to supply concrete evidence as to why he thinks it should be a "literal" representation by Paul.[314] The truth is, Paul, who urged his reader to obey the government in Romans 13:1–6, will not literally advocate a military tactic in the defence of his ministry. Bowens has argued that one should interpret this martial imagery from an apocalyptic point of view.[315] According to her, Paul uses it to "denote that all of humanity is entangled in the cosmic clash

---

308. According to Hauck, ἁγνότης is "used neither in classical Greek nor the LXX" (in *TDNT*, 1:124).

309. It can also mean, "'long-tempered' . . . which is a quality of God (LXX, Exod. 34:6)." Bruce, *Commentary on Galatians*, 253.

310. It is surprising to find Paul use πνεύματι ἁγίῳ here in the midst of other lists. Plummer (*Second Epistle*, 196) and Barrett (*Second Epistle*, 186–187) think that Paul might mean the "human spirit" as opposed to the "Holy Spirit." However, Thrall thinks that there is no problem in accepting Paul's uses of πνεύματι ἁγίῳ (*Corinthians 1–7*, 460).

311. Wan, *Power in Weakness*, 94; see also Harris, *Second Epistle*, 477.

312. Harris, 477.

313. Harris, 477.

314. Harris asks, "'But what are these weapons provided by God?' Probably the answer is found in the phrase [right and left]. . . . We should not, however take the next step and identify the sword." (*Second Epistle*, 477–478).

315. Bowens, "Investigating," 3–15.

between God and Satan."³¹⁶ Thus, it might be better if one understood Paul's "weapons of righteousness" more as psychological and spiritual warfare (see Eph 6:12). This makes sense because Paul had to fight the social prejudice that was hindering the progress of his ministry. He was fighting "right and left" the deeply ingrained traditions of Jewish hatred, as well as the prejudice of Greco-Roman society which blatantly disregarded disability.³¹⁷

The phrases "through glory and dishonour, through slander and praise" in 6:8a (διὰ δόξης καὶ ἀτιμίας, διὰ δυσφημίας καὶ εὐφημίας) describe correctly what Paul endured throughout his missionary work. He received "glory" from people who were amazed by what God was doing through him. For instance, the grateful and amazed people honoured Paul after healing a "lame man at Lystra" (Acts 14:8–12).³¹⁸ However, the people quickly turned on them and almost stoned Paul to death (Acts 14:19). Again, the Galatians treated Paul like "an angel of God – or Christ Jesus himself" in spite of his sickness (Gal 4:14).³¹⁹ Still, it is amazing to note how quickly the Galatians turned away from Paul when "people from James" came to visit them (Gal 2:12). Even the Corinthians themselves were not innocent of "slandering" Paul whom they thought was "fickle" (2 Cor 1:17) and "treated with contempt for his personal appearance and his speaking ability (10:10)."³²⁰ It seems Paul could not escape the negative societal attitude towards his disability.

In 6:8c–10, one notices that Paul constructs his self-commendation as antitheses, which, according to Bullinger, "is an oxymoronic usage."³²¹ Such is the beauty of Paul's composition that Danker suggests that Paul was deliberately composing these "elegant" sets of antitheses "since Greco-Romans respected people of extraordinary rhetorical ability as well as performance."³²² Probably, Paul did this to impress upon the Corinthians that he might be lacking in his oratorical skills, but he could very well match the best of ancient

---

316. Bowens, 14.
317. See Harris, *Second Epistle*, 477–478.
318. Harris, 478.
319. Harris, 479.
320. Harris, *Second Epistle*, 479.
321. Oxymoronic "is a smart saying, which unites words whose literal meanings appear to be incongruous, if not contradictory; but they are so cleverly and wisely joined together as to enhance the real sense of the words" (Bullinger, *Figures of Speech*, 817).
322. Danker, *Augsburg Commentary*, 94.

rhetoricians when it came to writing. Hughes also expresses his appreciation of Paul's antitheses, especially that of 6:10, stating, "Its almost lyrical intensity, its structural balance, and its genuine spontaneity have called forth the response of admiration and gratitude in all generations."[323] Indeed, the seven antitheses grab one's attention in the way Paul played with the combination of his words. A representation of these antitheses below will help to clarify this point.[324]

| A. What they think of Paul | | B. How Paul thinks of himself |
|---|---|---|
| As Deceiver | yet | Truthful |
| As Unknown | yet | Well-known |
| As Dying | yet | Living |
| As Punished | yet | Not Killed |
| As Distressed | yet | Always Rejoicing |
| As Very Poor | yet | Possessing Everything |

Thus, these antitheses reveal "two concurrent and paradoxical realities of Paul's apostolic life."[325] On one hand, Paul indicates how his opponents perceive his disability. On the opposing sides, he shows them the "real Paul." While they were concerned about his external appearances, they failed to gauge the depth of his true character. What is significantly evident after analyzing the structure of 6:4b–10 is "the gravity of Paul's appeal" to the Corinthians.[326] Harris suggests that these antitheses serve as "not merely self-commendatory . . . but may also serve . . . [a] polemical purpose."[327] Since Paul's defence here seems to go much deeper and more personal, it is probably better to consider his commendation as "polemic."[328] The shameful treatment, the prejudice, the injustice that Paul daily encountered and endured in his social milieu is alarming. At the same time, Paul's fighting spirit, revealed in

---

323. Hughes, *Second Epistle*, 238.
324. The inspiration for this representation is from Harris, *Second Epistle*, 479.
325. Harris, 480.
326. Hughes, *Paul's Second Epistle*, 47.
327. Harris, *Second Epistle*, 479.
328. Paul is still maintaining a decent tone to his argument so far, but the gloves are coming off in chapters 10–13.

his use of paradoxes here, is encouraging to say the least. He simply refuses to be bogged down by others' negative attitudes towards him; instead, he finds positivity from all his sufferings.

One may ask how similar is his catalogue of sufferings here as "self-praise . . . to the attitude of the ideal Cynic"?[329] For instance, Grindheim notes, "several of the devices Paul used for his self-defence resemble the conventions for self-praise in the Greco-Roman world, as they were outlined by Plutarch in his essay 'On praising oneself inoffensively' (*Moralia* 539 A-547F)."[330] However, it seems strange that if Paul was self-praising himself, then what should one make of his "earlier denials of self-commendation" in 2 Corinthians 3:1,[331] where he said: "Are we beginning to commend ourselves to you afresh – as though we needed, like some others, to have letters of commendation either to you or from you?" (NJB). It seems writers of antiquity did not normally employ self-praise. Actually, they frowned upon people who boasted or self-praised their achievements directly or indirectly. In fact, Dionysius of Halicarnassus criticized Plato for "praising himself in respect of his oratorical power," which according to him was "the most vulgar and most invidious of tasks" that an orator could do.[332]

Yet, why is Paul "commending" himself here? Moreover, why are scholars insisting that his "self-praise" is similar to the one practised by writers of antiquity? The answer to this lies in the writings of Plutarch. He believed that one could indulge in self-praise "when the occasion and the matter in hand demand that the truth" be told, and when it came to "defending your good name or answering a charge" that your opponents brought against you.[333] Mention may also be made of "Dio Chrysostom, the first-century CE philosopher and orator" who thought "self-praise" was acceptable "because it secures the attention, compliance, and imitation of the audience."[334] Thus, it seems reasonable to think that "Paul's *peristasis* catalog in 6:4b-10 functions as a self-commendation vouching for his integrity and competency as God's

---

329. Fitzgerald, *Crack*, 189.
330. Grindheim, *Crux of Election*, 100.
331. Oropeza, *Exploring Second Corinthians*, 405.
332. Dionysius, *Three Literary Letters*, 94–95.
333. Plutarch, "On Praising Oneself."
334. Dio Chrysostom, *The Fifty-Seventh Discourse* (Crosby, LCL), 417–429, quoted in Watson, "Paul and Boasting," 91.

prophetic minister."³³⁵ As Seneca pointed out, "it is not poverty that we praise, it is the man whom poverty cannot humble or bend,"³³⁶ thus, the purpose of 6:4b–10 is not to focus on the hardships, but rather on Paul's disabled body enduring triumphantly in the face of intense suffering and weakness.

Aristotle also believed that a rhetor needed to substantiate his speech with three things: "The first depends upon the moral character of the speaker, the second upon putting the hearer into a certain frame of mind, the third upon the speech itself, in so far as it proves or seems to prove."³³⁷ From the preceding analyses, the passage reveals that Paul was indeed appealing rather quite intensely to the Corinthian congregation to accept him for who he was and for his ministry. This appeal to his character was necessary if Paul wanted to persuade the Corinthians to consider him worthy of their trust.³³⁸ Again, Isocrates stated, "The man who wishes to persuade people will not be negligent as to the matter of character . . . the argument which is made by a man's life is of more weight than that which is furnished by words."³³⁹ Thus, Paul does not mainly desire "to create confidence in his listeners so that they will heed his words,"³⁴⁰ he also desires to show them that his disabled body is no pushover when it comes to enduring pain. Paul certainly makes use of his resilient character to score a point against those who considered his "unimpressive body" as of no consequence.

### 5.4.2.3 *Paul's* peristasis *from a sociological perspective*

From the above rhetorical analyses of Paul's hardships, there are some important sociological insights that one can also make. In 2 Corinthians 6:5, Paul mentions that he "worked extra hard" or "labored" (cf. NRSV) and has gone through "sleeplessness" (ἀγρυπνίαις) at nights. Why did he have to work extremely hard, and why did he have to tell them? According to Paul, he worked extremely hard to support himself so that he did not rely on the Corinthians

---

335. Oropeza, *Exploring Second Corinthians*, 405.
336. Seneca, *Letters from a Stoic*, 272–273.
337. Aristotle, *Rhetoric*, 1356a.
338. Aristotle wrote, "The orator persuades by moral character when his speech is delivered in such a manner as to render him worthy of confidence" (*Rhetoric*, 1356a).
339. *Isocrates*, 2:15.278.
340. Fitzgerald, *Crack*, 186.

for financial assistance (see 1 Cor 9:12; 2 Cor 11:8–9).³⁴¹ In fact, he uses the same Greek word κόπος in both 2 Corinthians 6:5 and 2 Corinthians 11:23. What kind of work did he do? In Acts 18:3, one finds that Paul's vocation was "tent-making." Now, what was the nature of his work, and did it socially stigmatize Paul?

Rapske has analysed in detail the social significance of Paul being a manual labourer. According to him, "while his handiwork might be greatly admired for its quality or beauty and while he himself might become wealthy from his labour . . . he was, to the eyes of better Greeks and Romans, a figure to be despised."³⁴² In other words, Paul's vocation as a tent maker was, unfortunately, to "the eyes of better Greeks and Romans" a vocation to be "despised."³⁴³ Moreover, Paul's vocation enabled him to carry his tool and travel from one place to another, which could also result in generating the social "stigma of rootlessness."³⁴⁴ According to Belcher and Deforge, "Social stigma occurs in situations where there is unequal social, economic, and political power and there is an opportunity to label, stereotype, separate (us versus them), lose status, and discriminate."³⁴⁵ Because Paul was an itinerant preacher who travelled from one place to another and worked with his hands to support himself, it is possible that he could "be conceived as the underclass (i.e., those belonging to the lowest and least privilege social stratum in society)."³⁴⁶

To shed further insights into the social stigmatizations of a manual labourer, this present study considers the case of Cerdon and his shoe store, where he employed thirteen slaves who worked tirelessly, often "sleepless until the noises of the dawn."³⁴⁷ From this, one can assume that shoe stores involved working with leather, and since they worked very hard, they hardly had time for leisure. From Acts 17:16–32, one learns that people in antiquity needed their leisure time to involve themselves in deep philosophical discussions,

---

341. Chow postulates from his study of 1 Corinthians that Paul's enmity with the Corinthians started because he refuse to "accept money from" them thus disrespecting "the convention of friendship or patronage" that was prevalent in antiquity (*Patronage and Power*, 188–189).
342. Rapske, *Book of Acts*, 100.
343. Rapske, 110.
344. Rapske, 100.
345. Belcher and Deforge, "Social Stigma," 929–946.
346. Belcher and Deforge, 930.
347. *Mimes of Herondas*, ch. 7.

and Greco-Roman society would despise manual workers who did not have time for this.[348] Paul freely admits that he laboured and toiled sleepless nights like those slaves in Cerdon's shoe store.[349] In the previous chapter,[350] this study mentioned that "tent-making" was regarded as "unnecessary," "useful only to those who lived for luxury and extravagance."[351] Thus, Paul would have been "stigmatized," "reviled or abused" because of his vocation which would have been deemed "slavish" and "useless."[352]

Paul's vocation must also be considered in connection with his refusal of the traditional "patronage" system. According to MacGillivray, patronage was "a voluntary, though often exploitative, reciprocal relationship that pervaded Roman society, whereby a gift from a superior obligated an exchange, usually of intangible commodities such as political support or public laud of the patron's munificence."[353] Patrons were prevalent in the Greco-Roman world where "in theory they were voluntary, but in practice social inferiors often had no choice but to engage in such relationships in order to be materially supported."[354] By the time Paul had come to Corinth, this system was widely in use because Corinth was "a city of increasing prosperity and obvious wealth" and this "attracted artists and sophists seeking patronage."[355] Winter mentions that even "famous orators, such as Dio Chrysostom, Aristides, Favorinus, and Philostratus . . . received wealth and fame in public life ($\pi o \lambda \iota \tau \epsilon \acute{\iota} \alpha$), education ($\pi \alpha \iota \delta \epsilon \acute{\iota} \alpha$), and the courts on arriving at various cities."[356]

For the Corinthians, "Patronage was not just a matter of economic and social power, but also a matter of honour and shame."[357] Thus, since Paul refused the time-honoured and culturally prevalent form of the patronage system practiced during that time (see 11:7–9), he could have invited their

---

348. See Witherington, *Acts of the Apostles*, 574.
349. Hock, *Social Context*, 35.
350. See section 4.4 of this present study.
351. Hock, *Social Context*, 36.
352. Hock, 36.
353. MacGillivray, "Re-Evaluating Patronage," 38.
354. Witherington, *Conflict & Community*, 414.
355. deSilva, *Introduction*, 557.
356. Briones, "Paul's Financial Policy," 247n159.
357. Witherington, *Conflict & Community*, 419.

displeasure.³⁵⁸ Paul's refusal amounted to a rejection of their protection, which in turn hurt their honour. Thus, in their eyes, Paul committed a grievous "sin" for "refusing to receive financial help from the Corinthians" (see 11:5, 7–11; 12:11–15).³⁵⁹ If these premises are true, then the Corinthians' rejection of Paul reeks of social discrimination. While they despised him because of his manual job, they would further stigmatize him for not accepting their financial help. It is possible that Paul, a disabled apostle, with a weak physical appearance and an inability to speak properly in public, had dared to reject their generous offer for financial help, which would have made them spite him and reject his ministry for others who would be more obliging than him.

### 5.4.2.4 Paul's unrestrained and emotional appeal

The last three verses of this rhetorical unit (6:11–13) reveal a further tension that was, as Harris has stated, an "unreciprocated affection" between Paul and the Corinthians.³⁶⁰ In 6:11, Paul uses the vocative Κορίνθιοι to address the Corinthian congregation. What is revealing about this vocative usage is Paul's emotional turmoil. It is proper that one recollects here the only other times Paul addressed his congregations with a vocative. The first is in Galatians 3:1, Ὦ ἀνόητοι Γαλάται (O foolish Galatians!), and the second one is in Philippians 4:15, Φιλιππήσιοι (O Philippians!). Scholars have rightly pointed out that when Paul employs the vocative, it is a "sign of strong feeling."³⁶¹ Paul's intention is clear in Galatians: he chastises them for their change of hearts, calling them "stupid" (NJB).³⁶² While the sense of "O Philippians!" is much more mellow, the underlying tension of Paul's concern for them is palpable.³⁶³ The same sense of rebuke is very much discernible in 2 Corinthians 6:11.

In this same verse, Paul tells them that he "opens his mouth and that his heart is enlarged" (τὸ στόμα ἡμῶν ἀνέῳγεν πρὸς ὑμᾶς . . . ἡ καρδία ἡμῶν πεπλάτυνται). He "opens his mouth to them" (τὸ στόμα ἡμῶν ἀνέῳγεν πρὸς

---

358. See Judge, "Social Identity," 214.
359. Carson, *From Triumphalism to Maturity*, 18.
360. Harris, *Second Epistle*, 490.
361. Barrett, *Second Epistle*, 193.
362. Furnish, *2 Corinthians*, 360.
363. Michael, *Epistle*, 219. But against this, see Furnish and other scholars' interpretation that this vocative in Philippians is "an expression of gratitude" (Furnish, *2 Corinthians*, 360; see also Loh and Nida, *Handbook*, 144; O'Brien, *Epistle*, 530).

ὑμᾶς) is a Greek idiom that means "to be completely open with, to conceal nothing from, and to speak the whole truth."³⁶⁴ This shows that Paul was completely frank with them. The "enlarging of his heart" (ἡ καρδία ἡμῶν πεπλάτυνται) also indicates that he is willingly opening his heart wide to them. According to Malina and Piltch, "An open heart involves sincerity, affection, goodwill, honesty – in sum a totally welcoming attitude bereft of all deceit and deception."³⁶⁵ Previously, in 6:3, Paul told them that he has given no reason for someone to take offence at him. Now, in 6:11, Paul once again is showing the Corinthians that he means what he said.

However, in 6:12, one observes that it is the Corinthians who are "restricting" (στενοχωρέω) him, thus jeopardizing their relationship. Paul emphatically tells them that the fault lies with them. While Paul was completely open to them, they were shutting him literally out of their "bowels" (σπλάγχνοις). As such, "If there is any shortage of space it is on their side, literally in their bowels."³⁶⁶ This accusation of Paul's is "certainly . . . a serious charge" directed at the Corinthians.³⁶⁷ Yet, if the Corinthian congregation were withholding their love and affection for Paul, he has every right to be angry because he had suffered all sorts of humiliation and hardships in his desire for the salvation of the Corinthian congregation.

As one observes in 6:13, Paul "speaks to them as children" (ὡς τέκνοις λέγω), and "as a fair exchange" (ἣν δὲ αὐτὴν ἀντιμισθίαν), he commands them to "enlarge" (πλατύνθητε) their heart for what he did for them.³⁶⁸ Indeed, the imperative, aorist passive πλατύνθητε (make broad, enlarged) is unequivocal; Paul does not leave them much room for negotiation. He wants the Corinthian congregation to stop acting like children. One recollects 1 Corinthians 3:1 where Paul calls them "babes," figurative for "immature." Francis, in his analysis of 1 Corinthians 3:1–3, believes that Paul calls them "babes" "because they were in fact being childish, a condition contrary to being spiritual."³⁶⁹ As such, Gundry's observation that "Paul is trying to shame the Corinthians by

---

364. Louw and Nida, *Greek-English Lexicon*, 1:415.
365. Malina and Pilch, *Social-Science Commentary*, 147.
366. Barrett, *Second Epistle*, 193.
367. Harris, *Second Epistle*, 490.
368. The imperative aorist passive πλατύνθητε, along with the vocative use of Corinthians, literally rendered the tone of Paul here: "Hey you Corinthians! Enlarge your hearts to me now!"
369. Francis, "As Babes in Christ," 43.

comparing them to children who need a good talking to" may not be too far off for what Paul had in mind the first time he uttered it.[370] It is very much likely that Paul wanted to embarrass them for not opening their hearts to him.

From a sociological point of view, it is interesting to note that in antiquity, tensions existed between parents and children even when there was a strong desire to obey one's parents. For instance, the fifth commandment specifically states, "Honour your father and mother" (Exod 20:12 and Deut 5:16). In addition, even in Greco-Roman society, obeying and taking care of one's parents was the normative practice. According to Bella, "Perictytone states: 'we should reverence parents both while living and dead, and never oppose them in anything they say or do.'"[371] One also reads of Diogenes Laertius who wrote, "The Stoics approve also of honouring parents and brothers in the second place next after the gods."[372] Similarly, Cicero stated, "Now, if a contrast and comparison were to be made to find out where most of our moral obligation is due, country would come first, and parents; for their services have laid us under the heaviest obligation."[373] Thus, taking care of parents is the obligation of children.

Nonetheless, not all was smooth sailing in a parent-child relationship in antiquity. Bella mentions a father who prayed, "O Lord Sarapis Helios, beneficent one. (Say) whether it is fitting that Phania my son and his wife should not agree now with his father, but oppose him [αντιλεγειν] and not make contract. Tell me this truly. Goodbye."[374] He also mentions another letter that read, "If you won't take me with you to Alexandria I won't write you a letter or speak to you or say goodbye to you; and if you go to Alexandria I won't take your hand nor ever greet you again."[375] Sometimes, because of the unruly behaviour of their children, parents, often the father, punished the child. Again, Bella writes, "With a reference to Livy (1.50.9), Eyben argued that: When father and son disagree, no discussion was possible, or even necessary."[376] Take the case of Scaurus, "who did not want any contact with

---

370. Gundry, *Commentary*, 707.
371. "Book 2. Ch. 10. 10–12," quoted in Balla, *Child-Parent Relationship*, 73.
372. Laertius, *Lives of Eminent Philosophers*, 1.17.120.
373. Cicero, *De Officiis*, 1.58.
374. Balla, *Child-Parent Relationship*, 58.
375. Balla, 59.
376. Balla, 59.

his son anymore because of the latter's cowardly behaviour on the battlefield, thus driving him to commit suicide (101 BC)."³⁷⁷ Seneca also weighed in by stating, "Would not he, who constantly punished his children by beating them for the most trifling faults, be thought the worst of fathers?"³⁷⁸

Paul, who considered the Corinthians his children (1 Cor 4:14–15), had every right to demand a "reward" (ἀντιμισθίαν, 2 Cor 6:13) from the Corinthians. He could punish them and still be within his rights, but the way Paul deals with the Corinthians suggests desperation on his part. This ought to warn any interpreters of Paul of the seriousness and far-reaching effects of disability during Paul's days. One hardly knows the result of Paul's attempt at defending his integrity, but now that Paul has so forcefully commended himself, one can only hope that the Corinthians took heed and ceased to be bothered about his disability. Nevertheless, it is humbling to realize that if one stripped away all the legends that have accumulated in Christian traditions,³⁷⁹ the real Paul that emerges is a pitiful yet proud human being who refused to bow down or go quietly in a culture that was extremely bigoted towards its disabled members.

## 5.5 Applying a DH to the Exegetical Analysis of 2 Corinthians 10–13

These last four chapters of 2 Corinthians again fall under the *probatio* of Paul's argument. For those scholars who consider these four chapters to constitute a different letter, there are differing opinions on how to differentiate the rhetorical arrangement of Paul's argument here.³⁸⁰ For instance, while Peterson prefers to arrange this unit as consisting of "*exordium* (10:1–6), *propositio* (10:1–11), *narratio* (10:12–18), *argumentatio* (11:1–12:18), and *peroratio* (12:19–13:10),"³⁸¹ Thrall sees it as consisting of the "*exordium* (10:1–11),

---

377. Balla, 59.

378. Seneca, *De Clementia*; cf. Seneca, "Of Clemency (De Clementia), Book I (1900)," trans. by Aubrey Stewart, Wikisource, accessed November 13, 2018, https://en.wikisource.org/wiki/Of_Clemency/Book_I#XVI.

379. See Thurén, *Derhetorizing Paul*, 35.

380. Ashley, "Paul's Paradigm," 53; Garland, *2 Corinthians*, 422–423; Lambrecht, "Fool's Speech," 305–322, 324.

381. B. K. Peterson, "Eloquence and the Proclamation of the Gospel in Corinth: Social Standards and Eschatological Crisis" (PhD diss., Union Theological Seminary, 1998).

*narratio* and *propositio* (10:12–18), *insinuatio* (11:1–15), *argumentatio* (11:16–12:18), *translatio* (12:19–21), *peroratio* (13:1–10)."[382] However, as discussed earlier, this study treats 2 Corinthians as one unit, therefore it will continue to interpret chapters 10–13 as a continuation and an expansion of Paul's comments on his sufferings and weaknesses mentioned in the previous chapters (i.e. 1–9).[383] Thus, along with Witherington, this study considers these four chapters as the *porbatio* of Paul's argument.[384]

These last four chapters, without a doubt, are Paul's most personal and rawest emotional confrontation with the Corinthian congregation yet.[385] Witherington recognizes this and states, "What has been simmering on a back burner in chs. 1–9 is brought to a roaring boil in chapters 10–13."[386] The analyses of the previous chapters so far has made one think that Paul was gracious in his defence of himself and his ministry from the socio-cultural prejudices of the Corinthians.[387] Carson is right to observe, "Quite clearly the Corinthians were culturally conditioned to be led astray in these directions."[388] However, in 2 Corinthians 10–13, Paul does not hold back his stinging criticisms, and he rebukes the Corinthians for their humiliating rejection of his authority on the grounds of his disability.

## 5.5.1 Rhetorical Unit of 2 Corinthians 10–13

Many scholars argue for the rhetorical unity of 2 Corinthians 10–13, and rightly so, because these last four chapters are united in certain ways. For instance, according to Moon,

> The last four chapters of 2 Corinthians stand as manifestly apart from the previous chapters, the pastoral admonitions (7:2–15) and encouragement of collection (8:1–9:15), in the tone, style and subject matter. Here is an aggressive apologetic and counter-attack against those within the church who still oppose Paul

---

382. Thrall, *Corinthians 8–13*, 597.
383. See deSilva, *Introduction*, 584.
384. Witherington considers the last chapter (13:5–10) as *peroration*, which is "a brief emotional appeal" (*Conflict & Community*, 471).
385. Carson, *From Triumphalism*, 1; see also Welborn, "Paul's Appeal," 31–60.
386. Witherington, *Conflict & Community*, 431.
387. See Carson, *From Triumphalism*, 19.
388. Carson, 19.

(13:5–10) and against his opponents from outside Corinth who stand in the shadows behind them (10:10, 11:4, 12–15, 21–23). Paul's upcoming visit also dominates this section in the hope that it will be a constructive time of healing, rather than a time of judgement for the church (10:2, 12:14, 20–21, 13:1–4).[389]

Moon's observation that a "common theme"[390] unites these chapters makes further sense as one considers Paul's use of the personal pronoun "I" specifically in these last chapters. There has been a lot of speculation about Paul's sudden reverting to using the singular pronoun "I" at the beginning of 2 Corinthians 10:1, and all throughout the unit, continuing his narration in the first singular pronoun.[391] While "some have seen in this an indication that at this point in the letter Paul began to write with his own hand as Gal. 6:11,"[392] there are others like Black who think that Paul was trying to make a distinction between him and Timothy, who may have been the other author.[393] However, scholars like Harris, Matera, Martin, and Garland would interpret this sudden use of the "I" as an indication of Paul's willingness to defend his apostolic honour.[394] Indeed, the issue here is "Paul's conduct" which is very personal in nature.[395] As such, it is not strange for Paul to change his tone suddenly to the more personal pronoun "I." In fact, whenever he wanted to stress a particular point or was under immense pressure or "intense conviction,"[396] Paul would resort to this use of the personal pronoun (see Gal 5:2 and 1 Thess 2:18).

Moreover, Witherington points out, "A sudden change in tone and atmosphere was not unusual in a document using forensic rhetoric, especially when the case was difficult and a firm appeal to the stronger emotions (*pathos*)

---

389. Moon, "Paul's Discourse," 76.
390. Moon, 76.
391. Kistemaker, *2 Corinthians*, 330.
392. Barrett, *Second Epistle*, 246.
393. Black, *Paul*, 133.
394. See Harris, *Second Epistle*, 666; Matera, *2 Corinthians*, 219; Martin, *2 Corinthians*, 302; Garland, *2 Corinthians*, 425.
395. Dodd, *Paul's Paradigmatic 'I'*, 30. This contrasts with Ellington, who downplayed Paul's personal use of "I" for a more inclusive way ("Not Applicable," 325–340).
396. Barrett, *Second Epistle*, 246.

near the end was required to win the audience."³⁹⁷ This strategy is called *Insinuatio* in rhetoric, and Greek and Roman writers employed it as a strategy in many of their writings. Take for example Demosthenes's writing, which was so similar to 2 Corinthians that Ford and Yong use it as their framework to study Paul's argument.³⁹⁸ While the "Greek rhetorical theory instructed orators to approach prejudice head on at the beginning of the speech so that they could successfully make their case,"³⁹⁹ on the other hand, the "Roman rhetorical theory instructed orators to approach prejudice and scandalous cases in an indirect manner, saving the difficult topics for much later in the speech."⁴⁰⁰ From this study's analysis of Paul's defence, it is more likely that Paul was adopting the Roman's *insinuatio*. In these last four chapters, as compared to the previous chapters analysed, Paul does not mince his words as he goes all out on a frontal assault in defence of his person, his integrity as well as his ministry.

Other indicators show how these four chapters constitute a rhetorical unit. First, this unit "begins and ends with an appeal using the verb παρακαλεω (10:1, 13:11)."⁴⁰¹ "This appeal of Paul appears again as a form of ultimatum in the opening (10:6) and closing (13:2)."⁴⁰² Second, Paul's "willingness to be bold in his dealing with them when he arrived,"⁴⁰³ which one finds in 10:2 and again in 13:10, indicates the opening and closing of this unit. Third, Paul's mentioning of the "Corinthians' obedience," which is "explicit" in "10:6 and implied in 13:1–10," and finally, his mentioning of "previous and/or current writing (10:11, 13:10)" all point to the rhetorical unity of 2 Corinthians 10–13.⁴⁰⁴

## 5.5.2 The Rhetorical Exigence: Corinthians' Negative Attitude to Paul's Disability

The rhetorical problem, as was discussed in the *exordium* at the beginning of this chapter, clearly reveals that Paul was grappling with the negative attitude

---

397. Witherington, *Conflict & Community*, 431.
398. Young and Ford, *Meaning and Truth*, 37–40.
399. Christian, "*Insinuatio*," 6.
400. Christian, 12.
401. Ashley, "Paul's Paradigm," 53.
402. Moon, "Paul's Discourse," 77.
403. Ashley, "Paul's Paradigm," 53.
404. Ashley, 53.

that the Corinthians had towards his disability. Likewise, in this rhetorical unit, one sees clearly the Corinthians' shaming of Paul whom they considered a "lesser" apostle (11:5) and "meek" (10:1). To them, "Paul is weak, too weak to be a true apostle and strong leader," thus sowing doubts in their mind.[405] The Corinthian congregation seemed convinced that Paul did not have the necessary credentials to be among the "super-apostles."[406] Their prejudice towards Paul was influenced by the social ramifications of "Paul's unimpressive and humble . . . appearance and manner [and] his lack of sophistic oratory."[407] As previously discussed, these accusations were socially stigmatizing in nature, most of all, in the way they connected his unimpressive body and his "contemptible speech" (λόγος ἐξουθενημένος, 2 Cor 10:10). The following sections discuss in detail the rhetorical exigence from a disability perspective.

### 5.5.2.1 Paul lacks the necessary credentials of the "super apostle"

The Corinthian congregation was convinced that Paul lacked the necessary documentation or credentials (10:12, 15–16, 18). According to Carson, Paul "does not even bother to present the appropriated letters of introduction and commendation (10:13–14; cf. 3:1) [but] he has to rely on self-commendation (10:12–18, 12:11; cf. 5:12, 6:4–10)" when he first preaches the gospel to the Corinthians.[408] There seems to be some truth in their accusation because Paul's counterargument reveals that his commendation came from the Lord (10:8, 13). According to Garland, "in the cut-throat competition for plaudits and pupils, one had to advertise oneself publicly with audacious praise while impugning the qualities of other contenders for honour."[409] Since Paul had no commendation from anywhere, he had to defend his right to preach the gospel to them.

### 5.5.2.2 Paul's unimpressive appearance and lack of oratory skills

Some of the starkest evidence of the shameful treatment of Paul because of his disability is to be found in 2 Corinthians 10:10: "His letters are weighty

---

405. Roberts, "Weak Enough," 298.
406. Thielman, *Theology*, 326.
407. Roberts, "Weak Enough," 298.
408. Carson, *From Triumphalism*, 17.
409. Garland, *2 Corinthians*, 452.

and strong, but his bodily presence is weak and his speech of no account" (ESV). A cursory reading of this text reveals a comparative line of accusatory thought in this verse. In the first place, this study concentrates on the Corinthians' claim that Paul's letters were "weighty and strong" (10:10a). The Greek word βαρύς (weighty) can mean legalistic or rules that are burdensome as well (see Matt 23:4); on the other hand, there is no ambiguity to the Greek word ἰσχυρός (strong), which reflects the effect of his previous letters to the Corinthians. Second, the Corinthians were counter arguing that Paul's appearance was "weak" (ἀσθενής, 10:10) and that his "speech" (λόγος) was "contemptible" (ἐξουθενημένος).[410] One is reminded of the Greek word ἀσθενής, meaning "weakness or powerlessness of various kinds," be it "literally, of bodily ailment, weak, ill, sick, and of physical or intellectual inability, inadequate," or "figuratively, of what is less effective weak, feeble, not strong."[411]

Thus, Paul's appearance must be evidently "weak" as in opposition to his "strong" letter. However, by saying that Paul was actually "ugly" and "despicable" in manner of speech, they point out the differences in the qualities between his written letters and actual delivery. The question, "If Paul was so skilful in his letter writing, why aren't they seeing his rhetorical prowess when he is speaking in public (see 10:9–10)?" may have been the uppermost in their minds. There is hardly a better explanation than to think that they suspected Paul of cheating when he composed his letters. Seen from this perspective, the accusations levelled at Paul by the instigators were squarely on Paul's integrity as well.

From a disability point of view, this accusation of the Corinthians reeks of stigmatization. How so, one may ask. In the previous discussion of *APT*, Paul was described as "a man small of stature, with a bald head and crooked legs."[412] The background study done previously has shown that the Greco-Romans, with their emphasis on excellent physical symmetry, were not kind to dwarfs. Not only were dwarfs unable to hold official positions in antiquity,[413] one also reads of Suetonius, who mentioned Emperor Augustus describing the

---

410. Gingrich, "ἐξουθενημένος can mean 1. Despise, disdain Lk 18:9; Ro 14:3, 10; 1 Cor 1:28, 16:11; Gal 4:14; consider of no account 1 Cor 6:4; amount to nothing 2 Cor 10:10. 2; reject with contempt Ac 4:11; 1 Th 5:20; treat with contempt Lk 23:11" (*Shorter Lexicon*, 70).

411. Zmijewski, "ἀσθένεια," 170.

412. Schneemelcher, *New Testament Apocrypha*, 2.239.

413. Dasen studied the ancient Egyptian and Greek dwarfs (*Dwarfs*, 212).

dwarfs "as *lusus natura* ('nature's abortions'), and of evil omen."[414] Paul may not have been a natural dwarf, but his small stature would not inspire much confidence in that kind of society. Gundry acknowledges that the society of those days considered "small stature" as "an abnormality."[415] Paul, a short man with crooked legs and a bald head, would have been socially an outcast to those who were not loyal to him.

Nevertheless, was baldness a sign of disability? From an examination of some records in antiquity, it certainly seems that way. For instance, "writing in the fourth century B.C., Aristotle referred to the 'deformity' of baldness (*Generation of Animals* 784)."[416] Again, Cicero, "in his discussions regarding mimes speaks of their general deformity, their baldness and their ridiculous grimaces."[417] Another instance where bald people were made the butt of a joke is to be found in "the *Historia Augusta* [where] the emperor Elagabalus" ordered, as was "the custom . . . to a dinner eight bald men . . . to call forth general laughter."[418] One may also come across the inscription of "Heraieus of Mytilene . . . upon a stele at the Temple of Asclepius at Epiraurus," where it reads: "He had no hair on his head, but an abundant growth on his chin. He was ashamed because he was laughed at by others."[419] All these examples show that having an abundance of hair was very important in antiquity, and that the resultant loss of hair was equally disabling. Sussman points out that in the Old Testament, being bald was "often regarded as a curse (Isa 3:24; Ezek 7:18; Amos 8:10). Complete baldness (total alopecia) and even the common male-type baldness disqualified priests from service in the sanctuary (Lev 13:40–41)."[420]

Moreover, a disability perspective allows one to connect the reason of why the Corinthians felt ashamed because Paul was not a skilful orator and was also ugly. The attitude of the ancient Greek society was truly intolerant and ruthless towards someone who spoke in public but did not have

---

414. Suetonius, *Augustus*, ch. 81.
415. Gundry, *Commentary*, 315.
416. Rose, *Staff of Oedipus*, 12.
417. Welborn, *Paul*, 121.
418. *Historia Augusta*, 29.3.
419. "IG IV 1.121; Stele 1, no. 19, Edelstein and Edelstein, 1945 and 1998, 233," quoted in Draycott, "Hair Today," 78.
420. Sussman, "Sickness and Disease," 6:11.

good physical features. The public looked down on, mocked, or despised speakers and leaders who exhibited physical problems that prevented them from speaking well in public. According to deSilva, this was a society where "display was as important as substance in public speaking. Even classical rhetorical theorists stressed the importance of delivery, posture, voice and stage presence . . . over substance and careful preparation of argument."[421] Case in point, one of the greatest ancient Near Eastern orators, Demosthenes, struggled against societal biases and ridicule because of his speech problem and bodily weakness before he could achieve fame. According to Plutarch, the first time Demosthenes spoke in front of the people, "he was interrupted by their clamours and laughed at *his* weakness of voice and indistinctness of speech and shortness of breath which disturbed the sense of what he said by disjoining his sentences."[422] Contrast the plight of Demosthenes against Alcibiades who suffered from lisping yet endured no ridicule or harmful attitude from the audience: Alcibiades had "excellent natural parts" and those who heard him speak thought that his lisping "made his talk persuasive and full of charm."[423] Clearly, the ancient society was biased.

If the Greco-Roman societal attitude was like this, then one can surmise that Paul would have met the same treatment at the hands of the Corinthians. Because Paul was disabled, he was not fit to be included among the "super-apostles" of Christ (see 2 Cor 11:5). To top it all, it is truly remarkable that Paul did not deny his problem (disability). Rather he acknowledged that he was an ἰδιώτης (unskilled) when it came to speaking (2 Cor 11:6).[424] The word ἰδιώτης can mean, first, "a person who is relatively unskilled or inexperienced in some activity or field of knowledge," and second, "one who is not knowledgeable about some particular group's experience, one not in the know, an outsider."[425] In this particular case, the use of ἰδιώτης by Paul about himself seems to be indicating that he was "unskilled in speaking." If Paul had exhibited a more manly and appealing physical appearance, his lack of oratorical skill would not have mattered much. However, as it is, his unimpressive appearance

---

421. deSilva, *Introduction*, 557.
422. Plutarch, *Demosthenes*, 4.3.
423. Plutarch, *Alcibiades*, 1.4.
424. See Becker, *Letter Hermeneutics*, 116.
425. Bauer et al., *Greek-English Lexicon*, s.v. "ἰδιώτης," , 468.

allowed the Corinthians to denounce further his contemptible speech. One is surprised at such kinds of judgementalism among the Corinthians. Paul was deeply hurt by their accusation which prompted him to defend his honour from a "human standard," and he knew it (see 2 Cor 11:18), but he could not help himself (2 Cor 12:11).

### 5.5.2.3 Paul's "thorn in the flesh": A cause for stigmatization

How does one consider the meaning and substance of Paul's "thorn in the flesh"? No doubt, this is a crucial *exigence* from a disability point of view. From what one understands of Paul's narration of his heavenly revelation in 12:1–9, the Corinthians and their instigators used this "thorn in the flesh" as an excuse to belittle his status as an apostle. Baird thinks that Paul lacks the "sort of ecstatic demonstration that certifies their mission" because of his inability to heal his "thorn in the flesh."[426] This made the Corinthians doubt the source or authenticity of his apostolic power (13:3).

There are different proposals and hypotheses on what this "thorn in the flesh" could be. Among the earliest interpreters, the Latin church fathers like Tertullian and others "take the thorn to be some form of physical illness,"[427] while "the Greek fathers, on the other hand, held that the thorn was persecution,"[428] with some identifying "the thorn as . . . the 'ministers of Satan' at Corinth, or the Corinthian congregation itself."[429] The Latin church fathers' physical sickness proposal ranged from the possibility that Paul might be suffering from "epilepsy" to "malarial infection" to "psychosomatic disorders."[430] Recently, Yarbro again noticed the argument that Paul's thorn in the flesh might be an indication of his suffering from bouts of epilepsy.[431] She believes

---

426. Baird, "Visions," 653.
427. Twelftree, "Healing," 379.
428. Russell, "Redemptive Suffering," 556.
429. See Mullins, "Paul's Thorn," 299–303; O'Collins, "Power Made Perfect," 216–227; McCant, "Paul's Thorn," 550–572.
430. See Plummer, *Second Epistle*, 351; Lightfoot, *Epistle*, 186–191; Bernard, *Second Epistle*, 110–111; Ramsay, *St. Paul*, 94–97; Bultmann, *Second Letter*, 224; Barrett, *Second Epistle*, 315; Nisket, "Thorn," 126; Minn, *Thorn that Remained*, 23–31; Marshall, "Metaphor," 315–316; Hughes, *Paul's Second Epistle*, 442–448; Furnish, *2 Corinthians*, 549–550.
431. Collins, "Paul's Disability," 165–183.

that "this shameful character would explain why he considered the disease to be a sort of counterweight to his vision and revelations."[432]

Chrysostom was one of the earliest proponents who believed that Paul was referring to "Alexander the coppersmith, the party of Hymenæus and Philetus, all the adversaries of the word" as the messenger of Satan.[433] Moreover, these "messengers" did their "Satan's business" by continually fighting against Paul, thereby becoming his "thorn in the flesh."[434] Recently, Mullin picked up Chrysostom's proposal and was confident that Paul referred to an enemy.[435] Nevertheless, during the Middle Ages, it was normative for interpreters to link Paul's thorn in the flesh "with sensual temptations or spiritual trials."[436] For instance, the Vulgate translated the "thorn in the flesh" as "*stimulus carnis*", and this no doubt influenced some interpreters who were interested in monastic traditions.[437]

Price was the first to suggest that Paul was referring to a literal "demon or malevolent angel" as his "thorn in the flesh."[438] According to Price, this "demon" was sent to punish "Paul's pride at the wonder of his experience."[439] Glessner took it a step further and proposed that while it may be possible that an "adversative angel" was the one responsible, "it *remained* with Paul in the form of a chronic, bodily infirmity."[440] Abernathy's work also suggests that "a literal demon was his 'thorn in the flesh.'"[441] This suggestion from Price and others may seem somewhat incomprehensible, but it is not altogether nonsensical because one reads of heavenly beings causing bodily pains in the Hebrew Bible (see Gen 32:25). One also comes across the narrative of the four rabbis who entered paradise only for one to die, another to be wounded, the third to become "a heretic," and only the last to remain

---

432. Collins, 174.
433. Chrysostom, "Homily 26."
434. Chrysostom.
435. Mullins, "Paul's Thorn," 303. However, Murphy-O'Connor objects to this interpretation, questioning whether "Paul would have prayed to be delivered from persecution" (*Paul*, 321); see also, Martin, *2 Corinthians*, 415).
436. Russell, "Redemptive Suffering," 556.
437. Russell, "Redemptive Suffering," 556.
438. Price, "Punished in Paradise," 33–40.
439. Price, 33–40.
440. Glessner, "Ethnomedical Anthropology," 27.
441. Abernathy, "Paul's Thorn," 69.

unharmed.[442] Nevertheless, despite the attractiveness of the story about "four rabbis" for the background story of Paul's "thorn in the flesh,"[443] the "gap of nearly a century between the event recorded in Corinthians" and the story of the four rabbis makes the connection improbable.[444]

Murphy-O'Connor is adamant that this "thorn in the flesh" cannot be a "psychic problem," for a suggestion along these lines requires a person to have an active imagination. According to him, Paul was unlikely tortured by "a real demon, who accompanied Paul on his heavenly journey," or that he was in "agony at the refusal of the Jews to respond to the gospel," or better still, Paul battled "sexual temptations, hysteria, depression."[445] For him, and rightly so, one should add, "somatic illness appears to have a better foundation."[446] In addition, as Park points out, Paul's use of σαρκί (12:7) is "understood to refer to Paul's physical body and thus is viewed as the sphere within which the affliction affecting the Apostle resided."[447] That is why there are quite a number of influential scholars like Bultmann, Knox, Ramsay, Deissmann, Lightfoot, Schweitzer, and Lietzmann who have swayed to this line of interpretation.[448]

The exact cause of Paul's "thorn in the flesh" may not be possible to ascertain; however, what is most certain is that no matter how one wants to interpret it, the results are the same. Paul's "thorn in the flesh" was a reason for him being stigmatized socially by the Corinthians and his opponents, thus making him more disabled. Galli is right on point with his comments that even if one is "not sure what Paul's 'thorn in the flesh' was . . . it is not a reach to see it as a physical disability."[449] For instance, if Paul's "thorn in the flesh" was epilepsy as some interpreters claim, then Kelly's examinations of "ancient texts" that "represent epileptics' physiological condition as having

---

442. "Chagigah 14b."

443. Morray-Jones extensively studies this as the background of his explanation on Paul's "thorn in the flesh" in 2 Cor 12:7 ("Paradise Revisited," 265–292); see also Baird, "Visions," 651–662.

444. Gottstein, "Four Entered," 71.

445. Murphy-O'Connor, *Paul*, 321.

446. Murphy-O'Connor, 321.

447. Park, "Paul's Skolops tē Sarki," 179.

448. Bultmann, *Theology*, 233; Knox, *Chapters*, 9; Ramsay, *Historical Commentary*, 422–428; see also Ramsay, *St. Paul*, 94–97; Deissmann, *St. Paul*, 62–63, 195; Lightfoot, *St. Paul's Epistle*, 186–191; Schweitzer, *Mysticism*, 154; Lietzmann, *Beginnings*, 113.

449. Galli, "Power," 7.

demonic origins" make much sense for they validate the instigators claim about Paul's apostleship.[450] The Greco-Roman and Jewish cultures did not leave much room for an objective interpretation of any kind of illness. Take the case of leprosy in the Hebrew Bible: the most disconcerting consequence of this disease was not on the leprous person's wellbeing but rather the effects their leprosy had on the society.[451]

If one accepts Paul's "thorn in the flesh" as some sort of disability that manifested occasionally and for all to see (like epilepsy), then it makes sense that it would have caused a further complication because of the societal attitude towards the particular problem. It seems that from the text, particularly 10:10 and 13:3 where they ask proof that Paul is speaking through Christ, the Corinthians allow their "superstition and prejudice" to overcome their respect for Paul – that is, if they had any at all from the start.[452] Paul had suffered physically, mentally, and spiritually from a "chronic, incurable, physical affliction that caused acute, intense, disabling, sudden pain" (see 12:8).[453] This "thorn in the flesh" occasioned the Corinthians to treat him badly and even to doubt his very leadership and authority as an apostle of Christ. Thus, Paul's thorn in the flesh is a proof of his intense sufferings from the social stigmatization because of his disability.[454]

### 5.5.3 *Probatio*: **Paul Defends Himself**

Judging by the nature of how Paul responds to the Corinthians in this rhetorical unit, one concurs with Garland that the instigators had "met with an embarrassing measure of success."[455] Paul needed to act decisively at this point or else the possibility of losing his congregation loomed large. Paul was very possessive of his church, and losing control of the congregation he

---

450. Kelley, "Punishment," 206.

451. See Pilch, *Healing*, 59; cf. Glessner, "Ethnomedical Anthropology," 25.

452. According to Betz, "2 Cor 12:7–10 shows illness was likely to be interpreted by common people as demons possession" (*Galatians*, 225).

453. Nash, "Paul's 'Thorn,'" 33.

454. According to Creamer this thorn in the flesh "bore directly on Paul's stature and authority before the Corinthians, and so had social consequences within the Corinthian community" (*Disability*, 73). One can also connect the "trial" of the Galatians if one thinks that Paul's "bodily ailment" was epilepsy, which no doubt would have had a social stigma attached to it.

455. Garland, "Paul's Apostolic Authority," 371.

had worked so hard for must have been difficult. Thus, Paul "pulls out all the stops, using irony, sarcasm, mock humility, and contrast to dissuade the Corinthians from being bullied or beguiled into submitting any further to his opponents."[456]

A cursory reading of 2 Corinthians 10–13 shows that Paul uses all sorts of tools at his disposal such as "the derogatory expressions he applies to them" that include, "super-apostles" (11:5; 12:11), "false apostles, deceitful workers" (11:13), "ministers of Satan in disguise" (11:14–15), and "fools" (11:19).[457] Paul even refrains from revealing their names and identities. Furnish believes that Paul deliberately withheld this information, and in doing so, he was "following the ancient rhetorical convention of denying one's enemies even such status as the use of their names could accord them."[458] Not just content to slander his opponents, Paul also resorts to "self-boasting" which probably "was considered an act of honor" in those days.[459] As he tries to woo back the Corinthians to his side, what one gets to see of Paul in this rhetorical unit is a man daring to go to the bitter end in his attempt to defend his honour while shaming those who oppose him. The following sections further break down and analyse Paul's *probatio*.

### 5.5.3.1 Paul portrays himself as military personnel

Paul "appeals" (παρακαλῶ, 10:1) to the Corinthians not to be superficial in their judgement towards him (10:7). If they continue to be so, Paul will discipline them like a military man or, as Larson prefers, "warrior."[460] Thus, Paul writes to them, "For the weapons of our warfare are not merely human, but they have divine power to destroy strongholds. We destroy arguments and every proud obstacle raised up against the knowledge of God, and we take every thought captive to obey Christ. We are ready to punish every disobedience when your obedience is complete" (NRSV, 2 Cor 10:4–6; cf. Eph 6:10–17). Paul, whom they considered disabled, would be "bold" and punish their disobedience until they became obedient (10:6). Paul uses words such

---

456. Garland, 371; Longman and Garland, *Romans–Galatians*, 524.
457. Furnish, *2 Corinthians*, 49.
458. Furnish, 49.
459. Garland, *2 Corinthians*, 452.
460. Larson, "Paul's Masculinity," 96.

as στρατεύομαι (lit. "do military service, serve in the army," 10:3),⁴⁶¹ ὅπλον (lit. "weapon," 10:4),⁴⁶² στρατεία, (lit. "campaign," 10:4),⁴⁶³ ὀχύρωμα (lit. "stronghold, fortress," 10:4),⁴⁶⁴ καθαίρεσις ("tearing down, destruction," 10:4),⁴⁶⁵ and αἰχμαλωτίζω (lit. "be scattered as captives,"10:5)⁴⁶⁶ to make his points clear.⁴⁶⁷

As Matera explains, Paul's language in these verses is very much military in nature, as it echoes the process of decimation that the Romans employed against the Greeks in 1 Maccabees 8:10: "The Romans took captive their wives and children; they plundered them, conquered the land, tore down their strongholds, and enslaved them to this day (1 Macc 8:10)."⁴⁶⁸ Paul is clear in his statement that he is not fighting a normal battle, but a battle to tear down "arguments" and "pretension" that hinder people from receiving "the knowledge of God."⁴⁶⁹ In the same way, in Ephesians 6:11 the Pauline letter argues that his fight is not against flesh and blood, but against the unseen "dark world and spiritual forces of evil." One also observes a parallel with Philo referring to "stronghold" as an intangible term. Philo stated, "For a strong building which is erected by means of plausible arguments is not built for the sake of any other object except that of averting and alienating the mind from honour due to God."⁴⁷⁰ Likewise, Paul is focusing on the breaking down of cultural prejudices and traditional bigotries that prevent people from opening their hearts to him and his gospel (see 6:11; 7:1).⁴⁷¹

Just as the immediate verse after the military metaphor suggests (see 10:10), Paul is quite concerned with the cultural practice of judging a person by the cover and the stigmatization that follows straight away. These cultural

---

461. Gingrich, "στρατεύομαι," in *Shorter Lexicon*, 186.
462. Gingrich, "ὅπλον," 140.
463. Gingrich, "στρατεία," 186.
464. Gingrich, "ὀχύρωμα," 145.
465. Gingrich, "καθαίρεσις," 97.
466. Gingrich, "αἰχμαλωτίζω," as "Fig. take captive, subdue Rom 7:23; 2 Cor 10:5," in *Shorter Lexicon*, 6.
467. Peterson, "Conquest," 259.
468. Matera, *2 Corinthians*, 223.
469. See Matera (*2 Corinthians*, 224) on the steps that Paul took to safeguard his authority and at the same time save the Corinthians.
470. Philo, "On the Confusion of Tongues," 26.129, in *Works of Philo: Complete and Unabridged*, 245.
471. Peterson, "Conquest," 259–262.

obstacles to his disability were all rooted in the mind; no wonder Paul talks of taking captives πᾶν νόημα ("all minds/thoughts," 2 Cor 10:5) in his attempt to tear down this perception that acted as a fortress. One sees Paul describing νοήματα in 2 Corinthians 2:11 as "use of the 'wiles' or 'nefarious 'designs' or 'manoeuvres' of Satan."[472] Thus, it is not far-fetched to suggest that Paul's use of military metaphors is to demolish the cultural biases against disability embedded deep within the Corinthians' consciousness.

### *5.5.3.2 Paul positively boasts of his sufferings and hardships*

Paul's baldness or lack of hair, his weak physical presence and short stature, his unappealing manner of talking, and his epilepsy, all make the reader understand how stigmatized Paul was by the Corinthians and their instigators. Paul seems to accept that their criticisms have some merit and that he lacks the sophistication and the well-built body that orators should possess. Therefore, in the bulk of the passages in this rhetorical unit (chapters 10–12), he does the next best thing he could, and that is "boasting" of what his "disabled" body can endure. In fact, it is interesting to note the similarity between the list of his sufferings mentioned in 4:8–9 and 6:4–8 to that of 11:23b–29. One would not be amiss to think of this list as the expansion or final version of the hardship list that Paul had previously mentioned in 2 Corinthians 1:8–9, 4:8–9, and 6:4–8.

In 2 Corinthians 11:23b–33, Paul narrates all the sufferings that he has let his body through for the sake of his ministry and for the sake of the Corinthians as well.[473] He has worked much harder than anyone else, he has "been in prison more frequently, been flogged more severely, and been exposed to death again and again" (11:23b). Then, he specifically mentions that he has been "lashed" forty (minus one) times five, which means he had received from the Jews 195 lashes on different occasions (11:24). According to Martin, this is a "statutory thirty-nine lashes, prescribed in Mishnah, *Makkot 3.10*, on the basis of Deut 25:2–3, which gave the maximum as forty."[474] The book of Acts is silent on how and when Paul received these lashes, but this

---

472. Harris, *Second Epistle*, 683.
473. Martyn, *Galatians*, 568.
474. Martin, *2 Corinthians*, 376.

kind of beating was specifically a Jewish synagogue punishment.[475] Because it is a synagogue penalty, Meeks believes that Paul was "lashed" as he first went to the Jews who rejected him and his message (see Acts 18:5).[476] Whatever the case may be, to be "lashed" 195 times requires someone with guts and endurance. Paul was right to boast of his receiving lashes since he wanted the Corinthians to respect his disabled body.

Paul continues his factual narrations stating that he was beaten three times with rods (τρὶς ἐρραβδίσθην, 11:25a). This beating with rods is a "technical punishment" of the Romans.[477] In Acts 16:22, one reads of Paul being beaten with rods even though as a Roman citizen he was supposed to be "exempted from this punishment."[478] However, this was not out of the ordinary for there were other cases where even Roman citizens were beaten with rods if they caused disturbances. For instance, Josephus recorded, "Florus who succeeded Albinus as procurator of Judea in A.D. 64/65 had soldiers of equestrian rank flogged, ignoring their rights as Romans."[479] If they beat Paul with the rod, does it also mean he was causing disturbances? Martin certainly seems to think so, writing, "Because he was treated as a social pest" they beat Paul with the rod.[480] One can further suggest from a disability perspective that his beating with the rod signifies prejudicial treatment. Looking at Paul's point of view in 1 Thessalonians 2:2, Paul was treated "shamefully" (ὑβρισθέντες). This Greek expression literally means, "Treat in an arrogant or spiteful manner, mistreat, scoff at, insult."[481] It was only after he told them that he had Roman citizenship that they treated him properly.[482] In a way, his "unimpressive appearance" must have been the cause of this unfavourable first impression.

He was stoned once, and this incident is concurrent with his stoning in Acts 14:5 and 19. Again, from a disability perspective, stoning is a shameful way to receive punishment. Stoning was essentially a Jewish punishment, and

---

475. Hengel, *Acts*, 109; Martin, *2 Corinthians*, 376.
476. Meeks, *First Urban Christians*, 26.
477. Martin, *2 Corinthians*, 377.
478. Martin, 377; Sherwin-White, *Roman Society*, 48–98.
479. Josephus, *The War of the Jews*, 2:308.
480. Martin, *2 Corinthians*, 377.
481. Gingrich, "ὑβρίζω," in *Shorter Lexicon*, 204.
482. Acts 22:22–29 and Acts 16:20–37 clearly show the difference between Paul mentioning his citizenship after and before being beaten. One observes here that Paul learned his lesson after his beating in Acts 16.

Paul's stoning indicates that the Jews considered him one of the "apostates" or "blasphemers" (Deut 17:5; 22:22–24; M. Sanh. 7.56–60).[483] One recollects the irony of Paul watching and acting as a witness when Stephen was stoned to death (Acts 7:58). Indeed, Paul has come full circle from someone who witnessed stoning to suffering being actually stoned to death. Why did Paul boast about his stoning? In spite of the shame associated with this cultural practice, Paul is not hesitant to boast about it. The most plausible explanation must be the fact that Paul endured such pain and lived to tell his story. It signifies his resilience and determination no matter how weak his appearance might be to them.

Paul then mentions that he has experienced shipwreck three times and has spent "a night and a day in the open sea" (11:25b). Although the incident Luke records in Acts 27 is "subsequent to the time of this writing," still one can use the picture that Luke paints to visualize what Paul means by experiencing "shipwreck."[484] One can only speculate whether or not Paul's narration of his experiences struck a chord in the hearts of the Corinthians and made them respect his disabled body, perhaps grudgingly. After these specific sufferings, Paul reverts to a more generalized description of his sufferings. Thus, one finds in 11:26–29 what Martin calls the continuation of "the 'catalogue of trials' . . . with a generalizing rubric."[485] In these verses, Paul quickly glosses over the additional description of his suffering that shows how resilient and strong his "weak physical body" is and how it could endure hardships and sufferings. He tells them of the hardships he faced on his "frequent journeys" where he was "in danger from rivers, danger from bandits, danger from my own people, danger from Gentiles, danger in the city, danger in the wilderness, danger at sea, danger from false brothers and sisters" (11:26 NRSV). He also lets them know of his "toil and hardship" and how he went "through many a sleepless night, hungry and thirsty, often without food, cold and naked" (11:27 NRSV). Finally, he reminds them of how constantly he worried about their welfare. He writes, "Besides other things, I am under daily pressure because of my anxiety for all the churches. Who is weak, and I am not weak? Who is made to stumble, and I am not indignant?" (11:28–29).

---

483. Martin, *2 Corinthians*, 377.
484. Martin, 377.
485. Martin, 378.

Such were the physical, emotional, and mental sacrifices that Paul endured for their sake; he is right to be indignant with their criticism and attempt to distance themselves from him.

Paul continues to boast of his escape at the hands of the Damascus governor under King Aretas in 11:32–33. Lim sees 11:30–33 as "a continuation of his boasting of his weakness" from 11:23b.[486] This seems to be the correct way of interpreting the flow of Paul's defence. However, Bishop thinks that the narration of how he escaped is "out of context, out of style [and] quite out of connection."[487] This is understandable given the fact that Paul punctuates his boasting narration from 11:23b in v. 30 by saying, "If I must boast, I will boast of the things that show my weakness" (NRSV). Because of this, there are those such as Bishop who think that Paul is breaking away from his boastings in the preceding verses and that he is on his way to boast genuinely of his weakness without attempting to sound positive.[488] In spite of the sudden change in tone, Martin correctly notes, "Paul's irony tempers his statement in v. 30, and paradoxically he parades the very evidence his opponents would ridicule."[489] Granted, the picture of him escaping is humiliating and helpless,[490] but, in the preceding verses, he boasts of his hardships as if they were the greatest achievements a person could experience. It is reasonable to think that Paul also wanted to flip this humiliating picture into a positive one. Paul, whom they considered weak and disabled, managing to escape the governor and his soldiers seriously echoes the successful escape of Joshua's spies with the help of Rahab (Josh 2:15–24).

Nevertheless, is Paul attempting to portray himself as a "war hero" as Welborn thinks?[491] It is very much doubtful that Paul would want to portray himself as a "hero," for if he did, he would not mention about his fleeing (ἐξέφυγον) like a coward.[492] In all his narration of sufferings, Paul prides himself on having met head-on any incident that came his way; as such, it seems reasonable to understand his escape as Paul boasting of getting away

---

486. Lim, "Sufferings of Christ," 181.
487. Bishop, "Does Aretas Belong," 189, also cited in Furnish, *2 Corinthians*, 540.
488. See Roberts, "Weak Enough," 296.
489. Martin, *2 Corinthians*, 383.
490. Martin, 384.
491. Welborn, "Runaway Paul," 117.
492. See Lambrecht, "Fool's Speech," 307.

from some powerful opponents in spite of the fact that he is disabled. Paul, indeed, is talking about a paradoxical irony where he freely acknowledges his weakness, not feeling ashamed but using it to control his narrative in a way that portrays him as someone determined, with endurance and stamina.

It is interesting to note that these lists of hardships in 11:23–33 are absent in Fitzgerald's attempt to interpret Paul's catalogues of hardships in 2 Corinthians. Fitzgerald is interested in 2 Corinthians 4 and 6 only. In these two chapters (4 and 6), Fitzgerald identifies Paul's narration of his hardship with that of the sage who ultimately credits his triumph over hardship "on the divine."[493] No wonder Fitzgerald leaves these lists of hardship (11:23b–29) out of his purview because they clearly fall into his "first basic level," which he terms as "the crudest and most self-offensive form of self-praise" as "the victory over hardship is a purely personal accomplishment."[494] Savage also states that 2 Corinthians 11:23–29 is "a list of personal afflictions so horrific that it would have elicited feelings of extreme contempt among his readers. By boasting of such humiliations, the apostle would seem to be revelling in his disgrace."[495] However, by narrating his personal achievements in this fashion, Paul clearly shows them that his body is as fit and strong as anyone claiming to be a "super-apostle."

One concurs with Glancy's observation that Paul's narration of his hardships "is consistent with the Greco-Roman rhetorical practice of acknowledging hardships, often as demonstrations of virile fortitude."[496] Paul does not hold back on his boasting: even if he boasts of his strength and superiority, he is simply telling the truth (11:31; 12:6). So, if one were to ask, "Why does he highlight his corporal abasement during a crisis of Corinthian confidence in his apostolic authority?"[497] The answer is quite clear. "The Corinthians have Paul's body on their minds" (see 10:1–11:6)[498] – that is, his weakness – and it is up to him to counteract his opponents' jibes. Thus, he opts to fight with the same weapon that his opponents were using: boasting even more than was permissible (see 10:13).

---

493. Fitzgerald, *Crack*, 114.
494. Fitzgerald, 113.
495. Savage, *Power through Weakness*, 75.
496. Glancy, "Boasting of Beatings," 118–119.
497. Glancy, 126.
498. Glancy, 127.

### 5.5.3.3 Paul positively spins his "thorn in flesh"

In 2 Corinthians 12:1-12, Paul boasts of the superior revelation that he has because of his "thorn in the flesh." There are four important views of Paul boasting about his visions and revelations. First, one can say that the instigators drove Paul to "foolish" boastings, as they doubted his apostleship while they themselves claimed that they were "super-apostles" who had come from Peter and company (12:11).[499] Second, he boasts because the instigators were pointing out Paul's apparent lack of an actual relationship with the earthly Jesus.[500] Third, he boasts because the instigators were probably condemning Paul's lack "of ecstatic demonstration that certifies their mission."[501] Fourth, Paul boasts in answer to the humiliating and socially ostracizing disability that he received and which his instigators were pointing out to question his apostolic credibility. These people credit his disability "to the agency of Personified Evil Spirits."[502]

While all these views are defendable to a certain degree, as they all point to Paul's inferiority as an apostle, the last point is most likely the one Paul has in mind when he boasts of his "visions and revelations from the Lord" (12:1). In regard to the first point, Paul has no reason to be jealous of these instigators because, as McClelland has shown, there is an absence of "undeniable proof" connecting the instigators as having come with the authority of the Jerusalem apostles, especially that of Peter.[503] Recently, Thrall renews the hypothesis that these instigators claimed Peter as their authority, and thus their commendation came directly from the Jerusalem leadership.[504] Roetzel,[505] as well as Albl,[506] also draw a connection to these instigators with Peter taking into consideration the incident of Paul publicly rebuking Peter in Galatians 2:11-14.[507] While Roetzel acknowledges that the evidence for this is

---

499. See Peerbolte, "Paul's Rapture," 173.
500. See Thrall, "Super-Apostles," 55.
501. Baird, "Visions," 653.
502. Neyrey, *Paul*, 169.
503. McClelland, "Super-Apostles," 83.
504. Thrall, "Super-Apostles," 55.
505. Roetzel, *2 Corinthians*, 105.
506. Albl, "For Whenever," 155.
507. Furnish also points out the possible connection of these instigators to those "reputed to be pillars Gal 2:9" (*2 Corinthians*, 503).

not strong, he still thinks it is "conceivable that they came from Antioch, the arena of the fiery exchange between Peter and Paul (Gal 2:11–14)."[508] However, McClelland has refuted this claim as he notes that scholars who supported this theory, especially Thrall, have been "unable to demonstrate any undeniable proof that the authority which the opponents may have claimed from Jerusalem actually existed."[509]

Concerning the second point, Wilson's opinion is worth noting. He is quite convinced that, "Either the life and teachings of the historical Jesus were not of interest to Paul or else they were simply not known."[510] However, Bruce is more optimistic as he feels that even though Paul "does not tell us much about [Jesus], in comparison with what we can learn from the Gospels [he is nonetheless] our earliest literary authority for the historical Jesus."[511] The third point, no doubt is attractive. If the "Hellenistic ideas [of] signs and wonders, visions and revelations" fascinated the Corinthians and their instigators,[512] they might have criticized Paul and his ministry. However, a closer analysis of 12:1–10 does not fully support the idea that Paul's boasting is in retaliation to these accusations. If he wanted to point this out, then he would have clearly used the first person pronoun and not the third person as he narrated his visions and revelations from the Lord ("I know a man"; "I know that this man"; "He heard"; "I will boast about a man like that, but I will not boast about myself," 12:2–5).

Nevertheless, in line with the fourth point, if one considers Paul boasting of his "visions and revelations" as a means of the origin of his despised weakness, it fits the tone and nature of argument well. As has been suggested in the rhetorical *exigence*, Paul may have suffered from a bout of epilepsy, and the instigators picked this up to prove to the Corinthians that he was inferior to them. This was a serious concern for Paul as the Corinthian congregation was starting to doubt the source or authenticity of his apostolic power (13:3). Thus, Paul interprets his apparent weakness as a source of strength. His opponents had taken his "thorn in the flesh" as a means to humiliate him, but he flips

---

508. Roetzel, *2 Corinthians*, 105.
509. McClelland, "Super-Apostles," 83.
510. Wilson, "If We Only."
511. Bruce, "Paul."
512. Gloer, "2 Corinthians," 176.

their argument on them and takes this opportunity to boast about his superior "visions and revelations of the Lord." Paul uses this information to convince the Corinthians of the genuineness of his apostolic authority and to validate that his disability was the consequence of his superior spiritual experiences.

One realizes how vital "this vision is . . . to Paul's claim to apostolic authority."[513] He explains to them how he got his "thorn in the flesh" by narrating his transportation to the third heaven. He writes, ἁρπαγέντα τὸν τοιοῦτον ἕως τρίτου οὐρανοῦ ("I know a person in Christ who fourteen years ago was caught up to the third heaven," 12:2 NRSV). Paul further specifies this third heaven as παράδεισον ("paradise," 12:4). This description indicates that Paul is aware of the prevailing Jewish apocalyptic thoughts about the different levels of the heavens.[514] How he was taken up remains a mystery; even he did not know it (12:3), but a closer inspection of the word ἁρπαγέντα (12:2), from the root ἁρπάζω (caught, to seize), should offer some insights into the actual incidents of Paul's transportation to the third heaven. The Greek word ἁρπάζω has assorted ranges of meaning but all involve a forcible snatching away of something or a person.[515] As such, it is best if one interprets ἁρπαγέντα as "of an ecstatic vision or experience *catch up or away*."[516]

The other places where ἁρπάζω is used are in Acts 8:39, 1 Thessalonians 4:17, and Revelation 12:5. What is interesting about these texts is that they all point to a literal process of physical displacement, the notion of transporting someone's physical body. Take for instance the case of Philip in Acts 8:39: it is clear that Philip was physically snatched away from "a desert road between Jerusalem and Gaza" (Acts 8:26) to "Azotus" (Acts 8:40), which is about 67.4 kilometres.[517] In the case of Paul, he refrains from saying outright how he found himself in paradise (12:3). It is interesting to note that Rowland sees nothing wrong with Paul's hesitation to describe his actual experience, for he thinks it was the prevailing style. However, as to bodily displacement

---

513. Morray-Jones, "Paradise Revisited," 271.

514. For example, in *The Book of the Secrets of Enoch,* ch. 22:1: "On the tenth heaven, (which is called) Aravoth, I saw the appearance of the Lord's face, like iron made to glow in fire, and brought out, emitting sparks, and it burns."

515. Friberg, Friberg, and Miller, "ἁρπάζω," in *Analytical Lexicon*, 4:75.

516. Friberg, Friberg and Miller, 4:75.

517. This is the distance between Jerusalem and Azotus as measured by Google Maps (accessed November 23, 2018, http://bit.ly/2R3K9zW).

or not, even Paul is unsure, but the textual evidence from the Greek word ἁρπαγέντα (12:2) suggests Paul found himself bodily in paradise.[518] There he heard inexpressible (ἄρρητα, lit. "too scared to tell") words (ῥήματα, 12:4), things that human beings are not permitted to tell (12:4b).[519]

After setting himself up with a narrative of boasting about the very ὑπερβολῇ τῶν ἀποκαλύψεων ("surpassing revelations," 12:7) Paul then goes on to explain how he got this disability (which may be epilepsy) in 12:7b–10. He blames "a messenger of Satan" (ἄγγελος σατανα) sent to κολαφίζῃ ("torment," 12:7) him. The Greek word κολαφίζῃ can mean literally, "strike with the fist, beat; be roughly treated," and figuratively, "of attacks of illness."[520] Whether one wants to interpret this figuratively or literally, it hardly changes the fact that Paul was crediting his disability to the work of Satan because of his superior revelations. The concern of Thornton that Paul considers the "messenger of Satan" as working for God is quite valid here because for Paul it did not matter, as God can use Satan as a messenger for punishment. Indeed, one finds Paul clearly blaming Satan for tormenting believers in 1 Corinthians 5:5 and 1 Timothy 1:20.[521] Thus for Paul, "Satan is simply acting in line with his malevolent nature."[522] Nonetheless, Glessner is on sure ground with his comments: "Paul goes out of his way to valorize the circumstances of the origins and persistence of his thorn."[523] In direct contrast against "the value system of his" opponents, Paul claims that his "illness was a direct result of his 'surpassingly great visions'" in which Satan had played his part.[524]

To be fair, Paul is very disappointed with the suffering he experienced because of his "thorn in the flesh." He specifically tells the Corinthians, "Three times I appealed to the Lord about this, that it would leave me" (2 Cor 12:8 NRSV). Dodd opines that Paul "resented bitterly" his "disability" for "he felt it an intolerable humiliation, thwarting his purpose and exposing him to

---

518. Rowland, *Open Heaven*, 385.

519. See Morray-Jones, "Paradise Revisited," 265–292, esp. 271, on the prohibitions of uttering "visionary experiences" in "hekhalot literature."

520. Gingrich, "κολαφίζω" in *Shorter Lexicon*, 111.

521. Thornton, "Satan," 151–152.

522. Smith, "Hand This Man," 207.

523. Glessner also correctly points out that this valorizing "suggests [Paul's] audience may have viewed his physical condition in other (less positive) ways," (in "Ethnomedical Anthropology," 27).

524. Glessner, 29.

contempt."[525] Murphy also paints a very bleak picture; he thinks, "the thorn reminds [Paul] that he has none of the qualities which the world considered essential prerequisites for the success of his mission."[526] Indeed, Paul "resented bitterly" his limitation, however Paul seems to have a positive mindset as he describes his visions in 2 Corinthians 12:1–12. Paul knew that he had to explain his "thorn in the flesh," and it is highly likely that he knew experiencing visions was a mark of spiritual superiority. For instance, while describing Jesus's vision in Mark 1:10, Palachuvati states, "Mark portrays Jesus throughout his narrative as actively involved in an ongoing communion with God."[527] Therefore, Paul spins his narrative in such a way that he achieves his intention, and that is to defend his disability by explaining its heavenly origin and to let them know that he needs this disability to keep him grounded in spite of the "surpassingly great revelations" he has received (12:7). From this explanation of the necessity of his "thorn in the flesh" comes one of the most profound theological insights of Paul: "For when I am weak, then I am strong" (12:10b).[528]

### 5.5.3.4 Paul's defence from a sociological point of view

One of the main components of a DH is making use of a sociological model to understand Paul's defence of his disability in the face of the intense criticism he endured at the hands of the Corinthians and their instigators. The Corinthians' main criticism of Paul was his weakness, or rather, his disability, which when comparing him to other "super-apostles" (12:11) made them want to reject Paul's authority over them. Throughout this rhetorical unit, therefore, it is not surprising to find Paul using the sociological model of parenting to chastise them for their criticism, as well as using it to explain and reclaim his authority over them.

Piltch defines parenting as the process by which parents "seek to instill appropriate positive values in the offspring in order to strengthen group or family cohesion."[529] In antiquity, "the cornerstone of the patriarchal and patrilineal social edifice is the father,"[530] and as such, "children are taught at

---

525. Dodd, *New Testament Studies*, 68.
526. Murphy-O'Connor, *Paul*, 322.
527. Palachuvattil, *"He Saw,"* 84.
528. Savage calls this statement a "paradox" (*Power through Weakness*, 1, 187).
529. Piltch, "Parenting," 128.
530. Piltch, 128.

very early age to subordinate personal ego to the authority of the father and/ or actual male head of the family."[531] Thus, one finds in 1 Timothy 3:4 that a man "must manage his own household well, keeping his children submissive and respectful in every way" (NRSV; see Titus 1:6). If the children disobey or are disrespectful, "frequent and severe physical punishment is the means of instilling such obedience and subordination."[532] It is not surprising to find proverbs such as, "Whoever spares the rod hates his son, but he who loves him is diligent to discipline him" (Prov 13:24; 23:13 ESV) and "Discipline your children while there is hope; do not set your heart on their destruction" (Prov 19:18 NRSV).

From a sociological point of view, Paul's insistence on taking care of the Corinthians as his children was not out of line with the prevailing culture of that time. This is because, "Fatherly love was a widely held ideal, an ideal that can be traced in numerous burial inscriptions as well as in Latin literature."[533] Some scholars think that the Greco-Roman and Jewish use of "father" as a metaphor influenced Paul. For instance, Quintilian wrote, "Let him, therefore, adopt a parental attitude to his pupils, and regard himself as the representative of those who have committed their children to his charge."[534] Epictetus also described that "the Cynic" in him considered himself "the father of all men" who deeply cared for his children.[535] Lassen draws attention to the inscription made by the Corinthians "dated AD 47–50" that reads, "To Tiberius Claudius Caesar Britannicus, son of Augustus, (and) to Tiberius Claudius Caesar Augustus Germanicus, *pontifex maximus, p P,* father of the fatherland."[536] Since Paul stayed in Corinth for around eighteen months (Acts 18:11), it seems likely that Paul would have noticed this inscription as well as the prevalence of the "father figure" in Corinth.[537] Aside from the Greco-Roman parental background, Myrick is confident that his Jewish background also equally influenced Paul.[538] For instance, in the Damascus scroll, one finds

---

531. Piltch, 128.
532. Piltch, 128.
533. Lassen, "Use," 129.
534. Quintilian, *Institutio Oratoria*, 2.2.5.
535. Epictetus, *Discourses*, trans. Long, bk 3.
536. Lassen, "Use," 134.
537. Lassen, 134; see also Larson, "Paul's Masculinity," 96.
538. Myrick, "Father's Imagery," 171.

that priests "shall love them [the people] as a father loves his children, and shall carry them in all their distress like a shepherd his sheep."[539] Indeed, as in 2 Corinthians 6:11–12 where Paul tells them that he loves and cares for them, he again unequivocally tells them that he loves them in 2 Corinthians 11:11.

Nevertheless, no matter how much Paul loved the Corinthian congregation, he had to punish them for they were clearly disrespectful to him. First, they criticized his dealings with them. They said that Paul acted "humble" when he was in their midst, but as soon as he was away, he became "bold" (10:1). Martin believes that Paul's uses of ταπεινος (humble) "carries a pejorative sense, implying that his enemies regarded Paul as pusillanimous."[540] One recollects the Corinthians' accusation of Paul's "fickleness" in 2 Corinthians 1:17. It is as if they thought that Paul was exhibiting a double-standard personality. They also disapproved of his "weak appearance and his contemptible speech" (10:10), which made them consider Paul an "inferior apostle." They were not pleased with his "disability" (10:10) and refused to "commend" him (11:2), besides questioning if Christ was really speaking through him (13:3). As Martin states, this was the Corinthians calling Paul, their spiritual father, "a charlatan and a bogus apostle with no right to be at Corinth.[541]

From a disability perspective, these criticisms and accusations were so personal that Paul had to respond as a wounded father who had been greatly disrespected by his children. Paul responds that he is not a weakling; in fact, he tells them he is "ready to punish every disobedience" until their "obedience is complete" (10:6 NRSV). Roberts claims that Paul "has a unique history of ministry without abuse with the Corinthians, which his rivals cannot claim."[542] While this assessment may be too optimistic, what is clear is that Paul claims his God-given authority over them (10:8), since he is the one who "pioneered the church in Corinth and is humanly responsible for the Corinthians' being Christians" (10:14).[543] As such, his "invoking an authoritative relationship over the congregation as its founding father" is not unnatural.[544] Like any

---

539. *Damascus Rule* 13, in Vermes, *Dead Sea Scrolls*, 97.
540. Martin, *2 Corinthians*, 303.
541. Martin, 303.
542. Roberts, "Weak Enough," 293.
543. Roberts, 293.
544. Lassen, "Use," 136; Best, "Paul's Apostolic Authority," 17.

well-meaning father in antiquity, he has the right to discipline them even if his words are harsher than usual.[545]

What is also at play here is the "honour and shame" value that is closely linked with the "parenting" model. According to Piltch, parenting "is intimately related to the core values of honor and shame, since kinship honor consists in loyalty to the family."[546] In the *exordium*, one recollects that the Corinthian Christians were out to shame Paul. Indeed, a cursory reading of these last chapters from a disability perspective reveals that Paul is trying his best to reclaim his lost honour in the eyes of the Corinthians. Here, one calls to mind Malina's explanation, "People get shamed when they aspire to a certain status and this status is denied them by public opinion."[547] What could have been the status claimed by Paul? The status claimed by Paul was his consideration that he was the Corinthians' "spiritual father" (1 Cor 4:14–15; cf. 1 Cor 2:6, "I planted the seed").

However, the Corinthians shamed him by rejecting Paul's status. They did this by accepting those "super-apostles" whom Paul sees as "false apostles, deceitful workmen, masquerading as apostles of Christ" (11:13). Paul even considers their preferences as shameful. He writes, "For you put up with it when someone makes slaves of you, or preys upon you, or takes advantage of you, or puts on airs, or gives you a slap in the face. To my shame, I must say, we were too weak for that!" (2 Cor 11:20–21a NRSV). The Greek word Paul uses for "shame" is ἀτιμίαν and can also mean dishonour and disgrace as well.[548] He uses the same word in 2 Corinthians 6:8, "in honour and shame," when he defends his personal integrity. Paul sarcastically retorts that in their rejection of his authority, they would welcome someone who "slaps" (δέρω) them in their face (cf. Mark 12:3, 5; Luke 22:63; John 18:23; Acts 22:19).[549] According to Martin, "The verb denotes a calculated insult (akin to the scene in Luke 22:63) and shares the Jewish imagery of directing a blow to a person's face as a way of humiliating him."[550] Paul, in a way, is implying that they treated him shamefully while they let someone treat them shamefully.

---

545. See Garland, "Paul's Apostolic Authority," 375.
546. Piltch, "Parenting," 128.
547. Malina, *New Testament World*, 52.
548. Gingrich, "ἀτιμίαν," in *Shorter Lexicon*, 29.
549. Gingrich, "δέρω," 43.
550. Martin, *2 Corinthians*, 303.

Again, from a disability perspective, one of the reasons his weak appearance might be a cause of shame to them is the notion that manliness inspires authority. Harrill has proposed that the opponents brought up his physical appearance as a means to "question Paul's manhood and right to dominate others."[551] Besides the Corinthians' accusation that Paul had a weak physical appearance, Paul also told them in his first epistle that he lived a celibate life and how he wished those unmarried and widows would be like him (1 Cor 7:8). However, Malina states that during antiquity a man's "honor is symboled by the testicles, which stand for manliness, courage, authority over family, willingness to defend one's reputation, and refusal to humiliation."[552] As such, a man's "masculinity is in doubt if he maintains sexual purity, that is, if he does not challenge the boundaries of others through their women."[553] It seems appropriate to think that the Corinthians would think lowly of a celibate Paul, as it would have seemed alien to their understanding of who a man should be. Barclay writes, "The very word *korinthiazesthai*, to live like a Corinthian, had become a part of the Greek language, and meant to live with drunken and immoral debauchery."[554] Therefore, in the understanding of the Corinthians, Paul was quite different.

Aside from this, the aesthetic appeal to the perfect body, which was at the heart of the Greek's love for the arts, may contribute significantly to the rejection of Paul's unimpressive body. One recollects the remarks made by Jenkins and Turner, "the Greeks invented the body in art or, at least, the idealized male body conceived as a thing of beauty and bearer of meaning."[555] Malina and Neyrey have commented, "When a person realizes he is being denied the status, he is or gets shamed; he is humiliated, and stripped of honour for aspiring to a value not socially his."[556] This seems to describe the situation of Paul who got "shamed" and "humiliated" for trying to attain a "status" that was enviable by the standard of the Corinthians and their instigators.

However, as one who considers himself their father, Paul has to punish them to regain his lost honour. How is he going to do it? Paul tells them that

---

551. Harrill, "Invective Against Paul," 189–213, esp. 211.
552. Malina, *New Testament World*, 47.
553. Malina, 47.
554. Barclay, *Letters*, 3
555. Jenkins and Turner, preface to *Greek Body*.
556. Malina and Neyrey, "Honor and Shame," 45.

he is going to be "bold" (10:1), and "issues warnings and insists that when he does come to Corinth, he will not be lenient."[557] Paul writes to them, "I warned those who sinned previously and all the others, and I warn them now while absent, as I did when present on my second visit, that if I come again, I will not be lenient" (13:2 NRSV). What is remarkable is the fact that this is not the first time Paul had to deal with those who "sinned" against him. The Greek words he uses in 13:2, προημαρτηκόσιν (sin beforehand) and προλέγω (tell before), are a clear indication the Corinthians had humiliated Paul in the past. It seems Paul cannot bear their sins of humiliating him anymore. Now he is ready to "not spare" them. Clearly, in 1 Corinthians 5:5 the Corinthians had already faced the wrath of Paul when their members committed the sin of incest. Given the effectiveness of Paul's punishment of those who sinned (see 2 Cor 2:6–11), it is possible that they would also heed his warning this time.

Scholars like Castelli also agree: "The paternal metaphor does not necessarily evoke a sense of kindness or love."[558] She is convinced Paul's authority as a father is moulded on the lines of the Roman *patria potestas* where "the power of the father had served as a paradigm of patriarchal authority and social order" in the Roman society.[559] This *patria potestas* gives "immense power over his offspring, the power to determine who was – or not – a member of the *famlilia*."[560] Nevertheless, it is possible that if he took up a strong stance against the Corinthians, "he himself may end up being ejected and irrevocably disowned."[561] Perhaps that is why Paul indicates the manner of how he will react when he meets them for the third time. He writes in 2 Corinthians 12:20–21,

> For I fear that when I come, I may find you not as I wish, and that you may find me not as you wish; I fear that there may perhaps be quarreling, jealousy, anger, selfishness, slander, gossip, conceit, and disorder. I fear that when I come again, my God may humble me before you, and that I may have to mourn over many who previously sinned and have not repented of the

---

557. Larson, "Paul's Masculinity," 96.
558. Castelli, *Imitation of Paul*, 109.
559. Saller, *Patriarchy*, 102; see also Burke, "Pauline Paternity," 61.
560. Vial-Dumas, "Parents," 308.
561. Martin, *2 Corinthians*, 472.

impurity, sexual immorality, and licentiousness that they have practiced (NRSV).

Martin asked, "Will Paul have such backing at his third visit" as he did when he punished the sexual offenders?[562] The tone of Paul's pleading in these verses, "afraid" (φοβοῦμαι, 12:20) that he will "grieve" (πενθήσω, 12:21) and be "humiliated" (ταπεινώσῃ, 12:21) in front of those who προημαρτηκότων ("sin beforehand," 12:21) suggests a more diplomatic approach. Martin's comment is notable here: "Perhaps this is Paul's way of saying that discipline is not necessarily a foregone conclusion.... While Paul will exercise parental discipline if necessary, he also has the heart of a pastor and exudes pastoral wisdom.... Paul hopes for the best, yet is prepared for the worst."[563]

## 5.6 Summarization

This chapter has analysed 2 Corinthians 1:3–11, 4:1–18, 6:3–13, and 10–13, respectively, by using a DH. What is most revealing from the analysis is the personal suffering that Paul underwent at the hands of the Corinthians because of his disability. The Corinthians and their instigators challenged Paul's personal integrity, authority, and credentials as an apostle as well as his ministry. Paul tries his best to reason with them. He appeals to their emotion, and (comma added) sometimes he threatens them as well. In this fight for survival of himself and his gospel among the Corinthians, one observes that Paul uses the rhetorical strategy of the Romans *insinuatio*, slowly building up the momentum of his arguments until the last four chapters, where he is very tough on them.

By employing a DH, one observes that Paul's disability and the Corinthians' prejudicial treatment are at the heart of his arguments in 2 Corinthians. First, in analyzing the *exordium* (i.e. 2 Corinthians 1:1–11), this study has established that Paul suffered from a serious illness in Asia. Even though the exact nature is unknown, Paul could have been suffering from epilepsy. This illness was a serious disability that the Corinthian Christians used to stigmatize him socially. Their treatment made Paul suffer even more emotionally and mentally. Paul does his best to explain that this disability is from God and that because of it,

---
562. Martin, 472.
563. Martin, 461.

they are themselves blessed. Second, in the first *probatio* (4:1–18) examined, the Corinthians criticized Paul's ministry, which was the result of his disability, thus, causing him intense suffering. He defends his ministry by pointing out to them that this ministry, even though it was the result of his suffering, allowed him to gain deeper insights into the sufferings of Jesus Christ. He argues that this ministry will give them hope for future perfection.

Third, in the second *probatio* (6:3–13) examined, Paul is made to suffer because the Corinthians criticized his personal integrity because of his disability. In this rhetorical unit, Paul defends his integrity by commending himself, listing out the many hardships that he underwent. He also tells them specifically that he loves and cares for them. He blames the Corinthians' unwillingness to open their hearts, causing him deep emotional sufferings. Fourth, in what is the last *probatio* (chs. 10–13) examined, the Corinthians made Paul suffer because they were unjustly comparing him to the other "super-apostles" and asking proof that Christ was really speaking through him. At the heart of this criticism lay his disability as well. Paul is very vocal in his defence. He then boasts of the various hardships he had suffered; he boasts of his superior visions and revelations. He also warns them sternly that when he comes to visit them again, he is going to punish them for making him suffer by their unwillingness to accept the disability that had been such a blessing to them.

In all these sufferings, it is significant to know that Paul "finds his sufficiency, his source of power and authority, neither in the wisdom of philosophy nor in the personal glory derived from wealth, social status and rhetorical *finesse*, but in Christ alone, in his sufferings, death and resurrection."[564]

---

564. Ogereau, "Paul's Leadership," 6.

CHAPTER 6

# A Critique of Paul's Sufferings and Weaknesses in 2 Corinthians from a Disability Perspective

## 6.1 Introduction

In the previous chapter, the important texts containing Paul's lists of weaknesses and sufferings were analysed, setting the stage for a final critique of 2 Corinthians. After a thorough exegetical enquiry into these selected passages, one can say with certainty that his opponents – that is, the Corinthian congregation as well as their instigators – took advantage of Paul's disability causing him to suffer much. One is also in a better position to gauge the personal existential struggle that Paul had with his disability. While it had been nothing but trouble for him, it soon turned out to be the one instrument for his redemption and hope for the future. Thus, these selected texts, 2 Corinthians 1:3–11, 4:1–18, 6:3–13, and 10–13, when analysed from a DH reveal remarkable insights into the nature of Paul's sufferings and weaknesses in 2 Corinthians.

Therefore, this present study is now in a strong position to answer the significance of analyzing Paul's suffering and weakness in 2 Corinthians from a disability perspective. In other words, what role does Paul's disability play in the present study's attempts for a deeper and more comprehensive understanding of his suffering and weakness in 2 Corinthians? To this end, this chapter will give a comprehensive critique of the exegetical analyses of Paul's suffering and weakness in 2 Corinthians from a disability perspective.

## 6.2 The Socio-Anthropological Dimension of Paul's Suffering and Weakness

One of the most significant findings from analyzing 2 Corinthians by employing a DH is the affirmation that Paul's disability gravely accentuated his suffering in his apostolic ministry. From the analysis of Paul's personal testimony, this study shows Paul was physically struggling from some sort of disabling ailment. He calls himself ἐκτρώματι (untimely born or abnormally born) in 1 Corinthians 15:8, which could indicate the possibility that he is describing the insults he had received from others.[1] He also describes his ἀσθένεια τῆς σαρκός (weakness of the flesh) in Galatians 4:13–14 and admits his fear that the Galatians would consider his condition ἐξεπτύσατε (lit. "to spit out," Gal 4:14).[2] Moreover, he brings attention to his opponents' jibe παρουσια του σωματος (unimpressive physical appearance) and ὁ λόγος ἐξουθενημένος (contemptible manner of speaking) in 2 Corinthians 10:10.[3]

The present study has analysed the Greco-Roman social dynamics of how they treated orators with or without physical weaknesses. One recollects here the injustice faced by Demosthenes who, despite being a skilled orator, was publicly jeered at because of his weak physical disposition.[4] In contrast, Alcibiades lisped when he talked, but the public still considered him a wonderful orator because he was physically beautiful.[5] In such an environment, one is not surprised to find that the Corinthians and their instigators would stigmatize Paul because of his weak physical appearance and contemptible manner of speaking (10:10). Paul openly talks about his σκόλοψ τῇ σαρκί (thorn in the flesh) in 2 Corinthians 12:7. This study leans towards the hypothesis that Paul is talking about his disability when he mentions his "thorn in the flesh," although the exact identification of this disability

---

1. George, "(Dis)abled Jesus," 118; see section 3.4.1 of this present study.
2. See section 3.4.1.2 of this present study.
3. See section 3.4.1.3 of this present study.
4. Plutarch, *Demosthenes*, 4.3.
5. Plutarch, *Alcibiades*, 1.4.

is up for debate.⁶ Additionally, in *Acts of Paul and Thecla*, one observes that Paul's physical description as "short, bald with crooked legs" does not inspire admiration. In conjunction with all these, Paul informs the Corinthians that he almost died of some illness while he was in Asia (2 Cor 1:8).⁷

To be fair, with the suffering and hardship catalogues mentioned by Paul in his defence in 2 Corinthians (4:8–9; 6:4–10; 11:23–33), it looks as if Paul was physically robust and that he had good health. Thus, this present study does not fault Harris's comment that "Paul must have been robust to survive all five floggings and resilient to face the last four."⁸ This present study's analysis of Paul's hardship catalogues also clearly shows that Paul boasted positively of his sufferings.⁹ However, what one cannot fail to notice and point out is the fact that he was clearly suffering from his disability along with the resultant social prejudice and stigmatization. Aside from the socially distasteful attitude that the Corinthians had regarding Paul's weak physical appearance and contemptible manner of speaking, one may also point out the effects of his "thorn in the flesh."

In the previous chapter, it has been observed that many scholars conjecture that Paul suffered from bouts of epilepsy.¹⁰ Recently, Kelly and Collins have discussed the social ramifications of having epilepsy in antiquity.¹¹ It is significant to know that epilepsy was not just physically disabling, but the social taboo attached with it made it much worse for the person having it.¹² The previous analysis also has shown a number of examples of how Greco-Roman and Jewish societies viewed their disabled.¹³ One recollects in particular the study of Jenkins and Turner which brought to light the Greco-Romans' love for perfection as revealed in their immaculate sculptures and art.¹⁴ In a society where a good and beautiful physical body triumphed over

---

6. See section 3.4.1.4 of this present study.
7. See section 5.2.2.1 of this present study.
8. Harris, *Second Epistle*, 802; cf. Hodge, *Commentary*, 617; McCant, *2 Corinthians*, 109.
9. See sections 5.5.3.2 and 5.5.3.3 of this present study.
10. See section 3.4.1.4 and section 5.5.2.3 of this present study.
11. Kelley, "Punishment," 206; Collins, "Paul's Disability," 174.
12. Kelley, "Punishment," 206; Collins, "Paul's Disability," 174.
13. See chapter 3 of this present study.
14. Jenkins and Turner, preface to *Greek Body*.

any imperfection or weakness (i.e. disability), one can only speculate on the magnitude of sufferings that Paul endured.

One recollects further that this present study understands disability as indicating a person's bodily limitation(s) or *imperfections* coupled with the negative social reaction to those bodily limitation(s) or *imperfections*. As such, disability does not just mean physical or mental inability, but more often than not, disability arises from the social stigmatization of what a person's limitation may be.[15] Indeed, there are times when the social mindset and derogatory caricature conjured up is a much more effective way of disabling a person than the physical limitations experienced. This seems particularly true when it comes to Paul. For instance, George's assessment of Paul's description in *APT* is right on point. According to him, "his unimpressive physical appearance was used as a point to discredit him of his apostolic status."[16] Because of his disability, his opponent questioned his personal integrity and credentials (see 10:12, 15–16, 18).[17] In a culture where leaders are not expected to exhibit these kinds of disability, one can hardly doubt that Paul, with his physical weakness (disability), would be further stigmatized as someone who should not have been a leader.

It is true that one cannot exaggerate/emphasize enough the importance and "services which were rendered to Christianity by Paul of Tarsus."[18] In fact, Paul has achieved a legendary status in modern Christianity, which makes people nervous to consider him or picture him as a struggling disabled man, suffering hostility and prejudicial attitudes from the people he was ministering to in his days.[19] Yet, this study cautions on the need to examine objectively the evidence of disability related to Paul.[20] Paul himself acknowledged that he was a "weak" man, "different" from the other apostles, that he was not trained in "rhetoric," and that his overall physical stature was not something he was

---

15. See section 2.2.4 of this present study.
16. George, "(Dis)abled Jesus," 118.
17. Martin, *2 Corinthians*, 303.
18. Farrar, *Life and Work*, 2.
19. Just consider the fact that scholars such as Ludemann (*Paul, the Founder of Christianity* and Maccoby (*Mythmaker: Paul and the Invention of Christianity*) strongly suggest that it was Paul and not Jesus who was responsible for the formation of Christianity. Such is the strength of scholarly opinions on this that N. T. Wright has had to refute this claim in his work *What Saint Paul Really Said*.
20. See Farrar, *Life and Work*, 6.

boastful of (see 10:10; 11:6, 21; 12:10). *APT* also describes Paul as someone who was bald,[21] and in a culture where bald people were mocked (see 2 Kings 2:23–24), Paul was very much a disabled and stigmatized man.[22] One must also not fail to mention that Paul's vocation as a tent maker was indicative of his social status. This present study has shown that Greco-Roman society looked down on manual labourers with scorn or derision because they associated these people with the slaves.[23]

Thus, the time in which Paul found himself was a society in which lofty ideals of human, particularly bodily, perfection were at the top of what one should desire and admire. It is not difficult to surmise that Paul would have met unfavourable treatment at the hands of the Corinthians. Because Paul was disabled, he was not fit to be included among the "super-apostles" of Christ (see 2 Cor 11:5). All the wounded cries and pleading to the Corinthians to open up their hearts and love him back, for he loved them very much (see 6:11–13; 11:11; 12:15) reveals a desperate man who suffered emotional and mental anguish because he had been rejected. Paul, who considered himself their spiritual father and very possessive of them (1 Cor 4:14–15; cf. 1 Cor 2:6), was hurt by their questioning whether Christ spoke through him at all since he was disabled (2 Cor 13:3). Thus, the present study on these selected texts of 2 Corinthians strongly suggests that Paul's disability was at the root of his physical, mental, and emotional suffering at the hands of the Corinthians and their instigators. As these accusations, and social stigmatization because of his disability, cut Paul to the heart, he fought back fiercely.

## 6.3 Paul's Disability Is at the Heart of His Suffering for His Ministry

One observes that while the tenor of his suffering echoes throughout the selected texts under evaluation, it is particularly evident in those texts that highlight his *peristasis* catalogues. In 4:1, Paul writes, "Therefore, since we have this ministry, as we received mercy, we do not lose heart" (NASB).

---

21. See section 3.4.2 of this present study.
22. See Draycott, "Hair Today," 78.
23. See section 5.4.2.3 of this present study.

Instead, he "renounced the things hidden because of shame, not walking in craftiness or adulterating the word of God, but by the manifestation of truth"; he commended himself "to every man's conscience in the sight of God" (4:2). He did not mind if he was "afflicted in every way" or "crushed" or "persecuted" or even "being delivered over to death" (4:8–9). He did not mind "beatings" or "imprisonments," and it did not matter if he was "dishonoured or shamed" for the sake of his ministry (6:4–10). He had faced plenty of floggings and was even stoned to death (11:24–27) because of his ministry. For him, the most important thing is that he gave "no cause for offense in anything, so that the ministry will not be discredited" (6:3 NASB). In other places, he writes, "For I am under compulsion; for woe is me if I do not preach the gospel" (1 Cor 9:16 NASB). What was so precious and significant about his ministry that Paul would sacrifice his comfort and face the ridicule of the Corinthians and their instigators? The following sections delineate the argument that Paul formulated his ministry on his weakness (i.e. his disability) which in effect was at the heart of his ministry.

## 6.3.1 Paul's Disability as Crucial Components of His Ministry

In the previous section,[24] one observes that Paul equates his ministry with that of a "treasure" (4:7). From the previous analysis of 4:1–18, one can, with confidence, describe the content of his ministry as "Jesus Christ is Lord" (v. 5), "Christ is the image of God" (v. 4b), "Jesus suffered and died" (v.10), and "God raises Jesus from the dead" (v. 14) and "gives hope for an eternal glory" (v. 17).[25] Another crucial aspect of his ministry involves the fallacy of Mosaic law, especially to Paul, and how he contrasts this fallacy of Moses's ministry with that of his own ministry (3:7–11; 4:3). Thus, his ministry revolves around convincing people that his ministry is about what Jesus had accomplished on earth and how, as the risen Christ, he gives hope for eternal life. Yet, the crux of the matter is, what made him formulate his ministry? What gave rise to his glorious ministry? Why was it so precious to him that he willingly suffered untold hardship for it? Moreover, why was the ministry of Moses so crucial to the development of his ministry? In the light of previous study,

---

24. See section 5.3.2 of this present study.
25. See Jervis, "God's Obedient Messiah," 22–23.

the straightforward answer to these questions is that Paul's precious ministry was the direct outcome of his disability.

Indeed, it is intriguing to read Paul's claim that his ministry is better and beyond the ministry of Moses. The ministry of Moses, or in other words, the law of Moses, seems to be integral in the development of Paul's ministry. Yet, so far, a satisfactory answer is still elusive, prompting scholars to call out Paul for being "inconsistent" in his understanding of Mosaic law.[26] The main problem seems to be what van Spanje points out: the failure to "make sufficient use of hermeneutical rules appropriate to the interpretations of Paul's letters."[27] The right questions have been asked, but the follow-through lacks the desired answers because scholars' hermeneutics do not allow them to seek the very source of Paul's problem with the ministry of Moses, as well as the reason Paul considered his ministry worthy of dying for.[28] Yet, ever since Stendahl pointed out the fallacy of the Western interpretation that was influenced by Baur,[29] things have been moving in the right direction when it comes to dealing with Mosaic law.[30] As of now, this present study acknowledges that scholars have come much closer to explaining the origin of Paul's ministry as having a problem with the Mosaic law, with "boundary" as the central issue.[31]

For instance, Dunn explains the issue of the boundary where "Paul has in mind the specific short-fall of his typical Jewish contemporary . . . who treated the law as a boundary to mark the people of God off from the Gentiles, who give a false priority to ritual markers."[32] Dunn is correct to assume that Mosaic law created barriers for the Gentiles. This understanding can be pushed further back to suggest that due to his disability, Paul, was already struggling with the law in regard to the exclusion of disabled people from the eschatological community.[33] This means that the "ethnocentric restrictions" perpetrated by

---

26. See Sanders, *Paul and Palestinian Judaism*, 518; Räisänen, *Paul and the Law*, 264.

27. Van Spanje, *Inconsistency in Paul?*, 249.

28. See footnote @@1044 of this present study for a discussion of Van Spanje's critiques of Räisänen's work.

29. Stendahl, "Apostle Paul," 200.

30. See Sanders, *Paul, the Law*, 68; Sanders, *Paul and Palestinian Judaism*, 497; Boyarin, *Radical Jew*, 136; Dunn, *New Perspective*, 8; Watson, *Paul*, 19.

31. Dunn, *New Perspective*, 8.

32. Dunn, 137.

33. See section 5.3.2.1 of this present study.

Mosaic law for the Gentiles were personally felt by Paul because of his disability.[34] In other words, this study suggests that Paul's inability to integrate himself fully into the fabrics of Mosaic law because of his disability is the reason he could later come up with the notion of ethnocentric "boundary."

Therefore, by employing a DH, this present study has found that Paul suffered much under the exclusive interpretation of Mosaic law that left out PwDs as they were unable to integrate fully into the socio-religious matrix of Paul's Judaism.[35] The injustice is most vivid when the law of Moses is interpreted to disallow the disabled to enter or be a part of the eschatological community. Why would the Israelites go to such great length to interpret and obey the Mosaic law to the letter (see Matt 23:23)? It seems the Israelites took on themselves to be strictly obedient to the interpretation of the Mosaic law. Theilman articulates that the "Jews of Paul's time believed that the foreign domination under which they lived was a result of their disobedience to the Mosaic Law" (Deut 28:1–31:29).[36] This makes sense because they would have reasoned that if they wanted to continue to enjoy their election and be a part of the eschatological community, then they had to obey Mosaic law to the letter (see 4 Macc 9:2).[37] To prove this point, one must allow Garlington to state it clearly. According to him,

> There is every reason to believe that Paul's contemporaries would have endorsed fully the outlook of their forebears, who said that Israel was to "walk in obedience to the law" (CD. 7.7), i.e., "to observe the whole law of the Lord" (TJud. 26.1; TGad. 3.1; Tash. 6.3), to "walk in perfection in all his ways" (CD. 2.16), "obeying all His instructions" (CD. 7.5; cf. 1QS. 1.3–5), "to act according to the exact tenor of the Law" (CD. 4.8) and to "cling to the covenant of the fathers" (1QS 2.9; 1 Macc. 2.50).[38]

The Mosaic law continued to make its presence felt heavily for Paul, the disabled Pharisee. The irony here is that such a person as Paul, who was legally an

---

34. Longenecker, *Eschatology*, 219; see Boyarin, *Radical Jew*, 136.
35. See section 5.3.2.1 of this present study.
36. Thielman, *Paul*, 49.
37. Thielman, *Paul*, 49; see also Elass, "Paul's Understanding," 270.
38. Garlington, *Obedience of Faith*, 258.

impeccably observant Pharisee (see Phil 3:5–6),[39] was nonetheless ostracized by that same law. One can only imagine a disabled and stigmatized Paul left frustrated by such rules and regulations that excluded him or any other PwD from being a member of the eschatological community. Again, Thielman is right to suggest, "Eschatological redemption is Paul's focus,"[40] as he struggled to find alternative interpretations to counter the present interpretation that excluded him and others who were disabled. Thus, without a doubt, his sufferings on account of his disability made him formulate a new ministry which became so precious to him that he would call it his "treasure" (2 Cor 4:7). It provided him with a new eschatological hope that was much more inclusive than the ministry of Moses. Regardless of whether one was disabled or not, in Paul's newfound ministry, all could participate in the eschatological redemptions if only they believed in Jesus Christ (see Gal 3:28).

## 6.3.2 DHs on the Christological Dimensions of Paul's Suffering and Weakness

Following the above discussion on the crucial role disability played in formulating Paul's ministry, this study is also in a strong position to further claim that the use of a DH enables the researcher to get a better grasp on how Paul incorporated the sufferings of Jesus into his ministry. Stegman has argued convincingly in his monograph that "the story of Jesus" is the "linchpin to Paul's argument in 2 Corinthians" and that "Paul extrapolated" the "ethos of Jesus, [his] attitudes, virtues, self-emptying mode of existence."[41] The significance of Jesus Christ and his sufferings to the ministry of Paul cannot be overstated. Indeed, all throughout his argument in 2 Corinthians, right from the start (1:5) to the end of his letter where Paul urges the Corinthians to test themselves if they are in Christ (see 2 Cor 13:5), one observes how important the story of Jesus is to Paul.[42] Even a cursory reading of Paul is unequivocally clear: "For we do not preach ourselves, but Jesus Christ as Lord (2 Cor 4:5),

---

39. Scholars think Paul belonged to the house of Shammaites who "were said to have inherited, and even to intentionally imitate, the stern and unbending character of their founder. To them it seemed impossible to be too stringent in applying the Law" (*New World Encyclopedia*, s.v. "Shammai").
40. Thielman, *Paul*, 241–242.
41. Stegman, *Character of Jesus*, 1–2.
42. Stegman, 1.

and "we preach Christ crucified" (1 Cor 1:23; 2:2). Pryor's observation supports this present study's claim,

> "Death of Jesus" refers to the crucifixion to which Paul is joined, and "life of Jesus" refers to His resurrection, which Paul understands as equivalent to God's redeeming power in the life and ministry of God's servant Paul. [ . . . ] The reference to Jesus highlights the strong link between the apostle and his association in the historic events of Jesus' life, which are the core of his preaching. Perhaps it is this combination of preaching content and participation in Jesus' life, death and resurrection which tips the balance for Paul in his choice of terminology.[43]

To be fair, scholars such as Bultmann, Thrall, Proudfoot, and Lim are all interested to know the connection between how Paul alludes to his sufferings and those of Jesus.[44] For example, in 2 Corinthians 4, where one finds the most elegant rhetorical construction of Paul's "*peristasis* catalogue,"[45] the name "Jesus" occurs seven times.[46] That is why Lim can state, "Paul had allowed the story of Jesus to redefine his understanding of his suffering."[47] While these scholars correctly point to Paul's sufferings as having a christological orientation, they do not seem to pursue the reason Paul specifically and unhesitatingly connects his sufferings to that of the story of Jesus, particularly his sufferings and weaknesses. Any discussion on Paul and Jesus that fails to take into consideration this crucial disability and its subsequent social stigmatization will always lack in conviction. Among the scholars, Dunn again comes closest to connecting the dots as he states,

> For Paul the loyal Jew, the curse of Deuteronomy 21:23 was the opposite of the blessings of the covenant (particularly Deut 27–28); to be cursed by God was to have the covenant revoked, to be put out of the covenant (27:58–68) – that is to be put in the position of the Gentile sinner. The crucifixion of Jesus meant

---

43. Pryor, "Paul's Use," 31–45.
44. See Bultmann, *Second Letter*, 16; Thrall, *Corinthians 1–7*; Proudfoot, "Imitation," 140–160; Lim, *Sufferings of Christ*, 150; Roetzel, "As Dying," 17; Kim, *Origin*, 333.
45. See Fitzgerald, *Crack*, 45.
46. Pryor, "Paul's Use," 40–41.
47. Lim, *Sufferings of Christ*, 149.

that God had rejected him, numbered him with the Gentiles, reckoned him as outside the covenant. The Damascus road Christophany must obviously have turned such a line of reasoning completely on its head, for it indicated clearly that God had accepted and vindicated this one precisely as the crucified. The immediate corollary for Paul would be that God must, therefore, favour the cursed one, the sinner outside the covenant, the Gentile.[48]

Dunn's line of reasoning is correct in the sense that the curse of Deuteronomy 21:23 is akin to putting someone outside the covenant, and what is immediately apparent in his explanation is the general "Jews and Gentiles divide." No doubt, his key hermeneutical principle, "boundary," influenced his interpretation.[49] In addition, this line of reasoning could be pushed back further by taking into consideration the personal nature of Paul's struggle as a PwD under the strict observation of Mosaic law. For Paul, the parallel between Jesus's curses putting him outside the covenant is precisely identical to his exclusion from the covenant's blessing because of his disability, which is also in a way his curse. At this point, one might well agree with Kim who wrote "that already in the pre-Christian period Dt 21.23 [Deuteronomy 21:23] was applied to crucifixion and that the crucified was regarded as accursed by God"[50] (cf. 4QpNah. 3–4, 1.7f, and the Temple Scroll of Qumran 64.6–13). The Damascus revelation changed all that because Paul saw firsthand the risen Jesus whom the Jews considered accursed, now being "exalted and enthroned by God" (2 Cor 12:2; Acts 9:5).[51] Such was the impact on Paul that he now considered Christ as "the end of the Law" (Rom 10:4, ESV, NASB). Thus, it is not surprising to observe Paul dwelling much on the crucified but risen Christ.

Paul must have found the social stigmatization and the discrimination Jesus suffered at the hands of his people very encouraging in his struggle to find acceptance in an unforgiving society that could not come to terms with his disability. For instance, when Paul writes that he is being "treated as a

---

48. Dunn, *Jesus*, 99–100.
49. See Dunn, *New Perspective*, 8.
50. Kim, *Origin*, 46; see also Wilcox, "Upon the Tree," 85–99.
51. Kim, *Origin*, 331.

deceiver" (πλάνος, 2 Cor 6:8), he seriously echoes the same way Jesus was being treated by the chief priests and the Pharisees who called him a "deceiver" (πλάνος, Matt 27:63 and John 7:12).[52] Besides this, Jesus's incarnation as a helpless babe (Phil 2:6–7), which George rightly describes as an "'able-bodied' eternal God taking over the human limitation, weakness and disabilities in multiple respects," was a cause for intense sufferings.[53] In addition, take the case of his illegitimate birth (Matt 1:18–19), which was a serious case for social discrimination.[54] Moreover, his earthly family being not so well-to-do (Luke 2:24; cf. Lev 12:8), they settled in Galilee, a place mistrusted by the Jews (see John 1:46; 7:52), and he presented no exceptional attributes to inspire much worth and respect in his fellow Jews.[55] Although not physically disabled, Jesus's upbringing and family seem to have been a cause of deep social stigmatization. One recollects the wounded cry (ἔκραξεν, "screaming wordlessly") of Jesus in John 7:28 when the people questioned his claims of being their Messiah.

All these hardships and sufferings that Jesus endured were to provide "dignity" to the marginalized, the destitute, and the disabled who were social outcasts.[56] For instance, take the case of Jesus dismantling the hypocritical interpretation of the observation of the Sabbath as laid down by the Mosaic law (see Exod 20:8–11) in Luke 13:10–16. Jesus answered the Pharisees who objected to his healing of the crippled woman by saying, "You hypocrites! Doesn't each of you on the Sabbath untie his ox or donkey from the stall and lead it out to give it water?" (Luke 13:15). Jesus was probably referring to the teaching of Mishnah, particularly that of Erubin 2:2 which says, "It is permitted to bring [the fence] close to the well, so long as the head and greater part of a cow will be inside [the enclosed space] when it drinks."[57] Moreover, Shabbat 16:8 states, "[If a Gentile] drew water to give water to his

---

52. See Harris, *Second Epistle*, 480; Scott, *2 Corinthians*, 150.
53. George, "(Dis)abled Jesus," 111.
54. See Robinson, "Birth of Jesus," 25.
55. According to Häkkinen, "The elite lived by depriving the Galilean rural population, with no direct connection to the ordinary people. Their agents collected taxes, and usually the villagers had the opportunity to deal with minor legal things themselves in local assemblies, the synagogues" ("Poverty").
56. McVerry, "Jesus."
57. Neusner, *Mishnah*, 210.

beast, an Israelite gives water to his beast after him."[58] Again, Shabbat 15:1 gives permission to tie or untie "a camel driver's knot, and a sailor's knot."[59] Without a doubt, Paul would be much emboldened in the face of extreme oppositions and criticisms of his weakness-and-suffering-marked ministry by the testimonies about Jesus's dealing with fierce oppositions.[60]

One must also not fail to note the intrinsic connection of Paul's identification of his suffering with that of Jesus's suffering and its relationship to Jesus's resurrection. Jesus died the death of a criminal, hanged on a tree, a symbol of a cursed man for all to see (Deut 21:23), and he was raised by God's power in a glorious resurrection. So long as Paul was convinced without an iota of doubt that Jesus rose from the dead, he was able to hold on to the promise of Jesus's glorious resurrection to his own future resurrection even though he suffered. In other words, the more he suffered personally, the closer he approached and identified with Jesus, and the more he suffered for the sake of Jesus, the more his hope and faith for "an eternal glory" (4:17) was strengthened.

Thus, Paul's identification with Jesus's suffering takes on an eschatological dimension. In fact, this eschatological dimension becomes the icing on the cake for his ministry. For Paul, the power of God that raised Jesus from the shameful death and glorified him became the most attractive part of aligning himself with Jesus. Elsewhere in his other letters, one discerns the effect of God's power over death on Paul's thoughts. For instance, Paul testifies to the Corinthian Christians, "For to be sure, he was crucified in weakness, yet he lives by God's power. Likewise, we are weak in him, yet by God's power we will live with him in our dealing with you" (2 Cor 13:4 NIV). As such, Paul considers all his sufferings as worth it because they are proof that just as he shared in the suffering of Jesus, God will reward him by resurrecting him and making him "whole" again (see 2 Cor 1:9–10; 4:14–18; 5:1–4; 13:4).

It should become clear now that after understanding the significance of Jesus's suffering, Paul would have interpreted and accepted his disability as something far more momentous than he had previously contemplated. Paul had been scorned and ridiculed for his weak bodily appearance and contemptible speech (2 Cor 10:10), and his sickness (possibly epilepsy) had left

---

58. Neusner, 199.
59. Neusner, 197.
60. See Wan, *Power in Weakness*, 14.

him vulnerable to open hostility from his opponents.[61] However, in all these, he found strength, hope, and above all comfort in the sufferings of Jesus Christ as he identified his sufferings with that of the "dying" (νέκρωσις) Jesus (2 Cor 4:10). One finds Paul's unswerving sense of optimism as pointing to the depth of his understanding of the sufferings of Jesus in relation to his own.[62] That is why he could emphatically say to the Corinthians, "Therefore I will boast all the more gladly of my weaknesses, so that the power of Christ may rest upon me. That is why, I am content with weaknesses, insults, hardships, persecutions, and calamities for the sake of Christ; for whenever I am weak, then I am strong" (2 Cor 12:9–10 NIV). He realized that his disability was no obstacle for him to be a part of the messianic community. Rather he had God on his side who glorified Jesus, a social outcast condemned to die like an accursed criminal. Paul now knew that as long as he remained faithful to Christ, his rejected body would also be glorified, for what "is sown in dishonour, it is raised in glory" and what "is sown in weakness, it is raised in power" (1 Cor 15:43).

## 6.4 The Purpose and Functions of Paul's Suffering and Weakness in 2 Corinthians

In chapter 5, this present study has shown that the Corinthian Christians were ashamed of Paul's disability and wanted to disassociate from him. In the *exordium*, this study established that Paul was dealing with the Corinthians' reaction to his suffering from a disabling illness that clearly manifested while he was in Asia (1:8).[63] As the exegetical analyses progress, it soon becomes clear why Paul had to defend his ministry also (4:1–5; 6:2). The Corinthians were mocking him for his "weak appearance and his contemptible speech" (10:10). They called him an "inferior apostle" (11:5; 12:11) and refused to "commend" him (12:11), and most of all, they questioned whether Christ was really speaking through him (13:3). They also were probably asking him why he considered his ministry, which they might have considered "dark and

---

61. See Belleville, *2 Corinthians*, 122.
62. See Wan, *Power in Weakness*, 79; Roetzel, *2 Corinthians*, 78.
63. See section 5.3 of this present study.

uninspiring," better than that of Moses.⁶⁴ It was in such situations that Paul had to argue for himself and the validity of his ministry. Thus, by applying a DH, this present study has shown that Paul's suffering and weakness in 2 Corinthians serves two rhetorical purposes and functions.

## 6.4.1 Interpreting His Suffering and Weakness as a Symbol of His Strength

In the chosen texts analysed, this study has found that Paul narrates all the sufferings he endured to tell the story of his superiority. The constant themes that reverberate in all the suffering and hardship that Paul narrates is how Paul considered his weakness and sufferings positively. What the Corinthians and their instigators thought of as his weakness, Paul actually represented to them as the symbol of his prowess and resilience, letting them know that his disabled body was far from shameful and useless. It is true that "Paul was hit hard and low by his opponents," and that he could not totally distance himself from the social stigmatization of his disability, but he sure did make an effort to defend his disability.⁶⁵

Some scholars such as Wan have found it difficult to come to terms with the fact that Paul is blatantly boasting about his hardships and sufferings. According to Wan,

> Paul could not engage his opponents by arguing with them directly, for to do so would have ceded to them the grounds and terms of the argument. To match strength for strength with his detractors would have been an endorsement of their operating premises that ministry is to be authenticated by power and strength. If Paul had done that, he might have been able to salvage his personal dignity but would have ultimately lost the debate.⁶⁶

However, this is precisely what Paul does. For he explicitly states, "Since many are boasting in the way the world does, I too will boast (11:18)," and "It is necessary to boast" (12:1 NRSV). Moreover, in 11:20–21 he

---

64. Savage, *Power though Weakness*, 111.
65. Wan, *Power in Weakness*, 13.
66. Wan, 14.

(comma added) further narrates, "To my shame I must say that we have been weak by comparison. But in whatever respect anyone else is bold – I speak in foolishness – I am just as bold myself" (NASB). In what can be termed as a "paradoxical irony," he gets back at them by boasting of his sufferings and hardships.[67] One has to admit that Paul considers boasting as "foolishness," and that there is nothing wise about self-commending (10:12; 11:16–17). Maybe his Jewish theological training made him hesitant because he quotes Jeremiah 9:24, "Let him who boasts boast in the Lord" (2 Cor 10:17). Nevertheless, he soon realizes that he cannot be modest about his disability when the Corinthians and their instigators assail his weaknesses. He has to fight back; he has to start boasting about his experiences to validate the virility of his "disabled and weak" body and in the process save himself, his honour, and most of all, the reputation of his ministry.

At this point, one needs to recollect briefly Paul's rhetoric as he commends himself, particularly in 2 Corinthians 1:8–9, 4:8–9, 6:8–10, and in 11:23b–33. As has been pointed out in the previous chapter, Paul employs the Romans' *insinuatio*, as is evident from the flow of his forensic arguments in these selected passages.[68] In 1:4, Paul reasons quite mildly that his affliction serves a greater purpose as it enables him to sympathize with those who are equally unfortunate. Furthermore, before he narrates the list of his sufferings in 4:8–9, Paul explains that all hardships he endured were to show that God gave him strength and that God did not abandon him because of his disability (4:7). In 6:3, Paul specifically informs the Corinthians that the lists of his sufferings and hardships were to commend him to all as his ministry was blameless. Finally, in 2 Corinthians 11:23b–27, Paul lets loose his fiery defence and starts to commend himself seriously by boasting of his sufferings and hardships. At one point, he goes so far as to brag, "Are they servants of Christ? I am a better one" (11:23a ESV); he thinks of himself "not in the least inferior to these super-apostles" (11:5 NRSV).

Paul gives evidence to his firm statement by stating that he is "working much harder than anyone else," imprisoned "more frequently," "flogged more severely," and "exposed to death again and again" (ὑπερβαλλόντως, lit. "above

---

67. Shillington, *2 Corinthians*, 223.
68. See section 5.6 of his present study.

measure," 2 Cor 11:23b).[69] This evidence may be "an exaggerated emphasis" as Martin calls it, but it is a necessity because of the spiteful and vindictive treatment of Paul's disability by the Corinthians and their instigators.[70] Enduring the Jewish practice of flogging for a total of 195 lashes on different occasions (v. 24) cannot but point to Paul's toughness, for others were known to have died after receiving "thirty-nine lashes."[71] Besides, his stories of being "stoned," "flogged," "beaten with rods," and "adrift in open sea," among other challenges (11:25–27), all commend his disabled body. Thrall sums it up well,

> By whatever standards of comparison anyone might choose, Paul can prove his equality with the rival missionaries – indeed, his superiority to them. Their equal in respect of race and ancestry, he is incomparably their superior as an agent of Christ. His evangelistic labours have been more numerous. Moreover, in the course of his missionary work he has suffered more varieties of persecution more frequently, and has endured many more potentially fatal dangers.[72]

On the other hand, as Savage remarks, it is possible that "a list of personal afflictions so horrific . . . would have elicited feelings of extreme contempt among his readers."[73] However, from the way Paul finds it necessary, his reputation and acceptance in the Corinthian congregation must be at an all-time low, and only a personal listing of hardships and triumphs could turn the tide in his favour.[74] This would validate Paul's claim that his disability is not a hindrance to the success of his ministry. Indeed, Paul seems to choose to publicize his sufferings precisely because it proves his point that he is superior to these so-called "super-apostles" (11:5).[75]

---

69. See Kistemaker, *Exploration*, 388, and Hock, *Social Context*, 35–37.
70. Martin, *2 Corinthians*, 376.
71. Harris uses the word "robust," but it is more fitting to use the word "tough," as robust can be misleading to describe a person with a physical problem. Also, according to Harris, "in *m. Makkot* 3.14 the possibility of a person's dying during or after the thirty-nine strokes is envisaged" (*Second Epistle*, 802).
72. Thrall, *Corinthians 8–13*, 722.
73. Savage, *Power though Weakness*, 63.
74. See Hodgson, "Paul the Apostle," 64.
75. See Savage, *Power through Weakness*, 75.

Another aspect of Paul's boasting about his sufferings and weaknesses has to do with the way he locates his disability as having a supernatural origin. As was mentioned in the previous chapter, his opponents maligned Paul because of his disabling "thorn in the flesh" (which may perhaps be his epilepsy or a different malady altogether).[76] Paul was angry with the Corinthians for blatantly believing the instigators' tale (12:11–12). Consequently, he had a point to prove and thus, Paul kept on "boasting although there is nothing to be gained," of the "visions and revelations from the Lord" (12:1). One recollects here the words written in Numbers 12:6, "Hear my words: If there is a prophet among you, I the LORD make myself known to him in a vision; I speak with him in a dream" (ESV). It is possible that Paul was equating himself to a higher calling compared to the depth of his opponents' spiritual status. Whatever the case may be, by connecting his visit to the "third heaven" (12:4) as the source of his disabling "thorn in the flesh" (12:7), Paul successfully manages to divert the negative impact of his disability to a more positive understanding.[77]

In connection to personal boastings of hardships, this present study has also questioned the validity of Fitzgerald's analysis of the *peristasis* catalogues. Fitzgerald analysed 2 Corinthians 4:8–9 and 6:8–10 only, while excluding the most detailed lists of sufferings and hardships that Paul narrates in 2 Corinthians 11:23a–33. Fitzgerald was concerned with personal boasting as long as it was with the help of "the divine."[78] Yet, when it comes to 2 Corinthians 11:23a–33, it seems Fitzgerald could not accept that Paul would blatantly boast of his sufferings and hardships apart from the divine. According to Fitzgerald's understanding, Paul's *peristasis* in 11:23b–23 would belong to what he called the "first basic level [which is] the crudest and most self-offensive form of self-praise [where] victory over hardship is purely a personal accomplishment."[79] However, given the severity of the circumstances or the situations that Paul found himself in, this present study sees no reason why Paul could not boast of his sufferings and hardship as his personal achievement.

---

76. See section 5.5.2.3 of this present study.
77. See section 5.5.3.3 of this present study.
78. Fitzgerald, *Crack*, 114.
79. Fitzgerald, 113.

Paul was indeed conscious of the fact that he left out the "divine," as he admits, "I am not saying as the Lord would, but as in foolishness, in this confidence of boasting. Since many boast according to the flesh, I will boast also" (2 Cor 11:17–18). Indeed, he goes so far as to call himself a "fool" for boasting the way his opponents boasted of their accomplishments (2 Cor 11:16–21), which clearly contradicts his previous statement, "But he who boasts is to boast in the Lord" (2 Cor 10:17 NASB). This study is aware that "self-praise was an odious business, and one that no decent person would indulge in, except in certain fairly clearly defined circumstances."[80] However, in antiquity, there were times when self-commendation became a necessity, like when a person was in danger of forfeiting his integrity.[81] Indeed, it is heartening to come across Xenophon who stated, "But these scars become the 'evidence' by which others could judge what manner of man he was."[82] Likewise, Paul's suffering and weakness because of his disability were his battle scars in his attempt to spread his gospel across the Mediterranean, and it seems he was proud of them.[83] They become his "badge of honor and his final emphatic argument against his opponents" and not something to be ashamed of or to be ridiculed.[84] Moreover, in the end, he always comes back to God who empowered him to face much trial and sufferings (see 2 Cor 11:31; 12:10; 13:4, 8).

## 6.4.2 Paul's Suffering and Weakness Was for the Corinthians' Salvation

Another significant purpose and function of Paul's argument is the eschatological advantage it opens up for the Corinthian congregation. In the previous analyses done on the *exordium*, one finds that Paul specifically informed the Corinthians that his weakness (θλιβόμεθα) was for their παρακλήσεως καὶ σωτηρίας ("comforts and salvation," 2 Cor 1:6).[85] One observes that the

---

80. Forbes, "Comparison," 8.
81. Oropeza, *Exploring Second Corinthians*, 405.
82. Xenophon, *Agesilaus*, 6.2.)
83. See Hafemann, *Suffering and Ministry*, 226.
84. Levasheff, "Jesus of Nazareth," 49; see also Black, "Paulus Infirmus," 87; Wilson, *What*, 80; Deffinbaugh, "Religious Affections"; "Paul's Prison Epistles"; cf. Christiansen, "Rhetoric," 204.
85. See section 5.2.3.3, "Statement 3: Paul's suffering is important for the Corinthians (1:6–7)."

structure of 1:6 exhibits a clear rhythmic flow that would have been ideal to be read aloud in a congregation:

εἴτε δὲ θλιβόμεθα,
    ὑπὲρ τῆς ὑμῶν παρακλήσεως καὶ σωτηρίας
εἴτε παρακαλούμεθα,
    ὑπὲρ τῆς ὑμῶν παρακλήσεως τῆς ἐνεργουμένης
    ἐν ὑπομονῇ τῶν αὐτῶν παθημάτων ὧν καὶ ἡμεῖς πάσχομεν.

From the above, what is also evident is Paul's logical train of thought as he attempts to convince the Corinthians. First, one observes the present indicative conditional beginning of the sentence, εἴτε δὲ θλιβόμεθα ("But if we are afflicted," NET). Paul acknowledges that he is indeed afflicted, and (comma added) his affliction is a point of criticism from the Corinthians.[86] However, from this conditional introduction, one can deduce that Paul is making the effort to present his "affliction" as the origin of something wonderful for them. The Corinthian Christians seem to lack the necessary faith to believe that Paul's affliction or his disability could result in something positive for them. Second, Paul qualifies his conditional introduction by stating immediately in this verse that it is for ὑπὲρ τῆς ὑμῶν παρακλήσεως καὶ σωτηρίας (their comforts and salvation). Now, the question here is how Paul connects his affliction (disability) with that of the Corinthian Christians' comfort and salvation. Furthermore, what does Paul mean by "salvation," and when he says this, is he putting himself up as the intermediary between them and their salvation?

To answer these questions, one needs to recollect from the previous analysis of this study that Paul's ministry (i.e. his gospel) is the outcome of his disability.[87] His law-free, inclusive gospel, formulated because of his disability, enables him to further include the Gentiles into the eschatological community at the end of ages.[88] This understanding puts Paul in a position to argue that the Corinthians will get a chance to enjoy comfort and salvation precisely because he was weak and suffering. The Greek word σωτηρίας (salvation) is an important word for Paul, as he tries to impart the importance of his disability

---

86. Garland, *2 Corinthians*, 67.
87. See section 6.3.1 of this present chapter.
88. See section 6.3.1.

to the Corinthians (see 6:1–3).⁸⁹ Scholars such as Furnish and Barnett have rightly pointed out the eschatological dimension of σωτηρίας, particularly when Paul employs it in his writings.⁹⁰ In 2 Corinthians 4:13–14, Paul mentions the process of salvation, which is to believe that God raised Jesus from the dead (4:13), and that the same God will raise those who died to be with Jesus eternally. Barnett has given a diagrammatical representation, particularly of 2 Corinthians 4:14, to show the eschatological reality of this process of salvation that Paul is describing:⁹¹

> Knowing that
>    (A) He who raised the Lord Jesus
>       (B) Also he will raise us
>          (C) And present [us] with you [to Jesus].

From this, one concurs with Barnett's interpretation that "the introductory phrase 'knowing that' gives the basis for the apostle's 'believing ... speaking' of the previous verse (4:13). . . . This verse supplies a reason – an eschatological reason – for Paul's verbal ministry."⁹² For Paul, believing in something entails an objective realization of what has happened in the past, a concrete event upon which one bases one's trust. In 2 Corinthians 4:13, Paul quotes Psalm 116:10, "I believed, therefore I spoke," and comments, "we also believe, therefore we also speak" (2 Cor 4:13 NASB). The use of aorist ἐπίστευσα (believed) and ἐλάλησα (spoke) immediately followed by the present indicative πιστεύομεν (believe) and λαλοῦμεν (speak) connects what has happened in the past to his present state. In a way, Paul is informing the Corinthian Christians that he bases his gospel (that was borne out of his disability) on factual events that had happened in the past.

What are these past factual events? The immediate first line that follows "knowing that" explains this: "God raised Jesus from the dead" (4:14a). Paul is unequivocal about the fact that Jesus rose from the dead. Aside from stating that he along with more than five hundred people saw the resurrected Christ (1 Cor 15:5–8), he persuasively warns the Corinthians, "If Christ has

---

89. Barnett, *Second Epistle*, 80.
90. Furnish, *2 Corinthians*, 120; Barnett, *Second Epistle*, 79.
91. Barnett, *Second Epistle*, 243.
92. Barnett, 242.

not been raised, your faith is worthless; you are still in your sins. Then those also who have fallen asleep in Christ have perished" (1 Cor 15:17–18 NASB). In this context, it is important to notice how Paul uses the aorist participle ἐγείρας (2 Cor 4:14a) as "indicating a completed act . . . occurring in the past."[93] Since Paul bases his hope on an actual event in the past, he is confident that the same God who was responsible for that event will be able to do it again in the future.[94] That is why Paul uses the future tense ἐγερεῖ (4:14b) and παραστήσει (4:14c) in his argument.[95] Therefore, in the face of the Corinthian Christians' seeming rejection of Paul's gospel because of his disability, he is strongly reminding them that they must stick with him or else they will be stuck in the past (see 1 Cor 15:18).[96]

Even from a cursory reading of the text in 2 Corinthians 1:6, it seems clear enough that Paul is telling them that his weakness and suffering arising out of his disability is instrumental for their comfort and salvation. This study agrees with Matera's assessment that Paul "certainly does not mean that he is the one who saves them."[97] It is more likely that when Paul says that his suffering and weakness because of his disability is for their salvation, he is implying that they played an integral part in their coming to Christ.[98] It is undeniable that Paul suffered much in the process of delivering his gospel to many parts of Asia Minor. Nevertheless, Paul is pointing to the origin of his gospel through which the Corinthians received their salvation, and that was his disability, which the Corinthian congregation was rejecting.[99] One may also question if Paul is making a threat to the Corinthian Christians. For instance, in Philemon, Paul is definitely making a threat, though subtle, for Philemon to accept his runaway slave (Phlm 1:19). In such a case, it is possible that Paul is using the same rhetorical strategy when it comes to dealing with the Corinthian congregation.

---

93. Barnett, 242.
94. See Savage, *Power through Weakness*, 181–182.
95. Barnett, *Second Epistle*, 242.
96. Cf. Savage who claims that the Corinthian Christians lack the necessary faith for future expectations (*Power through Weakness*, 181–182).
97. Matera, *2 Corinthians*, 42.
98. Cf. Garland's suggestion that Paul's "suffering affects their salvation" (*2 Corinthians*, 67).
99. See Barton and Osborne, *1 & 2 Corinthians*, 274.

Third, Paul seems to be suggesting in 1:6c that the Corinthians share in the same suffering that Paul suffered for their comfort and salvation (ὑπὲρ τῆς ὑμῶν παρακλήσεως τῆς ἐνεργουμένης ἐν ὑπομονῇ τῶν αὐτῶν παθημάτων ὧν καὶ ἡμεῖς πάσχομεν, "it is for your comfort that you experience in your patient endurance of the same sufferings that we also suffer"). In other words, as Thrall rightly understands, Paul "speaks of the sufferings of his readers, and says that they are the *same* as his own."[100] This particular argument has proven vexing for scholars who cannot understand how the Corinthian Christians suffered.[101] However, what is clear from 2 Corinthians 1:6c is that Paul wants the Corinthian Christians to endure patiently their suffering which is similar to what he himself was suffering.

From a disability perspective, it is clear that the Corinthian Christians were very critical of Paul's affliction or disability as the previous chapter has shown.[102] What seems to be obvious is the fact that because of the nature of Paul's affliction, it produced unwanted social stigmatization for him and those with whom he associated. It makes sense that as long as the Corinthian Christians were associating with the disabled and afflicted Paul, they too would suffer the same social discrimination that he was facing. Thus, it seems the best recourse for them was to keep their distance from Paul, for if they did not want to suffer the same fate, then they must reject him.[103] It seems as if the Corinthian Christians also wanted nothing to do with Paul's gospel, as it was born out of his suffering and his weakness. Associating with an afflicted and disabled Paul must have put a target on their backs.[104] Thus, as long as Paul suffered social stigmatization, the Corinthian Christians would also suffer the same ridicule.

Paul is reminding them that they must be willing to continue suffering the same stigmatization that he is suffering from. They must not be ashamed of his disability even though others might mock them for it. Because, as Barnett points out, "What they tend to despise in him is a part and parcel of what

---

100. Thrall, *Corinthians 1–7*, 110.

101. See Thrall, *Corinthians 1–7*, 110; Martin, *2 Corinthians*, 10; Baker, *2 Corinthians*, 68; Stegman, *Second Corinthians*, 40; Bultmann, *Second Letter*, 24.

102. See chapter 5 of this present study.

103. See Barnett, *Second Epistle*, 612–613.

104. See Hafemann, "Comfort and Power," 325–326.

brought life to them."[105] Elsewhere, "in 2 Corinthians 13:9, he writes with the fundamental conviction that it is precisely through his weakness that God's power is disclosed and is mightily effective for others (4:7, 12:9–10, 13:3–4; cf. 10:3–4)."[106] If the Corinthian Christians disassociate themselves from Paul's suffering, then they stand to lose their comfort and salvation precisely because they would be rejecting the one thing that brings them closer to Christ. In a way, one concurs with McCant's assessment that Paul's rhetorical strategy here "is but another instance of self-praise that Paul softens by saying it is all for 'the glory of God'" (see 4:15).[107] Thus, the core argument that Paul makes here is that as long as the Corinthian Christians willingly suffer and endure whatever consequences come their way because of their association with Paul, their reward is the eschatological comfort and salvation that his gospel promises (see 2 Cor 4:14–15).

## 6.5 Summarization

To summarise briefly the findings of this application of a DH to the exegetical studies of the selected 2 Corinthians texts (1:1–13; 4:1–18; 6:3–13; 10–13), one understands that there are different dimensions to Paul's sufferings and weaknesses in 2 Corinthians. First, the physical, mental, and emotional suffering of Paul was primarily because of his disability, and one can trace back every subsequent suffering he encountered as he spread his newfound gospel to his disability. Second, Paul listed out his sufferings and weaknesses because of his disability into an effective defence strategy. That is, Paul boasted of his sufferings in defence of, and at the same time in retaliation for, the accusation that he was not fit to be the Corinthians' apostle because of his disability. Paul pointed to his sufferings as the ultimate vindication that his disabled and weak body was very much durable and resilient to withstand untold hardships. He also used it to prove that he was also spiritually superior to the so-called "super-apostles."

Third, Paul intrinsically connected his weaknesses and sufferings because of his disability to the story of Jesus's sufferings, his life, death, and

---

105. Barnett, *Second Epistle*, 80.
106. Furnish, *2 Corinthians*, 579.
107. McCant, *2 Corinthians*, 48.

resurrection. It was precisely because of his suffering as a disabled man that his encounter with the risen Christ on the road to Damascus made so much sense. Lastly, Paul's weakness and suffering because of his disability became the foundation of his gospel and the source of his strength and hope for future glory in Christ. The suffering he endured because of his disability, both tangible and intangible, became the origin of his trail-blazing ministry. Thus, the greatest thing about Paul's defence of his disability in 2 Corinthians is that what his opponents deemed as weakness and a cause for rejection and stigmatization, Paul could counter and prove that it was the ultimate blessing from God.

CHAPTER 7

# Conclusion and Implications

## 7.1 General Conclusion

This research attempts to investigate and answer the primary question of how disability plays a role in understanding Paul's suffering and weakness in 2 Corinthians. After an exhaustive investigation, this present study finds that disability plays a very significant part in understanding Paul's suffering and hardship in 2 Corinthians. In fact this present study would go so far as to identify "disability" as the key hermeneutical tool for understanding Paul and his ministry to the Corinthians. The following briefly recapitulates how this present study has carried out its investigations and arrived at its conclusion.

In chapter 1, this study pointed out that various scholars interpret Paul's suffering and weakness as suffering for his apostolic ministry and imitating the suffering of Christ. However, considering the intensity of Paul's argument with the Corinthians in this particular epistle, this study suggested that the existing hypotheses are not satisfactory and that there must be another way to approach Paul's suffering and weakness in 2 Corinthians. It thus proposed analyzing Paul's suffering and weakness from a disability perspective. In order to carry out the said objective, it formulated an eclectic methodology called disability hermeneutics (DHs) with the help of sociological and rhetorical tools of interpretation to analyse the selected 2 Corinthians texts. The selected texts are 2 Corinthians 1:3–11, 4:1–18, 6:3–13, and 10–13.

In chapter 2, questions were asked about how this study should understand the term "disability" and how one should formulate the methodology to carry out its investigations into the selected 2 Corinthian texts. First, as to the question of the term "disability," this study makes its stand clear by defining "disability" as indicating an individual's emotional, physical, and mental suffering brought about by the physical defects or limitations that innately intertwine with negative societal impact. In other words, this present study has understood the mechanism of disability as undergoing a continuous relationship between physically impaired individuals and their social environments, in which an individual suffers physically, mentally, and emotionally because of societal attitudes towards what is considered *imperfection*, thus stigmatizing the individuals for their problems. With this definition established, this study has gone on to state that Paul was and could definitely be considered a "disabled" person.

Second, to the question of how this study would go about investigating Paul's suffering and weakness, it has formulated an eclectic methodology called a disability hermeneutic that would properly focus on the social and the rhetorical dimensions of Paul's arguments. Therefore, this DH is "a perspectival exegetical-interpretative engagement with the text where the reality of disability and the associate socio-cultural elements are intentionally foregrounded to gain insights" into the reason Paul talks so much about his suffering and weakness in 2 Corinthians.[1]

It is important to understand that this DH actively involves a perspectival reading of the texts under investigation. In fact, this conscious employment of disability as the lens through which the texts are analysed is what sets this present study apart from previous attempts by various scholars. Moreover, the addition of academically tested and accepted critical tools offsets the subjective allure of employing a perspectival reading of a given text. These critical tools are-(1) rhetorical criticism and (2) a sociological approach. Both these critical tools work in tandem to unveil the complex texture of the text as well as the cultural bias that Paul had to deal with in the process of defending his integrity and his ministry.

Chapter 3 employs a DH to analyse the presence of disability in the history, culture, and social and religious environments of the Greco-Roman and Jewish worlds. It asks important questions such as, "Was disability a problem to these people from the first century, and if so, how did this ancient society treat those with disability?" and "How disabled was Paul on the strength of

---

1. See section 2.4 of this present study.

this study's definitions of 'disability'"? After careful analysis, this study has found that there were indeed disabled people present in their midst, and these people were not treated fairly and justly. One recollects Garland's statement, "People with congenital deformities and disabilities experienced widespread stigma and discrimination because they exhibited physical and aesthetic deviations from the able-bodied norm . . . *which* inspired negative reactions, and sometimes even outright odium, among the able-bodied population."[2]

The PwD group hardly stood a chance against such social prejudice because right from the time they were born, every aspect of society seemed to be against them. Concerning Paul's disability, chapter 3 examines his own testimony from his writings, such as Galatians 4:13–14, 1 Corinthians 15:8, 2 Corinthians 10:10 and 12:7, and *APT*. In light of this study's definition of "disability," as well as from the knowledge of how first-century societies treated their disabled people, Paul's own testimonies are enough to validate the argument that he was disabled and would have been stigmatized greatly because of his disability.

Chapter 4 analyses the socio-rhetorical context of 2 Corinthians from a disability perspective. The purpose of this was to contribute background insights for the main exegesis found in chapter 5. This chapter asks questions such as, "What was the socio-historical context when Paul wrote his second epistle to the Corinthians?" It also analyses the literary unity of 2 Corinthians, as well as the opponents of Paul, from a disability point of view. Julius Caesar rebuilt the city of Corinth. He also repopulated the city with the likes of ex-Roman soldiers, freed slaves, and others who were trying to make a living out of the immense commercial opportunity presented by Corinth's seaport and strategic location. It is likely that there would have been disabled people among them, and given the fact that there seemed to be a stark contrast in terms of class distinction, this commercial opportunity did not help much those who were disabled and poor.

Paul's time coincided with a high value placed on those who were skilled in rhetoric. This study also acknowledges that the practice of rhetoric was rampant during Paul's writing of 2 Corinthians, and that there were some instances in his letter where one can see Paul having the knowledge of rhetorical skills. It supports the position of those scholars who argue for the unity of

---

2. Garland, *Eye*, 11.

2 Corinthians. This is mainly because from a rhetorical point of view, Paul's argument in 2 Corinthians seems to follow a rhetorical pattern employed by writers in antiquity. It seems likely that Paul was following the Roman's technique of *insinuatio* in the arrangement of his argument with the Corinthians.

Chapter 4 also analyses the major hypotheses of scholars concerning the identities of Paul's opponents as it pertains to his letter. These hypotheses include the suggestion that Paul's opponents were the Judaizers, while some have insisted that they were gnostics, pneumatics, divine men, or sophists. This present study contends that Paul's opponents in 2 Corinthians are most likely the Corinthian congregation, who may be to some extent instigated by those who did not like Paul and his gospel. If Paul was disabled, then it makes sense that the Corinthian Christians, because of their socio-cultural prejudice, would be reluctant to associate themselves with a disabled man.

This study particularly finds it significant that disability should play such a central role in the society's assessment of the skills of a particular rhetor. It has found that a direct correlation exists between physically attractive rhetors and the way they delivered their speech. The society of that time was very rude and prejudicial to those who were physically weak, even though they might have been great speakers, yet the people ridiculed them because of their physical weakness. On the other hand, a rhetor may have had some problem delivering a speech due to an existing condition such as lisping, but if he was physically attractive, the people were quite forgiving about accepting his disability.

Chapter 5 concentrates on the exegetical analysis of the selected texts – 2 Corinthians 1:3–11, 4:1–18, 6:3–13, and 10–13 – by using a DH. This study has chosen these texts because they contain most of Paul's catalogue of sufferings and hardships. By employing a DH, this study finds that in the *exordium* (1:1–11), Paul acknowledges the affliction that was causing him to be stigmatized by the Corinthians. This study supports the suggestions by some scholars that Paul's affliction might have been epilepsy, which was crippling him now and then. The Corinthians' prejudicial treatment because of his affliction made Paul suffer even more emotionally and mentally. Furthermore, in the first *probatio* (4:1–18) examined, this study finds that the Corinthians were likely very critical of Paul's ministry as it was the result of his disability. Paul defends his ministry by telling them that it was for their sake (4:15) because it gave them hope for future eschatological glory. Elsewhere, in the second *probatio* (6:3–13) examined, the study finds that Paul suffered much as his personal integrity was called into question because of his disability. Paul argues that even though he may be disabled, his conduct was without blemish. Therefore, they should not be withholding their affection but love him back the same way he loved them.

In the last *probatio* (chs. 10–13) examined, the context of Paul's emotional argument to the Corinthian is clear when one analyses it from a disability perspective. Paul was suffering from social stigmatization because of his disability. This present study has made it clear that when the Corinthians and their instigators labelled Paul as weak in appearance and contemptible in speech (10:10), they were actually being true to the socio-cultural practices of that time. In their eyes, Paul's disability made him weak, and because of that, they questioned his integrity and his ministry, and they seem to have lost all respect for him when they questioned if Christ was really speaking through him (13:3). One can only speculate how much Paul suffered as they compared his ministry to that of their instigators, whom Paul sarcastically calls the "super-apostles" (11:5; 12:11). Since the Corinthians' attack on Paul was very personal, it is not surprising that his defence was very vocal. What is apparent from the analysis of these last four chapters (2 Cor 10–13) is that Paul held nothing back as he tried to reclaim his lost honour and self-esteem, as well as the value of his ministry from which the Corinthian Christians were distancing themselves. In all these, what is clear is that the Corinthian congregation's biggest issue with Paul and his ministry is his weakness – that is, his disability.

Chapter 6 brings together all the findings and insights gained from the previous chapters to propose a comprehensive response to the research's primary question of the role of disability in Paul's suffering and weakness in 2 Corinthians. First, this study understands and points out the anthropological dimension of the sufferings that Paul endured because of his disability. Paul suffered even more emotional and mental cruelty to compound his physical suffering since his disability made him a target of scorn and derision to the Corinthians and their instigators. Second, from employing a DH, this study finds that it can contribute further to scholars' suggestions of Paul's treatment of the Mosaic law, particularly the ethnocentric boundary divide and the origin of Paul's gospel. This is done by suggesting that Paul's disability causes him to confront the strict interpretation of Mosaic law that excluded the PwD from the eschatological community.

Third, from this DH, this study finds that the story of Jesus's sufferings, his life, death, and resurrection made complete sense to Paul because of his disability for which he suffered much. Scholars know that Paul's encounter with the risen Christ on the road to Damascus was an important event in the life of Paul and some, like Kim, would even go so far as to suggest that it was the origin of his gospel.[3] However, from analyzing this point by employing a DH, this study finds that Paul's encounter of the risen Christ makes sense of the eschatological component of Paul's gospel rather than pointing to its origin. In other words, the Damascus incident was the *eureka* moment rather than the sole origin of Paul's gospel. Again, because Paul was disabled, the interpretation of the Mosaic law against disability excluded him from becoming a part of that eschatological community. In a way, they considered his disability a curse. However, on the way to Damascus, Paul saw the glorified Jesus Christ whom they thought was accursed by God. Thus, to Paul, the same God who glorified Jesus Christ would also accept his disabled body, and as long as he remained faithful to Christ, he would receive his eschatological glory.

Finally, from employing a DH, this study understands that the cause of disagreement between the Corinthians and Paul was the Corinthian Christians' stigmatization of Paul because of his disability. Paul was in danger of losing his apostolic authority over them as they started to question Paul's integrity and by extension, his ministry. In return, Paul narrates his sufferings and weaknesses as a defence strategy against the complaint that he was weak. Paul points to his sufferings and hardships as a positive indication that speaks to what his weak body could endure. Paul particularly took the opportunity to spin his stigmatized "thorn in the flesh" into a symbol of spiritual superiority over the so-called "super-apostles."

Paul's defence in 2 Corinthians proves one should not despise or condemn his disability because it made him realize the depths and comforts of God's mercy. Ultimately, Paul could accept that his disability was a blessing from God because whenever he was weak, God's power made him strong. In other words, Paul's weakness and suffering because of his disability became the foundation of his gospel and the source of his strength and hope for future

---

3. Kim, *Paul*, 293.

glory in Christ. Because of this, Paul did not mind suffering the hardships and humiliation that he received from the Corinthians. His focus was clear – as long as he was preaching the good news of Christ, he was happy to suffer (see 2 Cor 13:9). In sum, this study understands that disability was at the heart of Paul's suffering and weakness in 2 Corinthians.

## 7.2 Implications

The findings of this research – that disability plays a crucial role in the understanding of Paul's suffering and weakness in 2 Corinthians – have multiple implications. The following sections discuss the significance of this study.

### 7.2.1 The Use of DHs within New Testament Studies

The formulation of DHs for the present study can also have important implications for New Testament studies as a whole. It is true that this DH has been formulated specifically for studying Paul's Second Letter to the Corinthians. However, since the methodology being formulated consists of rhetorical criticism as well as the broad aspect of sociological criticism coupled with a disability perspective, there are reasons to believe that this DH can also work for other New Testament texts that show affinity to disability, particularly its social ramifications.

For instance, when it comes to analyzing New Testament books other than Pauline Epistles, the researcher is optimistic that this DH can be employed particularly to the four gospel narratives. Previously, in many of the chapters of this present study, it has been shown that Paul was very particular about connecting his suffering with that of Jesus's sufferings while on earth. While it may not amount to much, it was argued strongly that Jesus was also very much suffering from social stigmatization, ultimately dying the death of a criminal who was hanged on a cross, a symbol of being accursed. Already, scholars like George, John Mathew, and Sam Peedikayil Mathew have worked on analyzing Jesus and his mission from a disability perspective with varying successful results.[4] As such, it becomes a step in the right direction to incorporate the two other critical tools composing a DH – that is, rhetorical

---

4. George, "(Dis)abled Jesus," 101–125; Mathew, "Disability," 43. Mathew, "Jesus," 48.

and sociological criticism – to add depth for anyone who wishes to analyse the four gospel narratives.

## 7.2.2 Implications for Pauline Studies

This present study of Paul's sufferings and weaknesses in 2 Corinthians by employing a DH may contribute to Pauline studies as follows. First, as far as the researcher is aware, this present study is the first detailed analysis of any of Paul's letters by formulating a hermeneutic especially from a disability point of view. In the introduction chapter, this present study has shown that there have been many attempts by scholars to find the underlying cause of Paul's suffering and weakness in 2 Corinthians. Yet, there had been no serious work done on how to interpret and analyse Paul's suffering and weakness from the perspective of disability. One of the closest works focused on Paul's suffering and weakness was an article by Albl who specifically analysed Galatians 4:13-14 and 2 Corinthians 12:1-10 from a disability perspective.

Second, if this DH can be incorporated into studying Paul and his interaction with the Corinthian congregations, it is logical to pursue the possibility that other letters written by Paul can also make use of a DH to further shed light on how Paul was perceived by the Christian congregations he ministered to and planted. For instance, Paul's heartfelt letter to the Galatians, seen through a DH, might be able to shed interesting insights into the tension between Paul and his opponents as well as the Galatian congregation. Moreover, his statement in Galatians 3:28, "There is neither Jew nor Gentile, neither slave nor free, nor is there male and female, for you are all one in Christ Jesus" (NIV), when analysed through DHs would probably reveal to the reader that Paul came to this conclusion and revelation from his struggle with disability under Judaism (and the Mosaic law). Thus, in all likelihood, anyone interested in Paul's writings will have a new hermeneutical key that will help in their understanding of how Paul came to develop his theology. This new hermeneutical key is "disability."

## 7.2.3 Contributing to Disability Studies in Christian Academia

This present study also contributes to disability studies in larger Christian academia. It was briefly pointed out in the literature reviews of this present study (see chapter 1, section 1.4.1) that studying biblical texts and doing theology from a disability perspective came to the forefront with the publication of *The Disabled God: Towards a Liberatory Theology of Disability* by Nancy Eiesland in 1994.[5] After her, quite a number of works have been published that reveal the extent to which disability studies have swept the academic world of Christianity. Mention may be made of those who employ a disability perspective in the study of theology, such as Kathy Black and Jennie Weiss Block.[6] Block has proposed a model (called "the accessible God") based "on a social/minority group definition of disability, which highlights disability as an issue of oppressive structures and exclusion."[7] Another important work in this direction has been the work of Amos Yong who published the book *Theology and Down Syndrome: Reimagining Disability in Late Modernity*.[8] Then there is the work of Thomas E. Reynolds who published *Vulnerable Communion: A Theology of Disability and Hospitality* in which he seeks to reflect theologically on how Christians might think differently about disability and act differently towards people with disability.[9]

Mention may also be made of books such as *Embracing the Inclusive Community: A Disability Perspective, Doing Theology from a Disability Perspective, Sprouts of Disability Theology*, which are all collective works on disability subjects from various scholars.[10] Aside from these brief collections, there are many articles published in reputed journals that deal with disability from a Christian perspective. This present study has also mentioned that a biblical commentary from a disability perspective was recently published and is the very first of its kind. When it comes to Pauline studies, there is, so far, no monograph or book published that focuses solely on disability as its methodology. In that regard, this present study attempts to be the first published monograph that addresses Paul from a disability perspective. Thus, this possibility underscores the significance of this present study's contribution to wider Christian academia.

---

5. Eiesland, *Disabled God*.
6. Black, *Healing Homiletic*; Block, *Copious Hosting*.
7. Block, *Copious Hosting*, 82.
8. Yong, *Theology*, 201.
9. Reynolds, *Vulnerable Communion*, 14.
10. Longchar and Rajkumar, *Embracing*; Longchar and Cowans, *Doing Theology*; Rajkumar, *Sprouts*.

## 7.2.4 Implications to the Church and Her Members

Another important area where this study's findings can make an impact is to encourage the church to reflect deeper on the ways that disabled members are being treated.[11] At the beginning, this present study pointed out that some theologians accuse the church of perpetrating a theology that is not inclusive to disabled members. For instance, Eiesland, who is herself disabled, has touchingly stated, "Sadly, rather than offering empowerment, the church has more often supported societal structures and attitudes that have treated people with disabilities as objects of pity and paternalism."[12] One also recollects the charges levelled by Njoroge that the problem lies with the church and not the disabled.[13] There are many areas where the church is working to care for its disabled members; however, the focus here is on the possibility of the church doing much more for its disabled members.[14] A cursory reading of how the church has treated its disabled members indirectly or directly reveals a rather unpleasant result.

There are many testimonies of people with disabilities and families with disabilities who are reluctant to attend church services because of the negative attitude of other church members. For instance, in the US alone, about 80 percent of church members who have a PwD in their family are disinclined to attend church services because of the insensitive remarks they hear among churchgoers or even the pastors themselves.[15] Stumbo has collected quite a few reasons why parents feel unwelcome inside the church, among them are:

- My child is not welcomed in any of the children's activities, they said he is too disruptive.
- I took my child to Sunday School class, but they wheeled him to the corner, and he sat there until I came to pick him up.

---

11. This study is referencing the universal church, not any particular denomination.
12. Eiesland, "Encountering," 584–586.
13. Njoroge, "Not an Option," 7.
14. The formation of the Ecumenical Disability Advocates Network (EDAN) by World Council of Churches (WCC) in 1998 at the eighth WCC assembly held in Harare, Zimbabwe, is one such wide-sweeping attempt by the church to help the disabled as well as the non-disabled in the church (see http://www.edan-wcc.org/about-us/our-history/).
15. Stumbo, "Church and Disability."

- I asked the pastor if we could possibly have someone help my child during Sunday School, they told me they were not responsible to find me babysitters.
- When my child is loud, people stare at us and shake their heads. I even had people tell me that my child needs discipline, my child has autism and they know it![16]

In addition, Hentrich narrates the frustration he has felt when his disabled son is denied the sacrament of the Lord's Supper because "the church was concerned the boy couldn't understand its significance."[17] Just from these examples, one observes the exclusive and callous attitude meted out to disabled members by other church members. The pity is that even some pastors do not seem to care much about the plight of the disabled and their families.

In another case, Dingle reflects on the shame that her family endured inside the church because there was no ramp for a wheelchair to access the pulpit. She wrote of how uncomfortable she was when some church members hoisted up her youngest child who was in a wheelchair in front of the entire congregation so she could take part in a play.[18] What also hurt Dingle further was the fact that there were no ramps inside the church because, "Christian schools and churches successfully fought to be excluded from the requirements of the Americans with Disabilities Act (ADA), which was passed 27 years ago."[19] Indeed, *The ADA National Network Disability Law Handbook* exempted churches, mosques, and synagogues from complying with the rules laid out in this act.[20]

Besides ramps or any other obstacles inside the church, one of the most disturbing practices that a church perpetrates is the way the various church authorities across the world discriminate against disabled people by keeping them from becoming ministers working full time in church ministry. For instance, Karen Pitt reports that some Anglican members faced hardship while in seminary partly because they were discouraged from seeking help from

---

16. Stumbo.
17. "When Churches Discuss."
18. Dingle, "Churches."
19. Dingle.
20. Brennan, *ADA National Network*.

others.²¹ Morgan-Gurr, a "disabled woman in itinerant ministry," also feels that the biggest hurdle in her ministry is the fact that she is a PwD. According to her, "Some say I shouldn't be in ministry because my disability dishonours God. Others just want to 'fix' me either by prayer or random suggestions such as 'Are you harbouring an unforgiving spirit?'"²²

Even in some churches in the Northeastern parts of India, there are reports that there are some PwDs who are emotionally and mentally capable but are discouraged from becoming pastors. For instance, one of the Presbyterian pastors commented that the pastoral committee rejected the application of one candidate because he was short, dark in complexion, and had a soft voice.²³ This kind of stigmatization because of one's disability seems to be widespread and real judging by the fact that the United Methodist Association of Ministers with Disabilities (UMAMD) has passed legislation that includes, "Removing discrimination toward ordination candidates with disabilities; confirming that the ordination process ensures non-discrimination."²⁴ If a person is mentally and emotionally competent and has a normal intelligent quotient, such a person ought not to be restricted from achieving his/her dream of working in the church. As Louise Gosbell remarks, "It is in our diversity of gifts and our weaknesses that we together become this body" of Christ.²⁵

From the above, it is obvious that the church treats its disabled members unfairly in some circles and that the church does not utilize enough resources and flexibility of procedures towards them. What is ironic is the fact that the church derives its theology and its structures from the great apostle to the Gentiles, Paul himself, who was disabled. Farrar is right to point out how "hardly" it is "possible to exaggerate the extent, the permanence, the vast importance, of those services which were rendered to Christianity by Paul of Tarsus."²⁶ Yet, while most Christians venerate Paul, what one fails to see is the

---

21. Folkins, "Church."
22. Morgan-Gurr, "Disability Inclusion."
23. Personal interview. It seems that there is an unwritten rule whereby a person with visible defects does not have a chance to become a pastor because of the biases of the selecting committee as well as the congregation.
24. "Coalition Interview."
25. Delbridge, "People with Disability."
26. Farrar, *Life and Work*, 2.

Paul whom the Corinthian congregation despised, mocked, and looked down upon because of his "disability." If Paul was to come back to this present-day Christianity, one thinks that he would once again passionately argue in the same manner that he did to the Corinthian Christians.

From the findings of this present study, Paul was definitely suffering from some sort of disability, and the Corinthians and their instigators were stigmatizing him because of it. He himself acknowledged that he was a "weak" man, "different" from the other apostles, that he was not trained in "rhetoric," and that his overall physical stature was not impressive. His testimonies are clear: he was a disabled man who found strength and purpose in the risen Christ. It does not reflect well on the church when one observes the many Christian institutions and churches in Asia and around the world setting such high standards for a PwD to fit in their midst. If one accepts that the works done by the disabled Paul were the main factors in the formation of Christianity, there is no excuse for the church not to take care of its disabled members.

The fact that Paul was disabled should be prompting the church to be more open-minded. It must resolve itself to be more accommodating of those disabled members. The church ought to imitate Paul's attitude of considering oneself with humility, knowing that in some way, human beings are *all* imperfect and in need of the grace of Christ.

APPENDIX 1

# Index of Some Rare Greek Words for Disability

This appendix lists many Greek words pertaining to the modern term "disability" that are found scattered across Evelyne Samama's work, *The Greek Vocabulary of Disabilities*.[1]

| | |
|---|---|
| ἀβλεψια – lack of sight, blindness | κολοβος – maimed, undersized |
| ἀδυνατος – without strength | κολος – having a part lopped off, reduced to a stump |
| ἀγυιος – without limb | κωφος – blunt, dull, obtuse |
| αἶσχος – ugly | κυφος – bent forward, hunchbacked |
| ἄκαρος – blind | κυρτος – curved, hunchbacked |
| ἄλαλος – speechless | κυλλος – deformed, crippled, club-footed |
| ἀλαος – blind | λαπαρος – slack, loose, dislocated |
| ἀμφιγυηεις – with both feet crooked | λορδος – bent, backward |
| ἀνακουστος – not hearing | λοξος – oblique, slanting, sloping |
| ἄπους – without feet | μιλλος – flabby, dumb |
| ἄφωνος – voiceless, mute | μωρος – dull, sluggish, dumb, silly |
| ἄποτως – deaf, lit. far ear | μυκος – speechless, voiceless, mute |

---

1. Samama, "Greek Vocabulary," 121.

| | |
|---|---|
| ἄγχραν – short-sighted | μυλλος – crippled, twisted |
| ἀρρωστια – weakness | μυωψ – short-sighted |
| ἄρρωστος – weak | μυσαρος – foul, dirty, abominable |
| ἀσιδαρος – limping upon | νενιηλος – blinded |
| ἀσθενεια – naked | νυσος – lame, paralysed |
| βωβος – lame, handicap | ὀμματοστερης – deprived of eyesight, blind |
| βαττος – stammerer, lisper | παραλελυμενος – paralysed |
| βλαισος – bent, distorted designating a person with feet inward | πηρος – infirm, invalid, lame or blind |
| βλωμος – squinting | φοξος – sharp as in *sharp*-head |
| βαταλος or βαττολος – stammerer | φριξος – hairly, frizzy |
| χαβος – curved, weak | πιναρος – dirty, squalid |
| χαλαρος – slack, loose | πλαδαρος – flabby |
| Χωλος – lame, paralysed | πλαγιους – oblique, sloping, not straight |
| δυδειδης – unpleasant, ugly | ψαφαρος – friable, crumbling |
| δυσεργεια – unpleasant, ugly | ψελλος – speaking inarticulately |
| δυσκωφος – completely deaf | ψιλος – bald |
| ἔλλοψ – mute, dumb | ῥαιβος – distorted, bent inward |
| ἐνεος – speechless, mute | ῥαμψος – beak, bill portraying an image of crooked, bent, distorted form. |
| γαμψος – curved, crooked | ῥοικος – bow-legged |
| γαυσος – crooked, bent outward | ῥυσος – wrinkled |
| γρυπος – crooked, hook-nosed | σιλλος – squinted eyes |
| γυρος – curved, crooked | σιφλος – defect, crippled, maimed |
| ὑβος – hunchback, humpbacked | σκαμβος – crooked, bandy-legged |
| ἰσχνοφωνος – thin-voiced, weak-voiced | σκιμβος – lame, crooked |
| καδαμος – blind | σκολιος – twisted or crooked leg |
| καμψος – curved, bend as opposed to flexible | στραβος – squinted |
| καμπυλος – curved, bend | στρεβλος – twisted, crooked |

| | |
|---|---|
| κελλας – one eye | τετρωμενος – wounded, harmed, injured, damaged |
| κλαδαρος – quivering, invalid | τραυλος – suffering from a speech disorder, lisping, stammering |
| Κλαμβος – cocked, mutilated | τυφλος – blind, dark, clogged or blocked |

The observation of Evelyne Samama about the social impact of these "disabilities" is remarkable. According to her, "Many of these terms could be interpreted as mocking, either because of the vowel -α- or because of the geminate, often used in the vocabulary of derision. Denigration is a recurrent way of pointing at the physical defect. A rich and varied vocabulary connotes marked and imperfect bodies."[2]

---

2. Samama, 125

# Bibliography

## Primary Sources

Aeschylus. *Agamemnon*. In *Aeschylus*, edited by Herbert Weir Smyth. Vol. 2. Cambridge, MA: Harvard University Press, 1926. Perseus Digital Library. Accessed June 13, 2018. http://www.perseus.tufts.edu/hopper/text?doc=Perseus%3Atext%3A1999.01.0004%3Acard%3D1.

Aland, Barbara, Kurt Aland, Johannes Karavidopoulos, Carlos M. Martini, and Bruce M. Metzger, eds. *The Greek New Testament*. 4th revised edition with dictionary. Philadelphia, USA: United Bible Societies, 1983.

Alciphron. *Alciphron: Literally and Completely Translated from the Greek with Introduction and Notes*. Athens: Privately Printed for the Athenian Society, 1896. Accessed December 27, 2017. http://www.elfinspell.com/Alciphron3.html.

Aristotle. *Rhetoric*. In *Aristotle: Art of Rhetoric*, translated by J. H. Freese. Volume 22 of *Aristotle in Twenty-Three Volumes*. Cambridge, MA: Harvard University Press, 1926. Perseus Digital Library. Accessed July 10, 2018. http://bit.ly/2m7qz7N.

Athanassakis, Apostolos N., ed. *Hesiod: Theogony, Works and Days*, 2nd ed. Baltimore: Johns Hopkins University Press, 2004.

Baumgarten, Joseph M. *Studies in Qumran Law*. Leiden: E. J. Brill, 1977.

*The Book of the Secrets of Enoch*. Blackmask Online, 2001. Accessed January 28, 2017. https://wbaseem.files.wordpress.com/2013/08/the-book-of-the-secrets-of-enoch.pdf.

"Chagigah 14b." In *The William Davidson Talmud*. Sefaria. Accessed July 28, 2018. https://www.sefaria.org/Chagigah.14b?lang=bi.

Chrysostom, John. "Homily 26." Translated by Talbot W. Chambers. In *Nicene and Post-Nicene Fathers*, edited by Philip Schaff. Vol. 12. Buffalo: Christian Literature Publishing, 1889. New Advent. Accessed July 27, 2018. http://www.newadvent.org/fathers/220226.htm.

Cicero, M. Tullius. *De Officiis*. Translated by Walter Miller. Cambridge, MA: Harvard University Press, 1913. Perseus Digital Library. Accessed November 13, 2018. http://bit.ly/2RQa4eh.

———. *De Oratore*. In *M. Tulli Ciceronis: Rhetorica*, edited by A. S. Wilkins. Vol. 2. Oxford: Oxford University Press, 1902; Perseus Digital Library, n.d. Accessed February 11, 2018. http://www.perseus.tufts.edu/hopper/text?doc=Perseus%3Atext%3A1999.02.0120%3Abook%3D2%3Asection%3D1.

———. *Rhetorica ad Herennium*. Cambridge, MA, Harvard University Press, 1954. Bill Thayer. Accessed September 21, 2018. https://penelope.uchicago.edu/Thayer/E/Roman/Texts/Rhetorica_ad_Herennium/home.html

———. *Rhetorici libri duo qui vocantur de inventione*. Edited by Eduard Stroebel. Lipsiae: B. G. Teubneri, 1915. Perseus Digital Library. Accessed 21, 2018. http://www.perseus.tufts.edu/hopper/text?doc=Perseus%3Atext%3A2008.01.0683%3Abook%3D1%3Asection%3D1.

Dionysius of Halicarnassus. *Dionysii Halicarnasei Antiquitatum Romanarum quae supersunt*. Edited by Karl Jacoby. 4 vols. Leipzig: Aedibus B.G. Teubneri, 1885. Perseus Digital Library. Accessed December 28, 2017. http://www.perseus.tufts.edu/hopper/textopen_in_new.

———. *The Three Literary Letters*. Edited by W. Rhys Roberts. Cambridge: Cambridge University Press, 1901. Internet Archive. Accessed July 13, 2018. http://bit.ly/2zBOF49.

Elliott, James K., ed. *The Apocryphal New Testament: A Collection of Apocryphal Christian Literature in an English Translation*. Oxford: Oxford University Press, 1993.

Epictetus. *Discourses*. In *The Works of Epictetus: His Discourses in Four Books, the Enchiridion, and Fragments*. Translated by Thomas Wentworth Higginson. New York: Thomas Nelson and Sons, 1890. Accessed July 3, 2018. http://bit.ly/2KBbZ6F.

———. *The Discourses of Epictetus, with the Enchiridion and Fragments*. Translated by George Long. London: George Bell and Sons. 1890. Perseus Digital Library. Accessed August 2, 2018. http://bit.ly/2ABEehE.

Eusebius. *The Church History*. Translation and compiled by Paul L. Maier. Grand Rapids: Kregel Publications, 2007.

———. *The Ecclesiastical History*. Edited by Kirsopp Lake, J. E. L. Oulton, H. J. Lawlor, and William Heinemann. 2 vols. Cambridge, MA: Harvard University Press, 1926–1932. Perseus Digital Library. Accessed January 19, 2018, https://goo.gl/Jekb5Q.

Herodotus. *The History of Herodotus*. Translated by George Rawlinson. Internet History Sourcebooks Project. Accessed December 26, 2017, https://sourcebooks.fordham.edu/Halsall/ancient/herodotus-history.txt

Herondas. *The Mimes of Herondas*. Translated by M. S. Buck. New York: A. Koren, 1921. Accessed July 30, 2018. http://www.elfinspell.com/Mimes.html.

*Historia Augusta*. Translated by David Magie. Vol. 2. Cambridge, MA: Harvard University Press, 1924.

Hoffner, Harry. *Letters from the Hittite Kingdom*. Atlanta: Society of Biblical Literature SBL, 2009.

Holmes, M. W. *The Greek New Testament*. Atlanta: Society of Biblical Literature, 2011–2013. Logos Bible Software.

Homer. *The Iliad*. Translated by A. T. Murray. 2 vols. Cambridge, MA: Harvard University Press, 1924. Perseus Digital Library. Accessed December 27, 2018. http://www.perseus.tufts.edu/hopper/text?doc=Perseus:text:1999.01.0134.

Isocrates. *Isocrates in Three Volumes*. Vol. 2. Translated by George Norlin. Edited by T. E. Page, E. Capps, and W. H. D. Rouse. The Loeb Classical Library. London: William Heinemann Ltd, 1929. PDF.

Jones, David E. *A Missionary's Autobiography*. Translated by J. M. Lloyd. Mizoram: H. Liansailova, 1998.

Josephus. *Antiquities of the Jews*. In *The Works of Josephus: Complete and Unabridged*. Translated by William Whiston Peabody, Massachusetts: Hendrickson Publishers, 1987.

———. *Wars of the Jews*. In *The Works of Josephus: Complete and Unabridged*. Translated by William Whiston Peabody, Massachusetts: Hendrickson Publishers, 1987.

Justinus, M. Junianius. *Epitome of Pompeius Trogus' Philippic Histories*. Translated by S. Watson. Attalus. Accessed June 30, 2018, http://www.attalus.org/translate/justin5.html#36.1. 36

Laertius, Diogenes. *Lives of Eminent Philosophers*. Edited by R. D. Hicks. Cambridge, MA: Harvard University Press, 1972. First published 1925. Perseus Digital Library. Accessed November 13, 2018. http://bit.ly/2RR2Syq.

Lessing, Robert Reed, trans. *Scriptorium Classicorum Bibliotheca Oxoniensi— Aristotelis Ars Rhetorica*. Edited by W. D. Ross. Oxford: Clarendon, 1959.

Lipsius, R. A., ed. "Acta Pauli et Theclae." In *Acta apostolorum apocrypha*, edited by R. A. Lipsius, 235–271. Vol. 1. Leipzig: Mendelssohn, 1891. Accessed January 19, 2018. http://www.patrologia-lib.ru/apocryph/novum/a_paul.htm.

Lucian. *Lucian: Works with an English Translation*. Translated by A. M. Harmon. Cambridge, MA: Harvard University Press, 1913.

Lysias. *On the Refusal of a Pension*. In *Lysias*. Translated by W. R. M. Lamb. Cambridge, MA: Harvard University Press, 1930.

Martinez, Florentino Garcia, ed. *The Dead Sea Scrolls Translated: The Qumran Texts in English*. Translated by Wilfred G. E. Watson. 2nd ed. Grand Rapids: William B. Eerdmans, 1996.

Neusner, Jacob. *The Mishnah: A New Translation*. New Haven: Yale University Press, 1988.

Oribasius Latinus (fragments). Universitätsbibliothek, N I 3:13 + 15. Basel, Switzerland. Accessed December 14, 2017. https://www.e-codices.unifr.ch/en/list/one/ubb/N-I-0003-13-15.

Pausanias. *Corinth*. In *Attica and Corinth*, translated by W. H. S. Jones. Vol. 1 of *Description of Greece*. Cambridge, MA: Harvard University Press, 1918. Accessed December 26, 2017. https://sourcebooks.fordham.edu/Halsall/index.asp.

Philo. *The Works of Philo: Complete and Unabridged*. Translated by C. D. Yonge. New updated edition. Peabody, MA: Hendrickson publishers, 2011.

———. *The Works of Philo Judaeus: The Contemporary of Josephus*. Vol. 1. Translated by C. D. Yonge. London: George Bell & Sons, 1800.

Plato. *Republic*. In vols. 5–6 of *Plato in Twelve Volumes*, translated by Paul Shorey. London: William Heinemann, 1969. Perseus Digital Library. Accessed February 11, 2019 http://www.perseus.tufts.edu/hopper/text?doc=Perseus:text:1999.01.0168.

Plautus, T. Maccius. *Captivi: The Captives*. In *The Comedies of Plautus*, edited by Henry Thomas Riley. London: G. Bell and Sons, 1912. Perseus Digital Library. n.d.). Accessed January 11, 2018. http://www.perseus.tufts.edu/hopper/text?doc=Perseus:text:1999.02.0096.

Pliny the Elder, *Natural History*. With an English Translation in Ten Volumes, vol 8, libri 28–32: 28.7, page 27 by W. H. S. Jones Cambridge/Massachusetts: Harvard University Press/ London: William Heineman Ltd, 1963. https://archive.org/details/naturalhistory08plinuoft/page/26/mode/2up.

Plutarch. *Alcibiades*. In *Plutarch's Lives*, edited by Bernadotte Perrin. London: William Heinemann, 1919. Perseus Digital Library. Accessed December 27, 2017. http://www.perseus.tufts.edu/hopper/text?doc=Perseus:text:2008.01.0006.

———. *Cicero*. In *Plutarch's Lives*, edited by Bernadotte Perrin. London: William Heinemann, 1919. Perseus Digital Library. Accessed February 11, 2018. http://www.perseus.tufts.edu/hopper/text?doc=Perseus:text:2008.01.0016.

———. *Demosthenes*. In *Plutarch's Lives*, edited by Bernadotte Perrin. London: William Heinemann, 1919. Perseus Digital Library. Accessed September 7, 2018. http://www.perseus.tufts.edu/hopper/text?doc=Perseus:text:2008.01.0039.

———. "On Praising Oneself Inoffensively." In *Moralia*, translated by Phillip H. De Lacy and Benedict Einarson, 109–167. Cambridge, MA: Harvard University Press, 1959; Bill Thayer. Accessed July 13, 2018. http://bit.ly/2zCvBmC.

Quintilian. *Institutio Oratoria: Books 1–3*. Translated by H. E. Butler. Cambridge, MA: Harvard University Press, 1920. Bill Thayer. Accessed August 2, 2018. https://penelope.uchicago.edu/Thayer/E/Roman/Texts/Quintilian/Institutio_Oratoria/2A*.html#2.

Rosner, Fred. *Medicine in the Bible and the Talmud: Selection from Classical Jewish Sources*. Augmented Edition. New York: Ktav, 1995.

Schneemelcher, Wilhelm, ed. *New Testament Apocrypha 2: Writings Relating to the Apostles Apocalypses and Related Subjects*. Vol. 2. Translated and edited by R. Mc L. Wilson II. Louisville: Westminster John Knox Press, 1992.

Scurlock, Jo Ann, and Burton R. Andersen. *Diagnoses in Assyrian and Babylonian Medicine: Ancient Sources, Translations, and Modern Medical Analyses*. Urbana: University of Illinois Press, 2005.

Seneca. *Apocolocyntosis*. Edited by W. H. D. Rouse. London: William Heinemann, 1913. Perseus Digital Library. Accessed January 15, 2017. http://www.perseus.tufts.edu/hopper/text?doc=Perseus:text:2007.01.0029.

———. *De Clementia*. In *Moral Essays* In *Moral Essays*, edited by John W. Basore. Vol. 1. London: Heinemann, 1928. Perseus Digital Library. Accessed November 13, 2018. http://www.perseus.tufts.edu/hopper/text?doc=Perseus:text:2007.01.0015.

———. *De Constantia*. In *Moral Essays*, edited by John W. Basore. Vol. 1. London: Heinemann, 1928. Perseus Digital Library. Accessed December 28, 2017. http://bit.ly/2S2lIIc.

———. *De Ira*. In *Moral Essays*, edited by John W. Basore. Vol. 1. London: Heinemann, 1928. Perseus Digital Library. Accessed December 28, 2017. http://www.perseus.tufts.edu/hopper/text?doc=Perseus:text:2007.01.0014.

———. *Letters from a Stoic*. Vol. 2. Translated by Richard Mott Gummere. Los Angeles: Enhanced Media Publishing, 2016.

Sophocles. *The Oedipus Tyrannus of Sophocles*. Edited by Richard Jebb. Cambridge: Cambridge University Press, 1887. Perseus Digital Library. Accessed February 11, 2018. http://www.perseus.tufts.edu/hopper/text?doc=Perseus%3Atext%3A1999.01.0192%3Acard%3D1.

———. *The Philoctetes of Sophocles*. Edited by Richard Jebb. Cambridge: Cambridge University Press, 1898. Perseus Digital Library. Accessed February 11, 2018. https://goo.gl/2VMKGh.

Sorani. *De signis fracturarum, De fasciis, Vita Hippocratis secundum Soranum*. In vol. 4 of *Gynaeciorum*, edited by J. Ilberg. Leipzig: Teubner, 1927. Corpus Medicorum Graecorum/Latinorum. Accessed June 11, 2018. http://galen.bbaw.de/epubl/online/cmg_04.php?p=25.

Strabo. *The Geography of Strabo*. 3 vols. Edited by H. C. Hamilton and W. Falconer. London: George Bell & Sons. Perseus Digital Library. Accessed June 30, 2018.

http://www.perseus.tufts.edu/hopper/text?doc=Perseus%3Atext%3A1999.01.0239%3Abook%3Dnotice.

Suetonius. *Augustus*. In *The Lives of the Twelve Caesars: Augmented with the Biographies of Contemporary Statesmen, Orators, Poets, and Other Associates*, edited by J. Eugene Reed and Alexander Thomson. Philadelphia: Gebbie & Co., 1889. Perseus Digital Library. Accessed December 28, 2108. http://www.perseus.tufts.edu/hopper/text?doc=Perseus:text:1999.02.0132.

———. *Claudius*. In *The Lives of the Twelve Caesars: Augmented with the Biographies of Contemporary Statesmen, Orators, Poets, and Other Associates*, edited by J. Eugene Reed and Alexander Thomson. Philadelphia: Gebbie & Co., 1889. Perseus Digital Library. Accessed December 28, 2108. http://www.perseus.tufts.edu/hopper/text?doc=Perseus:text:1999.02.0132.

Tacitus, Cornelius. *A Dialogue on Oratory*. In *The Complete Works of Tacitus*. Edited by Alfred John Church and William Jackson Brodribb. New York: Random House, 1942. Perseus Digital Library. Accessed March 6, 2018. https://goo.gl/ovwa1K.

Tajra, Harry W. *The Martyrdom of St. Paul: Historical and Judicial Context, Traditions and Legends*. Tubingen: J. C. B Mohr, 1994.

Tertullian. "Concerning Baptism." In *Tertullian's Treatises Concerning Prayer and Baptism*, translated by Alexander Souter. London: SPCK, 1919. The Tertullian Project. Accessed January 19, 2018. http://www.tertullian.org/articles/souter_orat_bapt/souter_orat_bapt_04baptism.htm.

"Tractate Yoma: Chapter 1." Jewish Virtual Library: A Project of AIC. Accessed July 2, 2018. https://www.jewishvirtuallibrary.org/tractate-yoma-chapter-1.

Vermes, Geza. *The Dead Sea Scrolls in English*. 3rd edition. New York: Penguin, 1987.

Vogt, Katja. "Seneca." Stanford Encyclopedia of Philosophy. October 17, 2007. Accessed January 24, 2017. https://plato.stanford.edu/entries/seneca/).

Wright, Wilmer Cave., trans. *Philostratus and Eunapius: The Lives of the Sophists*. London: Heinemann, 1922.

Xenophon. *Agesilaus*. In *Xenophon: Scripta Minora*, translated by E. C. Marchant and G. W. Bowersock. Vol. 7 of *Xenophon in Seven Volumes*. Cambridge, Massachusetts: Harvard University Press, 1925. Perseus Digital Library. Accessed August 15, 2018. http://bit.ly/2KZxmdM.

## Secondary Sources

Abernathy, David. "Paul's Thorn in the Flesh: A Messenger of Satan?" *Neotestamentica* 35, no. 1–2 (2001): 69–79.

Albl, Martin. "For Whenever I Am Weak, Then I Am Strong." In *This Abled Body: Rethinking Disabilities in Biblical Studies*, edited by Hector Avalos, Sarah

J. Melcher and Jeremy Schipper, 145–158. SBL Semeia Studies 55. Atlanta: Society of Biblical Literature, 2007.

Amador, J. D. H. "Revisiting 2 Corinthians: Rhetoric and the Case for Unity." *New Testament Studies* 46 (2000): 92–111.

Andrews, Mary Edith. *The Ethical of Paul: A Study in Origin*. North Carolina: University of North Carolina Press, 1934.

Arcangeli, Alessandro. *Cultural History: A Concise Introduction*. London and New York: Routledge, 2012.

Ashley, Evelyn. "Paul's Paradigm for Ministry in 2 Corinthians: Christ's Death and Resurrection." PhD diss., Murdoch University, 2006. http://researchrepository.murdoch.edu.au/id/eprint/139.

Atkinson, Rebecca. "Viewpoint: Is it Time to Stop Using the Word 'Disability'?" *Ouch* (blog). *BBC*. September 30th, 2015. https://www.bbc.com/news/blogs-ouch-34385738.

Aune, D. E. *The NT in Its Literary Environment*. Philadelphia: Westminster, 1987.

Avalos, Hector. *Illness and Health Care in the Ancient Near East: The Role of the Temple in Greece, Mesopotamia, and Israel*. Harvard Semitic Monographs 54. Atlanta: Scholars Press, 1995.

———. "Redemptionism, Rejectionism, and Historicism as Emerging Approaches in Disability Studies." *Perspectives in Religious Studies* (Spring 2007): 91–100.

Avalos, Hector, Sarah J. Melcher, and Jeremy Schipper, eds. *This Abled Body: Rethinking Disabilities in Biblical Studies*. Semeia Studies 55. Atlanta: Society of Biblical Literature, 2007.

Bailey, Diana. *Ancient Civilization: Ancient Greece*. Minneapolis: ABDO Publishing, 2015.

Baird, William. "Visions, Revelation, and Ministry: Reflections on 2 Cor 12:1–5 and Gal 1:11–17." *Journal of Biblical Literature* 104, no. 4 (1985): 631–662.

Baker, W. R. *2 Corinthians*. The College Press New International Version Commentary. Joplin: College Press Publication, 1999.

Balla, Peter. *The Child-Parent Relationship in the New Testament and Its Environment*. Peabody: Hendrickson Publishers, 2003.

Balz, H. R., and Gerhard Schneider, eds. *Exegetical Dictionary of the New Testament*. Grand Rapids: Eerdmans, 1993.

Barclay, John M. G. "Paul among Diaspora Jews: Anomaly or Apostate?" *Journal For the Study of the New Testament* 60 (December 1995): 89–120.

———. "Paul and the Law: Observations on Some Recent Debates." *Themelios* 12, no. 1 (September 1986): 5–15.

Barclay, William. *The Letters to the Corinthians*. The New Daily Study Bible. Louisville: Westminster John Knox Press, 2002.

Barnett, Paul. *Paul: Missionary of Jesus*. Vol. 2 of *After Jesus*. Grand Rapids: Eerdmans, 2008.

———. *The Second Epistle to the Corinthians*. The New International Commentary on the New Testament. Grand Rapids: Eerdmans, 1997.

Barrett, C. K. *A Commentary on the Second Epistle to The Corinthians*. Black's New Testament Commentary. London: A. & C. Black, 1986.

———. "Pauline Controversies in the Post-Pauline Period." *New Testament Studies* 20, no. 3 (1974): 229–245.

Barton, B. B., and G. R. Osborne. *1 & 2 Corinthians*. Life Application Bible Commentary. Wheaton: Tyndale House, 1999.

Barton, Stephen C. "Social-Scientific Approaches to Paul." In *Dictionary of Paul and his Letters*, edited by G. F. Hawthorne, R. P Martin and D. G. Reid, 892–900. Downers Grove, Illinois: InterVarsity Press, 1993.

———. "Social Values and Structures." In *Dictionary of New Testament Background*, edited by Craig A. Evans and Stanley E. Porter, 1127–1134. Leicester/Downers Grove: InterVarsity Press, 2010.

Basselin, Timothy J. "Why Theology Needs Disability." *Theology Today* 68, no. 1 (2011): 47–57.

Bates, W. H. "The Integrity of 2 Corinthians." *New Testament Studies* 12 (1965): 56–69.

Bauer, W., F. W. Danker, W. F. Arndt, and F. W Gingrich. *A Greek-English Lexicon of the New Testament and Other Early Christian Literature*. Rev. 3rd ed. Chicago: The University of Chicago Press, 1987.

Baur, Ferdinand Christian. "The Christ-party in the Corinthian Church, the Conflict between Petrine and Pauline Christianity in the Early Church, the Apostle Peter in Rome." *Tübingen Zeitschrift für Theologie* 4 (1831): 61–206.

Becker, Eve-Marie. *Letter Hermeneutics in 2 Corinthians: Studies in 'Literarkritik' and Communication Theory*. Translated by Helen S. Heron and edited by Mark Goodacre. London: T&T Clark, 2004.

Belcher, John R., and Deforge, Bruce R. "Social Stigma and Homelessness: The Limits of Social Change." *Journal of Human Behavior in the Social Environment* 22 (2012): 929–946.

Belleville, Linda L. *2 Corinthians*. InterVarsity Press New Testament Commentary 8. Downers Grove: IVP, 1995.

———. "A Letter of Apologetic Self-Commendation: 2 Cor 1:8–7:16." *Novum Testamentum* 31 (1989): 142–163.

Benard, J. H. *The Second Epistle to the Corinthians*. The Expositor's Greek Testament. Grand Rapids: Eerdmans, 1961.

Berger, Ronald J. *Introducing Disability Studies*. Boulder: Lynne Rienner Publishers, 2013.

Bergson, Henri. *Laughter: An Essay on the Meaning of the Comic*. Translated by Cloudesley Brereton and Fred Rothwell. Mineola: Dover Publications, 2005.

Bertram, Georg. "στενοχωρία-A. Profane Usage." In vol. 7 of *Theological Dictionary of the New Testament*, edited by G. Kittel and G. Friedrich, translated by G. W. Bromiley, 604. Grand Rapids: Eerdmans, 1971.

Betz, Hans Dieter. *2 Corinthians 8 and 9: A Commentary on Two Administrative Letters of the Apostle Paul*. Hermenia Series. Minneapolis: Fortress Press, 1985.

———. *Galatians: A Commentary on Paul's Letter to the Churches in Galatia*. Hermenia Series. Philadelphia: Fortress Press, 1979.

———. *Paul's Apology in 2 Corinthians 10–13 and the Socratic Tradition*. Berkeley: University of California, 1970.

Bickenbach, J. S., S. Chatterji, E. M. Badley, and T. B. Ustun. "Models of Disablement, Universalism and the International Classification of Impairments Disabilities and Handicaps." *Social Science and Medicine* 48 (1999): 1173–1186.

Bishop, E. F. F. "Does Aretas Belong in 2 Corinthians or Galatians." *Expository Times* 64 (1953): 188–189.

Bitzer, Lloyd F. "The Rhetorical Situation." *Philosophy and Rhetoric* 1, no. 1 (January 1968): 6.

Björck, G. "Nochmals Paulus Abortivus." *Coniectanea JNeotestamentica* 3 (1938): 3–8.

Black, Clifton. "Rhetorical Criticism and the New Testament." *Proceedings* 8 (1988): 77–92.

Black, David Alan. *Paul, Apostle of Weakness: Astheneia and Its Cognates in the Pauline Literature*. Rev. ed. Eugene: Pickwick Publications, 2012.

———. "Paulus Infirmus: The Pauline Concept of Weakness." *Grace Theological Journal* 5, no.1 (1984): 77–93.

Black, Edwin. *Rhetorical Criticism: A Study in Method*. Madison: The University of Wisconsin Press, 1965.

Black, Kathy. *A Healing Homiletic: Preaching and Disability*. Nashville: Abingdon Press, 1996.

Bliss, Matthew Todd. "A Rhetorical Analysis of Paul's Epistle to the Colossians." PhD diss., University of Edinburgh, 1998. http://hdl.handle.net/1842/18734.

Block, Jennie Weiss. *Copious Hosting: A Theology of Access for People with Disabilities*. New York: Continuum, 2002.

Boardman, J., J. Griffin, and O. Murray. *The Oxford Illustrated History of The Roman World*. Oxford: Oxford University Press, 1988.

Bock, Darrell L. *Acts*. Baker Exegetical Commentary of the New Testament. Grand Rapids: Baker Academic, 2007.

Bockmuehl, Markus N. A. "Scriptural Completion in the Infancy Gospel of James." *Pro Ecclesia* 27, no. 2 (Spring 2018): 180–202.

Bond, Sarah E., and T. H. M. Gellar-Goad, "Foul and Fair Bodies, Minds, and Poetry in Roman Satire." In *Disability in Antiquity*, edited by Christian Laes. London: Routledge, Taylor & Francis Group, 2017: 222–231.

Bornkamm, Günther. "The History of the Origin of the So-Called Second Letter to the Corinthians." *NTS* 8 no. 3 (April 1962): 258–264.

Bowens, Lisa M. "Investigating the Apocalyptic Texture of Paul's Martial Imagery in 2 Corinthians 4–6." *Journal for the Study of the New Testament* 39, 1 (2016): 3–15.

Bower, E. W. "ΕΦΟΔΟΣ and INSINUATIO in Greek and Latin Rhetoric." *Catholic Quarterly* 8, no.3 (1958): 224.

Bowerstock, G. W. *Greek Sophists in the Roman Empire*. Oxford: Clarendon Press, 1969.

Boyarin, Daniel. *A Radical Jew: Paul and the Politics of Identity*. Berkeley: University of California Press, 1994.

Branscomb, Bennett Harvie. *Jesus and the Law of Moses*. Whitefish: Literary Licensing, 2013.

Brennan, Jacquie. *The ADA National Network Disability Law Handbook*. ILRU, 2015. ADA National Network: Information, Guidance, and Training on the Americans with Disabilities Act. Accessed December 18, 2018. https://adata.org/publication/disability-law-handbook.

Briones, David E. *Paul's Financial Policy: A Socio-Theological Approach*. London: Bloomsbury, 2013.

———. "Paul's Financial Policy: A Socio-Theological Approach." PhD diss., University of Durham, June 2011. https://www.scribd.com/document/362939329/Paul-s-Financial-Policy-A-Socio-Theological-Approach.

Bruce, F. F. *1 and 2 Corinthians*. New Century Bible. London: Oliphants, 1971.

———. *The Book of Acts*. Rev. ed. The New International Commentary on the New Testament. Grand Rapids: Eerdmans, 1988.

———. "Paul and the Historical Jesus." Lecture presented at John Rylands University Library, November 14, 1973. https://biblicalstudies.org.uk/pdf/bjrl/historical_bruce.pdf.

Bullinger, E. W. *Figures of Speech Used in the Bible: Explained and Illustrated*. Grand Rapids: Baker Books, 1990.

Bultmann, Rudolf. *The Second Letter to the Corinthians*. Edited by Erich Dinkler and translated by Roy A. Harrisville. Original German edition. Minneapolis: Augsburg Publishing House, 1976.

———. *Theology of the New Testament*. Vol. 2. Translated by Kendrick Grobel. New York: Charles Scribner's Sons, 1955.

Burke, Trevor J. "Pauline Paternity in 1 Thessalonians." *Tyndale Bulletin* 51, no. 1 (2000): 59–72.

Calvin, John. *The First Epistle of Paul to the Corinthians*. Translated by John W. Fraser. Edinburgh: Oliver & Boyd,1960.

"Canons of Rhetoric: Arrangement." Silva Rhetoricae: The Forest of Rhetoric. Brigham Young University. Accessed September 5, 2018. http://rhetoric.byu.edu/Canons/Arrangement/Exordium.htm.

Carson, D. A. *From Triumphalism to Maturity: An Exposition of 2 Corinthians 10–13*. Grand Rapids: Baker Book House, 1984.

Castelli, E. *Imitation of Paul: A Discourse of Power*. Louisville: Westminster John Knox, 1991.

Chow, John K. *Patronage and Power: A Study of Social Networks in Corinth*. Journal for the Study of New Testament Supplement Series 75. England: Sheffield Academic Press, 1992.

Christian, Timothy J. "*Insinuatio* and Paul's Areopagus Speech in Acts 17:22–31." Paper presented at the annual meeting of the Society of Biblical Literature, Boston, MA, November 20, 2017. http://bit.ly/2xgnMiQ.

Christiansen, Daniel L. "Rhetoric, Gender, Weakness, and Shame: Paul's Somatic Self-Presentation in the Corinthian Correspondence." PhD diss., University of Aberdeen, 2015. https://pure.uhi.ac.uk/portal/files/3077332/pdf.

Claasens, Juliana M. "Job, Theology and Disability: Moving Towards a New Kind of Speech." In *Searching for Dignity: Conversations on Human Dignity, Theology, and Disability*, edited by Julie Claassens, Leslie Swartz, and Len Hansen, 55–66. Stellenbosch: Sun Media, 2013.

Claasens, Julie, Leslie Swartz, and Len Hansen. *Searching for Dignity: Conversations on Human Dignity, Theology and Disability*. Stellenbosch: SUN Media Stellenbosch, 2013.

Clapton, Jayne, and Jennifer Fitzgerald. "The History of Disability: A History of 'Otherness.'" Renaissance Universal: Featuring *New Renaissance Magazine*. Accessed September 25, 2017. http://www.ru.org/index.php/human-rights/315-the-history-of-disability-ahistory-of-otherness.

"Coalition Interview with Evy McDonald of the United Methodist Association of Disabled Ministers (UMAMD)." *Love Prevails* (blog). October 13, 2015. https://loveprevailsumc.com/2015/10/.

Coenen, L. "νεκρός." In vol. 1 of *The New International Dictionary of New Testament Theology*, edited by Colin Brown, 443. Grand Rapids: Regency Reference Library, Zondervan Publishing House, 1986.

Collins, Adele Yarbro. "Paul's Disability: The Thorn in His Flesh." In *Disability Studies and Biblical Literature*, edited by Candida R. Moss and Jeremy Schipper, 165–183. New York: Palgrave Macmillan, 2011.

Conway, Colleen M. *Behold the Man: Jesus and Greco-Roman Masculinity*. Oxford: Oxford University Press, 2008.

Cookson, Peter W., Jr., and Alan R. Sadovnik. "Functionalist Theories of Education." In *Education and Sociology: An Encyclopedia*, edited by David L. Levinson, Peter W. Cookson Jr., and Alan R. Sadovnik, 267–271. New York: Routledge Falmer, 2002.

Cranfield, C. E. B. *A Critical and Exegetical Commentary on the Epistle to the Romans*. Vol. 1. International Critical Commentary. Edinburgh: T & T Clark, 2004.

Creamer, Deborah Beth. *Disability and Christian Theology: Embodied Limits and Constructive Possibilities*. American Academy of Religion. Oxford: Oxford University Press, 2009.

Danker, Frederick W. *Augsburg Commentary on the New Testament: 2 Corinthians*. Minneapolis: Augsburg Publishing House, 1989.

Dasen, Veronique. *Dwarfs in Ancient Egypt and Greece*. Oxford: Clarendon Press, 1993.

Davis, Lennard J. "Crips Strike Back: The Rise of Disability Studies." *American Literary History* 11, no. 3 (1999): 500–512.

de Boer, M. C. "Images of Paul in the Post-Apostolic Period." *Catholic Bible Quarterly* 42 (1980): 359–380.

Deffinbaugh, Bob. "Religious Affections: A Study of Paul's 2 Corinthian Correspondence." Bible.org, 2 February, 2009. Accessed 7 December, 2018. bible.org/book/export/html/6254.

Deines, Roland. "The Pharisees Between 'Judaisms' and 'Common Judaism.'" In *The Complexities of Second Temple Judaism*, edited by D. A. Carson, Peter Thomas O'Brien, and Mark A. Seifrid, 443–504. Vol. 1 of *Justification and Variegated Nomism*. Grand Rapids: Baker Academic, 2001.

Deissmann, A. *Light From the Ancient East*. Peabody: Hendrickson Publishers, 1995.

———. *St. Paul: A Study in Social and Religious History*. Translated by Lionel R. M. Strachan. Eugene: Wipf & Stock, 2004.

Delbridge, Tess. "People with Disability and Mental Illness Belong in Church." *Eternity*. 16 June, 2017. https://www.eternitynews.com.au/australia/people-with-disability-and-mental-illness-belong-in-church.

Denney, J. *The Second Epistle to the Corinthians*. London: Hodder and Stoughton, 1894.

deSilva, David A. *An Introduction to the New Testament: Contexts, Methods & Ministry Formation*. Downers Grove: IVP Academic, 2004.

de Souza, Vivian Tais Cunha, Walderi Monteiro da Silva Jr., Amelia Maria Ribeiro de Jesus, Daniela Teles de Oliveira, Helli Alkisti Raptis, Paulo Henrique Luiz de Freitas, and Shela Schneiberg. "Is the WHO Disability Grading System for Leprosy Related to the Level of Functional Activity and Social Participation?" *Leprosy Review* 87 (2016): 191–200.

Dewey, Arthur J., and Miller, Anna C. "Paul." In *The Bible and Disability: A Commentary*, edited by Sarah J. Melcher, Mikeal C. Parsons, and Amos Yong, 379–425. Studies in Religion, Theology, and Disability. London: SCM Press, 2018.

Dillon, Matthew. "Legal (And Customary?) Approaches to the Disabled in Ancient Greece." In *Disability in Antiquity*, edited by Christian Laes. London: Routledge, Taylor & Francis Group, 2017: 167–181.

Dingle, Shannon. "Churches Have a History of Excluding and Erasing People with Disabilities." *Houston Chronicle*. August 5, 2017. https://www.houstonchronicle.com/life/houston-belief/article/Churches-have-a-history-of-excluding-and-erasing-11736695.php

Dodd, Brian J. *Paul's Paradigmatic 'I': Personal Example as Literary Strategy*. Journal for the Study of New Testament Supplement Series 177. Sheffield: Sheffield Academic Press, 1999.

Dodd, Charles Harold. *New Testament Studies*. New York: Charles Scribner's Sons, 1954.

Drake Stanley Levasheff, "Jesus of Nazareth, Paul of Tarsus, and the Early Christian Challenge to Traditional Honor and Shame Values." PhD diss., University of California, Los Angeles, 2013. https://religiondocbox.com/Christianity/69242669-Ucla-ucla-electronic-theses-and-dissertations.html.

Draycott, Jane. "Hair Today, Gone Tomorrow: The Use of Real, False and Artificial Hair as Votive Offerings." In *Bodies of Evidence: Ancient Anatomical Votives Past, Present and Future, Medicine and the Body in Antiquity*, 77–94. London: Routledge Taylor & Francis Group, 2017.

Duff, Paul Brooks. "Paul's Elusive Opponents: Reading 2 Cor 3 without the 'False Apostles' of 2 Cor 11:13." *Biblical Research* 54 (2009): 37–59.

Dungan, D. L. *The Sayings of Jesus in the Churches of Paul*. Oxford: Basil Blackwell, 1971.

Dunn, Peter Wallace. "The Acts of Paul and the Pauline Legacy in the Second Century. PhD diss., University of Cambridge, 1999. https://actapauli.files.wordpress.com/2009/01/pwdunn1996.pdf.

Dunn, James D. G. *Jesus, Paul, and the Law: Studies in Mark and Galatians*. Louisville: Westminster John Knox Press, 1990.

———. *Jesus and the Spirit: A Study of the Religious and Charismatic Experience of Jesus and the First Christian as Reflected in the New Testament*. London: SCM Press, 1975.

———. *Neither Jew nor Greek: Christianity in the Making*. Grand Rapids: Eerdmans, 2015.

———. *The New Perspective on Paul*. Rev. ed. Grand Rapids: Eerdmans, 2008.

———. *Unity and Diversity in the New Testament: An Inquiry into the Character of Earliest Christianity*. Philadelphia: Westminster Press, 1977.

Dutch, Robert S. *The Educated Elite in 1 Corinthians: Education and Community Conflict in Greco-Roman Context*. London: T&T Clark, 2005.

Edersheim, Alfred. *Sketches of Jewish Social Life*. Grand Rapids: Christian Classics Ethereal Library, 1904. PDF. http://www.ccel.org/ccel/edersheim/sketches.html.

———. *The Life and Times of Jesus the Messiah*. Grand Rapids: Christian Classics Ethereal Library, 1953. PDF.

Edwards, Martha Lynn. "Philoctetes in Historical Context." In *Disabled Veterans in History*, edited by D. A. Gerber, 55–69. Michigan: Ann Arbor, 2000.

Eiesland, Nancy. *The Disabled God: Towards a Liberatory Theology of Disability*. Nashville: Abingdon Press, 1994.

———. "Encountering the Disabled God." *Publications of the Modern Language Association* 120, no. 2 (March 2005): 584–586. http://www.jstor.org/stable/25486188.

———. "Things Not Seen: Women with Physical Disabilities." In *Liberating Faith Practices: Feminist Practical Theologies in Context*, edited by Denise Ackermann and Reit Bons-Storm, 103–127. Leuven: Peeters, 1998.

Elass, Mateen Assaad. "Paul's Understanding and Use of the Concept of Election in Romans 9–11." PhD diss., Durham University, 1996. http://etheses.dur.ac.uk/5193/.

Ellington, Dustin W. "Not Applicable to Believers? The Aims and Basis of Paul's 'I' in 2 Corinthians 10–13." *Journal of Biblical Literature* 131, no. 2 (2012): 325–340.

Elliot, John H. "Patronage and Clientage." In *The Social Sciences and New Testament Interpretation*, edited by Richard L. Rohrbaugh, 148–149. Peabody: Hendrickson Publishers, 1996.

———. *What Is Social-Scientific Criticism?* Minneapolis: Fortress Press, 1993.

Ellis, E. Earle. "Paul and His Opponents: Trends in Research." In *Christianity, Judaism and Other Greco-Romans Cults*, edited by Jacon Neusner, 271–272. Leiden: E. J. Brill, 1975.

Esler, Philip Francis. *Galatians*. London: Routledge, 1998.

Farrar, F. W. *The Life and Work of St. Paul*. Vol. 1. Forward by Dr. Cyril J. Barber. Minneapolis: Klock & Klock Christian Publishers, 1902.

Fee, Gordon D. *Paul's Letter to the Philippians*. Grand Rapids: Eerdmans, 1995.

Findlay, Adam Fyfe. *Byways in Early Christian Literature*. Studies in the Uncanonical Gospels and Acts. Edinburgh: T&T Clark, 1923.

Fitzgerald, John T. *Cracks in an Earthen Vessel: An Examination of the Catalogues of Hardship in the Corinthian Correspondence*. Edited by J. J. M Roberts and Charles Talbert. Society of Biblical Literature Dissertations Series 99. Atlanta: Scholars Press: 1988.

Folkins, Tali. "Church May Create 'Envoy' for People with Disabilities: Hiltz." *Anglican Journal*. February 5, 2018. https://www.anglicanjournal.com/church-may-create-envoy-disabled-people-hiltz/.

Forbes, Christopher. "Comparison, Self-Praise and Irony: Paul's Boasting and the Conventions of Hellenistic Rhetoric." *New Testament Studies* 32 (1986): 5–18.

Fortenbaugh, William. *Aristotle's Practical Side: On his Psychology, Ethics, Politics and Rhetoric*. Leiden: Brill, 2006.

Francis, James. "'As Babes in Christ'—Some Proposals Regarding 1 Corinthians 3.1–3." *Journal for the Study of the New Testament* 7 (1980): 41–60.

Fraser, J. W. *Jesus and Paul*. Abingdon: Marcham Books, 1974.

Freedman, David Noel, ed. *The Anchor Bible Dictionary*. 6 vols. New York: Doubleday, 1996.

Fretheim, Terrence E. *Exodus*. Interpretation: A Bible Commentary for Teaching and Preaching. Louisville: John Knox Press, 1991.

Friberg, T., B. Friberg, and N. F Miller. *Analytical Lexicon of the Greek New Testament*. Vol. 4. Baker's Greek New Testament Library. Grand Rapids: Baker Books, 2000.

Furnish, Victor Paul. *2 Corinthians: A New Translation with Introduction and Commentary*. Anchor Bible. Garden City, NY: Doubleday & Company, 1984.

Galli, Mark. "The Power of Our Inability: The Glory and Failing of the Human Body – It's all God's Grace." *Christianity Today* 62, no. 4 (May 2018): 7.

Garland, David E. *1 Corinthians*. Baker Exegetical Commentary on the New Testament. Grand Rapids: Baker Academic, 2003.

———. *2 Corinthians*. Edited by E. Ray Clendenen. New American Commentary 29. Nashville, Tennessee: Broadman & Holman Publishers, 1999.

———. "Paul's Apostolic Authority: The Power of Christ Sustaining Weakness (2 Corinthians 10–13)." *Review and Expositor* 86 (1989): 371–389.

Garland, Robert. "Disabilities in Tragedy and Comedy." In *Disability in Antiquity*, edited by Christian Laes, 154–166. London: Routledge, Taylor & Francis Group, 2017.

———. *The Eye of the Beholder: Deformity and Disability in the Graeco-Roman World*. London: Duckworth, 1995.

Garlington, Don. *The Obedience of Faith: A Pauline Phrase in Historical Context*. N.p.: Wipf and Stock, 2009.

George, Roji T. "'(Dis)abled Jesus': Reading Jesus, His Mission, and the Jesus' Community for a (Dis)ability Perspective." *Bangalore Theological Forum* 46, no. 2 (2014): 101–124.

———, ed. *The Holy Spirit and Christian Mission in a Pluralistic Context*. Bangalore: SAIACS Press, 2017.

———. "Towards a Hermeneutic of (Dis)Ability." In *Disability Theology from Asia: A Resource Book for Theological and Religious*, edited by Anjeline Okola and Wati Longchar, 155–173. PTCA Study Series 17. Kolkata: EDAN-WCC/PTCA/ATEM/SATHRI/YTCS, 2019.

Georgi, Dieter. *The Opponents of Paul in Second Corinthians*. Philadelphia: Fortress Press, 1986.

Gevaert, Bert. "Perfect Roman Bodies." In *Disability in Antiquity*, edited by Christian Laes. London: Routledge, Taylor & Francis Group, 2017: 213–221.

Gingrich, F. Wilbur. *Shorter Lexicon of the Greek New Testament*. 2nd ed. Revised by Frederick W. Danker. Chicago: The University of Chicago Press, 1983.

Giroux, H. *Pedagogy and The Politics of Hope: Theory, Culture, and Schooling*. Boulder, CO: Westview Press, 1997.

Glessner, Justin M. "Ethnomedical Anthropology and Paul's 'Thorn' (2 Corinthians 12:7)." *Biblical Theology Bulletin* 47, no.1 (2017): 15–46.

Gloer, W. Hulitt. "2 Corinthians." In *Acts and Pauline Writings*, edited by Watson E. Mills, Richard F. Wilson, Roger A. Bullard, Walter Harrelson, Edgar V. McKnight, and Edmon L. Rowell Jr., 173–197. Mercer Commentary on the Bible 7. Macon: Mercer University Press, 1997.

Goodspeed, Edgar Johnson. "The Acts of Paul and Thecla." *The Biblical World* 17, no. 3 (1901): 185–190.

Gorman, Michael. *Apostle of the Crucified Lord: A Theological Introduction to Paul & His Letters*. 2nd ed. Grand Rapids: Eerdmans, 2017.

Gottstein, Alon Goshen. "Four Entered Paradise Revisited." *Harvard Theological Review* 88, no.1 (1995): 69–133.

Grafe, H. "Hindu Apologetics at the Beginning of the Protestant Mission Era in India." *Indian Church History Review* 6, no. 1 (June 1972): 43–69.

Grant, Robert McQueen. "The Description of Paul in the Acts of Paul and Thecla." *Vigiliae Christianae* 36, no. 1 (March 1982): 1–4.

Grindheim, Sigrud. *The Crux of Election: Paul's Critique of the Jewish Confidence in the Election of Israel*. Tübingen: Mohr Siebeck, 2005.

Grundmann. "ἀνάγκ-outside the NT." In vol. 1 of *Theological Dictionary of the New Testament*, edited by G. Kittel and G. Friedrich, translated by G. W. Bromiley, 345. Grand Rapids: Eerdmans, 1964.

Guenther, Heinz O. "Gnosticism in Corinth?" In *Origins and Method: Towards a New Understanding of Judaism and Christianity, Essays in Honour of John C. Hurd*, edited by Bradley H. Mclean, 44–81. JSNTSS 86. London: Bloomsbury, 1993.

Gundry, Robert H. *Commentary on the New Testament: Verse-by-verse Explanations with a Literal Translation*. Peabody, MA: Hendrickson Publishers, 2010.

Hafemann, Scott. "The Comfort and Power of the Gospel: The Argument of 2 Corinthians 13." *Review and Expositor* 86 (1989): 325–344.

———. *Paul's Message and Ministry in Covenant Perspective: Selected Essays.* Eugene: Cascade Books, 2015.

———. "Suffering: Paul's Suffering as an Apostle." In *Dictionary of Paul and His Letters*, edited by G. F Hawthorne, R. P. Martin, and D. G. Reid, 919–921. Downers Grove: InterVarsity Press, 1993.

Häkkinen, Sakari. "Poverty in the First-Century Galilee." *Harvard Theological Studies Theological Studies* 72, no. 4 (2016): 1–9. Doi.org/10.4102/hts.v72i4.3398.

Hansen, G. Walter "Rhetorical Criticism." In *Dictionary of Paul and His Letters*, edited by Gerald F. Hawthorne, Ralph P. Martin, and Daniel G. Reid, 822–826. Downers Grove: InterVarsity Press, 1993.

Harrill, J. Albert. "Invective against Paul (2 Cor 10:10): The Physiognomies of the Ancient Slave Body, and the Greco-Roman Rhetoric of Manhood." In *Antiquity and Humanity: Essays on Ancient Religion and Philosophy Presented to Hans Dieter Betz on His 70th Birthday*, edited by Adela Yarbro Collins and Margaret M. Mitchell, 189–213. Tübingen: Mohr-Siebeck, 2001.

———. *Slaves in the New Testament: Literary, Social, and Moral Dimensions.* Minneapolis: Augsburg Fortress Publishers, 2006.

Harris, W. V. "Child-Exposure in the Roman Empire." *The Journal of Roman Studies* 84 (1994): 1–22.

Harrison, Roland K. "Lame." In vol. 3 of *the Interpreter's Dictionary of the Bible: An Illustrated Encyclopedia*, edited by George Arthur Buttrick, 59–60. New York / Nashville: Abingdon Press, 1962.

Harvey, A.E. *Renewal Through Suffering: A Study of 2 Corinthians.* Edinburgh: T&T Clark, 1996.

Hauck, Friedrich. "ἁγνότης." In vol. 1 of *Theological Dictionary of the New Testament*, edited by G. Kittel and G. Friedrich, translated by G. W. Bromiley, 124. Grand Rapids: Eerdmans, 1964.

———. "μωμος." In vol. 4 of *Theological Dictionary of the New Testament*, edited by G. Kittel and G. Friedrich, translated by G. W. Bromiley, 829. Grand Rapids: Eerdmans, 1967.

Hawthorne, Gerald F. *Paul's Letter to the Colossian.* Edited by Stephen E. Hawthorne. Lulu.com, 2010. PDF.

Hester. "The Unity of 2 Corinthians: A Test Case for a Re-discovered and Re-invented Rhetoric." *Neotestamentica* 33 (1999): 411–432.

Hock, Ronald F. "Paul and Greco-Roman Education." In *Paul in the Greco-Roman World: A Handbook*, edited by J. Paul Sampley, 198–227. Harrisburg: Trinity Press International, 2003.

———. *The Social Context of Paul's Ministry: Tentmaking and Apostleship.* Minneapolis: Fortress Press, 1980.

Hodge, Charles. *A Commentary on 1 & 2 Corinthians*. Geneva Series Commentary. Edinburgh: The Banner of Truth Trust, 1983.

Hodgson, Robert. "Paul the Apostle and First Century Tribulation Lists." *Zeitschrift Für Die Neutestamentliche Wissenschaft Und Die Kunde Der Älteren Kirche* 74, no. 1–2 (1983): 59–80.

Holladay, Carl. *Theios Aner in Hellenistic-Judaism: A Critique of This Category in New Testament Christology*. Society of Biblical Literature Dissertations Series 40. Missoula: Scholars Press, 1977.

Horrell, David G. *The Social Ethos of the Corinthian Correspondence: Interest and Ideology from 1 Corinthians to 1 Clement*. Edited by John Barclay, Joel Marcus, and John Riches. Studies of the New Testament and Its World. Edinburgh: T&T Clark, 1996.

———. "Social Sciences Studying Formative Christian Phenomena: A Creative Movement." Academia. Accessed September 18, 2018. http://bit.ly/2pjDbdO.

———. "Social-Scientific Interpretation of the New Testament: Retrospect and Prospect." In *Social- Scientific Approaches to New Testament Interpretation*, edited by David G. Horrell, 3–38. Edinburgh: T&T Clark, 1990.

Horsley, Richard A. *1 Corinthians*. Edited by Victor Paul Furnish. Abingdon New Testament Commentaries. Nashville: Abingdon Press, 1988.

House, Paul R. *Old Testament Theology*. Downers Grove, Illinois: IVP, 1998.

Howard, David M. "Rhetorical Criticism in Old Testament Studies." *Bulletin for Biblical Research* 4 (1994): 87–104.

Howards, Gregory T. *Dictionary of Rhetorical Terms*. Bloomington: Xlibris Corporation, 2010.

Hudson, D. Dennis. *Protestant Origin in India: Tamil Evangelical Christians, 1706–1835*. Edited by R. E. Frykenberg and Brian Stanley. Studies in the History of Christian Mission. Grand Rapids: Eerdmans, 2000.

Hughes, Frank W. "Rhetorical Criticism and the Corinthians Correspondence." In *The Rhetorical Analysis of Scripture: Essays from the 1995 London Conference*, edited by Stanley E. Porter, Thomas H. Olbricht, 336–350. Journal for the Study of the New Testament Supplement Series 146. Sheffield: Sheffield Academic Press, 1997.

Hughes, Philip Edgcumbe. *Paul's Second Epistle to the Corinthians*. Grand Rapids: Eerdmans, 1862.

———. *The Second Epistle to the Corinthians*. Edited by F. F. Bruce. The International Commentary on the New Testament. Grand Rapids: Eerdmans, 1982.

Ironside, H. A. *Addresses on The Second Epistle to the Corinthians: Expository Sermons Preached in The Moody Memorial Church*. Chicago: Western Book and Tract, 1939.

Jayakumar, Samuel. *Dalit Consciousness and Christian Conversion: Historical Resources for a Contemporary Debate*. Delhi: ISPCK, 1999.

Jenkins, Ian, and Victoria Turner. *The Greek Body*. Los Angeles: Getty Publications, 2009.

Jervis, Ann. "God's Obedient Messiah and the End of the Law: Richard N. Longenecker's Understanding of Paul's Gospel." In *Gospel in Paul: Studies on Corinthians, Galatians and Romans for Richard Longenecker*, edited by Richard N. Longenecker, L. Ann Jervis, and Peter Richardson, 21–37. Journal for the Study of the New Testament Supplement Series 108. Sheffield: Sheffield Academic Press, 1994.

*Jewish Encyclopedia*. S.v. "Pharisees." By Kaufmann Kohler. Accessed July 2, 2018. http://www.jewishencyclopedia.com/articles/12087-pharisees.

Jowett, Benjamin. "On the Interpretation of Scripture." In *Essays and Reviews*, 330–433. 7th ed. London: Longman, Green, Longman & Roberts, 1861.

Joy, Gracie. "Obstetrics and Gynaecology in the Ancient World." *The Histories* 3, no. 1 (2016): article 7. Accessed December 12, 2018. htp://digitalcommons.lasalle.edu/the_histories/vol3/iss1/7.

Judge, E. A. "The Early Christians as a Scholastic Community." *Journal of Religious History* 1 (1960–61): 4–15.

———. "Paul as a Radical Critic of Society." *Interchange* 16 (1974): 191–203.

———. "Paul's Boasting in Relation to Contemporary Professional Practice." *ABR* 16 (1968): 37–50.

———. "The Social Identity of the First Christians." *Journal of Religious History* 11 (1980): 201–217.

Judge, E. A. *The Social Pattern of the Christian Groups in the First Century: Some Prolegomena to the Study of New Testament Ideas of Social Obligation*. London: Tyndale Press, 1960.

Kaiser, Walter C., Peter H. Davids, F. F. Bruce, and Manfred Brauch. *Hard Sayings of the Bible*. Downers Grove: InterVarsity Press, 1996.

Kaplan, Deborah. "The Definition of Disability: Perspective of the Disability Community." *Journal of Health Care Law and Policy* 3, no. 2 (2000): 352–364. https://digitalcommons.law.umaryland.edu/jhclp/vol3/iss2/5/.

Kasch, Wilhlem. "συνίστημι." In vol. 7 of *Theological Dictionary of the New Testament*, edited by G. Kittel and G. Friedrich, translated by G. W. Bromiley, 897. Grand Rapids: Eerdmans, 1971.

Kee, Howard Clark. *Jesus in History: An Approach to the Study of the Gospels*. San Diego: Harcourt Brace Jovanovich, 1977.

Keifert, Patrick R. *Welcoming the Stranger: A Public Theology of Worship and Evangelism*. Minneapolis: Fortress Press.

Kellenberger, Edgar. "Mesopotamia and Israel." In *Disability in Antiquity*, edited by Christian Laes, 47–60. London: Routledge, Taylor & Francis Group, 2017.

Kelley, Nicole. "'The Punishment of the Devil was Apparent in the Torment of the Human Body': Epilepsy in Ancient Christianity." In *Disability Studies and Biblical Literature*, edited by Candida R. Moss and Jeremy Schipper, 205–221. New York: Palgrave Macmillan, 2011.

Kennedy, George A. *New Testament Interpretation through Rhetorical Criticism. Studies in Religion*. Chapel Hill: University of North Carolina Press, 1984.

Kennedy, J. H. *The Second and the Third Epistles of St. Paul to the Corinthians*. London: Methuen, 1900.

Kierkegaard, S. *Edifying Discourses*. Vol. 2. Minneapolis: Augsburg Publishing House, 1962.

Kim, Seyoon. *Paul and the New Perspective: Second Thoughts on the Origin of Paul's Gospel*. Tübingen: Mohr Siebeck, 2002.

———. *The Origin of Paul's Gospel*. Eugene: Wipf & Stock, 2007.

Kistemaker, S. J., and W. Hendriksen. *Exposition of the First Epistle to the Corinthians*. New Testament Commentary 18. Grand Rapids: Baker Book House, 2001.

Klijn A. F. J. "The Apocryphal Acts of the Apostles." *Vigiliae Christianae* 37, no. 2 (1983): 193–199.

Knox, John. *Chapters in a Life of Paul*. Nashville: Abingdon-Cokesbury, 1950.

Knox, Wilfred Lawrence. *St. Paul and the Church of Jerusalem*. Cambridge: Cambridge University Press, 2010.

Koptak, Paul E. "Rhetorical Criticism of the Bible: A Resource for Preaching." *The Covenant Quarterly* 54, no. 3 (August 1996): 26–32.

Koptak, Paul E. *Exploration of the Second Epistle to the Corinthians*. New Testament Commentary. Grand Rapids: Baker Books, 1997.

———. "Rhetorical Criticism of the Bible: A Resource for Preaching." *The Covenant Quarterly* 54, no. 3 (August 1996): 26–32.

Kramer, W. *Christ: Lord, Son of God*. Translated by B. Hardy. Studies in Biblical Theology 5. Naperville. IL: Allenson, 1966.

Kruse, Colin G. "Afflictions, Trials, Hardships; Call, Calling; Ministry; Servant, Service; Virtues and Vices." In *Dictionary of Paul and His Letters*, edited by G. F. Hawthorne, R. P. Martin, and D. G. Reid, 19–20. Downers Grove: InterVarsity Press, 1993.

Kummel, W. G. *Introduction to the New Testament*. Translated by A. J. Mattill. London: Abingdon Press, 1966.

Laes, Christian, ed. *Disability in Antiquity*. London: Routledge, Taylor & Francis Group, 2017.

———. "Learning from Silence: Disabled Children in Roman Antiquity." *Arctos* 42 (2008): 85–122.

———. "Silent History? Speech Impairment in Roman Antiquity." In *Disabilities in Roman Antiquity: Disparate Bodies a Capite ad Calcem*, edited by Christian

Laes, C. F. Goodey, and M. Lynn Rose, 145–180. Mnemosyne Supplement 356. Leiden and Boston: Brill, 2013.

Laes, Christian, C. F. Goodey, and M. Lynn Rose, eds. *Disabilities in Roman Antiquity: Disparate Bodies a Capitead Calcem*. Mnemosyne Supplement 356. Leiden: Brill, 2013.

Lambrecht, Jan. "The Fool's Speech and Its Context: Paul's Particular Way of Arguing in 2 Cor 10–13." *Biblica* 82 (2001): 305–322.

Larson, Jennifer. "Paul's Masculinity." *Journal of Biblical Literature* 123, no. 1 (2004): 85–97.

Lessing, Robert Reed. "Preaching like the Prophets: Using Rhetorical Criticism in the Appropriation of Old Testament Prophetic Literature." *Concordia Journal* 28, no. 4 (October 2002): 395.

Levasheff, Drake Stanley. "Jesus of Nazareth, Paul of Tarsus, and the Early Christian Challenge to Traditional Honor and Shame Values." PhD diss. University of California, Los Angeles, 2013. https://escholarship.org/uc/item/1cf4r8sd.

Levin, Yigal. "Jesus, 'Son of God' and 'Son of David': The 'Adoption' of Jesus into the Davidic Line." *Journal for the Study of the New Testament* 28, no. 4 (2006): 415–442.

Liachowitz, C. H. *The Social Construction of Disability*. Philadelphia: University of Pennsylvania Press, 1988.

Lietzmann, H. *The Beginnings of the Christian Church*. New York: Charles Scribner's Sons, 1949.

Lieu, Judith, and J. W. Rogerson. "Rhetorical Criticism." In *The Oxford Handbook of Biblical Studies*, 617–618. Oxford: Oxford University Press, 2006.

Lightfoot, Christopher. "The Roman Empire (27 B.C.–393 A.D.)." In *Heilbrunn Timeline of Art History*. New York: The Metropolitan Museum of Art, 2000. Accessed February 5, 2019. https://www.metmuseum.org/toah/hd/roem/hd_roem.htm.

Lightfoot, J. B. *The Epistle of St. Paul to the Galatians*. Grand Rapids: Zondervan, 1957.

Lim, Kar Yong. *Metaphors and Social Identity Formation in Paul's Letters to the Corinthians*. Eugene: Pickwick Publication, 2017.

———. *'The Sufferings of Christ Are Abundant in Us' (2 Corinthians 1:5): A Narrative-Dynamics Investigation of Paul's Sufferings in 2 Corinthians*. Library of New Testament Studies 399. London: T&T Clark, 2009.

Lindgård, Fredrik. *Paul's Line of Thought in 2 Corinthians 4:16–5:10*. Tübingen: Mohr Siebeck.

Linton, Simi. *Claiming Disability: Knowledge and Identity*. New York: New York University Press, 1998. Accessed December 28, 2018. http://www.disabilitymuseum.org/dhm/edu/essay.html?id=21.

Litfin, A. Duane. *St. Paul's Theology of Proclamation: 1 Corinthians 1–4 and Greco-Roman Rhetoric*. Cambridge: Cambridge University Press, 1994.

Littell, Josh. "Why Were New Born Children Left to Die in Ancient Rome?" *Lucius' Romans* (blog). University of Kent. June 15, 2016. https://blogs.kent.ac.uk/lucius-romans/2016/06/15/why-were-new-born-children-left-to-die-in-ancient-rome/.

Long, Fredrick J. *Ancient Rhetoric and Paul's Apology: The Compositional Unity of 2 Corinthians*. Society for New Testament Studies Monograph Series 131. Cambridge: Cambridge University Press, 2004.

Longchar, A. Wati, and Gordon Cowans, eds. *Doing Theology from a Disability Perspective*, Rev. ed. Manila: The Association for Theological Education in South East Asia, 2011.

Longchar, A. Wati, and R. Christopher Rajkumar, eds. *Embracing the Inclusive Community: A Disability Perspective*. Bangalore: BTESSC/SATHRI, NCCI & SCEPTRE, 2010.

Loh, I. Jin, and Eugene Albert Nida. *A Handbook on Paul's Letter to the Philippians*. New York: United Bible Societies, 1995.

Longenecker, Bruce. *Eschatology and the Covenant: A Comparison of 4 Ezra and Romans 1–11*. Bloomsbury Academic Collections. London: Bloomsbury Publishing, 2015.

———. *Paul, Apostle of Liberty*. Grand Rapids: Eerdmans, 2015.

Longenecker, Richard N. *Galatians*. Word Biblical Commentary. Dallas: Word, 1990.

Longman, Temper, III, and Garland, David E. *Romans–Galatians*. The Expositor's Bible Commentary 11. Grand Rapids: Zondervan, 2008.

Loubser, Johannes A. "Reconciling Rhetorical Criticism with Its Oral Roots." *Neotestamentica* 35, no. 1–2 (2001): 95–110.

Louw, J. P., and E. Nida. *A Greek-English Lexicon of the New Testament: Based on Semantic Domains*. 2 vols. New York: United Bible Societies, 1996.

Ludemann, Gerd. *Paul, the Founder of Christianity*. Amherst: Prometheus Books, 2002.

Luniya, B. N. *Evolution of Indian Culture*. Agra: Lakshmi Narain Agarwal, 1997.

Luther, Martin. *Commentaries on 1 Corinthians 7 and 1 Corinthians 15*. Vol. 28 of *Luther's Works*. American ed. St. Louis: Concordia, 1973.

MacArthur, J. *2 Corinthians*. Chicago: Moody Publishers, 2003.

Maccoby, Hyam. *The Mythmaker: Paul and the Invention of Christianity*. New York: Barnes & Noble, 1998.

MacDonald, Dennis Ronald. "Apocryphal and Canonical Narratives About Paul." In *Paul and the Legacies of Paul*, edited by William S. Babcock, 55–70. Dallas: Southern Methodist University Press, 1990.

MacGillivray, Erlend D. "Re-evaluating Patronage and Reciprocity in Antiquity and New Testament Studies." *Journal of Greco-Roman Christianity and Judaism* 6 (2009): 37–81.

Malherbe, Abraham J. *Paul and the Thessalonians*. Philadelphia: Fortress Press, 1987.

———. "A Physical Description of Paul." *Harvard Theological Review* 79, no. 1–3 (January 1986): 170–175.

———. *Social Aspects of Early Christianity*. 2nd ed. Eugene: Wipf & Stock, 2003.

Malina, Bruce J. *The New Testament World: Insights from Cultural Anthropology*. Rev. ed. Louisville: Westminster John Knox Press, 1993.

Malina, Bruce J., and Jerome H. Neyrey. "Honor and Shame in Luke-Acts: Pivotal Value of the Mediterranean World." In *The Social World of Luke-Acts: Models for Interpretation*, edited by Jerome H. Neyrey, 25–66. Peabody: Hendrickson Publishers, 1991.

Malina, Bruce J., and John J. Pilch. *Social-Science Commentary on the Letters of Paul*. Minneapolis: Fortress Press, 2006.

Marcincola, John. "Speech in Classical Historiography." In *A Companion to Greek and Romans Historiography*, edited by John Marincola, 118–146. West Sussex: Wiley-Blackwell, 2011.

Marshall, Peter. *Enmity in Corinth: Social Conventions in Paul's Relations with the Corinthians*. Tübingen: J.C.B. Mohr, 1987.

———. "A Metaphor of Social Shame." *Novum Testamentum* 25 (1983): 315–316.

Martin, Dale B. *The Corinthian Body*. New Haven: Yale University Press, 1995.

Martin, Douglas. "Nancy Eiesland Is Dead at 44; Wrote of a Disabled God." *The New York Times*. March 21, 2009. https://www.nytimes.com/2009/03/22/us/22eiesland.html.

Martin, Ralph P. *2 Corinthians*. Word Biblical Commentary 40. Waco: Word Books Publisher, 1986.

Martin, Troy W. "Invention and Arrangement in Recent Pauline Rhetorical Studies: A Survey of the Practices and the Problems." In *Paul and Rhetoric*, edited by J. Paul Sampley and Peter Lampe, 48–118. New York: T&T Clark, 2010.

Martyn, J. Louis. *Galatians*. Anchor Bible 33A. New York: Doubleday, 1997.

Marxsen, W. *Introduction to the New Testament*. Translated by G. Buswell. Oxford: Blackwell, 1968.

Maschmeier, Jens-Christian. "2 Corinthians." In vol. 1 of *The Oxford Encyclopaedia of the Books of the Bible*, edited by Michael D. Coogan, 148–158. New York: UOP, 2011.

Matera, Frank J. *2 Corinthians: A Commentary*. Edited by C. Clifford Black, John T. Carroll and Beverly Roberts Gaventa. The New Testament Library. Louisville: Westminster John Knox Press, 2003.

Mathew, John. "Disability and the Inclusive Community: Re-reading the New Testament from a Disability Perspective." In *Embracing the Inclusive Community: A Disability Perspective*, 43–52. Bangalore: BTESSC/SATHRI, NCCI & SCEPTRE, 2010.

Mathew, Sam Peedikayil. "Jesus and Persons with Disabilities: A Re-reading of the Synoptic Gospels from a Disability Perspective." In *Sprouts of Disability Theology*, edited by Christopher Rajkumar, 48–59. Nagpur: National Council of Churches in India, 2012.

McCant, J. W. *2 Corinthians*. Sheffield, England: Sheffield Academic Press, 1999.

———. "Paul's Thorn of Rejected Apostleship." *New Testament Studies* 34 (1988): 550–572.

McClelland, S. E. "'Super-Apostles, Servants of Christ, Servants of Satan': A Response." *Journal for the Study of the New Testament* 17 (1982): 82–87.

McDougall, Sara. *Royal Bastard: The Birth of Illegitimacy, 800–1230*. Oxford: Oxford University Press, 2017.

McGee, J. Vernon. *2 Corinthians*. Pasadena: Thru the Bible Books, 1977.

McReynolds, Kathy "The Gospel of Luke: A Framework for a Theology of Disability." *Christian Education Journal* 13, no. 1 (2016): 169–178.

McVerry, Peter. "Jesus: Social Revolutionary?" *CatholicIreland.net*. November 30, 1999. https://www.catholicireland.net/jesus-social-revolutionary/.

Meeks, Wayne A. *The First Urban Christian: The Social World of the Apostle Paul*. New Haven: Yale University Press, 1983.

———. *The Moral World of the First Christians*. Edited by Wayne A. Meeks. Library of Early Christianity. Philadelphia: The Westminster Press, 1986.

Meeusen, Michiel. "Plutarch's 'Philosophy' of Disability." In *Disability in Antiquity*, edited by Christian Laes. London: Routledge, Taylor & Francis Group, 2017: 197–210.

Melcher, Sarah J. "Introduction: Setting the Stage." In *The Bible and Disability: A Commentary*, edited by Sarah J. Melcher, Mikeal C. Parsons, and Amos Yong, 1–27. Studies in Religion, Theology, and Disability. London: SCM Press, 2018.

Melcher, Sarah J., Mikeal C. Parsons, and Amos Yong, eds. *The Bible and Disability: A Commentary*. Studies in Religion, Theology, and Disability. London: SCM Press, 2018.

Menzies, A. *The Second Epistle of the Apostle Paul to the Corinthians*. London: Macmillan, 1912.

Meyer, Jason C. *The End of the Law: Mosaic Covenant in Pauline Theology*. New American Commentary Studies in Bible & Theology. Nashville: B & H Academic, 2009.

Michael, J. H. *The Epistle to the Philippians*. Moffatt New Testament Commentary. London: Hodder and Stoughton, 1928.

Michaelis, Wilhlem. "πασχω: The Greek and Hellenistic World." In vol. 5 of *Theological Dictionary of the New Testament*, edited by G. Kittel and G. Friedrich, translated by G. W. Bromiley, 905. Grand Rapids: Eerdmans, 1967.

———. "The LXX and Judaism: Pseudepigrapha and Rabbinism." In vol. 5 of *Theological Dictionary of the New Testament*, edited by G. Kittel and G. Friedrich, translated by G. W. Bromiley, 910. Grand Rapids: Eerdmans, 1967.

Minn, H. R. *The Thorn that Remained*. Auckland: G. W. Moore, 1972.

Mitchell, Alexandre. "The Hellenistic Turn in Bodily Representations." In *Disability in Antiquity*, edited by Christian Laes, 182–196. London: Routledge, Taylor & Francis Group, 2017.

Mitchell, Margaret M. *Paul and the Rhetoric of Reconciliation: An Exegetical Investigation of the Language and Composition of 1 Corinthians*. Hermeneutische Untersuchungen zur Theologie 28. Tubingen: Mohr Siebeck, 1991.

Moffatt, James. *An Introduction to the Literature of the New Testament*. 3rd rev. ed. Edinburgh: T&T Clark, 1918.

Moon, Jang-Hwan. "Paul's Discourse for the Corinthians' Edification: A Socio-Rhetorical; Interpretation of 2 Corinthians 10–13." PhD diss., University of Stellenbosch, December 2004. https://scholar.sun.ac.za/bitstream/handle/10019.1/16066/pdf

Morgan-Gurr, Kay. "Disability Inclusion: Why It's about More than a Ramp." *Christian Today*. July 26, 2018. https://www.christiantoday.com/article/disability-inclusion-why-its-about-more-than-a-ramp/130083.htm.

Morray-Jones, C. R. A. "Paradise Revisited (2 Cor 12:1–12): The Jewish Mystical Background to Paul's Apostolate, Part 2: Paul's Heavenly Ascent and Its Significance." *Harvard Theological Review* 86, no. 3 (1993): 265–292.

Moss, Candida, and Jeremy Schipper, eds. *Disability Studies and Biblical Literature*. New York: Palgrave Macmillan, 2011.

Muilenburg, James. "Form Criticism and Beyond." *Journal of Biblical Literature* 88, no. 1 (March 1969): 1–18.

Mullins, T. Y. "Paul's Thorn in the Flesh." *Journal of Biblical Literature* 761 (1957): 299–303.

Munck, Johannes. *Paul and the Salvation of Mankind*. Atlanta: John Knox Press, 1959.

———. "Paulus Tanquam Abortivus: (1 Cor 15:8)." In *New Testament Essays in Memory of Thomas Walter Manson 1893–1958*, edited by A. J. B. Higgins, 180–193. Manchester: Manchester University Press, 1959.

Murphy-O'Connor, Jerome. *Paul: A Critical Life*. Oxford: Oxford University Press, 1996.

———. *The Theology of the Second Letter to the Corinthians*. Edited by J. D. G. Dunn. New Testament Theology. Cambridge: Cambridge University Press, 1991.

Myrick, Anthony A. "'Father's Imagery in 2 Corinthians 1–9 and Jewish Paternal Tradition." *Tyndale Bulletin* 47, no. 1 (May 1996): 163–171.

Nash, Charles Harris. "Paul's 'Thorn in the Flesh' in Its Bearing on His Character and Mission." *Review & Expositor* 28, no. 1 (January 1931): 33–55.

*New World Encyclopedia*. S.v. "Shammai." Accessed August 19, 2018. http://www.newworldencyclopedia.org/p/index.php?title=Shammai&oldid=990554.

Neyrey, Jerome H. *Paul, in Other Worlds: A Cultural Reading of His Letters*. Louisville: Westminster John Knox Press, 1990.

Nisbet, Patricia. "The Thorn in the Flesh." *Expository Times* 80 (1969): 126.

Njoroge, N. "Not an Option: Ministry with and for Persons with Disabilities." *Ministerial Formation* 92 (2001): 5–8.

O'Brien, Peter Thomas. *The Epistle to the Philippians: A Commentary on the Greek Text*. The New International Greek Text Commentary. Grand Rapids: Eerdmans, 1991.

O'Collins, G. G. "Power Made Perfect in Weakness: 2 Cor 12:9–10." *The Catholic Biblical Quarterly* 42 (1980): 216–227.

Ogereau, Julien. "Paul's Leadership Ethos in 2 Cor 10–13: A Critique of 21st Century Pentecostal Leadership." *APS* 13 (2010): 6. http://aps-journal.com/aps/index.php/APS/article/view/105/102.

Olbricht, Thomas H. "An Aristotelian Rhetorical Analysis of 1 Thessalonians." In *Greeks, Romans, and Christians: Essays in Honor of Abraham J. Malherbe*, edited by D. L. Balch, E. Ferguson and W. A. Meeks, 216–236. Minneapolis: Fortress Press, 1990.

———. "Rhetorical Criticism in Biblical Commentaries." *Currents in Biblical Research* 7, no. 1 (October 2008): 11–36.

Oliver, Michael. *The Politics of Disablement: A Sociological Approach*. New York: St. Martin's Press, 1990.

———. *Understanding Disability: From Theory to Practice*. New York: St. Martin's Press, 1996.

Olyan, Saul M. *Disability in the Hebrew Bible: Interpreting Mental and Physical Differences*. Cambridge: Cambridge University Press, 2008.

Omanson R. L., and J. Ellington. *A Handbook on Paul's Second Letter to the Corinthians*. UBS Handbook Series. New York: United Bible Societies, 1993.

Omerzu, Heike. "The Portrayal of Paul's Outer Appearance in the Acts of Paul and Thecla: Reconsidering the Correspondence between the Body and Personality in Ancient Literature." *Religion & Theology* 15, no. 3–4 (2008): 252–279.

Oostendorp, Derk William. *Another Jesus: A Gospel of Jewish-Christian Superiority in 2 Corinthians*. Kampen: J. H. Kok, 1967.

Oropeza, B. J. *Exploring Second Corinthians: Death and Life, Hardship and Rivalry.* Atlanta: SBL Press, 2016.

Palachuvattil, Joy. *"He Saw": The Significance of Jesus' Seeing Denoted by the Verb εἶδεν in the Gospel of Mark.* Roma: Editrice Pontifica Universita Gregoriana, 2002.

Park, David Michael. "Paul's Skolops tē Sarki: Thorn or Stake (2 Cor 12:7)." *Novum Testamentum* 22, no. 2 (April 1980): 179–183.

Parkes, J. *Jesus, Paul and the Jews.* London: Student Christian Movement Press, 1936.

Parry, R. St. John. *The First Epistle of Paul the Apostle to the Corinthians.* The Cambridge New Testament. Cambridge: Cambridge University Press, 1926.

Parsons, Mikeal C. "The Character of the Lame Man in Acts 3–4." *Journal of Biblical Literature* 124, no. 2 (Summer 2005): 295–312. Doi: 10.2307/30041014.

———. "His Feet and Ankles Were Made Strong: Signs of Character in the Man Lame from Birth." In *Disability Studies and Biblical Literature*, edited by Candida R. Moss and Jeremy Schipper, 151–164. New York: Palgrave Macmillan, 2011.

Patrick, Dale, and Scult, Allen. *Rhetoric and Biblical Interpretation.* Sheffield: Almond Press, 1990.

Patterson, Stephen J. "Paul and the Jesus Tradition: It Is Time for Another Look." *Harvard Theological Review* 84, no. 1 (January 1991): 23–41.

Paul, John, II. *Crossing the Threshold of Hope.* Edited by Vitterio Messori. New York: Alfred A. Knopf, 1995.

"Paul's Prison Epistles: Paul and the Philippians." Birmingham Theological Seminary. Accessed December 7, 2018. http://btsfreeccm.org/local/lmp/lessons.php?lesson=PPE5text.

Peerbolte, Bert Jan Lietaert. "Paul's Rapture: 2 Corinthians 12:2–4 and the Language of the Mystics." In vol. 1 of *Experientia: Inquiry into Religious Experience in Early Judaism*, edited by Frances Flannery, Collen Shantz, and Rodney A. Werline, 159–176. Society of Biblical Literature, Symposium Series 40. Atlanta: SBL, 2008.

Penner, Erwin. *A Guide to New Testament Greek.* Toronto: Clements Publishing, 2002.

Peterson, Brian K. "Conquest, Control, and the Cross: Paul's Self-Portrayal in 2 Corinthians 10-13." *Interpretation* 52, no. 3 (1998): 258–270.

———. *Eloquence and the Proclamation of the Gospel in Corinth.* SBL Dissertations Series 163. Atlanta: Scholars Press, 1998.

———, "Eloquence and the Proclamation of the Gospel in Corinth: Social Standards and Eschatological Crisis." PhD Diss., Union Theological Seminary, 1998.

Pherigo, L. P. "Paul and the Corinthians Church." *Journal for Biblical Literature* 68 (1949): 341–351.

Philipps, Gerald M. "The Place of Rhetoric in the Babylonian Talmud." *Quarterly Journal of Speech* 43, no. 4 (1957): 390–393.

———. "The Practice of Rhetoric at the Talmudic Academies." *Speech Monographs* 26 (1959): 37–46.

Pilch, John J. *Healing in the New Testament: Insights from Medical and Mediterranean Anthropology*. Minneapolis: Fortress Press, 2000.

Piltch, John. "Parenting." In *Biblical Social Values and their Meaning: A Handbook*, edited by John J. Pilch and Bruce J. Malina, 126–128. Peabody: Hendrickson Publishers, 1993.

Piper, John. *Disability and the Sovereign Goodness of God*. Edited by Tony Reinke. Minneapolis: Desiring God Foundation, 2012.

Pitt-Rivers, Julian. "Honour and Social Status." In *Honour and Shame: The Values of Mediterranean Society*, edited by John G. Peristiany, 19–77. The Nature of Human Society Series. Chicago: University of Chicago Press, 1966.

Plummer, A. *A Critical and Exegetical Commentary on the Second Epistles of St. Paul to the Corinthians*. International Critical Commentary. Edinburgh: T & T Clark, 1915.

Porter, Stanley E. "Introduction to the Study of Paul's Opponents." In *Paul and His Opponents*, edited by Stanley E. Porter, 1–5. Leiden: Brill, 2005.

———. "When It Was Clear That We Could Not Persuade Him, We Gave Up and Said, 'The Lord's Will Be Done (Acts 21:14)': Good Reasons to Stop Making Unproven Claims for Rhetorical Criticism." *Bulletin for Biblical Research* 26, no.4 (2016): 533–545.

Potts E. Daniel. *British Baptist Missionaries in India, 1837: The History of Serampore and Its Mission*. Cambridge: Cambridge University, 1967.

Price, Robert M. "Punished in Paradise: An Exegetical Theory on 2 Corinthians 12:1–10." *Journal for the Study of the New Testament* 2, no.7, (1980): 33–40.

Proudfoot, Merrill. "Imitation or Realistic Participation: A Study of Paul's Concept of 'Suffering with Christ.'" *Interpretation* 17, no. 2 (April 1963): 140–160.

Pryor, John W. "Paul's Use of Iēsous: A Clue for the Translation of Romans 3:26?" *Colloquium* 16 (1983): 31–45.

Pudsey, April. "Disability and Infirmitas in the Ancient World: Demographic and Biological Facts in the Longue Duree." In *Disability in Antiquity*, edited by Christian Laes, 22–34. London: Routledge, Taylor & Francis Group, 2017.

Punt, Jeremy. "The Others' in Galatians Texts and the Negotiation of Identity." In *Soundings in Cultural Criticism: Perspectives Methods in Culture, Power and Identity in the New Testament*, edited by Francisco Lozada Jr. and Greg Carey, 45–56. Minneapolis: Fortress Press, 2013.

Räisänen, Heikki. *Paul and the Law*. 2nd ed. Wissenschaftliche Untersuchungen zum Neuen Testament 29. Eugene: Wipf & Stock, 1983.

Raj, Ebe Sunder. *Conversion: A National Debate*. Mussoorie: Nivedit Good Book Distributors, 2004.

Rajkumar, Christopher, ed. *Sprouts of Disability Theology*. Nagpur: National Council of Churches in India, 2012.

Ramsay, W. M. *The Church in the Roman Empire Before A. D. 170*. London: Hodder & Stoughton, 1890.

———. *A Historical Commentary on St. Paul's Epistle to the Galatians*. New York: G. P. Putnam's Sons, 1900.

———. *St. Paul the Traveler and Roman Citizen*. London: Hodder & Stoughton, 1935.

Raphael, Rebecca. *Biblical Corpora: Representation of Disability in Hebrew Biblical Literature*. The Library of Hebrew Bible/Old Testament Studies. New York: T&T Clark, 2007.

———. "Images of Disability in Hebrew Prophetic Literature." Paper presented at the annual meeting of the American Academy of Religion, Atlanta, November 23, 2003.

Rapske, Brian. *The Book of Acts and Paul in Roman Custody*. Vol. 3 of *The Book of Acts in Its First Century Setting*. Grand Rapids: Eerdmans, 1994.

Reynolds, Thomas E. *Vulnerable Communion: A Theology of Disability and Hospitality*. Grand Rapids: Brazos Press, 2008.

Rice, Joshua. *Paul and Patronage: The Dynamics of Power in 1 Corinthians*. Eugene: Pickwick, 2013.

Roberts, Mark Edward. "Weak Enough to Lead: Paul's Response to Criticism and Rivals in 2 Corinthians 10–13: A Rhetorical Reading." PhD diss., Vanderbilt University, 2002. http://citeseerx.ist.psu.edu/viewdoc/download?doi=10.1.1.615.2289&rep=rep1&type=pdf.

Robinson, Rowena. *Christians of India*. New Delhi: Sage Publications, 2003.

Robinson, Ryan. "The Birth of Jesus: Solidarity with the Outcast." Anabaptist Redux. May 19, 2018. https://anabaptistredux.com/.

Rodd, Cyril S. "On Applying a Sociological Theory to Biblical Studies." *Journal For the Study of the Old Testament* 6, no. 19 (February 1981): 95–106.

Roetzel, Calvin J. *2 Corinthians*. Abingdon New Testament Commentaries. Nashville: Abingdon, 2007.

———. "'As Dying, and Behold We Live': Death and Resurrection in Paul's Theology." *Interpretation* 46 (1992): 5–18.

Rohrbaugh, Richard L., ed. *The Social Sciences and New Testament Interpretation*. Peabody: Hendrickson Publishers, 1996.

"Romulus and Remus: Roman Mythology." *Encyclopædia Britannica*. Accessed December 28, 2017. https://www.britannica.com/biography/Romulus-and-Remus.

Rose, Martha Lynn. "Ability and Disability in Classical Athenian Oratory." In *Disability in Antiquity*, edited by Christian Laes, 139–153. London: Routledge, Taylor & Francis Group, 2017.

———. *The Staff of Oedipus: Transforming Disability in Ancient Greece*. Ann Arbor: The University of Michigan Press, 2003.

Rowland, Christopher. *The Open Heaven: A Study of Apocalyptic in Judaism and Early Christianity*. London: SPCK, 1982.

Russell, Ronald. "Redemptive Suffering and Paul's Thorn in the Flesh." *Journal of the Evangelical Theological Society* 39, no. 4 (December 1996): 550–570.

Saller, Richard P. *Patriarchy, Property and Death in the Roman Family*. Cambridge: Cambridge University Press, 1994.

Samaha, Adam. "What Good Is the Social Model of Disability?" *University of Chicago Public Law & Legal Theory Working Paper* 166 (2007): 1–69. Accessed November 23, 2017. https://chicagounbound.uchicago.edu/cgi/viewcontent.cgi?article=1377&context=public_law_and_legal_theory.

Samama, Evelyne. "The Greek Vocabulary of Disabilities." In *Disability in Antiquity*, edited by Christian Laes, 121–138. London: Routledge, Taylor & Francis Group, 2017.

Sanders, E. P. *Judaism: Practice and Belief, 63 BCE–66 CE*. London: SCM Press, 1992.

———. *Paul and Palestinian Judaism: A Comparison of Patterns of Religion*. Philadelphia: Fortress Press, 1977.

———. *Paul, the Law, and the Jewish People*. Philadelphia: Fortress Press, 1977.

Sandnes, Karl Olav. "Paul and Socrates: The Aim of Paul's Areopagus Speech." *Journal for the Study of the New Testament* 15, no. 50 (1993): 15–16.

Savage, Timothy B. *Power Though Weakness: Paul's Understanding of the Christian Ministry in 2 Corinthians*. Edited by Margaret E. Thrall. Society for New Testament Studies Monograph Series 88. Cambridge: Cambridge University Press, 1996.

Schellenberg, Ryan S. *Rethinking Paul's Rhetorical Education: Comparative Rhetoric and 2 Corinthians 10–13*. Early Christianity and Its Literature. Atlanta: Society of Biblical Literature, 2013.

Schipper, Jeremy. "Disability in the Hebrew Bible." *Teaching the Bible: A e-Newsletter for Public School Teachers by Society of Biblical Literature*. Accessed September 11, 2017. https://www.sbl-site.org/assets/pdfs/TBv2i8_SchipperDisability.pdf.

———. *Disability Studies and the Hebrew Bible: Figuring Mephibosheth in the David Story*. New York: T&T Clark, 2006.

———. "Embodying Deuteronomistic Theology in 1 Kings 15:22–24." In *Bodies, Embodiment, and Theology of the Hebrew Bible*, edited by S. Tamar Kamionkowski and Wonil Kim, 77–89. New York: Bloomsbury Publishing, 2010.

Schlier, H. "θλίβω, θλῖψις, in Secular Greek." In vol. 2 of *Theological Dictionary of the New Testament*, edited by G. Kittel and G. Friedrich, translated by G. W. Bromiley, 139. Grand Rapids: Eerdmans, 1964.

———. "thlíbō (to press, afflict), thlípsis (pressure, affliction)." In *Theological Dictionary of the New Testament*. Abridged in One Volume, edited by Geoffrey W. Bromiley, Gerhard Friedrich, Gerhard Kittel. Translated by G. W. Bromiley and Gerhard Friedrich. Grand Rapids, Michigan: Eerdmans, 1985.

Schmithals, Walter. *Gnosticism in Corinth: An Investigation of the Letter to the Corinthians*. Translated by John E. Steely. Nashville: Abingdon Press, 1971.

Schütz, John Howard. *Paul and the Anatomy of Apostolic Authority*. New Testament Library. Louisville: Westminster John Knox Press, 2007.

Schweitzer, Albert. *The Mysticism of Paul the Apostle*. New York: Seabury, 1931.

Scott, James M. *2 Corinthians*. New International Biblical Commentary: New Testament Series 8. Peabody, MA: Hendrickson Publishers, 1998.

Segal, Jerome M. *Joseph's Bones: Understanding the Struggle Between God and Mankind in the Bible*. London: Penguin, 2007.

Sen, Ronojoy. "Secularism and Religious Freedom." In *The Oxford Handbook on the Indian Constitutions*, edited by Sujit Choudhry, Madhav Khosla, and Proatab Bhanu Mehta, 885–902. Oxford: Oxford University Press, 2016.

Shakespeare, Tom. "The Social Model of Disability." In *The Disabilities Study Reader*, edited by Lennard J. Davis, 195–203. 5th ed. New York: Routledge, Taylor & Francis Group, 2017.

Sherwin-White, A. N. *Roman Society and Roman Law in the New Testament*. Oxford: Clarendon, 1963.

Shillington, V. George. *2 Corinthians*. Believers Church Bible Commentary. Scottdale: Herald Press, 1998.

Smith, David Raymond. "Hand This Man Over to Satan: Curse, Exclusion and Salvation in 1 Corinthians 5." PhD diss., Durham University, 2005. https://core.ac.uk/download/pdf/108966.pdf.

Smith, Morton. *New Testament, Early Christianity, and Magic. Studies in the Cult of Yahweh*. Vol. 2. Edited by Shaye J. D. Cohen. Leiden: E. J. Brill, 1966.

Smith, Phil. "Drawing New Maps: A Radical Cartography of Developmental Disabilities." *Review of Educational Research* 69, no. 2 (1999): 117–144.

Snyder, Sharon L., Brenda Jo Brueggemann, and Rosemarie Garland-Thomson. "Introduction: Integrating Disability into Teaching and Scholarship." In *Disability Studies: Enabling the Humanities*, edited by Sharon L. Snyder,

Brenda Jo Brueggemann, and Rosemarie Garland-Thomson, 1–12. New York: Modern Language Association, 2002.

Solevåg, Anna Rebecca. *Negotiating the Disabled Body: Representations of Disability in Early Christian Texts*. Early Christianity and Its Literature 23. Atlanta: SBL Press, 2018.

Souter, A. *A Pocket Lexicon to the Greek New Testament*. Oxford: Clarendon Press, 1917.

Stählin, Gustav. "προσκοπή." In vol. 6 of *Theological Dictionary of the New Testament*, edited by G. Kittel and G. Friedrich, translated by G. W. Bromiley, 747. Grand Rapids: Eerdmans, 1969.

Stambaugh, John E., and David L. Balch. *The New Testament in Its Social Environment, Library of Early Christianity*. Edited by Wayne A. Meeks. Philadelphia: The Westminster Press, 1986.

Stanley, D. M. *Boasting in the Lord: The Phenomenon of Prayer in Saint Paul*. New York: Paulist, 1973.

Stegman, Thomas. *The Character of Jesus: The Linchpin to Paul's Argument in 2 Corinthians*. Analecta Biblica 158. Roma: Ed. Pontificio Istituto Biblico, 2005.

———. *Second Corinthians*. Catholic Commentary on Sacred Scripture. Grand Rapids: Baker Academic, 2009.

Stendahl, Krister. "The Apostle Paul and the Introspective Conscience of the West." *Harvard Theological Review* 56, no. 3 (July 1963): 199–215.

———. *Paul Among Jews and Gentiles*. Philadelphia: Fortress Press, 1976.

Stephenson, A. M. G. "A Defence of the Integrity of 2 Corinthians." In *The Authorship and Integrity of the New Testament*, 82–97. Society for the Promotion of Christian Knowledge Theological Collections 4. London: SPCK, 1965.

Stowers, Stanley K. *Letter Writing in Greco-Roman Antiquity*. Philadelphia: The Westminster Press, 1986.

———. "Social Status, Public Speaking and Private Teaching: The Circumstances of Paul's Preaching Activity." *Novum Testamentum* 26, no. 1 (January 1984): 59–82.

Stumbo, Ellen. "The Church and Disability." *Ellen Stumbo* (blog). April 1, 2014. https://www.ellenstumbo.com/confessions-pastors-wife-church-forgetting-us/.

Sumney, Jerry L. *Identifying Paul's Opponents: The Question of Method in 2 Corinthians*. Library of New Testament Studies. London: Bloomsbury Publishing, 2015.

———. "Studying Paul's Opponents: Advances and Challenges." In *Paul and His Opponents*, edited by Stanley E. Porter, 7–58. Leiden: Brill, 2005.

Sussman, Max. "Sickness and Disease: Baldness." In vol. 6 of *The Anchor Bible Dictionary*, edited by D. N. Freedman, 7–55. New York: Doubleday, 1996.

Swaro, Dasarathi. *The Christian Missionaries in Orissa: Their Impact on Nineteenth Century Society*. Calcutta: Punthi Pustak, 1990.

Sweeney, Marvin. *1 and 2 Kings: A Commentary*. Old Testament Library. Louisville: Westminster John Knox, 2007.

Swinton, John. "Who Is the God We Worship?: Theologies of Disability: Challenges and New Possibilities." *International Journal of Practical Theology* 14, no. 2 (2010): 273–307.

Swinton, John, and Brock, Brian. *Disability in the Christian Tradition: A Reader*. Grand Rapids: Eerdmans, 2012.

Tabor, James D. *Paul and Jesus: How the Apostle Transformed Christianity*. New York: Simon & Schuster, 2012.

Tasker, R. V. G. *The Second Epistle of Paul to the Corinthians*. Grand Rapids: Eerdmans, 1978.

Tate, W. Randolph. *Biblical Interpretation: An Integrated Approach*. 3rd ed. Grand Rapids: Baker Academic, 2008.

Theissen, Gerd. *The Social Setting of Pauline Christianity: Essays on Corinth*. Edited and translated by John H. Schütz. Edinburgh: T&T Clark, 1982.

Thielman, Frank. *Theology of the New Testament: A Canonical and Synthetic Approach*. Grand Rapids: Zondervan, 2005.

Thiselton, Anthony C. *The First Epistles to the Corinthians: A Commentary on the Greek Text*. The New International Greek Text Commentary. Grand Rapids: Eerdmans, 2000.

Thomas, John Christopher. *The Devil, Disease and Deliverance: Origins of Illness in New Testament Thoughts*. Sheffield: Sheffield Academic Press, 1998.

Thomson, Rosemarie Garland. *Extraordinary Bodies: Figuring Physical Disability in American Culture and Literature*. New York: Columbia University Press, 1997.

Thornton, T. C. G. "Satan-God's Agent for Punishing." *Expository Times* 83 (1971-1972): 151–152.

Thrall, Margaret E. *A Critical and Exegetical Commentary on the Second Epistle to the Corinthians 1–7*. Edited by J.A. Emerton, C. E. B. Cranfield, and G. N. Stanton. International Critical Commentary. London: T&T Clark, 2004.

———. *A Critical and Exegetical Commentary on the Second Epistle to the Corinthians 8–13*. Edited by J. A. Emerton, C. E. B. Cranfield, and G. N. Stanton. International Critical Commentary. London: T&T Clark.2004.

Thurén, Lauri. *Derhetorizing Paul: A Dynamic Perspective on Pauline Theology and the Law*. Tübingen: Mohr Siebeck, 2000.

Tolbert, Mary Ann "Writing History, Writing Culture, Writing Ourselves: Issues in Contemporary Biblical Interpretation." In *Sounding in Cultural Criticism: Perspectives Methods in Culture, Power and Identity in the New Testament*, edited by Francisco Lozada Jr. and Greg Carey, 17–30. Minneapolis: Fortress Press, 2013.

Tolmie, Donald Francois. "A Rhetorical Analysis of the Letter to the Galatians." PhD diss., University of the Free State Bloemfontein South Africa, April 2004. https://docplayer.net/35011700-A-rhetorical-analysis-of-the-letter-to-the-galatians.html.

Trentin, Lisa. "The 'Other' Romans: Deformed Bodies in the Visual Arts of Rome." In *Disability in Antiquity*, edited by Christian Laes., 233–247 London: Routledge, Taylor & Francis Group, 2017.

Tuckett, Christopher. *Reading the New Testament: Methods of Interpretation.* Philadelphia: Fortress Press, 1987.

Twelftree, G. H. "Healing, Illness." In *Dictionary of Paul and His Letters*, edited by Gerald F. Hawthorne, Ralph P. Martin, and Daniel G. Reid, 379–381. Downers Grove: Intervarsity Press, 1993.

Ucko, Hans. "Christian Perspective on Vulnerable Groups: The Elderly and the Disabled." In *Religious Perspectives on Human Vulnerability in Bioethics*, edited by Joseph Tham, Alberto Garcia, Gonzalo Miranda, 143–152. Advancing Global Bioethics 2. New York: 2014.

"UPIAS Founding Statement." UPIAS. Accessed September 25, 2017. http://www.leeds.ac.uk/disability studies/archiveuk/UPIAS/UPIAS.pdf.

Van Spanje, Teunis Erik. *Inconsistency in Paul? A Critique of the Work of Heikki Räisänen.* Tübingen: Mohr Siebeck, 1999.

Veerbrugge, Verlyn D. "1 Corinthians." In *Romans–Galatians*, edited by Tremper Longman III and David E. Garland. Vol. 11 of *The Expositor's Bible Commentary*. Rev. ed. Grand Rapids: Zondervan, 2008.

Vergeer, Charles. *The Letters of the Apostle Paul: Controversies and Consequences.* Cambridge: Cambridge Scholars Publishing, 2017.

Vial-Dumas, Manuel. "Parents, Children and Law: Patria Potestas and Emancipation in the Christian Mediterranean during Late Antiquity and the Early Middle Ages." *Journal of Family History* 39 no. 4 (2014): 307–329.

Vlahogiannis, Nicholas. "Disabling Bodies." In *Changing Bodies, Changing Meanings: Studies on the Human Body in Antiquity*, edited by Dominic Montserrat, 13–36. London: Routledge, 1998.

Voorwinde, Stephen. "Paul's Emotions in 2 Corinthians: Part 1 (Chapters 1–7)." *Vox Reformata* (2015): 66–105.

Wallace, Daniel. "2 Corinthians: Introduction, Argument, and Outline." In *New Testament Introductions and Outlines*. Bible.org, February 2, 2009. https://bible.org/seriespage/8-2-corinthians-introduction-argument-and-outline.

———. *Greek Grammar Beyond the Basic: An Exegetical Syntax of the New Testament.* Grand Rapids: Zondervan, 1996.

Walton, Steve. "Rhetorical Criticism: An Introduction." *Themelios* 21, no. 2 (January 1996): 4–9.

Wan, Sze-kar. *Power in Weakness: Conflict and Rhetoric in Paul's Second Letter to the Corinthians*. Edited by Howard Clark Kee and J. Andrew Overman. The New Testament in Context. Harrisburg: Trinity Press International, 2000.

Wasserman, David. "Philosophical Issues in the Definition and Social Response to Disability." In *Handbook of Disability Studies*, edited by Gary L. Albrecht, Katherine D. Seelman, and Michael Bury, 219–222. Thousand Oaks, CA: Sage, 2001.

Wasson, Donald. "Claudius." *World History Encyclopedia*, 18 October 2011. Accessed January 24, 2017. https://www.ancient.eu/claudius/.

Watson, Duane F. *Invention, Arrangement and Style: Rhetorical Criticism of Jude and 2 Peter*. Society of Biblical Literature Dissertations Series 104. Atlanta: Scholars Press 1988.

———. "Notes on History and Method." In part 2 of *Rhetorical Criticism of the Bible: A Comprehensive Bibliography with Notes on History and Method*, by Duane Frederick Watson and Alan J. Hauser. Leiden: E. J. Brill, 1994.

———. "Paul and Boasting." In vol. 1 of *Paul in the Greco-Roman World: A Handbook*, edited by J. Paul Sampley, 90–112. 2nd ed. London: Bloomsbury, 2016.

Watson, F. "2 Cor 10–13 and Paul's Painful Letter to the Corinthians." *Journal of Theological Studies*, no. 35 (1984): 324–346.

———. *Paul, Judaism and the Gentiles: A Sociological Approach*. Society for New Testament Studies Monograph Series 56. Cambridge: Cambridge University Press, 1986.

Weima, Jeffrey A. D. "What Does Aristotle Have to Do with Paul?: An Evaluation of Rhetorical Criticism." *Calvin Theological Journal* 32, no. 2 (November 1997): 458–468.

Weinel, H. *St. Paul: The Man and his Work*. Translated by G. A. Bienemann. Edited by W. D. Morrison. Eugene: Wipf & Stock, 2005.

Weiss, Johannes. *Earliest Christianity: A History of the Period A.D. 30–150*. Vol. 1. Translated by Frederick C. Grant. New York: Harper & Row, 1959.

Welborn, L. L. "Paul's Appeal to the Emotions in 2 Corinthians 1.1–2.13; 7.5–16." *Journal for the Study of the New Testament Supplement Series* 2 (2001): 31–60.

Wenham, J. W. *The Elements of New Testament Greek*. Cambridge: Cambridge University Press, 2003.

"When Churches Discuss Disability without Disabled People." *Crippledscholar* (blog). September 5, 2016. https://crippledscholar.com/2016/09/05/when-churches-discuss-disability-without-disabled-people/.

Wicher, Edward A. "Ancient Jewish Views of the Messiah Author." *The Biblical World* 34, no. 5 (1909): 317–325.

Wilcox, Max. "Upon the Tree: Deut. 21:22–23 in the New Testament." *Journal of Biblical Literature* 96, no. 1 (March 1977): 85–99.

Wilder, Courtney. *Disability, Faith, and the Church: Inclusion and Accommodation in Contemporary Congregations*. Santa Barbara: Praeger, 2016.

Wilfred, Felix. *Asian Dreams and Christian Hope: At the Dawn of the Millennium*. Delhi: Indian Society for Promotion of Christian Knowledge, 2003.

Wilkinson, John. *The Bible and Healing: A Medical and Theological Commentary*. Grand Rapids: Eerdmans, 1998.

Wilson, Barrie A. "If We Only Had Paul, What Would We Know of Jesus?" Paper presented at International Conference on the Arts & Humanities, January 2008, Honolulu, HI. Accessed August 8, 2018. http://www.barriewilson.com/pdf/If-We-Only-Had-Paul.pdf.

Wilson, Geoffrey B. *2 Corinthians*. A Digest of Reformed Comment. Edinburgh: The Banner of Truth Trust, 1979.

Wilson, Mark. "Treasures in Clay Jars." *Bible History Daily*. Biblical Archaeology, updated October 16, 2020. https://www.biblicalarchaeology.org/daily/biblical-artifacts/artifacts-and-the-bible/treasures-in-clay-jars/.

Wilson, S. G. "From Jesus to Paul: The Contour and Consequences of a Debate." In *From Jesus to Paul: Studies in Honour of Francis Wright Beare*, edited by P. Richardson and J. C. Hurd, 1–21. Waterloo, Ontario: Wilfrid Laurier University Press, 1984.

Wilson, William. *What, Why and How?: The Plan for Our Redemption*. Longwood: Xulon Press, 2007.

Winter, Bruce W. "The Entries and Ethics of Orators and Paul (1 Thessalonians 2:1–12)." *Tyndale Bulletin* 44, no. 1 (1993): 55–74.

———. *Philo and Paul Among the Sophists*. Edited by Richard Bauckham. Society for New Testament Studies Monograph Series 96. Cambridge: University Press, 1997.

Witherington, Ben, III. *Acts of the Apostles: A Socio-Rhetorical Commentary*. Grand Rapids: Eerdmans, 1998.

———. "'Almost Thou Persuadest Me . . .': The Importance of Greco-Roman Rhetoric for the Understanding of the Text and Context of the NT." *Journal of The Evangelical Theological Society* 58, no. 1 (March 2015): 63–88.

———. *Conflict & Community in Corinth: A Socio-Rhetorical Commentary on 1 and 2 Corinthians*. Grand Rapids: Eerdmans, 1995.

———. *New Testament Rhetoric: An Introductory Guide to the Art of Persuasion in and of the New Testament*. Eugene: Cascade, 2009.

———. *Paul's Narrative Thought World: The Tapestry of Tragedy and Triumph*. Louisville, Kentucky: Westminster John Knox Press, 1994.

World Health Organization. "Disability." World Health Organization. Accessed November 21, 2017. http://www.who.int/topics/disabilities/en/.

———. *International Classification of Impairments, Disabilities and Handicaps*. Geneva: World Health Organisation, 1980.

Wright, N. T. *The Climax of the Covenant: Christ and the Law in Pauline Theology*. London: T&T Clark, A Continuum Imprint, 1991.

———. *Paul and His Recent Interpreters: Some Contemporary Debates*. Minneapolis: Fortress Press, 2015.

———. *What Saint Paul Really Said: Was Paul of Tarsus the Real Founder of Christianity?* Grand Rapids: Eerdmans, 2014.

Wuellner, Wilhelm. "Rhetorical Criticism and Its Theory in Culture-Critical Perspective: The Narrative Rhetoric of John 11." In *Text and Interpretation: New Approaches in the Criticism of the New Testament*, edited by P. J. Hartin and J. H. Petzer, 171–186. Leiden: E. J. Brill, 1991.

———. "Where is Rhetorical Criticism Taking Us?" The Catholic *Biblical Quarterly* 49, no. 3 (July 1987): 448–4634.

Yadin, Yigael. "A Midrash on 2 Sam. 7 and Ps. 1–2 (4Q Florilegium)." *Israel Exploration Journal* 9 (1959): 95–98.

Yong, Amos. *The Bible, Disability, and the Church: A New Vision of the People of God*. Grand Rapid: Eerdmans, 2011.

———. *Theology and Down Syndrome: Reimagining Disability in Late Modernity*. Waco: Baylor University Press, 2007.

Young, Frances M. *Brokenness and Blessing: Towards A Biblical Spirituality*. Grand Rapids: Baker Academic, 2007.

Young, Frances M., and David F. Ford. *Meaning and Truth in Second Corinthians*. Eugene: Wipf & Stock, 1973.

Zedda, Maria "In the Loop: Models of Disability: Is the Religious Model Still Relevant Today?" *Wideaware* (blog). Updated September 25, 2017. http://blog.wideaware.co.uk/archive/7/models-of-disabilityis-the-religious-model-still-relevant-today.

Zmijewski, J. "ἀσθένεια." In *Exegetical Dictionary of the New Testament*, edited by H. R. Balz and Gerhard Schneider, 170. Grand Rapids: Eerdmans, 1993.

Langham Literature, with its publishing work, is a ministry of Langham Partnership.

Langham Partnership is a global fellowship working in pursuit of the vision God entrusted to its founder John Stott –

> *to facilitate the growth of the church in maturity and Christ-likeness through raising the standards of biblical preaching and teaching.*

**Our vision** is to see churches in the Majority World equipped for mission and growing to maturity in Christ through the ministry of pastors and leaders who believe, teach and live by the word of God.

**Our mission** is to strengthen the ministry of the word of God through:
- nurturing national movements for biblical preaching
- fostering the creation and distribution of evangelical literature
- enhancing evangelical theological education

especially in countries where churches are under-resourced.

**Our ministry**

*Langham Preaching* partners with national leaders to nurture indigenous biblical preaching movements for pastors and lay preachers all around the world. With the support of a team of trainers from many countries, a multi-level programme of seminars provides practical training, and is followed by a programme for training local facilitators. Local preachers' groups and national and regional networks ensure continuity and ongoing development, seeking to build vigorous movements committed to Bible exposition.

*Langham Literature* provides Majority World preachers, scholars and seminary libraries with evangelical books and electronic resources through publishing and distribution, grants and discounts. The programme also fosters the creation of indigenous evangelical books in many languages, through writer's grants, strengthening local evangelical publishing houses, and investment in major regional literature projects, such as one volume Bible commentaries like the *Africa Bible Commentary* and the *South Asia Bible Commentary*.

*Langham Scholars* provides financial support for evangelical doctoral students from the Majority World so that, when they return home, they may train pastors and other Christian leaders with sound, biblical and theological teaching. This programme equips those who equip others. Langham Scholars also works in partnership with Majority World seminaries in strengthening evangelical theological education. A growing number of Langham Scholars study in high quality doctoral programmes in the Majority World itself. As well as teaching the next generation of pastors, graduated Langham Scholars exercise significant influence through their writing and leadership.

To learn more about Langham Partnership and the work we do visit **langham.org**

www.ingramcontent.com/pod-product-compliance
Lightning Source LLC
Chambersburg PA
CBHW070234240426
43673CB00044B/1781

Rhodian Munyenyembe brings to the many controversies related to the Church of Central Africa Presbyterian (CCAP) a rigorous scholarly research. Being strong on sources and weak on controversy, the book makes a unique contribution to all the manifold discourses on church unity. The book is a major contribution to the development of an indigenous church historiography for Malawi.

**Dr Klaus Fiedler**
Professor of Theology and Religious Studies,
Mzuzu University, Malawi
Emeritus Professor of Missiology,
Evangelical Theological Faculty, Leuven, Belgium

Rhodian Munyenyembe assesses the historical relationship of the founding Synods of the Church of Central Africa Presbyterian (CCAP) in Malawi. Tracing their roots back to their mother churches in Scotland, the Netherlands and South Africa, Dr Munyenyembe argues that they are historically rooted in the theology of the 16th-century reformers and in the revivals of the 17th, 18th and 19th centuries, a shared history that offers them potential basis for unity. He observes that during the missionary period the Synods enjoyed an intricate interconnectedness and cooperation. However, the desire to maintain some characteristics of their mother churches and the interest of those churches to maintain influence on their daughter Synods, coupled with the local cultural, social and economic undercurrents, continue to stifle the development of an organic relationship among the Synods within the CCAP family. The result, Dr Munyenyembe argues, is that the CCAP remains a loosely connected set of autonomous Synods or "denominations," rather than a single denomination, and that this accounts for their troubled relationship today. Dr Munyenyembe's book offers a well-informed and balanced treatment of this complex relationship, and will remain, for a long time, indispensable for understanding current disputes in the CCAP to those interested in the history of the church in Malawi.

**Jonathan Nkhoma**
Associate Professor,
Mzuzu University, Malawi